£10

Off '

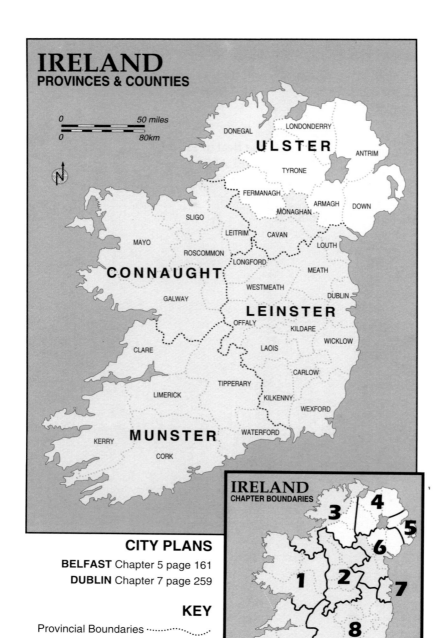

IRELAND
PROVINCES & COUNTIES

0 ——— 50 miles
0 ——— 80km

N

DONEGAL LONDONDERRY

ULSTER ANTRIM

TYRONE

FERMANAGH
ARMAGH DOWN
MONAGHAN
SLIGO
LEITRIM CAVAN
MAYO
ROSCOMMON LOUTH
LONGFORD
CONNAUGHT MEATH
WESTMEATH
GALWAY DUBLIN
LEINSTER
OFFALY
KILDARE
WICKLOW
CLARE LAOIS
CARLOW
TIPPERARY
LIMERICK KILKENNY
WEXFORD
MUNSTER WATERFORD
KERRY
CORK

IRELAND
CHAPTER BOUNDARIES

3 4
5
6
1 2 7
8
9

CITY PLANS
BELFAST Chapter 5 page 161
DUBLIN Chapter 7 page 259

KEY
Provincial Boundaries ··············
County Boundaries ··············

Off The Beaten Track

IRELAND

Rosemary Evans

MOORLAND PUBLISHING

The
Globe
Pequot
press

Published by:
Moorland Publishing Co Ltd,
Moor Farm Road West, Ashbourne,
Derbyshire, DE6 1HD England

ISBN 0 86190 402 8 (UK)

The Globe Pequot Press,
6 Business Park Road,
PO Box 833, Old Saybrook,
Connecticut 06475-0833

ISBN 1-56440-477-3 (USA)

The right of Rosemary Evans as author
of this work has been asserted by her in
accordance with the copyright, Designs
and Patents Act, 1993.

Cover photograph:
Jerry Mulvihill's Bog Village — Kerry Bog
Museum, Ballycleave, County Kerry
(*International Photobank*)

Rear cover photograph:
Making the most of an old petrol
pump, Beara Peninsula, County Cork
(*Stephen Hopkins*)

Black and white illustrations have been
supplied as follows:

Stephen Hopkins; Ron Scholes;
Northern Ireland Tourist Board;
Mr Brian Lynch/Monaghan County
Museum; David Malone, Lough
Muckno Leisure Park

Colour illustrations have been supplied
as follows:

Stephen Hopkins; Ron Scholes;
Northern Ireland Tourist Board

Origination by:
Forest Graphics (Nottm) Ltd

Printed by:
Wing King Tong Co Ltd, Hong Kong

MPC Production Team:
Editorial: Tonya Monk
Editorial Assistant: Christine Haines
Design: Ashley Emery/Dick Richardson
Cartography: Alastair Morrison

British Library Cataloguing in Publication Data:
A catalogue record for this book is available from the British Library.

Library of Congress Cataloging-in-Publication Data
Evans, Rosemary.
  Ireland/Rosemary Evans.
  'Off The Beaten Track'   p. cm.
  Includes index.
  ISBN 1-56440-477-3
  1. Ireland—Guidebooks. I. Title.
DA980. E93 1994
914.1504'824 — dc20
          94-29279
          CIP

Contents

Note on Maps

The maps for each chapter, while comprehensive, are not designed to be used as route maps, but to locate the main towns, villages and places of interest.

Opening Times for Visitor Attractions

The opening times given in the Further Information section for each chapter were current at the time of compilation. However, changes will inevitably occur and you are advised to use the telephone numbers given to make your own enquiries. Where access is irregular or intricate, the likely pattern only of opening hours is indicated and you should telephone before setting out.

Public holidays can affect opening times. Some facilities will open longer hours, others close altogether, and you should take this into account when planning your itinerary.

Public holidays in Ireland, North and South

New Year's Day, St Patrick's Day (17 March)
Easter Monday, 25 and 26 December.

Other public holidays

In the Republic — Good Friday, first Monday in June, first Monday in August, last Monday in October.

In Northern Ireland — May Day, last Monday in May, Orangeman's Day (12 July), last Monday in August.

Acknowledgements

I am grateful to the following people who, wittingly or unwittingly, gave assistance in the preparation of this book: Jim Blewitt, Myrtle Boal, Wilfrid Capper, Paddy Dillon, Laurence Flanagan, Brian Fox, Mr Roy Gibson (RVH), Doreen McBride, Bill Maguire, Marion Meek, and Ian Robertson (Arles). Most of all to my husband, David, who provided the framework, drove the miles and kept the coffee coming.

Dedication

To the shades of my mother and father

Introduction

Not since the Vikings sailed up the Shannon and fell on Clonmacnois could Ireland be said to be on the way to anywhere in particular. Indeed this whole island — the most peripheral part of the European Union's periphery — and every bog and townland, lough and drumlin on it, can fairly be said to be off the beaten track.

The island, which really was full of saints and scholars then, was the first conquest of those fearsome Scandinavian warriors who ran berserk over all of Europe and kept on going until they reached Constantinople and the Russian steppes. In the thousand years since that time newcomers to Ireland have, on the whole, been delighted with what they find. They soon discover that, in common with all Irish people, they have no desire to go elsewhere. They like it here. Even the Vikings, who had to be forced out because they made a nuisance of themselves, only thought about leaving after a tremendous battle at Clontarf in 1014.

Do not imagine that such love of country is at odds with the melancholy tradition of leaving Ireland for other lands. On the contrary, the reality of mass Irish emigration — on a scale surely unmatched in Western Europe, a fact embedded deep in the Irish psyche — has only ever been for reasons of economic necessity. For these same economic reasons, Official Ireland is determined to get itself *on* to the beaten track as quickly as possible and there are signs, in both the north and the south, that it is beginning to succeed. If, as Irish tourist chiefs say, tourism is a 'sunrise industry' independent travellers will make a point of avoiding high noon. Go now!

Rosemary Evans

7

1 • Connaught

Roscommon, Mayo and Galway

There are no motorways in Mayo. In fact, there are rather few roads of any sort, and not many either in Connemara, that lovely part of Connaught which lies west of Lough Corrib. An advantage of this is the near impossibility of losing your way, and it reinforces the sense of remoteness engendered by the strange Mayo landscape of glitzy white mountains and treeless black bog, with the vastness of the Atlantic stretching away into the sunset.

The mountains of the west of Ireland are not particularly high, there is not a Munro among them, but their shimmering quartzite forms rise dramatically from a flat plain. There are famous solitary cones like Nephin and Croagh Patrick, and Errigal in Donegal, and the glittering horseshoe ridge of Mweelrea which rises straight out of the sea at fiord-like Killary Harbour, and those peakiest of Irish peaks, the Twelve Bens north-east of Clifden.

If you cross from North to South via the B52 (R282) at Garrison in Fermanagh, you are passing directly between the ancient provinces of Ulster and Connaught. Facts of history more than the force of the old heroic legends have ensured that these names, Ulster and Connaught, resonate longer in the popular imagination than those of Ireland's other ancient provinces, Leinster and Munster. The notorious utterance about Connaught was Oliver Cromwell's 'Hell or Connaught' — the choice he prescribed in 1653 for Irish landowners whose estates east of the Shannon were confiscated following the 1641 rebellion. They were 'transplanted' to isolated Connaught and allocated land which in theory was the same acreage. However, the war had been expensive and Parliament's debts were large. Forfeited estates were parcelled out to English investors — 'adventurers' who had underwritten the cost of the war — and to the army, officers and men, in lieu of pay.

That was what normally happened after an Irish rebellion. It was not unusual. What was different about the Cromwellian confiscations was the systematic way in which they were done, and the scale

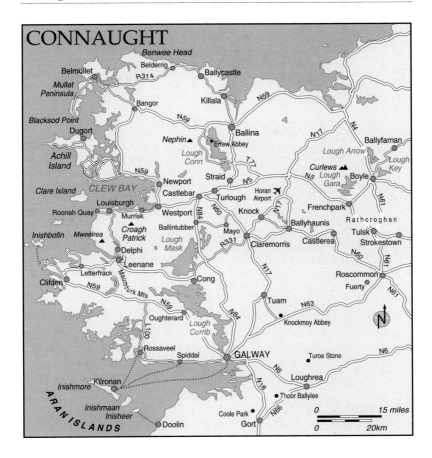

of them. Any shortfall was made good by confiscating more land, and so in practice the Irish ended up with somewhat less than half the land they had lost. The ex-soldiers sold their tiny shares to the officers who sold them on, with most of the land ending up as blocks in the hands of large-scale entrepreneurs.

The enduring Irish dislike, or folk memory, of the privilege signalled by Anglo-Irish big houses is stronger in some parts of Ireland than in others, and there can be problems of presentation when owners decide to let the paying public in. **Strokestown Park**, a seventeenth-century mansion south-east of Elphin, County Roscommon, on the N5, is an example. Until recently the house was the seat of the Gore Booths and Pakenham Mahons. The new owner has turned the elegant vaulted stables into an interpretive centre relating to the years of famine and emigration. The house was remodelled in

Strokestown is arranged along two broad streets

the 1730s by Richard Cassels, who was the architect of many stately houses in Ireland, including Powerscourt, Russborough and Leinster House which is now the Irish parliament building. At Strokestown he added the handsome Palladian wings. The outstanding feature of the gardens is a magnificent herbaceous border.

Strokestown village is arranged along two broad streets intersecting at right angles. Indeed the street running west-east is so broad that a stray German plane was able to land on it during World War II. At one end of the street is an octagonal church, now used as a genealogy/heritage centre. The other end is closed by the entrance to the demesne. The owner of Strokestown during the famine years, Major Denis Mahon, was murdered by his tenants in 1847 after word got back to the village that he was profiteering from 'coffin ships' — the leaky boats that crossed the Atlantic to America carrying Irish emigrants, including some of his own evicted tenants. Regulars in the pub just outside the demesne will tell you more about this wicked major.

The beautiful ruined church of **Boyle Abbey**, on the bank of the river that links Lough Gara to Lough Key and runs on to the Shannon, is one of the most rewarding medieval site visits in Connaught. A Cistercian foundation dating from 1148, Boyle was an early daughter-house of Mellifont Abbey near Drogheda, County Louth, and was the most influential abbey in medieval Connaught, were brought to Ireland from Clairvaux in 1142 by St Malachy. They built Mellifont, their first Irish monastery, on land granted by the king of Oriel. However, the life style of the Irish monks so displeased the austere French monks that they went back to France in unforgiving mood. Not even St Bernard himself could induce them to return to Ireland.

Rome was not built in a day and neither was Boyle. Its abbots, who were all Irish, included the famous religious poet, Donnchadh Mór O Daly (died 1244). Another was the thirteenth-century abbot who became much involved in the 'conspiracy of Mellifont', a row with the English Cistercians that rumbled on for more than a decade. Unlike Mellifont, Boyle was a wholly Gaelic foundation and yet its architecture is a curious jumble, with many imported and contradictory features. The Romanesque style of the arches on the south side of the long nave had gone out of fashion by the time the north side was built, and so rounded arches and cylindrical piers face pointed Gothic arches and square piers in a delightful disharmony. Carvings of beasts, trumpet-scallops and little human figures adorn the capitals at the west end of the nave. At the east end is a large square tower and a tall thirteenth-century English lancet window. The English master mason who was employed at Christ Church in Dublin almost certainly worked at Boyle too.

The turbulent history of Ireland from the tenth to the mid-seventeenth century left almost every ancient Irish church and monastery ruined and roofless. In 1202 Boyle was plundered by the Normans (with help from the local O'Conors), in 1235 it attracted the attention of Maurice Fitzgerald, justiciar of Ireland, and in 1659 it was smashed by Cromwellian soldiers. A model in the restored gatehouse shows how it would have looked originally.

Boyle town was part of the Rockingham estate, granted to Sir John King in 1617. As was the convention, the driveway to the big house was also the town's high street and the Kings' handsome U-shaped town house, the most distinguished building in Boyle, dominates the main street. Abandoned by the Kings almost 200 years ago, it became a barracks and was in turn abandoned by the military and left to decay. The county council has rescued it and admirably restored it for public use.

The Kings moved out to a palatial stately home on the Rockingham estate which is now a forest park. The mansion has vanished, destroyed by fire in 1957. Just how palatial it was can be guessed at by the quality of the stables, church, gatehouse, gazebo and other estate buildings which survive, more or less intact. An avenue of mighty beech trees, over half a mile (1km) long, is an outstanding feature of the demesne which borders **Lough Key**, a beautiful nearly circular lake with fine views of low mountains, and sprinkled with wooded islands.

There has been much planting of conifer trees in the park and there are some graceless tourist amenities. However, you can hire a boat to explore some of the thirty or so islands on the lough. Castle Island close to the shore was a seat of the MacDermots of Moylurg, once rulers of this whole region. The remains of their castle had a folly castle added by the Kings in the nineteenth century to give a more interesting profile. The island is famous for an important sixteenth-century manuscript known as the *Annals of Lough Cé*, a sort of local history of Lough Key, which is said to have been written here at the behest of the scholarly Brian MacDermot (died 1592). The manuscript is preserved in Trinity College, Dublin. Another interesting island to stop at is Trinity Island. The ruined priory here was built in 1217 by the White Canons, an order founded at Prémontré by St Norbert, archbishop of Magdeburg, who was a friend of St Bernard. The White Canons served as parish priests, though they had the same constitution as the Cistercians and were just as sternly ascetic.

Edward King, a fellow of Christ's College, Cambridge, was a scion of the King family of Boyle. He was drowned aged 25 when crossing the Irish Sea from Chester in 1632, and that might have been the end of it, except that his untimely death was the subject of *Lycidas*, Milton's great pastoral elegy:

> 'At last he rose, and twitched his mantle blue
> Tomorrow to fresh woods, and pastures new.'

Harpers, Crannogs and Miracles

From Boyle take the scenic route north towards the Arigna mountains, skirting the west bank of the lough, to **Ballyfarnan** to see the ruined fourteenth-century church of **Kilronan** where the celebrated Gaelic composer and harper Turlough O'Carolan (1670-1738) is buried. Left blind by smallpox, O'Carolan was apprenticed to a harper at the age of 14. For the rest of his life he enjoyed the patronage of Mrs Mary MacDermot Roe (1659-1739). She nurtured his talent at a time when the Irish social order was disintegrating and aristocratic patrons were hard to come by. When he was 21 she gave him a horse and a servant and got him the travel permit which all harpers, pipers and other wandering musicians needed at that period.

For the next 50 years O'Carolan travelled around Connaught and Ulster on horseback, moving between the houses of the old Irish noble families and repaying their hospitality with an endless stream of songs of praise and 'planxties', harp tunes that accompany dances. The influence of the Italian composers Vivaldi and Corelli, much in vogue in Dublin at that period, is apparent in some of the 200 melodies accredited to him. When he died, at Mrs MacDermot Roe's home at Alderford outside Ballyfarnan, ten harpers came to the wake which went on for 4 days. He is buried in the MacDermot Roe family vault on the north side of the church.

Another Irish harper, a legendary one, gave his name to the hill called **Keshcorran**, the Hog of Corran (1,188ft/362m). It has a rather eerie aspect, with a line of small shallow caves along the top, and dominates the minor road running north-west from Boyle to Ballymote. There are numerous myths associated with the hill, some of which feature Cormac McArt, high king of Ireland ruling at Tara in about AD250. Cormac is said to have been reared on this very hill by a lady wolf. Excavations have uncovered the bones of Great Elk, reindeer, bears and other creatures long extinct in Ireland.

The mountain roads around here give wonderful views of three big loughs — Lough Key, Lough Gara and Lough Arrow. The Curlew mountains, not very high but distinctive, rise to the north-west of Boyle, with the Bricklieve range beyond and, in the north-east, the coal-rich Arigna mountains. There is still some small-scale mining near Arigna and several well preserved sweat houses.

The **Drumanone dolmen** is 2 miles (3km) west of Boyle along a grassy lane off the R294, on the north side of the Sligo-Dublin railway line. It has one of the largest capstones in Ireland. Dolmens, the name derives from the Breton meaning 'stone table', are neolithic tombs where one huge flat stone is balanced on three or more unhewn upright stones. Drumanone's capstone has slipped off its five stubby legs but still impresses by its size — 14ft by 10ft (4m x 3m). While the dolmens of Ireland are not so big, nor so thick on the ground as in Brittany, there is a pleasant informality in the way they stand at the side of the road, in the corner of a field, or in someone's front garden.

Lough Gara upstream from Boyle is notable for its great number of crannogs, artificial islands from about AD500, some of which were in use up until the seventeenth century. Crannogs (from *crann* meaning 'tree' in Gaelic) are found predominantly in Ireland and are a striking feature of Irish lakes and shallow stretches of inland rivers. They were built from timber, with layers of brushwood, stone, peat, clay, anything handy that would give bulk, floated out or carried over in dug-out boats. The whole mass was anchored to the bottom of the lake, and a little house with a protective fence was built on top.

Fear of marauders or wild animals, perhaps a hostile land environment, swamps, bogs, it is not at all clear what led these Celtic farmers to undertake such a tremendous labour. At Lough Gara the level of the lake was lowered during drainage work in 1952 and, as the water fell, more and more crannogs popped up — over 360 of them.

Frenchpark 9 miles (14km) south-west of Boyle (R361) is the birthplace of Douglas Hyde (1860-1949), ardent pioneer of the Irish language revival, first professor of Irish at the National University (UCD), and first president of Ireland (1938-45). However, he is mostly remembered for founding the Gaelic League to promote the Irish language and Irish culture, in particular games and dancing. There is a Douglas Hyde interpretive centre in Frenchpark open during the summer.

People do not seem as grateful to Hyde as one might expect them to be. He is held responsible for allowing the League to become politicised and the language to be hijacked by political nationalism. Far from having saved Gaelic, spoken as their native language by 600,000 Irish people when the League was founded (1893), he is associated with its decline. Poor Hyde is a scapegoat for the disappointment over the decline of Gaelic of which there are now barely 10,000 native speakers. His house, Ratra Park, on the outskirts of the village, is not open to the public but his grave is at the Anglican parish church nearby (Churchstreet). The graveyard is a little untended, neglected even, perfect for a poet and Gaelic scholar, but not quite as spruce as one might expect for Ireland's first president.

Rathcroghan (Rathcruachan, Cruachan) near Tulsk in County Roscommon is the capital of the pagan kingdom of Connaught. Ask at the heritage centre in Strokestown village for a map of the monuments. Associated with some of the key characters in the legends of Ireland, Rathcroghan is a very important archaeological site, as yet undeveloped and with the scantiest of signposting but nonetheless on a par with the royal seats of Tara in County Meath and Emain Macha (Navan Fort) near Armagh.

The area designated covers about 3 square miles (8sq km) and encompasses the graves of the Firbolg kings, the palace of Queen Maeve, the crowning mound of the Celtic kings of Connaught and many other sacred and profane places. There are more than seventy prehistoric monuments of ritual origin and whole series of ring-forts, early Christian farmsteads. The ring-forts are on broad ridges overlooking the plain, at a slight distance from the ritual monuments.

The crowning place of the kings of Connaught is a small grassy mound just south of Tulsk off the N61. A much more impressive

The Hill of Rathcroghan, where the Celtic kings of Connaught were once crowned

earthwork is the Hill of Rathcroghan, a flat-topped circular mound 20ft (6m) high with a diameter of 280ft (85m), off the N5 3 miles (5km) north-west of Tulsk on the left side of the road. According to tradition Queen Maeve of Connaught had her palace on the top. It is hard to warm to Maeve. She seems to have combined the least appealing traits of Lady Macbeth, Clytemnestra and Grendel's mother, and had some unattractive ones of her own.

An area immediately south of the Hill of Rathcroghan is particularly rich in monuments including stones carved with ogham characters. There is also a souterrain associated with the Firbolgs, the legendary agricultural people from Greece who invaded Ireland in neolithic times. The tall red sandstone pillar nearby marks the burial place of Daithi, described as the last pagan king of Ireland. According to the *Book of Leinster* he died after being struck by lightning while he was off raiding in Gaul. Daithi is said to be the ancestor of the O'Dowds, and why not.

A little further south along this same road (N61) is **Roscommon** town, with its huge ruined royal fortress and Dominican priory, both built in the thirteenth century. The priory is mentioned in the *Annals of Lough Cé* as being founded by Phelim O'Conor (died 1265) whose effigy lies in a niche in the chancel guarded by eight gallowglasses — medieval mercenaries hired by the Irish kings to fight the Normans.

One little gallowglass is armed with a battle axe, the other seven have swords, and they are wearing chain mail. Phelim's effigy has been mutilated, hardly the fault of the gallowglasses, since they were carved only at the end of the fifteenth century. The effigy is one of two surviving early Irish royal tomb-effigies; the other is in the Cistercian abbey church at Corcomroe, County Clare.

Roscommon castle, on the outskirts of the town, has a striking twin-towered gatehouse and four massive corner towers. It is almost symmetrical, similar in plan to Harlech and Beaumaris in north Wales, and was part of the Norman attempt to establish a presence for the Crown west of the Shannon. There are two other castles near here which were built for the same purpose: Athlone castle is one, the other is the little-visited Rinndown castle south-east of Roscommon on a peninsula jutting into Lough Ree. (To see Rinndown take the N61 to Lecarrow, then a minor track passing close to the ruins. They are so draped in ivy that it is hard to see what a great castle Rinndown must have been.) Barely 4 years after Roscommon was completed in

The town of Roscommon takes its name and origin from St Coman who founded a monastery here in early Christian times

Roscommon castle was built by the Normans to govern west of the Shannon

1269, it was flattened by the Irish but rebuilt and, with an English garrison back in residence by 1280, captured in 1340 by the O'Conors and held by them for most of the next 200 years, retaken by Lord Deputy Sir Henry Sidney in 1569, remodelled in the sixteenth century, and changed hands several more times before the Cromwellians put it permanently out of action in 1652 by dismantling the fortifications. A fairly average career for an Irish castle.

It is a remarkable fact that throughout these upheavals, the local Dominicans managed to stay on in the town. They were there for 600 years, including throughout the period of the penal laws when all monks and friars were supposed to have been expelled from Ireland. The price of staying could be high, and there were massacres. For instance at **Fuerty**, a few miles west of Roscommon (R366), some 100 priests were done to death in the Franciscan church. The graveyard adjacent to the ruins has interesting slabs and headstones with Irish inscriptions dating from about 1720.

From Roscommon take the N60 through **Castlerea** to **Clonalis House**, just west of the town, a Victorian mansion which is open to visitors, and you can also stay overnight. It is the ancestral estate of the O'Conors of Connaught, perhaps the noblest of all Irish families, or septs. Twenty-four kings of Connaught, the first one in the fourth century AD, came from this family, and so did eleven high kings of Ireland, including the last two high kings — Turlough O'Conor

(1088-1156) and his son Rory O'Conor (1116-98) who was forced to surrender sovereignty to the Normans in 1186. Lest there be any doubt of the family's royal antecedents, the lumpy coronation stone of the kings of Connaught sits at the front door of the house, brought from Rathcroghan presumably for safe-keeping.

The mansion has an unprepossessing exterior but it is full of treasures, portraits, furniture and a fascinating O'Conor archive going back sixty generations and running into thousands of documents. Actually there are two Clonalis Houses on the estate. The family abandoned the Georgian house because they thought its low-lying position by the river was unhealthy and they moved into the present large mansion in 1880. Whereas most people might be expected to demolish a redundant house, the O'Conors left theirs standing, decaying picturesquely.

Among many notable objects preserved in the Victorian mansion is a seventeenth-century chalice from penal times which was made to be taken apart and the sections hidden separately. The harp which belonged to Carolan is also here, a survivor from that same period when Irish musical instruments were proscribed and could be seized. It is one of a dozen or so early Irish harps still in existence. The oldest is the fourteenth-century 'Brian Boru's Harp' preserved in Trinity College, Dublin. The Irish harp is a sturdy instrument — as seen on Guinness cans — with a thick outward-curving fore-pillar and a sounding box made from a single piece of willow.

In 1720 the O'Conors regained possession of their confiscated family estate at Belanagare a few miles from Clonalis. Things nearly went wrong again when the youngest brother of the antiquary Charles O'Conor (1710-91) became a Protestant and claimed the estate which, under the penal laws of the time, he was entitled to do. Charles just managed to buy him off.

A nineteenth-century Charles O'Conor stood for US president in 1872 against Ulysses S Grant. Another member of the Connaught sept was General Sir Luke O'Connor (1832-1915) who enlisted as a private in the British army and won a Victoria Cross in the Crimean war at the battle of Alma in 1855.

Enfin Mayo. Moving from one Irish county into another has certain similarities with crossing a US stateline. People generally are very conscious of belonging to a particular county — so different from the way of things in England and Wales where tinkerings with boundaries have consigned many old counties to folk memory, shapes on embroidery samplers, names on pre-packaged supermarket cheese. In Ireland, however, the system provides a universal and

The Bank of Ireland at Roscommon

convenient frame of reference. For example, Gaelic football, car registrations, a person's accent and even someone's sense of humour are highly county-specific, and talk of the '26 counties' (the Republic), the 'six counties' (Northern Ireland) or the concept of a '32-county' state is an extension of this. Yet the shiring of Ireland in about 1600, dividing it into counties in the English fashion, was an alien form of administration, much resented when it was imposed, not least because some Irish landowners lost their land during the process. But now the Irish are very attached to their counties and the system continues virtually unchanged since the early seventeenth century.

The N60 continues to the small market town of **Ballyhaunis**, where you might detour briefly to see an impressive ogham standing (leaning now) stone at Braghlaboy, signposted off the Island Lake road. Then return to the N60 which runs on to **Claremorris**, a crossroads village and railway junction set in the green flatlands of the Plains of Mayo. The county name derives from the ancient settlement of **Mayo** ('plain of the yew trees') between Claremorris and Lough Carra. Now a blink-and-miss ruin at a bend in the road, Mayo was an important seventh-century monastery founded by Bishop Colman of Lindisfarne specially for his English adherents. They quarrelled with the Irish monks at his Inishbofin monastery, so he transferred them to a new monastery here, known thereafter as

Clonalis House, Castlerea, ancestral home of the O'Conors of Connaught

Mag nEo na Sachsan ('Mayo of the English'). Commuting between the two must have had its difficulties.

The Marian shrine of **Knock**, the Lourdes of Ireland, is 6 miles (10km) from Ballyhaunis, west along the R323. The small folk museum in the middle of the town gives some background and an insight into the violent political climate of 1879, the year the Virgin Mary appeared here in a vision. Radical forces were abroad. The Land League of Mayo, a tenant farmers' rights organisation which soon became a national movement, led to rents being withheld and evictions on a large scale. It brought with it a sinister baggage of intimidation and murder. Bands of macho young law enforcers roamed the countryside at night. There were reports of orgies, and mutilations such as ear-cutting, priests' ears sometimes, and satanic acts of animal torture. In the midst of this madness a *deus ex machina* was greatly to be wished. On 21 August 1879, fifteen villagers saw apparitions of Mary, Joseph, John the Baptist and sundry angels on the gable wall of Knock parish church. After 2 hours the apparitions vanished but the village was never quite the same again.

The happening is said to have had a sobering effect on the local gangsters. A commission of enquiry held by the archbishop of Tuam declared the vision to be authentic. However, it was 100 years before the trickle of pilgrims began to resemble if not yet a torrent, at least a stream occasionally in spate. In 1976 a vast basilica church for 20,000 people opened for business and the pope came here in 1979. The original poor village, its wretchedness is well documented, swelled in the twinkling of an eye to a religious emporium of chapels, statues, carparks and tat shops. Apparition-watchers sit on benches ranked before the original gable wall, now glassed over, hoping for a reappearance. Holy water is available from a row of taps nearby. The pilgrims' fervency is intense, and ordinary visitors tend not to linger.

Emigration has left much of Mayo as empty as Calabria. People are still leaving in search of jobs and in some areas, the empty houses are new, modern houses. Even the local sports scene feels the pinch: no sooner has a decent Gaelic football team been put together than the best players leave to work in England or New York. In such circumstances it seemed almost like another miracle when a tiny but perfectly formed modern airport opened in the middle of this impoverished region in 1986. Horan International Airport is its official title, named for the energetic parish priest who brought the project to fruition. Cities with large Irish populations like Luton and Manchester are now only an hour away and it is a godsend for construction workers coming home for a break from the building sites of England. There is also a sad one-way traffic in the coffins of emigrants, the fulfilment of their last wish, to be buried at home in Ireland.

On now to the small monastic church of **Ballintubber** down a minor road (signposted) off the Ballinrobe-Castlebar road (N84) north of **Lough Carra**. Avert your eyes, if you can, from the crude statuary littered around outside and think instead about Cathal 'Red Hand' O'Conor, the king of Connaught who founded the abbey for the Augustinians in 1216. Although the abbey was banned in 1524 and burned in 1653, Catholic services have been held here more or less continuously up to the present day. The church has been well restored, and preserves its original fine carved capitals in the chancel similar to those at Boyle, though with more flourishes than the sculptor at Boyle would have been allowed. Ballintubber shares a feature with another Cistercian house: its round-headed windows are like the windows at Knockmoy Abbey in County Galway. Those medieval master masons certainly got around. From Ballintubber there is a traditional pilgrim's path, recently reopened, to Croagh Patrick. Its distinctive cone is clearly visible some 15 miles (24km) to the west. Known as the Tóchar Phádraig or 'Patrick's causeway' (since the saint is said to have trod it himself), the walk is 22 miles (35km), including the stony scramble up to the summit, or 44 miles (70km) if you insist on walking back.

The road beyond Ballintubber curls round the north end of Lough Carra to the atmospheric ruins of **Moore Hall**, birthplace of George Moore (1852-1933), novelist and writer of some fine short stories. His ashes are buried on an island in the lough. Though he lived mostly in Dublin and especially London, Moore drew greatly on his rural Irish childhood. *The Lake*, for example, well describes the countryside around Lough Carra and his most successful novel, *Esther Waters*, used his father's racing stables as background. He spent the last 22 years of his life being lionised by London literati at 121 Ebury Street, 'that long, lacklustre street', in SW1.

Moore Hall was destroyed during the Civil War in 1923 when Colonel Maurice Moore, George Moore's brother, was a senator in the first Free State government. In the first 2 months of that year the houses of thirty-seven senators went up in smoke. Among them was the Connemara mansion of Oliver St John Gogarty (1878-1957), the flamboyant Dublin wit and poet (and ENT surgeon), who later rebuilt it as a hotel (Renvyle House Hotel, north of Letterfrack) and threw parties there for his friends. It was Gogarty who ferried George Moore's funerary urn across Lough Carra in a rowing boat in 1933. Wealthy, influential and immensely privileged though these southern Unionist families were, by 1923 their political power had gone for good.

Lough Carra is the most northerly, and smallest, of a chain of three excellent fishing lakes — **Lough Mask** and **Lough Corrib** are the others — separating mountainous Connemara and south-west Mayo from the flattish agricultural lands to the east. The village of **Cong** (*cunga* 'neck') is named for its position on the narrow strip of land dividing Mask and Corrib loughs. It is an agreeable base for anglers, and for potholers and speleologists who come to explore the limestone caves and underground streams. An attempt to link the loughs by canal in the late 1840s failed when the water vanished into the porous limestone. You can still see the dry canal and its never-quite-finished locks. The market cross in the village main street has a medieval inscription on the base commending the O'Duffys, a family which produced cohorts of priests, abbots and bishops. One archbishop of Tuam was Cadhla O'Duffy who, as Rory O'Conor's ambassador, went on a vain mission to the court of Henry II in 1175.

The village is adjoined by **Ashford Castle**, a Victorian castellated former stately home of the Guinness family. Now a swanky hotel with an opulent interior, its most famous guest to date is US president Reagan. Tourists are invited to explore the magnificent grounds, though unless you are a staying guest (or look like one) there is an entrance fee. A riding centre caters for horsy visitors. Outside the entrance to the demesne, the lovely little ruin of Cong Abbey, an Augustinian house founded by Turlough O'Conor, stands on the site of an older, seventh-century monastery. Turlough's son Rory spent his last gloomy years here after surrendering the high kingship of Ireland to the Normans. The ruin retains four enchanting doorways, the best being a slype doorway with foliage carvings on the capitals. The cloister arcade, dating from about 1220, was reconstructed with Guinness money in 1860. For some reason a deplorably ugly church has been built up against the monument.

Captain Boycott and the Land Leaguers

Lough Mask House, the residence of Charles Boycott, the retired army captain who was Lord Erne's Mayo land agent in the 1870s, is just north of Cong opposite the island of Inishmaine. When Captain Boycott refused to reduce rents by 25 per cent as demanded by the Land Leaguers, the locals ostracised him. In 1880, unable to find anyone locally to harvest his crops, he drafted in 50 Orangemen from Cavan to do the work. The indignation of the Mayomen was such that 1,000 policemen were needed to protect the harvesters. The operation cost the government £10,000. From these events the English language acquired the word 'boycott'.

Castlebar is the county town of Mayo and has an airport and a large pink slab of a county hall to prove it but, despite the fame of the 'Castlebar Races', no race course. The reference is a gleeful recollection of the occasion in 1798 when General Humbert, commanding a small French force, chased the English garrison out of town. John Moore (of Moore Hall), president of the 'Republic of Connaught' for one week, is buried on the green. The Michael Davitt museum adjacent to the Dominican friary at **Straid**, on the way to Ballina (N5/N58), is a rewarding visit for background to the Land League. The Fenian leader was born in the village in 1846. A modern mini version of Davitt's campaign has been going on in Castlebar for the past 20 years. When Lord Lucan vanished after the murder of his children's nanny in 1974, residents of Castlebar stopped paying ground rents due to him. They are willing to pay when he comes to collect, in person. On a short stretch of the N5 (Castlebar-Swinford road) within a few miles of each other, are two fine round towers, a curiously fat one near **Turlough** with a church built inches away (2 inches) and, at **Meelick**, a slimmer one with no cap but with a cross-carved slab bolted on to the bottom.

From Castlebar, rather than following the N60 to Westport and then the Newport road snaking round to Achill Island, take the scenic route between Lough Conn and Lough Cullin to **Ballina** (pronounced ballynar), the first town General Humbert captured after landing at Killala. Between here and the flat chocolate-brown Mullet peninsula is some wonderful rugged Atlantic scenery, old abbeys, quirky little settlements and great views of the Nephin Beg mountains across the bog. At the eastern end of the range the glitzy cone of Nephin (2,646ft/807m) rises close to Lough Conn. Ruined **Errew Abbey** stands at the end of a peninsula in the lough, where peat cutting has exposed ancient pine tree stumps and pieces of petrified wood lie on the spongy ground. A tiny oratory known as the 'Church of the Black Nun', is a few yards north of the abbey. It has immensely thick walls.

All kinds of dramas have been enacted at Ballina's congenial Imperial Hotel. Humbert found it a comfortable if temporary billet when he passed through in 1798. In the Civil War that followed the Anglo-Irish Treaty of 1921, the hotel was a pro-Treaty (provisional government) headquarters but was captured by Michael Kilroy's anti-Treaty (Republican) forces. In November 1990 it was the scene of jubilation when Mary Robinson, who was born in Ballina, was elected president of Ireland.

Opposite the five-arch bridge over the Moy river, and dwarfed by the adjoining cathedral, the ruined church of **Ardnaree** friary is tucked away behind a high wall. Founded for the Augustinians by the O'Dowds, the church has an elegant but tiny west doorway. The members of this family, who controlled all the north coast of Mayo up until the fifteenth century, were noted for their great height. For example, the O'Dowd leader killed at the Boyne in 1690 was said to be 7ft (2m) tall. He must have bent low to get through this door.

Drive across the railway track just before the station to see the dolmen of the **Four Maols**, on rising ground on the left. As dolmens go, it is not very special but it is associated with a tantalisingly obscure sixth-century crime. A rather shady bishop was murdered by four of his pupils. What drove them to the deed is not recorded, only their names are known: Maol Cróin, Maol Seanaidh, Maol Da-Lua and Maol Deoraidh. Maol means 'bald', or shaven, perhaps they were druids. They were hanged at Ardnaree (*Ard na Riaghadh*, 'Hill of the Executions') near where the friary was later built, then brought across the river and buried close to this 3,000-year-old pagan tomb.

The river at Ballina, birthplace of Mary Robinson, Ireland's first woman president

A weathered, wordless grave slab which has been jammed underneath the dolmen does not appear to be of great antiquity.

Killala's gardens are full of the pink mallow even in December and the mild climate supports tender plants that brighten the prevailing grey stone and whitewash livery of the coastal settlements. The town itself has a small cathedral with a fine slender steeple, a round tower with a disconcerting bulge in the side part way up, and at least two busts of General Humbert. The temptation to dawdle is considerable. Two splendid fifteenth-century Franciscan friaries, Rosserk Abbey and Moyne Abbey, on the road from Ballina should not be missed. Two miles (3km) beyond Killala, Rathfran Abbey and the very tall Breastagh ogham stone are signposted at **Palmerstown** where an impressive 11-arch bridge spans the Cloonaghmore river. The megalithic tombs just west of **Ballycastle** village on the land side of the road are two of many in the area. Five miles (8km) down the road a large prehistoric farm has been uncovered at **Céide Fields.**

Killala has a round tower and a cathedral with a fine slender steeple

Field patterns, stone-walled animal enclosures and megalithic tombs, including a superb court grave at Behy, were discovered in the cut-away bog. The settlement, reckoned to cover over 2,500 acres (1,000 hectares), has been dated to 3,000BC and is well interpreted at the visitor centre. A second, smaller neolithic farming landscape has been uncovered at **Belderrig** 5 miles (8km) further west.

The grandeur of the view from Benwee Head, a huge headland buttressing north-west Mayo against the Atlantic, has few equals in good weather. Access is via Kilgalligan village, and involves a 15-minute walk across rough grass. The jagged Stags (or Stacks) of **Broadhaven** 2 miles (3km) offshore are home to birds and seals, with great fishing in the deep water, though landing a boat is not feasible. These inhospitable rocks were recently on the market, a snip at £18,000.

It is a quick and pleasant drive to Belmullet from the Gaeltacht village of Glenamoy. North-west Mayo is a Gaeltacht enclave, a designated Irish-speaking district which is officially supported in an attempt to preserve the language. Although the number of native speakers continues to decline, there is widespread interest in Irish. Anyone wishing to learn it can attend classes in a Gaeltacht area, staying in the home of native speakers. **Belmullet**, the main settlement of this region which is still known by its Norman barony name of Erris, is a haphazard kind of town, at the edge of the time zone, surrounded

Rosserk Abbey, a fifteenth-century Franciscan foundation

by peat, mud and water, and at its most untidy at low tide. The lopsided square, with a vegetable stall marooned in the middle, is enlivened during the annual fair and sea-angling festival in August. It is possible to stay quite comfortably at the Western Strands (see Accommodation section), the town's dilapidated hotel, despite a startling message in the lounge bar, 'Whoever invented diets should be dragged into the street and shot'. The road from Belmullet down to Blacksod Point at the south tip of the peninsula passes, after 3 miles (5km), the turning to ruined Cross Abbey. Directly opposite the ruin, about a mile (2km) offshore, is **Inishglora** island which is associated with the sixth-century saint, Brendan the Navigator, and has interesting medieval churches, bee-hive huts and a holy well. This is one of several islands around the Mullet peninsula with monastic remains which are visitable by boat or curragh in summer.

And now east across the thin Mayo blanket bog. Somewhere along this lonely road a local troublemaker received summary justice at the hands of the men of Erris. According to J.M Synge, his antisocial behaviour included striking the parish priest and father-ing two sets of twins out of wedlock:

> 'And when you're walking out the way
> From Bangor to Belmullet,
> You'll see a flat cross on a stone
> Where men choked Danny's gullet.'

Great beehives of hand-won peat are piled up wherever you look. A surprising number of people claim to enjoy cutting peat, and many have their own little bit of bog, or a share of one. It is an immense manual labour, cutting and turning and stacking. How much peat is cut by hand each year, who can say? It is certainly only a fraction of what is stripped by mechanised methods from the deep raised bogs of the Midlands. But what is this belching chimney in the middle distance? Oh dear, Mayo has its own power station here at Bellacorick, and bulldozers are scraping the peat off the bog to feed the monster.

People go to **Achill** for the sea fishing and sailing, and for beautiful beaches like Keel Strand, 2 miles (3km) plus of silky sand. It is Ireland's largest island. Access is over the chunky peninsula of Corraun and across the bridge spanning Achill Sound and then through a straggle of B&B places, garages and fast food outlets, abuzz with tourists in the summer, but quiet in winter. It seems unlikely now but until the 1930s the Midland Great Western Railway ran a passenger service all the way to Achill Sound. Contrary to appearances, it is possible, by asking, to find accommodation and places to eat at any time of the year. The main road through the middle of the rocky island passes little Keel Lough — rich in brown trout and some sea trout and jam-packed with swans in winter — and ends at Keem Strand, a picturesque south-facing anchorage for yachts and fishing boats, and a haunt of the basking shark. These huge harmless creatures, some 35ft (11m) long and weighing up to six tons, used to be commercially hunted at Keem, caught in nets and harpooned from curraghs. You do not see that today, though there is plenty of offshore shark fishing, porbeagle especially, between April and July. The steep heathery slopes of **Croaghan**, a 2,200ft (671m) mountain occupying the entire west end of the island, come steeply down to the sea at Keem Strand. The view from Croaghan's summit is the best of all the Achill peaks. Paul Henry (1876-1958), who painted Whistlerish Mayo landscapes, lived on Achill between 1912 and 1919. His wife Grace, also an artist, intrigued the islanders by painting by moonlight at Dooagh bridge.

The self-possessed holiday settlement at **Dugort** on the north side of Achill is a former protestant mission founded by clergyman Edward Nangle in 1834. The mission buildings — orphanage, print shop, infirmary, small hotel, and Mr Nangle's residence — are arranged in a neat terrace fronting on to a flowery green. All teaching and preaching was in Gaelic and food and clothing was provided to those who hearkened to Mr Nangle's message. It seems there were many converts during the 1845-49 famine though most of them reconverted afterwards. Two miles (8km) away on the slopes of Slievemore mountain there is an interesting 'booley' village where herdsmen and their families lived during 'booleying', the seasonal movement of cattle to summer pastures. The place has long since tumbled down but you can count the tiny floor plans of some seventy cabins. Achill has several other ruined villages, though whether these are booley or merely 'deserted' villages is hard to say. Here and there one comes on the old graveyards of victims of famine and shipwrecks, with separate ones for unbaptised infants, and there are numerous standing stones, dolmens and stone circles. Ask at Dugort about boats visiting the Seal Caves which run underneath Slievemore. Visitable islands off Achill include tiny **Inishgalloon** opposite Purteen harbour which is much used by sea anglers, and two larger islands, Inishbiggle (boats from Bull's Head) and the more interesting **Achillbeg** which has an elaborate promontory fort and various defensive ramparts facing out to sea. Boats to Achillbeg leave from Cloghmore.

From Achill it is a short run to Westport via Burrishoole Abbey and Newport. A bit of Newport Bay comes right up to the graveyard at **Burrishoole**. This fifteenth-century Dominican friary was later turned into a fortified garrison. A stumpy tower and a charming two-light ogee-headed window in the north wall are features of the ruined church. **Newport** has an outsized railway viaduct and, across the river from the wide main street lined with small gaily painted houses, an elegant Georgian mansion, now a hotel popular with anglers who come here for sea trout and salmon.

The delightful town of **Westport** was laid out to a formal plan in 1780 for Peter Browne, second earl of Altamont, and it is one of the nicest towns in Ireland for strolling around. Altamont was an improving landlord, made immensely rich by marriage to a West Indies sugar heiress. He enlarged Westport House, home of the Brownes, earls of Altamont and marquesses of Sligo, and developed the town at the edge of the demesne. The Carrowbeg river was diverted through the town, canalised and spanned by a fine eighteenth-century stone bridge and several other steep little bridges. The stream flows between Georgian malls, overhung by lime trees, a pleasant wateriness reminiscent of Venetian Treviso. The town has an unusual octagonal market square graced by a statue of St Patrick and, across the stream from the Catholic church, a pleasant old coaching/railway inn where Thackeray stayed in 1842. The earl also developed Westport Quay as a commercial port and built huge warehouses along the quays but its heyday was short. The town declined after the linen trade moved north, the railway came, and in the nineteenth century the port's main trade was emigrants sailing to America. Westport now is a prosperous place with a congenial atmosphere. Warehouses have been converted to restaurants, with Atlantic fish prominent on the menu, and sea anglers come for the sport in Clew Bay.

Westport House, the only stately home in Mayo open to the public, has a variety of interesting features and objects to see. The beautiful dining room was designed by James Wyatt (1746-1813), the English architect who dominated Irish country house architecture for over 30 years. Family portraits, landscapes, horses and a Rubens *Holy Family* are among the numerous paintings, with Chinese wallpaper, naval prints, glass, silver and furniture all of interest. A number of tourist attractions, including a mini-zoo, have been introduced at Westport to help meet the cost of maintaining the fabric of the house.

The two columns at the front of the library are copies of pillars from the Treasury of Atreus at Mycenae. The original pillars were discovered in the house in 1906 and were sold to the British Museum. They had been whisked to Westport from Greece by the second marquess, Howe Peter Browne (1788-1845) and stashed in the basement. He was a friend of Lord Byron and the same age, and tended to get into scrapes. Travelling with Byron in Greece in the summer of 1810 he bribed two sailors from a British warship to sail his yacht — Byron called it 'Sligo's scrape with the Navy'. When he got home he was jailed for 4 months and fined £5,000.

The holy mountain **Croagh Patrick** is the object of extraordinary pieties on the last Sunday in July, known as Garland Sunday, when thousands of pilgrims, some barefoot, swarm up the erosion-scarred, statue-studded mountain. St Patrick spent 40 days fasting and praying on the top of Croagh Patrick, and it was up here that he performed the bell-ringing ceremony necessary to rid Ireland of snakes. Each time he rang his bell he threw it over a precipice (Lugnanarrib) whereupon hordes of reptiles, lemming-like, hurled themselves after it. Hovering about were friendly spirits who caught and returned the bell to the saint for him to repeat the procedure, until every snake and toad in Ireland had gone. A heady mix of Christian mysteries and Celtic animism hangs about the mountain and its pilgrimages. Garland Sunday approximates to Lughnasa, the festival of Lugh, a pre-Christian deity well known throughout the Celtic world. Known as 'many-skilled', Lugh was a wonderfully versatile god, equal to any eventuality, an ideal ally in an uncertain world. Lughnasa (1 August) was one of the four great feasts of the old Celtic calendar when people celebrated the season's successful cattle-raising.

The obvious approach to Croagh Patrick is from the capacious carpark with a conveniently adjacent pub at Murrisk, 5 miles (8km) west of Westport on the R335 coast road to Louisburgh. The small ruined church nearby is a fifteenth-century Augustinian friary founded by the O'Malleys, the celebrated clan of Mayo sea rovers who included among their number Grace O'Malley (c1530-c1600), ruler of western Mayo, a fiery pirate leader who impressed Sir Philip Sidney as 'a most famous feminine sea captain'. She had a power base on Clare Island at the entrance to Clew Bay.

There is a wondrous view from the summit across the sparkling islands of the inner waters of Clew Bay. Prominent on the mountain itself is the modern chapel that has been cemented to the top for the purposes of confession and Holy Communion, thereby adding quite a few extra feet to the Ordnance Survey's official height of 2,510ft (765m). However, when it comes to commercial developments on the mountain, the Catholic church and environmentalists find themselves actually in alliance. A plan to start gold mining on the mountain is being resisted and an application to install a cable car to the top — thus taking the penance out of the pilgrimage — has come to nothing. The fame of Croagh Patrick might lead one to expect a fair number of walkers all year round but it is virtually deserted except in summer, and the pub at Murrisk may not be open.

Clare Island is 25 minutes by boat (or curragh on sunny days) from Roonah Quay beyond **Louisburgh**, a pretty village with a peaceful harbour and sandy beach. Nearby at Old Head are the remnants of an ancient Atlantic oakwood. Clare Island was the centre of an international survey of flora and fauna in 1909 when a team of scientists arrived here en masse to study the biology of this most western part of the European continent. Looking at the stony, hedgeless, treeless place, it is hard to believe that over 8,000 different species were identified. The castle known as Grace O'Malley's Castle stands four-square at the east end of the island. It served as a coastguard station in the nineteenth century, and later as a police station. At least as interesting is a fifteenth-century ruined church a mile (2km) to the west, standing on the site of a Cistercian hermit cell which has disappeared. Fragmentary traces of medieval painting survive on the plastered ceiling of the chancel vault and on a tomb canopy. The O'Malley motto, inscribed on a round-headed arch at the entrance to the chancel, enshrines the clan's prowess at sea: *terra marique potens* — 'powerful on land and sea'.

Driving south from Louisburgh across desolate moorland, the grim riven cliffs of **Mweelrea** (*maol riabhach*, bald brindled mountain) rise inhospitably to 2,688ft (820m), the highest point in Connaught. This is by far the more dramatic of the two north-south routes crossing the peninsula from Clew Bay to Killary Harbour. The road runs up to a spectacular pass between Mweelrea and the Sheefry Hills, where Doo Lough (Black Lake), a long sombre sheet of water flanked by steep mountains, appears on the right and, beyond the roadside memorial to victims of the 1845-49 famine, the deserted village of **Delphi** a little way downstream. Plans to mine gold in this beautiful valley have been frozen for the time being. If you must climb Mweelrea, and it really is not for beginners, the south end of Doo Lough, where there is space for parking, is a good place to start from. As usual, getting on to the mountain is the hardest part. Scrabble your way across the stream north of the upmarket fishing lodge (walkers are not encouraged to go through the hotel's grounds) and persevere over the tussocky bog. Once you get up to the skyline, you can make for the first summit knowing that the worst is over. You are on a splendid broad highway, with less than 100ft (30m) between the three peaks that form the horseshoe — Ben Lugmore, Ben Bury and Mweelrea itself — and the views are superlative.

A good centre for walkers wanting to explore the Maumturks and the Twelve Bens (or Pins) is **Leenane**, where the village pub has a collection of stills (photographic ones) from *The Field* which was filmed here, with Richard Harris playing the flinty-hearted peasant.

The scenic walk along the south side of **Killary Harbour** gives a tremendous view of Mweelrea across the water. Mussels are farmed in the deep water at the landward (east) end of the fiord — much deeper than at the other end. Rosro Cottage, the house where Ludwig Wittgenstein found solitude in 1948 to work on *Philosophical Investigations*, published after his death in 1951, is now a youth hostel. There cannot have been too many distractions in this still austerely lovely place.

Connemara and the Aran Islands

The road to Clifden via the Quaker village of Letterfrack (N59) passes mock-Tudor **Kylemore Castle**, a girls' school run by Benedictine nuns, fast disappearing under rhododendrons the size of triffids, and also **Connemara National Park** which encompasses four of the Twelve Bens, including Benbaun, the tallest (2,395ft/730m). A less direct route, but dramatic and wild, is the road through the Inagh Valley which divides the Twelve Bens from the Maumturk range of mountains.

The cloisters at Cong Abbey in County Mayo. The interesting ruins display beautiful Romanesque-style carvings on several doorways (Chapter 1)

Statue of St Patrick at the beginning of the pilgrim path to the summit of Croagh Patrick, County Mayo (Chapter 1)

*Bar in Clifden,
County Galway
(Chapter 1)*

*Blind street musician
in Galway city
(Chapter 1)*

Capital of Connemara, **Clifden** has a superb setting on a rocky inlet above the sea, with the Twelve Bens rising beyond the town's church spires. It is at its most boisterous and picturesque in August when hundreds of shaggy little ponies come to town for the Connemara Pony Show. These diminutive animals are very hardy and will graze on seaweed and coarse seashore grasses when there is nothing else to eat. Prized for their riding and jumping abilities and sweet temperament, many of them end up as pets for lucky children.

Inishbofin, 7 miles (11 km) offshore, is easily visited as a day trip from Clifden in good weather. The ferry goes from Cleggan. The trip out gives ever-changing perspectives of Connemara and the Twelve Bens. If you intend staying overnight on the island, there are a couple of hotels, and you can hire bicycles.

Cromwell's Barrack, the seventeenth-century castle guarding the harbour, is not in good shape. It was once a 24-gun star fort, and the island was garrisoned until about 1700. Most of the prisoners held here were priests and monks. The remains of St Colman of Lindisfarne's monastic foundation are a mile (1km) north-east of the harbour close to a pretty beach. Colman returned to Ireland and came to Inishbofin after the Celtic church was defeated by the Roman church at the Synod of Whitby (664) in Northumbria. The argument was over the question of the calendar, in particular the method for calculating Easter, a wrangle that had been going on for 500 years.

If the weather is vile, as it can be in Connaught, make for **Galway** city. It has a disproportionate number of wet weather facilities! Bookshops, art galleries, theatres, pubs, restaurants, and 'the crack'. This last means good conversation, and you can find it in any of the establishments mentioned. Gateway to Connemara, cultural centre of the Gaeltacht, folk capital of the West, the old city has undergone a big urban renewal programme over the past decade but still has an intimate, convivial feel about it and a strong cultural identity. Students at University College Galway follow courses in Gaelic and English and the university has an archive of spoken material in all the Celtic languages. The Druid Lane theatre company's productions have an international following and another company performs entirely in Irish Gaelic.

Festivals are big business in Galway: the arts festival in July, the oyster festival at Clarinbridge in September, and the Galway Races, a week of horse racing in late July/early August, all bring their quota of freespenders into town.

The city's best feature is its waterfront. Three bridges span the broad Corrib river and you can join a cruise boat at Wood Quay in

summer for trips on Lough Corrib, or you might hire a rowing boat.
Opposite the cathedral upstream, at the salmon weir bridge, there is
a fine run of spring salmon, with hundreds of fish readying themselves to leap, a tremendous spectacle if you happen to be there in
March or April.

Buildings of interest include the fourteenth-century church of St
Nicholas, with a fine bell of eight peals and a memorial to James
Lynch Fitzstephen, mayor of Galway in 1493. The Lynch family
provided eighty-four mayors of Galway in the fifteenth and sixteenth centuries. This one is specially remembered for his 'act of
justice': he condemned his own son to death for murder and, since no
one else would do it, personally carried out the sentence himself and
hanged him. The Lynches were prosperous merchants, trading with
Bordeaux and Spain, and their fine house, called Lynch's Castle, at
the corner of Abbeygate Street is one of very few surviving merchant
mansions. Now a bank, it dates from about 1600. The home of Nora
Barnacle (1884-1951), wife of James Joyce, is a tiny house in Bowling
Green. It has been fixed up and is open to the public.

The **Aran Islands** are about 30 miles (48km) south-west of Galway, or 18 minutes by air from Carnmore airport if you are in a hurry.
For administrative purposes, the islands belong to County Galway
but they look like bits of detached Burren. In fact that is what they are
— a continuation of the Burren limestone ridge, with the same great
slabs of fractured slaty limestone and the strange vegetation of
Mediterranean and arctic-alpine plants. A patchwork of limestone-
floored fields, with tiny cultivated plots here and there, is a striking
feature. Every little paddock is enclosed by high dry-stone walls that
run all the way round. No gates! The locals unpick a wall to allow
animals through, and build it up again behind them — an activity
that truly indicates the agreeable pace of life on these islands.

A 30-minute trip on one of the numerous daily ferries that leave
from Doolin, County Clare, in summer brings you to little bun-
shaped Inisheer (East Island, population 250). Next comes Inishmaan
(Middle Island, population 300), and then long thin Inishmore (Big
Island, population 900).

The ferries from Spiddal, Rossaveel and Galway city come in to
Kilronan, the main town on **Inishmore**, at the north end of Killeany
Bay. It is a good base from which to visit some of the most remarkable
prehistoric and early Christian antiquities in Ireland. There are too
many to mention them all here.

The bus from Kilronan runs up to the west end of the island, with
stops on the way, and there are minibus tours of main attractions.

You can hire a bicycle, but walking is the best way to get around. In the sand dunes at the south end of the island, beyond Killeany village and the air strip, are the remains of St Enda's monastery, including a small church, St Enda's grave and the graves of another 120 saints. Enda (Einne or Eany) came to Aran in AD490 and evangelised the Firbolg inhabitants. He is credited with introducing monasticism to Ireland and an astonishing number of saints seem to have traipsed halfway across Ireland at the end of the fifth century to learn from him. St Jarlath came from Tuam, Finnian came from Clonard and Ciaran, Finnian's pupil, who later founded Clonmacnois, came too.

Inishmore has four tremendously impressive prehistoric stone forts. The best known, Dun Aengus, takes its name from a Firbolg chief. It is a semicircular citadel on the edge of a 250ft (76m) sheer cliff. Some authorities say that it is only half a fort, and that the other half fell into the sea. Two concentric walls form a horseshoe-shaped defence round the fort, and then comes a prehistoric tank trap: a broad band of thousands of nasty-looking upright stones staked close together in the ground, mightily effective in slowing down an enemy charge. Beyond these stone stakes, or *chevaux de frise,* is yet another wall. Equally interesting is Dubh Cathair (Black Fort), west of Killeany village, which has a similar *chevaux de frise* on the landward side of an immense wall, with two rows of stone houses on the sea side.

St Kieran's (Ciaran) church is a mile (2km) up the road from Kilronan on the right. Other important remains along or off this road are: Oghil stone fort; the Church of the Four Beautiful Saints — one of whom was St Berchan (died AD545), an unusually ugly saint, nicknamed 'flat-face'; Dun Onaght stone fort; a wonderfully preserved beehive-shaped monastic cell or clochan; and the Seven Churches site where people go to be cured at St Brecan's grave.

In summer you may be able to get to **Inishmaan** by curragh but there are other boats too. This little island has no fewer than eight national monuments, including the great stone fort of Dun Conor on the highest point and Kilcanonagh chapel (Church of the Canons), a fine oratory with a flat-headed doorway. J.M Synge (1871-1909) set his play *Riders to the Sea* on Inishmaan, and a thatched cottage where he sometimes stayed is preserved. Inisheer's proximity to the County Clare coast brings tourists in summer to buy Aran sweaters. The island is dominated by a large rock with a battered O'Brien castle on it. Among antiquities here are the remains of a church associated with Gobnat, a sixth-century lady saint who could order swarms of bees to do her bidding.

*Aughnanure Castle on the shores of Lough Corrib, near Oughterard, is a fine
example of a fifteenth-century fortified dwelling*

Cistercian **Knockmoy**, 7 miles (11km) south-east of Tuam, was founded in 1189 by the same 'Red Hand' O'Conor who underwrote Ballintubber for the Augustinians. On this occasion he had just beaten the English under Almeric St Lawrence and the abbey at Knockmoy , meaning 'Hill of the Slaughter', was intended to mark his victory. On the north wall of the chancel is a medieval mural. You can make out the black outlines of an angel, Christ giving a blessing, the martyrdom of St Sebastian and, further up the wall, the medieval *memento mori* tale of the Three Live Kings and the Three Dead Kings. The colours have all faded away. 'Red Hand' is thought to have retired to Knockmoy and died here in 1224. It is therefore rather disappointing to learn that the thirteenth-century canopied tomb niche is occupied by some other personage.

Pause a while at **Loughrea** to see the modern Irish stained glass in St Brendan's cathedral, which has a rose window by Evie Hone (1894-1955) who was influenced by the religious paintings of Georges Rouault. She was the most talented of the artists who worked at the Tower of Glass, a stained-glass workshop started in Dublin by Sarah Purser, a successful portrait painter. Purser did the window of St Brendan 'the navigator' at Loughrea.

Stories about St Brendan's legendary sea voyages and his miraculous encounters with monsters of the deep circulated throughout medieval Europe but facts about the saint are rather few. He was already an old man in AD560 when he established his foundation at **Clonfert**, not far from Clonmacnois (but on the west bank of the Shannon). Clonfert cathedral, actually a small church on the site of Brendan's monastery, has a very fine twelfth-century Irish-Romanesque doorway, with six recessed planes and a row of grotesques within the tall pediment. The innermost plane is a different colour. It is a fifteenth-century, limestone, addition.

The famous **Turoe Stone** is signposted off the R350 at Bullaun hamlet 4 miles (6km) north of Loughrea. This 3ft (1m) tall phallic-shaped white granite stone is richly decorated with abstract swirly motifs in the La Tène style (from the Celtic site found in Lake Neuchâtel, Switzerland) dating from 400BC.

The stone was removed from Feerwore, a pre-Christian site some miles away, and placed in the grounds of a private house so that an eye could be kept on it. Now bobbittised and neatly fixed in concrete, it is surrounded by a narrow circular cattle grid. The beeves of Ireland have always enjoyed a good scratch on a convenient field monument. They will lean on it, sit on it or lie underneath it at the first opportunity. Ireland's field monuments are prey to numerous other

*The famous Autographed Tree at Coole Park, where Lady Gregory entertained
leading figures of the Irish literary revival into the 1920s*

hazards — vandalism, accidents, theft (if the stone can be levered on to a lorry) — and the weather. The guardians of the Turoe Stone might as well have gone the whole hog and erected a shelter to shield it from the weather.

The N66 south-west from Loughrea to Gort passes, first, ruined **Roxborough House**, birthplace of the cultural nationalist Lady Gregory (1852-1932), friend and patron of W.B Yeats (1865-1939). Look out for the signpost for **Thoor Ballylee**, the sixteenth-century tower house where Yeats lived from time to time in the 1920s. The tower is now a Yeats Museum, much visited in the summer.**Coole Park**, 2 miles (3km) north of Gort on the N18, is also on the literary summer schools circuit. From 1880 it was the home of Lady Gregory and a centre of the Irish literary revival up until the 1920s. The estate was bought in 1927 by the Free State government which, having no interest in preserving the house, allowed a building contractor to dismantle it. However, the demesne with its beautiful lake, which Yeats celebrated in *The Wild Swans at Coole*, is open to the public as a wildlife park. A large copper beech in the walled garden, the Auto-graphed Tree, was Lady Gregory's arboreal visitors' book. The initials of famous guests like Augustus John, John Masefield and George Bernard Shaw, can still be seen, carved on the trunk. It is the most visited tree in Ireland.

Further Information
— Connaught —

Places to Visit

Aughrim
Near Ballinasloe, Co Galway
Battle of Aughrim Interpretive Centre
☎ (091) 63081 (See chapter 2)

Ballintubber Abbey
Co Mayo
Information on Croagh Patrick pilgrim path.
☎ (094) 30709/66597

Ballycastle
Co Mayo
Céide Fields Visitor Centre
Open: daily March to end of October.
☎ (096) 43325/43256

Boyle
Co Roscommon
Boyle Abbey
Open: daily mid-June to mid-September 9.30am-6.30pm.
☎ (079) 62604

King House (heritage centre)
Open: every day except Monday.
☎ (079) 63242

Castlerea
Co Roscommon
Clonalis House
Guided tours in summer 12noon-5pm every day except Monday. Other times by arrangement.
☎ (0907) 20014

Clare Island
Co Mayo
Centre for Island Studies
Clew Bay
☎ (098) 25048

Connemara National Park
Co Galway
Guided walks in high summer. Visitor centre open May to September inclusive.
☎ (095) 41054/41006

Foxford
Co Mayo
Woollen Mills
Visitor centre/shop
Open: Monday to Friday, 7 days all year.
☎ (094) 56104

Frenchpark
Co Roscommon
Douglas Hyde Centre
Open: every afternoon except Monday May to September, or contact curator Deirdre O'Gara at B&B (50 yards away).
☎ (0907) 70016

Galway city
A 1½-hour cruise around Lough Corrib leaves from the harbour (Wood Quay) at 1pm, 3pm and 4.30pm, late June to August only.
☎ (091) 68903

Gort
Co Galway
Thoor Ballylee
Open: every day 10am-6pm Easter to end of September.
☎ (091) 31436

Coole Park
National Park, always accessible.
☎ (091) 31804

Knock
Co Mayo
Knock Folk Museum
Open: all day from 10am every day May to October.
☎ (094) 88100

Letterfrack
Co Galway
Kylemore Castle
Open: daily 10am-6pm mid-March to end October. Closed Good Friday.
☎ (095) 41146

Louisburgh
Co Mayo
Grace O'Malley Heritage Centre
Open: daily 10am-6pm Easter to end
October.
☎ (098) 66195

Straid
Co Mayo
*Michael Davitt National Memorial
    Museum*
Open: in summer 10am-6pm daily,
except Sunday morning and Monday.
Closed lunchtime (1-2pm).
☎ Castlebar (094) 21207

Strokestown
Co Roscommon
Strokestown Park House Famine Museum
Open: June to September 12noon-5pm
every day except Monday.
☎ (078) 33013

County Heritage Centre
St John's
Church Street
Information/map of Rathcroghan
monuments.
Open: May to September 9.30am-
5.30pm weekdays (except Monday),
2-6pm Saturday and Sunday.
☎ (078) 33380/(079) 62414

Westport
Co Mayo
Westport House
Open: every afternoon May to
September plus mornings July and
August.
☎ (098) 25430

Travel

Ferries to the Islands
Clare Island ferry ☎ (098) 26307
Inishbofin Island ferry ☎ (095) 44642/
    45806
Arans (Inishmore)
    from Galway harbour ☎ (091) 62141
    from Rossaveel ☎ (091) 68903
    from Spiddal ☎ (099) 61266
    from Doolin, Co Clare ☎ (065) 74006

To Inishmore by air from Galway
(Carnmore airport): book by phone
with Aer Arann: ☎ (091) 93034.

Tourist Information Offices

Open: all year.

Galway
Co Galway
Victoria Place
Eyre Square
☎ (091) 63081

Knock (Horan) Airport
Co Mayo
Kilkelly
☎ (094) 67247

Westport
Co Galway
The Mall
☎ (098) 25711

2 • The Midlands

Leitrim, Cavan, Longford, Westmeath, Western Offaly

Wherever you start from, it takes a long time to get to Connaught, and more likely than not you will find yourself first traversing the land of the little lakes, the understated hinterland on its east side, the Irish Midlands. Precisely where the Midlands begin or end is difficult to say. Like the Barbarians vis-à-vis the Greeks, the region tends to be defined negatively. The part described here, spurned by tourists and in large part indifferent to them, encompasses Leitrim, Cavan, Longford, Westmeath and western Offaly.

An intermittent local dream envisions Ireland's first euroroute, which will run up the eastern seaboard from Rosslare to Belfast, detouring in a huge loop across the island to Connaught. This would spare Dubliners the tedium of jolting through the Midlands and would bring the splendours of Connemara within the Dublin ambit. Worse things have happened! In the meantime, there is no point in rushing. The roads do not allow it and besides, there are interesting things to see on the way.

The A4 from Enniskillen in Fermanagh runs between the two Macnean loughs to the Belcoo/Blacklion border crossing and then on to the N16. 'Welcome to Lovely Leitrim!' says a faded notice at **Glenfarne**, a hamlet caught in a time warp. A faintly lettered 'men at work' sign warns of ghostly gangs mending earlier generations of potholes. There are milk churns in the ditches, gently decaying stone walls, and a community hall with the words 'The Ballroom of Romance' painted on the side. This semi-derelict building is instantly recognised by couch potatoes as the setting for William Trevor's televised story of the same name, a poignant evocation of a rural Ireland where men drink and women wait.

Leitrim is disdained as the Cinderella of Irish counties, with too many lakes, too many rivers, and land so waterlogged and so poor, it is said that the snipe fly over it upside down because they know there is nothing down there worth eating — except for the fish. This is an excellent area for fishing, coarse angling especially. **Drumshanbo**

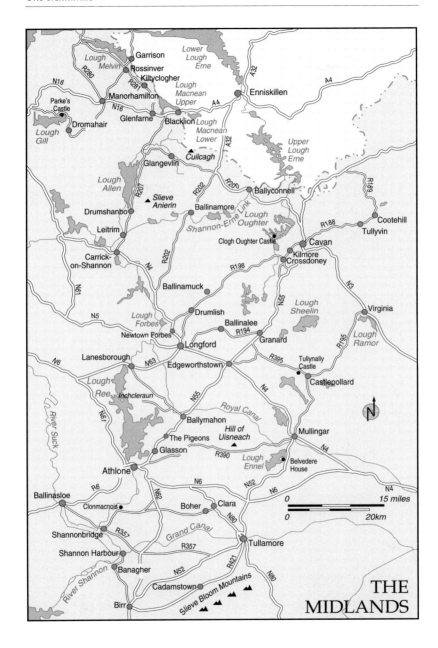

THE MIDLANDS

at the south tip of pike-filled Lough Allen is a spruce little village with steep streets and raised pavements, much patronised by pike fishermen. It was once a centre for iron smelting, using local timber to fuel the furnace. The iron was mined in the Iron Mountains, the bare hills that dominate the landscape to the east, particularly on Slieve Anierin (Mountain of Iron, 1,927ft/587m). Smelting stopped when there were no more trees to cut down.

The smaller lakes in the area are full of fish too. The reopening of the Victorian canal between Ballinamore and Ballyconnell in 1994 has again linked the Shannon with the Erne system and has created the longest leisure waterway in Europe — 500 miles (805km) of navigable water from Belleek to Limerick. The original through route was not a success and was in operation for barely a decade. There were engineering problems and the route was very slow compared with other inland waterways, but the main reason for its swift demise was one of timing. It was all too late: by the time the last weir was built and the last lock opened, goods were already being transported so much faster by Ireland's ever-widening network of railways. When the navigation trustees came to assess traffic on the waterway between its official opening in 1860 and 1869 they were dismayed to find that only eight boats had passed through and only £18 had been collected in tolls.

Along the 38-mile (61km) route there are 16 locks and no fewer than 34 bridges. It passes through beautiful varied countryside, several large lakes, including islanded Lough Garadice which has a pleasant harbour at the east end, then some smaller lakes before joining the Woodford river. The county takes its name from the sleepy Shannonside village of **Leitrim**, with its fragment of a medieval O'Rourke castle, a spreading chestnut tree and a fine stone bridge where the weeds and the wilderness of the past 120 years have been cut back from the rejuvenated canal.

Carrick-on-Shannon 4 miles (6km) south enjoys a summer influx of visitors. The town is well geared to supply the flotillas of boats that crowd the marina in summer. People on cruising holidays and hungry anglers come scrambling up from the river and make a beeline for Carrick's cake shops and delicatessens. Under the town's generously proportioned bridge is an arts/crafts centre — a good place to take refuge if it happens to be raining.

Between Rossinver and Blacklion, hamlets on the south side of the border corresponding to Garrison and Belcoo on the north side, there are some introspective little settlements, wary of strangers. You are unlikely to come on them unless you are lost, or unless at Glenfarne

Carrick-on-Shannon, a favourite resort for angling and cruising holidays

you take the Kiltyclogher road (R281), soon passing the lane to **Laghty Barr**. There is a mass rock along here, a clandestine open-air altar used for Roman Catholic worship during the eighteenth century when the penal laws were at their worst. Services are still sometimes held in these quiet leafy places, especially in summer.

The thatched cottage of Sean MacDermott, a revolutionary who fought in the Dublin General Post Office at Easter 1916 and one of the signatories of the proclamation of the Republic, is preserved at Laghty Barr as a national monument. Around 1900 MacDermott was working as a conductor on the trams in Glasgow and Belfast, but by 1907 he was setting up Sinn Féin offices all over Ireland and was treasurer of the Supreme Council of the Irish Republican Brotherhood (IRB). The cottage is surrounded by rhododendron bushes except on the lake side which has a fine view across Upper Lough Macnean into Fermanagh. A little further on, at Kiltyclogher crossroads, you come on a statue of MacDermott. 'Patriot executed by the British in 1916,' it says. MacDermott was a strange figure — even the president of the Supreme Council called him 'a weird bird'. Known for extreme ruthlessness, he was severely disabled by polio in 1912. All seven signatories of the proclamation were executed.

In this border country you occasionally pass what at first look like milestones. A closer look reveals that they are in fact memorials to local men who died in various violent ways in the Civil War in the 1920s. Despite the eerily sectarian preoccupations of the locals and the physical manifestations of the border, concrete barriers, broken bridges, roads going nowhere and so on, it is still possible to register the attractiveness of the countryside, with waterfalls on the County River, rounded hills and fine distant views.

Between Kiltyclogher and Lough Melvin is a 3-mile (5km) section of the great linear earthwork known as the **Black Pig's Dyke** (*'Cleann na muice duibh'* — Trench of the Black Pig) which is said to have been thrown up in prehistoric times as a defensive frontier to keep Ulster's enemies out. There is a shorter section between Kiltyclogher and Lough Macnean, and more sections to the east in a jiggly line all the way to Newry. It is difficult to see how these sections joined up, if they ever did, but there certainly seems to have been some kind of Iron Age south-facing frontier. The archaeologists are still working on it.

Five steep roads converge at **Manorhamilton** (*Cluainín* in Irish) where the scent of fresh laundry and fragrant peat fires hangs in the air. The Irish Peatland Conservation Council has made converts here, with 'Save Ireland's Bogs' notices posted in shop windows. Prominent features are an immense purple church and, high above the village on the north side, the picturesque ivy-covered ruins of a castle built by Sir Frederick Hamilton who was granted the manor by Charles I in the 1630s (and thus a 'planter'). A road sign directs you to Rosclogher Abbey on the shore of Lough Melvin and, on a fortified island (crannog) in the lake, the ruins of **MacClancy's Castle**. In 1588 nine Spanish Armada survivors, including Captain Francisco de Cuellar, found refuge in this castle. The hospitality was generous if rather basic. De Cuellar was puzzled that his rescuers drank only buttermilk. The Irish, he wrote in a letter to Philip of Spain, 'do not drink water, although it is the best in the world'.

A scenic bit of road with views of Lough Gill runs south-west from Manorhamilton down to **Dromahair** on the bank of the Bonet river. W.B Yeats celebrated the name of this little village in his poem *The Man Who Dreamed of Faeryland* which begins:

> 'He stood among a crowd at Dromahair;
> His heart hung all upon a silken dress.
> And he had known at last some tenderness
> Before earth took him to her stony care.'

Take the footpath from the village to visit **Creevelea Abbey**, the last pre-Reformation friary to be founded in Ireland (Franciscan, 1508).

If you are heading for Sligo, skirting round the east side of **Lough Gill**, stop off at the strangely shaped rock known as O'Rourke's Table for a superb view down the lake, and stop again at **Parke's Castle**, a seventeenth-century plantation castle which has a well preserved fortified courtyard or 'bawn', with two massive flanker towers.

People are thin on the ground in Leitrim and there is rather little industry, and less agriculture than there used to be. Dairy farmers especially are selling out to planters — tree planters, that is. In some places the countryside is draped with dark bird-free belts of tax-loss sitka spruce and lodgepole pine, growing on what was farmland. They present a rather cheerless aspect.

The Shannon river rises on the north-west side of the Cuilcagh mountain ridge 2 miles (3km) from Tiltinbane in County Fermanagh. It re-emerges in Cavan at Shannon Pot, a much visited small dark round pool. The R206, a minor road going north from Glangevlin towards Blacklion, passes close to Shannon Pot. The Cavan Way, a 17-mile (27km) signposted trail from Dowra to Blacklion through wild border country, passes even closer. However, to see the real source of Ireland's mightiest river, you have to climb the mountain itself. For that you need proper boots and a good map: sheet 26 in the Ordnance Survey (NI) Discoverer series, scale 1: 50 000 (about 1 ¼ inches to 1 mile) is best.

The development of the Ulster Way means that the best known approaches to **Cuilcagh** are from the Northern Ireland side. However, the mountain is equally accessible from County Cavan at Bellavally Gap, about 10 miles (16km) from Ballyconnell on the R200. On the Northern side, a fully waymarked section of the Ulster Way, starting from the carpark at Florence Court Forest Park, brings you to the summit of Cuilcagh (2,188ft/667m). Another favoured Fermanagh approach, from the carpark at Cladagh Glen past the Marble Arch Caves, comes up to Tiltinbane (1,881ft/573m) at the west end of the Cuilcagh ridge where you have one foot in the Republic and the other in the North. Views from the ridge are spectacular, including the whole of the Erne system and, to the south, Lough Allen and the Shannon. For most of their length the Erne and the Shannon are not at all riverlike but resemble chains of lakes that only remember they are rivers when they rush to meet the Atlantic.

The Erne rises in Lough Gowna on the Cavan/Longford border and flows lazily northwards through mazy **Lough Oughter** (pronounced 'oota'), a labyrinthine lake dotted with little wooded islands. It looks just like Upper Lough Erne, which indeed is what it becomes a few miles further on. At the south end of Oughter there are pleasant lakeside walks in **Killykeen Forest Park**, approached off the Killeshandra/Crossdoney road. You can rent one of the Scandinavian-style chalets (self-catering) in the forest park. The circular tower of **Clogh Oughter Castle** rises 60ft (18m) from its crannog in the lough about 2 miles (3km) north-west of Cavan town. You can get a fishing boat across for a closer inspection. It has the appearance of a cylindrical tower house but started out as a thirteenth-century stronghold of the O'Reillys.

The Protestant bishop of Kilmore, William Bedell (1571-1642) who translated the bible into Irish Gaelic (not published until 1686), spent his last 2 years in this castle as a prisoner of the rebels of 1641 — a time when Protestant bishops could expect to be locked up. Bedell believed that the best way to convert the Irish was through the medium of their own language. There were not many converts by all accounts but when he died his captors buried him with some reverence. His grave is at **Kilmore** halfway between Cavan town and Crossdoney (R198) in the grounds of the Anglican cathedral which, though modern, has a fine twelfth-century carved doorway that was brought here from an island monastery on Lough Oughter.

Another famous death at Clogh Oughter was that of Owen Roe O'Neill, the charismatic professional soldier who routed the Scots under Robert Monroe at Benburb, County Tyrone, in 1646. Described as 'the only Irish battle of annihilation' — Monroe lost 3,000 men and the Irish a mere 40 — this textbook victory was thrown away because the Irish could not agree among themselves about what to do next. Three years later Owen Roe became mysteriously ill and was brought here to die, poisoned they say.

Driving around you cannot help but be aware that pig slurry has been liberally applied to the green fields of Cavan. Pigmeat is an important agricultural product in both parts of the island north and south, though nowadays you can travel from Bantry to Ballymena without a single porcine sighting. The production units in Cavan and Monaghan are said to be the largest in Europe. Invisible they may be, shut up in sheds, but the pigs take a smelly revenge. Muckspreading is apparently the only safe and economic way to dispose of their manure. No one wants a repeat of the disaster in 1989 when thousands of gallons of pig slurry killed the fish in Lough Sheelin, a lovely lough south of Cavan town, and it seems that so long as the rivers stay clean and the trout lakes unpolluted, most people are resigned to hold their noses.

An old roadside telephone box and letter box in southern County Galway (Chapter 1)

The Cross of the Scriptures, Clonmacnois Visitor Centre, County Offaly (Chapter 2)

Mullaghmore, County Sligo (Chapter 3)

Enniskillen Castle, County Fermanagh (Chapter 3)

Almost every hamlet in the county can call itself an angling centre. The narrow roads wiggle along in an irresolute manner but always fetch up at a village with a river or a lake or both on the doorstep. In the eighteenth century **Belturbet** on the Erne was already a popular resort for boating and fishing, and no wonder, given its position at one end of this tremendous natural waterway running 50 miles (80km) down to Belleek. John Wesley, on one of his many visits to Ireland in the late 1740s, noted 'Sabbath breakers, drunkards and common swearers in abundance' among Belturbet's inhabitants. Today it is a tidy little town that welcomes visitors who come here for the fishing.

The pretty little plantation town of **Virginia**, which has a well kept Anglican parish church at the end of an avenue of trimmed yew trees, is attractively sited on the shore of Lough Ramor. Founded by James I and named after his aunt, Elizabeth I, the town has managed to hang on to its original name. A local speciality is Ryfield cheese, a rich matured cheddar type cheese in a black wax coat.

The Anglican parish church is a prominent feature of almost all the plantation settlements. The long main street of **Cootehill**, an attractive market town on the Monaghan border, is dominated by the Anglican church closing the view at the end. The unlikeable parliamentarian Sir Charles Coote was granted lands here in the seventeenth century. Just north of the town, on Dromore Lough, there are still Cootes at **Bellamont Forest** which, rather confusingly, is not a forest but a house (private) — a handsome redbrick Palladian mansion with ashlar facings designed in 1728 by Sir Edward Lovett Pearce. It was called Coote Hill until it was inherited by a rather absurd Coote (also Charles) who insisted on speaking French all the time and changed the name of his house after getting himself created earl of Bellamont (silent 't') in 1767. A famous libertine, he had at least six illegitimate children by four different mothers, one of whom inherited the house. From Cootehill the R188 to Cavan passes through **Tullyvin** village, yet another little plantation village, this one with an unusual circular green.

Cavan town, from which the county takes its name, has been much altered by hefty injections of money from the International Fund for Ireland, though this largesse does not seem to have extended to repairs and maintenance. The roads around Cavan have some awesome potholes. Like almost everything in this town, which was the chief seat of the Breffny O'Reillys, the Franciscan monastery was burnt and flattened over and over. Owen Roe was buried here, according to a plaque on the church tower where the friary used to be. It is also the burying place of another heroic soldier, Myles The Slasher O'Reilly — killed in battle near Lough Sheelin in 1646 — whose military style appears to have been tactical rather than strategic. There are still plenty of soldiers in Cavan, based in the large new army barracks, with patrol duties along a 37-mile (60km) stretch of border with no fewer than thirty-five crossings to the North, all of which are supposed to be patrolled by the Cavan-based military. The O'Reilly crowning place was at Shantemon Hill 3 miles (5km) north-east of Cavan off the Cootehill road (R188) where there are five standing stones (Finn McCool's Fingers).

One blithe spirit who alighted in Cavan was the songwriter, entertainer and painter Percy French (1854-1920) who lived at number 16 Farnham Street, an agreeable eighteenth-century terrace, in the 1880s. He spent 5 years here as a Board of Trade engineer — 'inspector of drains' he called himself. Later he toured the country on his bicycle every August, entertaining people in countless Irish towns and seaside resorts, making them laugh. He wrote the placenames of Ireland into his merry songs — Cavan itself, Ballyjamesduff, Cootehill, and many others — and he also painted hundreds of watercolours. The mists and bogs, the wide landscapes, the distant mountains beyond the watery flatness, a solitary tree, these typical features of the Irish Midlands are instantly recognisable in his pictures. To see them, however, requires a little planning. There are a few in the Ulster Museum, Belfast, and Armagh County Museum has an album of Percy French paintings and poems (accession no. 3-43) but most of his paintings, of Cavan, his native Roscommon, and Donegal and Connemara, are scattered all over Ireland in private houses.

Taking the N55 south-west from Cavan you are soon into County Longford, passing through **Granard** where the main road swerves sharply in the town centre to circumvent an improbably high Norman motte built by Hugh de Lacy in 1191. The motte has been made even higher by a disfiguring statue of St Patrick on the top. Follow the swerve on to the R194 Longford road.

To describe **Longford** as a cathedral town is somewhat misleading but that is what it is — of the Catholic diocese of Ardagh and Clonmacnois. The grey limestone cathedral dedicated to St Mel was built almost entirely by public donations, starting in 1840, and it was 53 years before the finishing touches were put to its pepperpot belfry, a monument to the generosity of the impoverished people who paid for it. St Mel's crozier (tenth century) is preserved in the diocesan museum behind the cathedral.

The grey limestone cathedral of St Mel, Longford, was begun in 1840 and not completed until some fifty years later

The town seems wilfully bereft of visitor facilities, though a small museum, focusing on the 1920s' Civil War, has been started up in the old post office. The public library in the town's carpark also has occasional exhibitions. The Labour peer Frank Pakenham, of the tribe that took its name from here, would be hard pressed to recommend anywhere congenial to stay. The oldest thing in the place is a fragment of the castle built in 1627 by his ancestor, the first earl of Longford. The sole remaining structure of any nobility is the courthouse, and it has a leaky look, a building under threat. The characterful workhouse where the father of Longford poet Padraic Colum (1881-1972) was master, has been replaced by a modern hospital building.

County Longford Literati

Colum was a friend of James Joyce. Active in the Irish literary revival, he wrote several plays for the Abbey Theatre, including *Thomas Muskerry*, a gloomy drama about a workhouse master. His best poems were some early pastoral lyrics, most notably the haunting lyric *She moved through the fair*. A plan to erect a plaque to Colum, who was born in the town, was recently thwarted by local people who felt the workhouse connection was one they did not want to be reminded of.

Three miles (5km) up the Carrick-on-Shannon road (N4) is the jaunty nineteenth-century castle of the earls of Granard, **Castle Forbes**. It overlooks Lough Forbes, one of the Shannon lakes. The castle is private but it is possible to walk in the gardens. The grave of Thomas Hanna, one of the last of the harpers (died 1869), is in the grounds. Half a mile (1km) beyond the castle entrance, you might want to turn east through Drumlish to follow the signs to **Ballinamuck** village, scene of a famous battle between a French expeditionary force and government troops in 1798, the year of the United Irishmen's rising. General Humbert and his French commandos landed at Killala, County Mayo, to support the rising — too late as it turned out. The rebels had already been crushed. Even so, several thousand Connaught peasant farmers joined the invaders, eager to fight for 'France and the Blessed Virgin'. They won a stylish battle at Castlebar but surrendered to government troops under General Lake here at Ballinamuck. The fight was hopelessly unequal and the French soon surrendered but the Connaught men fought on. Afterwards very many of these peasant insurgents were slaughtered. There are various monuments in and around the village, and memorials in Tubberpatrick cemetery 3 miles (5km) to the north.

Oliver Goldsmith (1730-74) and, more obviously, the novelist Maria

Edgeworth (1768-1849) whose family settled here in the sixteenth century, are literary figures associated with Longford county, though if there is any intellectual life here now it is well hidden. Goldsmith was born at (probably) Pallas, 14 miles (22km) south of Longford on the Athlone road, and that is where a birthplace plaque has been erected, although there is no house. The 'Goldsmith Country' trail hots up further along the N55 in neighbouring Westmeath, claimed as the country of *The Deserted Village*, a long elegaic poem published in 1770. The crossroads hamlet of Lissoy where Goldsmith grew up, has vanished. The poem is little read these days, even in England, but in Ireland it is frequently and selectively quoted. The village of the title is said to be an Irish village (viz. Lissoy) destroyed by unjust laws and grasping landlords. After inspecting various signposted features in the village of **Glasson** on this theme, the visitor will be ready for a pint in the 'Three Jolly Pigeons', a roadside hostelry named after the inn in Goldsmith's comedy *She Stoops to Conquer*. Goldsmith went to London in 1752 and never returned to Ireland.

By contrast Maria Edgeworth, often called the 'first Anglo-Irish novelist', spent almost all her long life in **Edgeworthstown**, presiding over the extended Edgeworth family and, as a very old lady in the 1840s, ministering to the needy during the years of famine and cholera. Periodic efforts to rid this dispirited little town of the name Edgeworthstown, in favour of 'Mostrim' (from *Meas Troim*, frontier of the elder tree) are a reminder of the ancient resentments towards landlords, absent or not. Even the admirable Edgeworths who gave so much more than they took, were not exempt.

Edgeworthstown House, the Georgian mansion where Maria Edgeworth lived (signposted) was at the centre of a cultured Anglo-Irish circle that included the Pakenhams, earls of Longford, the Granards, and the Huguenot Lefroys, chief justices of Ireland. It is now an old people's home. However, you can visit the school which was founded by Maria's father, Richard Lovell Edgeworth (1744-1817), an inventor and radical educationalist who had four wives, two of whom, shockingly for the times, were sisters. Maria was his eldest daughter, the second of his twenty-two children.

Anyone, Protestant or Catholic, could attend Mr Edgeworth's school and school uniform, a linen smock worn over the pupil's own clothes, was compulsory. This innovatory little school is now a museum with a collection of Edgeworth mementoes, photographs, scaled drawings and plans made by Mr Edgeworth, Maria's spectacles, and books belonging to her. Edgeworthstown House was filled with his labour-saving gadgets. One device was an ingenious water pump which automatically paid a halfpenny for each half hour it was worked. Beggars calling at the house were despatched in the direction of this pump.

Maria Edgeworth's moral tales for children started as stories for her younger brothers and sisters, and she wrote many novels. *Castle Rackrent*, a racy tale of eccentric and incompetent Irish squires (a sort of eighteenth-century *Porterhouse Blue*), is recognised as the first truly regional and historical novel. Her literary admirers included Sir Walter Scott who acknowledged his debt to her Irish novels and came on a visit here in 1825. Richard Lovell was inclined to 'edit' Maria's literary efforts but *Castle Rackrent* somehow evaded his blue pencil.

Richard Lovell's cousin, the Abbé Henry Essex Edgeworth de Fermont, born in the rectory in 1745, was Louis XVI's confessor and attended him on the scaffold. The abbé's father had gone to live in France where he became a Catholic. The first Irish Edgeworth was also a man of the cloth, a sixteenth-century Anglican bishop of Down and Connor. Part of the library from Edgeworthstown House, which included many books on theology, is now in St Mel's diocesan seminary. The Edgeworth family vault is at St John's church where there are Edgeworth memorials and some more personal effects, including a table with marble inlay, a present from Walter Scott to Maria.

The home of the Lefroys, **Carriglas Manor**, 6 miles (10km) northwest of Edgeworthstown House on the Ballinalee road from Longford (R194), has fared somewhat better. Lefroys still live there and give guided tours in summer (and B&B if you want it). The present frontage with its slender battlemented turrets, is nineteenth century but the outstanding feature of Carriglas is the superb stables with fine courtyards and entrance arch designed by James Gandon in about 1795.

'The small towns of Ireland by bards are neglected,' wrote John Betjeman of towns in the Irish Midlands. He did not mean it of course. They are neglected, but less by the bards than anyone else!

Across the border now into County Westmeath for a look at a really big 'big house'. **Tullynally Castle**, the Pakenham/Longford family home, is about 12 miles (19km) east of Edgeworthstown, near Castlepollard, a tidy village with a large triangular green. Called Pakenham Hall until recently, Tullynally is open to visitors on summer afternoons. This is one of the biggest castellated country houses in Ireland, a fine confection of turrets, battlements and towers all joined together to make a tremendously long frontage. It was one of the first houses in the British Isles to have central heating.

Richard Lovell Edgeworth devised the system for the second earl who shared his interest in inventing useful things. The huge Victorian kitchen, a veritable museum of nineteenth-century gadgets and domestic appliances, a magnificent kitchen garden and walks through the ancient oakwoods are outstanding features of a tour of Tullynally.

The **Hill of Uisneach** is a prominent feature on the road from Mullingar to Athlone. There are various burial mounds and other evidence of occupation from ancient times when the flat top was a druidic assembly point. Even if this is not a sufficient reason to climb the 250ft (76m) to the summit, the tremendously long view certainly is. If Ireland can be said to have a centre, this small hill surrounded by a vast undulating boggy plain with low grey cloud above, must surely be it. Well, not quite, the precise middle of Ireland is signposted and can be inspected a little further down the road: it is a large solitary boulder, probably a glacial 'erratic', weirdly shaped like a cat about to pounce, and known as the Catstone.

Because the region is flat no doubt the ruined castles, big houses and especially the churches are noticeable in a way they would not be in more varied countryside. It must be said that the mansions are rather easier on the eye than say, the Church of St Peter and St Paul (1937) in Athlone or the twin-towered 1930s' cathedral at Mullingar, both very big churches which do not add to the appeal of either of these County Westmeath towns.

However, many of the houses present a melancholy aspect. After the famine, the country house gentry lost their tenants and their income and then it was downhill all the way. The farmers who took over the bankrupt estates were interested in the land, not the elegant houses with their beautiful demesnes. Without the battalions of servants needed to run them and emptied of their families, these architectural exemplars of the Enlightenment gradually became derelict. An estimated quarter of all the country houses in Ireland at the turn of the century have been burnt (by accident or maliciously), pulled down or most often, allowed to fall down.

A typical example is **Tudenham Park** 3 miles (5km) south of Mullingar, a three-storey mansion built in 1742 for George Rochfort who was a younger brother of Robert Rochfort, Lord Bellfield. Used as a hospital in World War I it was a military billet in World War II. Now it is just a shell open to the elements, on the bank of Lough Ennell close to a caravan park. More or less next door, Robert Rochfort's villa, **Belvedere House**, is still in one piece and is open to the public. It was always much the prettier of the two houses. In the

The cathedral of Mullingar

grounds there is an ice house — forerunner of the fridge-freezer — a walled garden, gazebo and the famous 'Jealous Wall', a sham ruin built by Robert in 1760 to screen the view of his house from George's house. How this folly got its name is hard to know, since it was not George but a third brother, Arthur, who was alleged to have had an affair with Robert's wife. These quarrelsome Rochforts owned all the country round Mullingar.

Mullingar itself is a cattle market town almost entirely surrounded by the old Royal Canal that used to be a commercial link with Dublin 53 miles (85km) away. There is a military museum with an IRA section (the 'old' IRA) in the barracks past the canal, and also the usual ecclesiastical museum. This one has penal crosses and vestments belonging to St Oliver Plunkett, the Catholic archbishop of Armagh who was dragged off to England and hanged, drawn and quartered at Tyburn in 1681, the last Catholic to be martyred there. He was canonized in 1975. One wonders why, with such a very large cathedral, these objects could not be located inside it.

'Ath' is from the Irish for 'ford', and **Athlone** straddles the Shannon where it flows south from the tip of Lough Ree, the midpoint of Ireland's greatest river. Half the town is in Leinster and half in Connaught. Despite this strategically important position, a long battling history, an immensely fortified Norman castle, enormous church and, most recently a bypass, Athlone is curiously lacking in

Ireland's greatest river, the Shannon at Athlone

presence.

The town was defended by Colonel Richard Grace's Jacobite forces after the battle of the Boyne but, following a famous episode at the bridge in June 1691, was captured for William of Orange by the Dutch commander Ginkel. William rewarded him by creating him earl of Athlone. Ginkel assembled a large field army, as many as 25,000 men, at the Shannon here, determined to cross the river en route to capture Galway and Limerick for William. The Irish defenders on the Leinster side were forced across the bridge to the Connaught bank. As they fell back they managed to break two of the bridge's nine arches but the attackers placed planks across the gap.

What happened next recalls the heroic action of 'How Horatius kept the bridge' one of Macaulay's *Lays of Ancient Rome* (deplorable glamorised history, but heady). The action at Athlone was this: realising that the enemy was about to cross, a Jacobite sergeant named Custume and ten of his men leapt down from the broken bridge and started throwing the planks into the river. They were all killed by shot from the Leinster bank but twenty more men led by a lieutenant took their place. All but two of these were also killed but not before they had thrown down the last plank and stopped the advance.

Athlone has a different bridge now. The old one was dismantled in 1844 but the town barracks perpetuate Sergeant Custume's name.

A patriotic poem by Macaulay's contemporary, Aubrey de Vere (1814-1902), also celebrates the defence of Athlone bridge. It begins: 'Does any man dream that a Gael can fear?'. Although a supporter of the Union of Great Britain and Ireland, de Vere wrote a pamphlet called *English Misrule and Irish Misdeeds* criticising aspects of government policy in Ireland.

The episode at Athlone bridge ended badly for the defenders. Their commander, the haughty Marquis de Saint-Ruth, threw away the victory by taking time off for rest and recreation. Ginkel suddenly attacked again and this time the Williamites got across the river. The fighters then betook themselves to **Aughrim** ridge, about 18 miles (30km) south-west of Athlone where the last big pitched battle in Ireland was fought on 12 July 1691. About 4,000 Jacobites and 2,000 Williamites were killed and General Saint-Ruth himself had his head struck off by a cannonball. Victorious, Ginkel pressed on to take Galway and then Limerick, so breaking the last Jacobite link with France. There is a memorial cross at the castle ruins in Aughrim village on the N6 from Ballinasloe, and an interpretive centre nearby.

Athlone's most famous son is the Irish tenor John McCormack (1884-1945) who was born in a house off Mardyke Street (plaque). There is also a rather mediocre bust of him on the promenade, but haste you to the folk museum in the castle to hear the glorious

The Battle of Aughrim Interpretive Centre contains many mementos of the last great battle fought in Ireland, 1691

McCormack voice on old 78rpm records played on his own gramophone. He made over 500 recordings. He was a great operatic star, acclaimed in America and London, and he toured Australia with Nelly Melba in 1911. His extraordinary popularity however came after he turned to the concert stage. In 1932 a million people crowded into Phoenix Park, Dublin, to hear him sing.

You can hire a cruiser or join an excursion boat in summer at Coosan Point 2 miles (3km) north of the town centre to explore the islands scattered over Lough Ree, before going downstream to Clonmacnois. Inchmore, Inchbofin and Hare Island, which has some magnificent oak trees, are all interesting monastic sites. North-east of Inchbofin, on Saints' Island — no longer an island but a peninsula reached by road from Ballymahon, County Longford — are the remains of a fifteenth-century church, part of the priory of All Saints founded in the thirteenth century. Its most famous scholar was Augustine Magraidan (died 1405), who was one of the compilers of the *Annals of All Saints*. Further up this 18-mile (29km) long lake the island of **Inchcleraun** is particularly rich in early Christian monuments, with numerous ruined churches, and a tiny sixth-century mortuary house known as Dermot's Church. St Dermot was the teacher of St Ciaran of Clonmacnois. As late as the nineteenth century local boatmen claimed that they had seen Dermot walking along the waves from Inchcleraun. A legend relates how Queen Maeve of Connaught was killed here by a sling stone fired at her by an enemy (probably an Ulsterman) from the shore while she was bathing. The sling or the stone or the Ulsterman must have had magical powers since Inchcleraun is a good mile from the shore. In summer there are boat trips to the island from Elfeet Bay opposite (access off the Lanesborough/Ballymahon road R392).

Clonmacnois Saints, Kings and Plunderers

And now to the monastic ruins of **Clonmacnois** (pronounced Clonmakneesh), burial place of the kings of Connaught and Tara and a place of religious instruction and scholarship which was second in importance only to Armagh. Above all it was the centre of Irish art and literature for more than 600 years. Standing by the river on a *clon* or *cluain* (a meadow) at the end of an esker ridge above the bogland, the monastery was founded in AD547 by St Ciaran and, being richly endowed from the beginning, was plundered many times. The monastery remains comprise sculptured high crosses, round towers, eight churches and a cathedral. The collection of carved grave slabs, many of which are inscribed in Irish, and the wonderfully decorated

Clonmacnois, centre of Irish art and literature for six centuries

tenth-century Great Cross (Cross of the Scriptures) have recently been removed to the adjacent visitor centre for protection. The most prominent single feature is O'Rourke's Tower or Great Belfry, a large topless round tower which may have been twice its present height of 62ft (19m) before it was struck by lightning in 1135, only 10 years after the belfry was finished. It seems that the monks went on using it, unrepaired, for 400 more years. The cathedral has a fine ornamented north door with the figures of three saints, Patrick, Francis and Dominic, over the top. It and the choir vault date from the fifteenth century. The west doorway incorporates part of the original tenth-century church built by Flann, king of Tara. Rory O'Conor, last of the high kings of Ireland, is buried north of the altar. Outside the wall of the cemetery are the remains of the Nuns' Church, an exquisite little twelfth-century Romanesque church built by Dervorgilla, wife of Tiernan O'Rourke of Breffny. It has a beautiful west door and chancel arch.

The first plunderers of Clonmacnois, the Vikings, came upstream in the ninth century and the last, the English garrison at Athlone, came downstream in 1552. It seems that only locals and pilgrims came along the narrow ridgeway, still called the Pilgrims' Path, from the direction of Ballynahown. The most outlandish if brief episode in the monastery's history was in AD845 when the Viking king Thorgestr (Turgesius) installed his wife Ota as a high priestess. He was killed soon afterwards by the king of Meath. What happened to Ota is not recorded.

The tenth-century Cross of the Scriptures at Clonmacnois

Clonmacnois is still used for worship, though it is sufficiently far from Dublin not to be overwhelmed either by worshippers, nor yet by visitors. There is a pilgrimage here on the feast of St Ciaran, 9 September, and on the following Sunday. A new Roman Catholic altar was built in 1969, and Anglican services are occasionally held in one church, Temple Conor.

Precious book shrines, crosses and croziers fashioned by the metal-workers of Clonmacnois include the great oak silver-sheathed Cross of Cong, patterned with lacy gilt bronze panels and translucent rock crystal bosses, the finest of all surviving medieval Irish reliquaries. Made in about 1123 by order of Turlough O'Conor (who is also buried in the cathedral here) and taken to Cong Abbey by his son Rory O'Conor, it is in the National Museum, Dublin. Also in Dublin is the eleventh or twelfth-century *Book of the Dun Cow*, one of many illumi-nated manuscripts made here, preserved in the Royal Irish Academy. St Manchan's Shrine, on the other hand, a yew-wood box embossed with metalwork and cloisonné enamel made in about 1130 also for Turlough O'Conor, may be seen in the Catholic church at **Boher** 12 miles (19km) due east of Clonmacnois on the road to Clara, a small manufacturing centre on the Brosna river.

All of Offaly between the Shannon and the heathery Slieve Bloom hills is desolate raised bog, with isolated villages like Clara and the neat little settlements of Kilcormac, and Rochfortbridge (which is just over the Westmeath border), dotted here and there, sustained by the large-scale commercial exploitation of the bogs. There are some 2.5 million acres of peatlands in the Republic and turf is a major industry. About 20 per cent of electricity is generated by peat burning. In addition to supplying the power stations, the govern-ment's peat development board, Bord na Mona, produces milled peat for compressing into the briquettes that are so convenient for domestic use, cleaner than coal and wonderfully fragrant. The board also markets bog moss (sphagnum), the light peat from the upper layers of Midland bogs, as a soil conditioner and for use as livestock bedding.

On the largest raised bogs, like the Bog of Allen and the extensive deep bogs in Longford, Westmeath and Offaly, peat 'harvesting' is wholly mechanised, and different from the labour-intensive handcutting on the blanket bog of Connaught where the peat forms a thin undulating layer. First the bog has to be drained to prevent the giant machines from sinking. Then huge bucket dredgers cut the peat from vertical faces up to 12ft (3m) deep. Next, the machines chew it up, spread it out, cut it into sods, leave it for 3 or 4 weeks to dry, lift it into small piles, and leave it for another week or so before collecting it into storage ricks which are then covered in polythene.

All this has had a startling effect on the landscape and a more insidious effect on the local flora and fauna. Ireland generally has fewer bird species than Great Britain, and boglands are particularly under-birded. All the more reason then, to worry about the over-wintering snipe and white-fronted geese which find their raised bog habitat shrinking each year. Pressure from the 'green' lobby is reducing the use of sphagnum as the major constituent of composts sold to amateur gardeners. However, only a tiny proportion of exploited bog, as little as one per cent, is harvested for sphagnum. Every little helps, you may think, as you drive across the sombre landscape.

A 1,600-acre (640-hectare) raised bog nature reserve at **Clara** is open to the public as a tourist attraction from spring to autumn. It is one of two Offaly bogs (the other is at Raheenmore, north-west of Portarlington) to have been studied recently by an Irish-Dutch team of botanists and geographers. Rare flora at Clara include two interesting insect-trapping plants, yellow-flowering bladderworts and sundews. The bog is also the habitat of green hairstreaks, orange tips and numerous other species of moth. Another raised bog of international importance is Mongan Bog, close to Clonmacnois.

There were men living here 9,000 years ago, before the peat was formed. Traces of habitation were discovered during an excavation in 1977 at Boora Bog, near the Ferbane power station cooling towers north of Kilcormac. Since 1750 about eighty bog bodies, mostly from medieval times, have been recovered from Irish bogs, the majority from blanket bog. Skeletons of that prehistoric ruminant quadruped called the Great Irish Elk or Giant Deer have been discovered in the preserving peat too, and no Midlands museum is complete without a few Great Elk antlers. The poor creature, we are told, grew too big for its environment and so died out. A very large specimen, over 7ft (2m) high and with a 12ft (4m) antler span, can be seen in the Natural History Museum in Dublin.

Tullamore, county town of Offaly, is a convenient centre for walkers intent on exploring the Slieve Blooms, and has good restaurants and pubs much used by the local people. If a Tullamorian offers you a glass of port and a cigar accept his hospitality, for this is the town of Tullamore Dew whiskey and Irish Mist liqueur. Prosperity came after the Grand Canal opened in 1798, linking Tullamore to Dublin and soon after, to the Shannon. Some canal architecture remains and the waterway, with its bridges, well maintained towpaths and locks where hire cruisers congregate in summer, is an attractive feature of the town. Off the N52 Bir road south-west of the centre, **Charleville Forest Castle**, a spectacular castellated Gothic house by Francis Johnston, is open to the public. Built in the early 1800s, its interior is exceptionally fine.

Name-changing, monument-moving and suchlike manifestations of the revisionism of history seem not to have reached Offaly. The war memorial in Tullamore commemorates 'the men of Offaly, King's County' who died in both great world wars. World War I memorials have disappeared from so many market places and village squares in Ireland: this doubly unambivalent monument is a rarity. The name 'King's County' throws a light on that brief period, 1553-58, when Mary Tudor was queen of England. Her restoration of papal supremacy in the country earned her the soubriquet 'Bloody Mary'. The king in point is not, as might be expected, an average British monarch, but Philip II of Spain, who married Mary in 1554. When the land round here was shired, she named County Laois 'Queen's County' after herself, and the adjoining county, Offaly, in

Bord na Mona peat cutter, Clonmacnois & West Offaly Railway. The 5-mile railway carries milled peat to the electricity generating station from Blackwater Bog near Shannonbridge

honour of her consort. Thirty years after Mary's death Philip sent the Spanish Armada invasion fleet against Elizabeth I, her half-sister.

For a scenic drive around the Slieve Blooms, take the minor road T9 (R421) from Kinnitty, on to Drimmo and Clonaslee. The area within this rough triangle is under-visited, low key, low profile, and that is true of the 'mountains' themselves — gentle walking country, with Arderin the highest hill at only 1,700ft (518m). **Cadamstown**, a tiny place with a tea shop and post office on the edge of the Slieve Bloom Environment Park, was once an important stop on the road from the Rock of Cashel to the Hill of Tara. Paddy Heaney's mill on the Silver River has been partially restored and there are walks along the banks, overhung with sycamore and beech and planted with flowers.

The *dramatis personae* at **Shannonbridge** are the smoking chimneys of the enormous electricity generating station and its giant pylons striding across the bog. There are rail trips around the Blackwater Bog on the little Clonmacnois & West Offaly Railway on 5 miles (8km) of narrow-gauge track, which is still in use for transporting milled peat to the power station. To span the river at Shannonbridge a sixteen-arch bridge was needed, and the engineers have contrived to offset this extravagance by economising on the width. It is a curiously narrow bridge, controlled by traffic lights.

The broad and lazy Shannon is guarded at strategic points all the way from Athlone downstream to Loop Head at the river mouth, a distance of some 120 miles (193km), by all kinds of batteries, martello towers and other impressive fortifications built in Napoleonic times, strong enough to hold out until troops could be mustered from garrisons to the east. At Shannonbridge the massive fortifications on the Connaught (west) bank were built in 1804 in case of a repeat of the French landing at Killala in 1798. To see the frowning aspect these monumental structures presented to the potential invader you need to drive from west to east, or at least stop on the Connaught side, to look back at them. The main Ballinasloe to Tullamore road passed through a fortified gateway before reaching the river bridge. These early nineteenth-century defences on the Shannon are a reminder that the threat of invasion from the west was a real possibility.

There is a fine martello tower at Banagher, a short way downstream from Shannonbridge, and another at Meelick, further down again. Like the martellos in Britain, the Irish towers were built in a hurry, but whereas the English ones were built of brick, the Irish martellos are made of the best quality ashlar granite and are very handsome. One usually associates defences like these with coastal sites and, in the Irish context, most particularly with the coast around Dublin and at Cork harbour. It is strange to see martellos so far from the sea.

One of the most appealing small towns in Ireland, with Georgian malls, squares and townhouses laid out round the castle, **Birr** was built on the bank of the Camcor river mainly by the second earl of Rosse. His forebear Laurence Parsons, a native of Leicestershire, was granted the land in 1620. Particular features to note on a town walkabout include Emmet Square and the old coaching inn, Dooly's Hotel (an agreeable place to stay), dating from 1747 but rebuilt after some nineteenth-century carousing members of the Galway Hunt set it on fire. In the middle of the square a tall Doric column, also dating from 1747, used to be topped by a statue of the Duke of Cumberland, soldier son of George II, who crushed the rebellion at Culloden with notorious severity in 1745, earning himself the name 'Butcher Billy'. One assumes the statue was put up as a warning to the Irish. The bogeyman was taken down in 1925.

Arthur Bell Nicholls, whom Charlotte Brontë married in 1854,

The narrow-gauge railway at Shannonbridge

without much enthusiasm on her part, was rector of Birr. His was the rather uninspiring church opposite the castle gate. This and the other parish church, St Brendan's Catholic church down by the bridge, were both built in 1817 by the second earl. Next to the Catholic church is an accomplished stone-built convent designed in the 1840s by A.W.N Pugin. It has a delightful Irish round tower at the corner. Looking at the stonework one is reminded of the fact that Pugin used the best local stone and the most skilled masons. In John's Place, in front of the building with an Ionic portico, there is a statue of the third earl of Rosse, the famous astronomer William Parsons (1800-67). He was a benevolent landlord, remembered for spending a major part of his Irish revenues on relief works in the 1846-47 famine.

Birr Castle is best known nowadays for its outstanding ornamental gardens, arboretum and lake, which are open to visitors all year (the castle itself is private). The clipped box hedges, 34ft (10m) high, are mentioned in the *Guinness Book of Records*. In the nineteenth century, however, Birr was a world centre for astronomical research. In 1845 William Parsons spent £20,000 on building a telescope with a reflector 72 inches in diameter, the world's largest reflecting telescope at the time, and for the next 75 years. Astronomers came from all over the world to observe the heavens through the Birr Leviathan which was slung in chains between two huge piers. Rosse himself discovered the spiral structure of nebulae.

The giant speculum, or mirror, was given to the Science Museum in London in 1914. The 58ft (18m) long tube in which it was mounted lies in the castle demesne between castellated masonry walls which one might at first glance think was a garden folly. This noble remnant, and a scale model of the original, is on display all year round. Birr had and still has close connections with the older observatory at Armagh and astronomical meetings are held at the castle by courtesy of the seventh earl whose home this is. A large archive of drawings, photographs and notes made by those nineteenth-century scientists is the castle's chief treasure. Astronomical instruments including equipment used by the fourth earl (1840-1908), also an astronomer, to measure the heat of the moon, are displayed in the stable block (in summer only). The fourth earl's younger brother, Sir Charles Parsons (1854-1931) was an engineer who developed the steam turbine used in turbine-propelled battleships.

Mary, Countess of Rosse, wife of the third earl and mother of these clever boys, who were educated at home by tutors, was the pioneer photographer, Mary Wilmer Field. Another talented woman in the family was the artist and naturalist Mary Ward (1827-69) who, as 'The Hon Mrs W', illustrated her own books on the microscope and published such articles as *The Natterjack Toad in Ireland*. How clever they all were!

Further Information
— The Midlands —

Places to Visit

Athlone
Co Westmeath
Athlone Castle
The castle is open April to October every day. The museum is closed on Sundays.
☎ (0902) 92912

Aughrim
Near Ballinasloe, Co Galway
Battle of Aughrim Interpretive Centre
☎ (091) 63081

Birr
Co Offaly
Birr Castle Demesne
Open: daily all year.
☎ (0509) 20110/20056

Cavan
Co Cavan
Cavan Crystal
Dublin Road
Tours of the factory Monday to Friday all year. The shop and video show are also open on Saturday, and on Sunday afternoon. Factory tour/shop.
☎ (049) 31800

Clara Bog
Co Offaly
Guided tours from April to October, and other times by appointment.
Always accessible.
☎ (0506) 52566 (Offaly Tourism)

Clonmacnois
Co Offaly
Shannonbridge
Site and visitor centre open every day,
9am-7pm in summer, shorter hours in
winter.
☎ (0905) 74195/74134

Edgeworthstown
Co Longford
For access to *Edgeworth Memorabilia,* ask
at Tourist Office/Heritage Centre in
Main Street.
☎ (043) 71801

St John's Church
If church is locked ask at adjacent
rectory for access. Keyholder: Jack
Stewart (house opposite hotel).

Longford
Co Longford
Longford Museum
Open: daily June to September 2-6pm.
☎ (043) 46735

St Mel's Diocesan Museum
Limited access June to September only:
Monday and Wednesday 11am-1pm,
Saturday 1-3pm, Sunday 4-6 pm.
☎ (043) 46566

Carriglas Manor
3 miles (5km) north-east of Longford
on Granard road (R194). Guided tours
in summer. Closed Tuesday and
Wednesday.
☎ (043) 45165

Mullingar
Co Westmeath
Belvedere House and Gardens
Open: May to end September every day
from 12noon.
☎ (044) 40861

Mullingar Military Museum
Column Barracks
Open: by arrangement.
☎ (044) 48391

Mullingar Museum
Market House
Open: weekday afternoons in summer.
☎ (044) 48650

Parke's Castle
Co Leitrim
Five Mile Bourne, Lough Gill.
Open: daily mid-June to September.
Closed Monday in spring.
☎ (071) 64149

Shannonbridge
Co Offaly
Blackwater Bog Tour
Open: April to October every day. Tour
(45 minutes) 10am-5pm on the hour.

Tullamore
Co Offaly
Charleville Forest Castle
Open: weekend afternoons in April and
May, and Wednesday to Sunday
12noon-5pm June to September.
☎ (0506) 21279

Tullynally Castle
Co Westmeath
Near Castlepollard
Gardens open every day 10am-6pm
April to October. The house is open
from mid-July to mid-August, after-
noons only.
☎ (044) 61159/61289

Travel
Boat Trips on the Shannon River
From Coosan Point, Athlone, every day
in summer.
☎ (0902) 94630/72892/85163

Shannon-Erne Waterway Ltd
Ballinamore, Co Leitrim
☎ (078) 44855

Tourist Information Offices
Open: all year.

Cavan
Co Cavan
Farnham Street
☎ (049) 31942

Mullingar
Co Westmeath
Dublin Road
☎ (044) 48650

3 • The North West
Lakes & Mountains

Sligo, Fermanagh, West Tyrone and Donegal

To say that **Sligo** has associations with the poet William Butler
Yeats (1865-1939) and the painter-writer Jack Butler Yeats (1871-
1957) may be to understate the case. The Yeats' connection is a staple
of the region's tourist industry. There is an established Yeats' summer school, a 65-mile (105km) signposted Yeats' trail to places
mentioned in the poems and a startlingly long-legged larger-than-
life bronze statue of the poet, by Rowan Gillespie, outside the Ulster
Bank in Stephen Street in Sligo town. Since both the poet and the
painter drew inspiration and subject matter from this region, the
proliferation of Yeats' pubs, Yeats' sandwich bars and Yeats' cafés is
not unexpected.

Make for the county library to see a collection of the poet's letters,
first editions of his works, photographs and other memorabilia in
the museum. The art gallery in the same building contains drawings
and paintings by Yeats *père*, John B Yeats (1839-1922), who was a
celebrated portrait painter, and works by Paul Henry and George
Russell (*AE*) as well as a collection of Jack B Yeats' paintings and
illustrations. Jack contributed to *Punch* for over 30 years and also
wrote for the *Manchester Guardian*. In addition to painting all the
mountains, bays and beaches for miles around, his subjects included boxing matches, fairs, livestock markets, donkey races and
the most wonderful pictures of horses, all very intuitive and lively,
the paint laid on quickly in broad strokes, giving an unfinished look.
His famous early watercolour, *Memory Harbour* (1900) is of the
harbour at Rosses Point 5 miles (8km) by road north-west of Sligo.
However, like many of his best known pictures, this is in a private
collection. Other public collections are in the National Gallery and
the Hugh Lane Gallery, Dublin, and in the Ulster Museum, Belfast.

Sligo Abbey, a Dominican friary founded in 1252 by Maurice
Fitzgerald, is the only old building left in the town. It was damaged
by fire in 1414 and very thoroughly ruined in the 1641 rebellion but

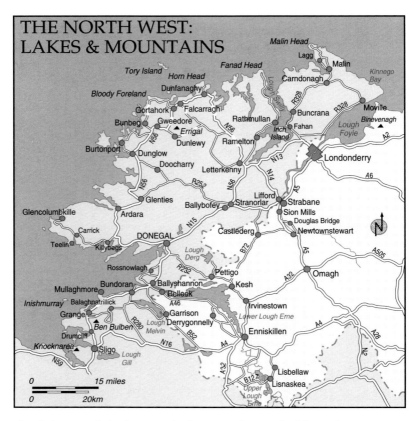

THE NORTH WEST:
LAKES & MOUNTAINS

the cloister and the lancet windows on the south side are in comparatively good shape. The town has two cathedrals, both called St John's. The Anglican one has a massive west tower and, inside, a brass memorial to Susan Yeats, née Pollenfex, mother of W.B and Jack B.

West of the town the solitary limestone chunk of **Knocknarea** rears up to nearly 1,100ft (335m). On the summit is an enormous cairn 35ft (11m) high and 200ft (61m) across. It has not been excavated but may conceal a passage grave, the tomb of Maeve, harridan queen of Connaught and bane of the kings of Ulster. More than once she came close to conquering her northern neighbours but was always routed at the eleventh hour by the Ulster warrior Cuchulain. There is a fine view of Slieve League and all of County Sligo from here. Round the base are some ruined 'satellite' passage graves, similar to those at Knowth and Dowth in the Boyne Valley. A very extensive cemetery of megalithic tombs at Carrowmore south-east of

Knocknarea has been greatly damaged by gravel extraction but is worth seeing anyway.

The Lake Isle of Innisfree on the south-east side of Lough Gill is approached by minor roads off the leafy R287. Out of season or at dusk you may have the view all to yourself, but be careful not to fall into too deep a reverie about the Nine Bean Rows or you might drive off the end of the little jetty.

The N15 north from Sligo town runs past **Drumcliff** parish church where W.B's grandfather was vicar. The poet spent holidays in Sligo with his Pollenfex maternal grandparents and is buried here. This is a very ancient holy place, the site of a monastery founded in AD574 by St Columba, with pleasant walks along the Drumcliff river and the striking table top of Ben Bulben dominating the landscape. Nearby at Cooladrumman the saints slew the druids in the 'Battle of the Books' — the battle of Culdrevny (Cul Dreimne) in AD561. The fight was between St Columba (of the northern Uí Néill tribe) and Dermot (Diarmaid mac Cerbaill), high king of the southern Uí Néill tribe, ruling at Tara. According to one version of the story, there was an argument about a book of psalms belonging to St Finnian of Moville. Columba had copied it without permission. After Dermot was asked to adjudicate, Columba had to give up his copy. 'To every cow her calf,' Dermot said, adding, 'To every book its little book'. Having lost the copyright dispute, Columba took his revenge at Cul Dreimne.

On the left side of the road is the stump of a round tower and on the right side beside the track to Drumcliff church is a high cross, actually parts of two crosses, with carvings of biblical scenes and fantastic animals and some fine, if rather weathered, interlacing. In 1938 Yeats wrote his own epitaph in the poem *Under Ben Bulben* and describes the scene, including his own grave (but not the present obtrusive overhead tangle of power lines). Tourist buses from Sligo cruise down the track to the church and the passengers get out to read the inscription on the poet's very plain gravestone near the porch:

> 'Cast a cold eye
> On life, on death.
> Horseman, pass by!'

A minute later they are all aboard again. After a well practised three-point turn the bus glides away.

Lissadell House, a large austere house overlooking Sligo Bay a few miles west of Drumcliff, was built in the 1830s by Sir Robert Gore-Booth, grandfather of the Gore-Booth sisters, the poetess Eva, and Constance. Better known as the nationalist Countess Markievicz,

Constance took part in the 1916 rising, was condemned to death but soon released, and in 1918 became the first woman to be elected to the British House of Commons though, being a member of Sinn Féin, she never took her seat. At the time of the famine, the philanthropic Sir Robert mortgaged his estate to feed the local people. The house is open to the public on summer afternoons.

At **Streedagh**, west off the N15 at Grange, there is a memorial to the dead of the Armada vessels that were wrecked here on 20 September 1588. Some 1,100 corpses were washed up on the strand. The three galleons wrecked that day were among twenty-four big ships of the Spanish Armada fleet that foundered off the Irish west coast on their way home after the failed invasion of England. Many of the ships were great floating pantechnicons, with tall turrets and high sides, heavily loaded with invasion equipment — siege guns, gun carriages, muskets, pikes, axes, spades, campaign tents and mules — and about 20,000 infantrymen. This lumbering force was attacked off Plymouth by the English fleet and then broken up by fire ships off Calais. The greatest enemies, however, were the ferocious autumn gales and the rocky Irish coast. Alarmed at the prospect of thousands of well armed soldiers coming ashore in Ireland, where the native population was sympathetic, the Lord Deputy of Ireland ordered the summary execution of all Spaniards who got ashore. In December 1588 the governor of Connaught wrote to Queen Elizabeth that almost all the survivors who got ashore from the twelve to fifteen ships wrecked off Connaught and Clare had been 'put to the sword'. However quite a few lucky ones, including Captain Francisco de Cuellar who wrote an eye-witness account of the disaster at Streedagh, were rescued by friendly northern chieftains who were at loggerheads with the English, notably the O'Neills, MacSweeneys, and the O'Rourkes and their vassal MacClancy chiefs, princes of Breffny.

On Inishmurray 4 miles (6km) offshore from Streedagh Point, are the extensive and interesting ruins of a monastery founded by St Molaise in the early sixth century. Inside a surrounding wall, which is 13ft (4m) high in places and may predate the monastery, are several primitive churches and altars, pillar stones, a beehive monastic cell and cross-carved grave slabs. The Vikings came this way in AD802 and plundered the monastery. To the visitor these remains may seem slight, in an Irish context they are well preserved. No one lives on Inishmurray now. Poteen-making, the mainstay of the tiny local economy, received a boost in about 1910 with the arrival of a large copper still, a light-hearted but valuable gift from a prominent whiskey distiller (legal), who had recently visited the island. However, its benefits did not last long and the last islanders left in 1948.

The bare headland over to the north-east is Mullaghmore Head and the big house clearly visible from here is **Classiebawn Castle**, a Victorian-baronial house built by the English statesman Lord Palmerston (1784-1865) when he was prime minister. His family's vast estate in County Sligo was acquired in 1609. As an absentee landlord, quite a good one, Palmerston financed many building projects on his Irish estates but hereabouts he is remembered for not arranging assisted passages to America for his destitute tenants during the famine. When he was (Whig) foreign secretary Palmerston secured Belgian independence and, as prime minister he supported Italian nationalism — but not of course any Irish manifestation of either of these! Irish independence did not figure on mainstream political agendas of the time and, viewed from the larger island, Ireland was still 'Little Britain'. Great Britain was so called to distinguish it from the smaller island called Little Britain, rather as ornithologists distinguish the great spotted woodpecker from the lesser spotted woodpecker, one being bigger than the other but both being perfectly formed. Such earnest explanations are not taken at face value in Ireland, however.

More recently Classiebawn was a holiday home of Lord Louis Mountbatten. He and his fishing party, including a young boat-hand from the village, were blown up in their boat by terrorists in 1979 while out in the harbour tucked in behind the headland. From Mullaghmore, reached along the R279 from Cliffony, boats go round the headland to Inishmurray, a 14-mile (22km) trip each way. Or you may be able to get a boat from Rosses Point. The trip is about the same distance and takes about 80 minutes.

In the 1922-23 Civil War there was fighting in the mountains of Sligo, both in the Ox range and in the Dartry mountains north of Sligo town. In one murky incident four young men who had escaped up **Ben Bulben** (1,730ft/527m) were caught and summarily executed just short of the top. Bulben is the best known of the Dartry peaks, partly because Yeats wrote about it but also because of its position at the west end of the range. Seen from the N15 it gives the appearance of being a solitary mountain. Highest mountain in the Dartry range, **Truskmore** (2,120ft/646m), forms a dramatic feature of the **Gleniff Horseshoe** scenic drive, signposted off the N15 about 4 miles (6km) north of Drumcliff. The pub at **Ballaghnatrillick** where the drive begins and ends, sells good Guinness, and there is a good view from here of Benweeskin mountain. You can drive up to the top of

The fine court tomb at Creevykeel near Cliffony

Truskmore, with parking near the TV mast, and walk round the Horseshoe, staying high above the glen.

The Ordnance Survey maps are clear about **Bundoran**, a popular seaside town. It is in County Donegal, on that tiny bit of the ancient province of Ulster south of the Erne estuary. It is topographically similar to coastal Sligo but separated from it by a sliver of Leitrim. The county boundaries here have always been odd, an oddness replicated when the North-South border was drawn in 1921. The Irish writer Benedict Kiely, who was born (1919) and grew up near Omagh, County Tyrone, recalls that when he was a child 'the Protestants went to see the sea at Portrush in County Antrim, the Catholics at Bundoran in County Donegal. The sea was sectarian. That may no longer be the case — not to that extent.' Travellers heading for *echt* Donegal will not linger in Bundoran and so are unlikely to discover whether it is or not.

The countryside from Ballyshannon up to Donegal town is undulating, with small smooth hillocks (called drumlins), not at all wild or peaty. One could spend a couple of hours in this betwixt-and-between area before turning east into Fermanagh.

The handsome former barracks beside the bridge across the Erne estuary at **Ballyshannon** is a reminder of the town's development as a British garrison in the eighteenth century after the O'Donnells had been displaced. However, the river crossing was already of strategic importance at the time when Niall of the Nine Hostages was seizing Tara in the fifth century. The local bard is William Allingham (1824-89) and the poet is well remembered. The town bridge is Allingham Bridge and his bust is displayed in the AIB bank on Main Street, the building where he was born. His best known poem *The Fairies*, published in 1850, recreates the spirit world of superstitious old Ireland:

> 'Up the airy mountain,
> Down the rushy glen,
> We daren't go a-hunting
> For fear of little men.'

A white marble slab marks his grave on Mullaghnashee hill in St Anne's churchyard. This distinctive knoll was the home of Niall's son, Conall Gulban and it is his name that forms part of the old name for Donegal: Tyrconnell (*Tir Conaill*, Land of Conall).

The road to **Rossnowlagh**, a popular surfing centre with a beautiful sandy beach, passes close to the scant remains of Assaroe Abbey, an 1178 Cistercian foundation. Apart from a few fragments of wall held together by ivy, only the cemetery has survived, with a tomb of the O'Clerys, a scholarly tribe who provided teachers to the O'Donnell chieftains of Tyrconnell for 300 years. A famous O'Clery was Michael O'Clery (1575-1643) the learned Franciscan lay brother who oversaw the compilation of the *Annals of the Four Masters*, a chronicle of Irish history starting in 2958BC, 40 years before the Flood, and ending in AD1616 at the death of Hugh O'Neill. Michael (christened Thady) was born at Kilbarron Castle, the ruined O'Clery fort on the shore a mile (2km) beyond Assaroe. He and his three assistants, the 'Masters', compiled the history between 1632 and 1636 and dedicated it to their patron, Fergal O'Garra, prince of Coolavin. Exactly where they wrote it is uncertain. There is a memorial obelisk in Donegal town centre though Donegal 'Abbey', the Franciscan monastery to which Michael was attached, was destroyed by a gunpowder explosion in 1601. The chronicle is a fascinating, bloodthirsty seven-volume work of scholarship, full of plagues, invasions, battles, saints and virgins.

The collection of the Donegal Historical Society is squeezed into one room at the modern Franciscan friary at Rossnowlagh. There are some interesting items but it would be nice to see them properly displayed, in Donegal town.

The N16/A4 road from Sligo to Enniskillen starts well enough, running up the valley of the Drumcliff river along the southern flank of the Dartry range. Seven miles (11km) out from Sligo the road peaks at Glencar Lough. If you have no time to visit the lovely waterfalls at the eastern end of the lake, stop anyway to look back down the valley: Drumcliff church is clearly visible at the far end some 4 miles (6km) away. Then follows a tedious winding stretch through dull country. Just before the border with Northern Ireland, at Blacklion, long shallow Lower Lough Macnean comes into view and the scenery improves. There is a view of the pretty upper lough from the long stone bridge that connects Blacklion to Belcoo, County Fermanagh.

Easy access to Fermanagh's lakeland began when the motorway was built from Belfast and opened up the land route to the south-west corner of Ulster. Now that Lough Erne has been linked into the mighty Shannon system by an ingenious canal, the area seems set to attract visitors in greater numbers. For the time being, however, the whole of this watery, forested region is agreeably empty of crowds. Certainly for cruising there is nowhere in Europe with so much water for so few boats as **Lough Erne**. A long sinuous waterway, 50 miles (80km) from end to end, Lough Erne is divided in two by a constriction in the middle where the county town of Enniskillen stands. The lower lake, navigable down as far as Belleek, is 5 miles (8km) wide in places, with quite big waves when the wind gets up. The shallow upper lake is a jigsaw of heavily wooded islands with rather little open water. Even good navigators armed with the navigation guides of the Ordnance Survey, can get happily confused by the maze of lookalike islands and headlands.

A glance at the map shows virtually all major roads in the county converging on **Enniskillen** on its island between the upper and the lower lake, and the result is considerable congestion around the town. The traffic engineers have tackled the circulation problem by building loop roads and improving the bridges. This solution, and the fact that parking regulations are enforced, means that traffic gridlock, an exasperating feature of many Irish towns, rarely happens in Enniskillen. The roads, plus the spread of housing estates on neighbouring hillsides, have effectively deprived the visitor of any sense of being on an island. Still, as a good shopping centre, with first-rate angling facilities and accommodation, the town is a convenient base for exploring this interesting region.

The highway between the ancient provinces of Ulster in the north and Connaught in the south went across the narrows at Enniskillen, and the whole area is rich in prehistoric monuments and Celtic and early Christian antiquities. The best of these sites, and they include

Devenish Island — perhaps the single most rewarding visit in Fermanagh — are on islands in Lough Erne, reached by waterbus, ferry or private cruiser. At the same time, you can drive to a number of ruined monasteries and early churches on islands that are now joined to the mainland by bridges.

In the Middle Ages there was a chain of island monasteries down the lake — convenient stopping places for pilgrims on their way to St Patrick's Purgatory, an important shrine on Lough Derg in County Donegal. Water transport was the main way of travelling around. Bishop Chiericati, a papal nuncio who passed through Fermanagh in 1517, found the county 'full of robbers, woods, lakes and marshes'. The lakeside is high and rocky in parts, and overland travel was hard going. The Maguires, chieftains of Fermanagh, policed the lake with a private navy of 1,500 boats which were stationed at Enniskillen Castle and Hare Island.

The castle at Enniskillen was the most important of a ring of castles — Crum, Portora, Tully, Archdale, Crevenish and Caldwell — round the lough shore which the planters used to control the waterway in the seventeenth and eighteenth centuries. The English first captured it in 1594. The Maguires got it back but were expelled again in 1607, after which the whole of Enniskillen was granted to Sir William Cole. As constable, and captain of the king's longboats, Cole enlarged the castle, built the fairytale Water Gate and established the plantation town. The Water Gate, which is really just a short length of wall flanked by two towers with nothing behind it, is best seen by boat, approaching from the upper lake. There are always a few anglers under its romantic towers, pole fishing for eels from the river bank.

Enniskillen was the only stronghold in Fermanagh to escape destruction in the seventeenth century. Cole's garrison successfully defended it against Roderick Maguire during the 1641 rising, and again in 1688 when the town rallied to William of Orange. The Enniskilleners were able to stop Jacobite troops at Belleek and prevented a large Irish force from joining the attack on Londonderry, and they formed William's personal guard at the battle of the Boyne. Two famous regiments, the Royal Inniskilling Fusiliers and the Inniskilling Dragoons, originated from this time (the town later changed the I for an E). Napoleonic battle trophies and other militaria of the Inniskilling regiments, both long since merged with other regiments, occupy several floors in the castle keep. The ground floor of the keep, which has an incongruous slate roof but dates from the castle of Hugh the Hospitable (died 1428), contains objects from the county museum collection, including an ogham stone and gro-

Enniskillen's main street

tesque stone idols (originals) and, presumably for educational purposes, copies of the mysterious carvings on White Island, Lower
Lough Erne.

At the east end of the town a delightful Victorian town park of
humpy hillocks has been squeezed on to the slopes of Fort Hill. Not
far from the cast-iron bandstand, with its clock tower and cupola, is
a very tall Doric column with a statue of Sir Galbraith Lowry Cole
(1772-1842) on the top. Sir Galbraith was one of Wellington's generals in the Peninsular War and is holding a fearsome-looking cavalry
sabre in his left hand. To share his panoramic view of the lakes, you
need to climb the 108 steps up the spiral staircase.

Enniskillen's long main street changes its name half a dozen times
as it curves and wiggles from East Bridge to West Bridge, up and
down two slight hills. The highest point of the street is occupied by
St Macartan's cathedral which, like several other Anglican cathedrals in Ulster, including even Armagh, looks more like an English
parish church than a cathedral. This one is interesting as a repository
of the town's military memory. The chancel contains a full length
martial portrait of General Sir Galbraith Lowry Cole, still brandish-
ing his sabre. A bell in the cathedral tower was cast from cannon used
at the battle of the Boyne (1690), colours of the Inniskilling regiments
hang in the light and airy late-Georgian interior and the names of all
the Fusiliers killed since the battle of Waterloo are recorded in a book
of remembrance. Other notable features are a seventeenth-century
font and a curious stone tablet to one William Pokrich (died 1628)
which has half its inscription upside down.

Devenish Island

Opposite St Macartan's is an immensely tall and thin nineteenth-century Catholic church, St Michael's, with a long nave and steep roof. A window in the south aisle portrays St Molaise, the abbot-founder of Devenish monastery, holding the Devenish Gospel Shrine. Atmospheric Blake's Of The Hollow (1887) down the street is Enniskillen's best known musical pub. At this point there is a pronounced dip, or hollow, in the road, hence its name. It has a characterful Victorian shopfront and pine-boarded snugs inside. Further along, high up on the town hall tower, are niche statues of a Fusilier and a Dragoon. A brass plate in the lobby commemorates brave Captain Oates of the Sixth Inniskilling Dragoons, who walked out into a blizzard on Scott's tragic return journey from the South Pole in March 1912. The chapel in the Convent of Mercy in Belmore St, below Fort Hill, contains good modern stained glass, including windows by Michael Healy (1879-1941), one of the four principal artists associated with the Tower of Glass (An Túr Gloine) workshop established in 1903 by Sarah Purser (1848-1943). She was a painter who made a fortune on the London stock market and spent it promoting Irish arts and culture.

Ruined Portora Castle (1613), which commanded the entrance to Lower Lough Erne, is in the grounds of **Portora Royal School**, founded by James I in 1608 and moved to this site above the river in

1777. The castle's ruinous state is partly the result of an experiment by the chemistry class of 1859. A large oil painting of Oscar Wilde (1854-1900), the school's most famous old boy, adorns the entrance hall. Other pupils included the dramatist Samuel Beckett (1905-89) and Henry Francis Lyte (1793-1847), the divine who wrote the hymn 'Abide with me'. Lyte also collected books on a big scale: it took London dealers 16 days to auction off his library, mostly antiquarian religious books, after his death. Patriotic Nurse Edith Cavell, shot by the Germans in 1915 for helping Allied soldiers escape over the Dutch border, ought to count as a famous old boy of Portora: she was a friend of the headmaster's wife and ministered to boarders in the school sanatorium.

The Islands and Antiquities of Lower Lough Erne

There are about 100 islands, big and small, on the lower lake. Devenish, Inishmacsaint and White Island have the most extensive and interesting monastic remains.

Devenish Island, 2 miles (3km) downstream from the town, is the site of a sixth-century monastery founded by St Molaise (died AD563), one of the 'twelve apostles of Ireland'. Arbiter in the quarrels of the Ulster chieftains, and mentor of St Columba, Molaise had 1,500 students attached to Devenish. The monastery was raided

One of many magnificent views across Lower Lough Erne

by Vikings in the ninth century and burned in 1157 but then remained an important religious centre until the early seventeenth century. The island's greatest treasure, the *Soiscél Molaise*, an early eleventh-century book shrine, is in the National Museum, Dublin. Follow the path up from the east jetty, past a remarkable succession of ecclesiastical remains.

Ruined Teampull Mór, the lower church, dates from about 1225 and has a fine south window of that period. It was greatly extended in about 1300 and was in turn a Culdee monastery and the parish church of Devenish. The Culdees (*Céli-Dé* — Companions of God) were a strict Celtic anchorite order founded at the end of the eighth century. Killadeas, a small angling and boating resort down the lake on the east shore, is named after the Culdees. The arms of the Maguires of Tempo appear in two places outside their sixteenth-century burial chamber here, and the graveyard below the church contains some interesting stones, including an eleventh-century cross-carved slab.

St Molaise's House is a tiny twelfth-century church with thick walls which once supported a stone roof. Though much ruined, it still has a sturdy look about it.

The round tower, a perfect twelfth-century example, has a setting as beautiful as any of the dozen or so complete round towers that survive in Ireland. Over 80ft (24m) high, with a decorated cornice round the conical cap, it has five floors which are ascended by interior ladders. The four windows at the top gave the sentry an all-round view of strangers approaching over the water, and he could sound his bell to warn the brethren. The door of the tower, 9ft (2m) off the ground, faces the entrance to St Molaise's House and so the monks — having snatched up books and relics from the church — could hurry to the safety of the tower, pull up the outside ladder and hope for the best. There are traces a few yards away of an earlier round tower, perhaps destroyed by Vikings who arrived on Lough Erne in AD837 and established a base at Belleek. Their long boats had no difficulty in reaching the island monasteries.

Beyond the round tower are the ruins of St Mary's, an Augustinian priory, built by the master mason Matthew O'Dubigan in 1449 when, according to an inscription on the south wall, Bartholomew O'Flanagan was prior. The O'Flanagan sept supplied the last prior of St Mary's too, and also many of the priests for Inishmacsaint. The most notable feature is the north door to the chancel which has elaborate carvings. The east window was taken to the Anglican parish church at Monea hamlet (at the B81/C443 junction, a mile

The mysterious stone figures of White Island, Lower Lough Erne

(2km) south-west of Monea Castle) where it was reset in 1890. The site museum preserves a female head from the west door into the nave. Note the unusual design of a pretty fifteenth-century cross in the graveyard. The Augustinian priory and the Culdee monastery down the hill co-existed in apparent harmony until both were abandoned in 1603 at the dissolution of monasteries in Fermanagh.

The ferry to Devenish leaves from Trory Point, signposted at the B82/A32 junction 3 miles (5km) north of Enniskillen.

Inishmacsaint Island also had a sixth-century monastery, one of the thousands that sprang up all over Ireland in the generation after St Patrick's death. This one was founded in about AD523 by St Ninnid who, like St Molaise, studied under St Finnian at Clonard. The island has an ancient rath, a ruined twelfth-century church, and a striking high cross with splayed arms and a broad shaft. Fourteen feet (4m) high, it lacks the usual Celtic circle, and it seems that the tenth-century stone carver was called away before he could finish it. There is a public jetty.

White Island's seven stone figures, lined up on the far wall of a roofless twelfth-century church, are first glimpsed through a Romanesque doorway as you walk through trees from the jetty. Dating from the ninth or tenth century, these Christian statues have a distinctly pagan mien and their significance has been much debated. The build-

The Bishop's Stone at Killadeas

ers of a later church used them as ordinary masonry stones but sockets on the heads indicate they were intended as supports. From left to right: a female fertility figure (*sheelnagig*) with a wide alluring smile; a seated man holding a book; an abbot with bell and crozier; another priestly figure scratching his chin; a man with a kiss-curl fringe holding two griffins by the scruff of their necks; a second curly-haired man with sword, shield and a big brooch; the seventh figure is unfinished. The eighth stone, a medieval sour-faced mask, is unconnected with the others. Look out for an eleventh-century gravestone in the church. A prominent feature of the site is a large enclosing bank west of the church. This earthworks must have been there already when the little church was built inside.

Killadeas and **Boa Island** are interesting sites which can be reached by car. The Bishop's Stone in Killadeas churchyard, near an old Irish yew, depicts on one side a little cleric walking briskly, and on another side a grotesque moonface with slack mouth — a ninth-century Charles Laughton. Note an even earlier cross-ornamented slab nearby.

Older than these, and unparalleled in Ireland is the two-faced Celtic idol in Caldragh cemetery on Boa Island. Between the heads is a deep libation stoup. Both faces have staring eyes, pointed chins and arms crossed over their chests. Just behind the Janus is the 'Lusty Man', a smaller idol, with an outsize head and shapely, womanly arms. He, or she, was brought here from nearby Lustymore Island — hence the name. Boa Island, a long and narrow island joined to the mainland by bridges, is easily reached. The A47 from Kesh to Belleek runs right across it. Caldragh is signposted beyond the turning to Lustybeg jetty.

Ned Allingham, reclusive brother of the poet William Allingham, once lived on Lustybeg, a thickly wooded island which is now popular for self-catering holidays. People come for the boating and angling and stay in log-cabin holiday chalets. The island's restaurant is open to anyone. To cross to Lustybeg, pick up the telephone on the jetty and state your business: a man will emerge from the nearby pub and ferry you over!

The Islands of Upper Lough Erne

The maze of islands in the shallow, reedy upper lake are better known for their natural beauty and wild birds than for their monastic sites. There are about sixty altogether, most of them are uninhabited, some with ruined mansions and abandoned cottages, others with colonies of nesting birds (restricted access in the breeding season) or wild goats who run up and steal your picnic sandwiches. However, a few islands still retain traces of the religious communities that flourished here in early Christian times. Three which can be reached by either car or boat are Inishkeen, Cleenish and Galloon.

Inishkeen, accessible by a causeway 3 miles (5km) south-east of Enniskillen off the A4, has a rath at either end, and strange carved stones in old St Fergus' cemetery — a god's head with antlers and an angel sitting in a boat, or it could be a devil boiling in a cauldron. The *Annals of Ulster* report that, in 1421, Hugh Maguire slew the three sons of Art Maguire on Inishkeen. Opposite the northern tip of the island, across the picturesque reach used by the rowing club, is a Georgian house with a battlemented tower incorporated into it. The tower is a remnant of Lisgoole Abbey, a twelfth-century monastery which passed from Augustinians to Franciscans in the sixteenth century. At Lisgoole, in 1631, Brother Michael O'Clery and other learned friars compiled the *Book of Invasions*, an intricate synthesis of pagan myths and Christian beliefs.

Cleenish, reached across a metal bridge south-east of Bellanaleck, had a celebrated abbot, St Sinell, tutor to St Columbanus, the austere Irish missionary who went to Europe in AD589 and founded famous Celtic monasteries at Luxeuil, France, and at Bobbio near Milan. The island has some distinctive carved gravestones. The father of Field Marshal Sir Claude Auchinleck (died 1981) was a native of Cleenish. On Inishrath, a small island further upstream, members of the Hare Krishna sect have turned an 1840s' mansion into a Hindu shrine. The wooded demesne of Crom Castle, home of the earls of Erne, occupies a long headland west of Galloon. The National Trust now looks after more than 1,000 acres (400 hectares) of the estate and there is a visitor centre. Down by the jetty a romantic plantation ruin, Old Crom Castle, built in 1611 and home of the Crichton family until an accidental fire destroyed it in 1764. Nearby is an enormous yew tree, the biggest in Ireland. The Woodford river, the northern end of the new Shannon-Erne link, debouches into Lough Erne just south of here. Boats arriving from Leitrim village, at the other end of the link, will have been on the move for about 13 hours. Though it is only 38 miles (61km) there are 16 locks to negotiate.

Galloon, 3 miles (5km) south-west of Newtownbutler, supports a small farming community. Whooper swans are common round here and, until recently, the rough grassy fields that stretch down to the water's edge were an important breeding site for corncrakes. Now you have to be lucky to hear that unmistakable 'crex crex'. The churchyard contains fragmentary remains of two very weathered tenth-century crosses. The worn sculpture on the taller cross in- cludes the Fall, Daniel in the lions' den, and the sacrifice of Isaac. On the smaller cross you may be able to make out the Last Judgment, the Adoration of the Magi and the baptism of Christ. There are also some fine eighteenth-century grave slabs carved with skull and crossbones, coffins, sand timers, and other melancholy reminders of the end of things.

The main attraction of **Lisnaskea** is the excellent river and lake fishing around it. A large unphotogenic ruined castle at the end of the town's well-pubbed main street has been there since 1618. In the market place is an Adam and Eve carved cross, very worn, brought from Galloon island. The second earl of Enniskillen put it here to improve appearances in 1841. A Lisnaskea publican's collection of 'folk' objects, including recipes for making poteen, illicit whiskey, is displayed in the local library. To see grave slabs similar to those on Galloon, take the B127 and turn off to the atmospheric ruins of **Aghalurcher** Old Church, chief burying place of the Maguires in

medieval times. Generations of Balfours and Galbraiths, local planter
families, also had themselves buried here, beneath some fine tomb-
stones. The church itself was abandoned in 1484, the year a Maguire
slew a kinsman on the altar.

At Smith's Strand off the B127, the Share Holiday Village caters for
disabled and able-bodied people who want to enjoy activity holidays
in each other's company. All the facilities are purpose-built. An
interesting cruise of the upper lake leaves from here. The boat is a sort
of Viking longship with an engine. It chugs peacefully around the
islands and long wooded tongues of land, passing the Crom estate,
Gad Island and the Hare Krishna folk on Inishrath. The islands
shelter nesting great-crested grebe, whooper swans and, on
Inishfendra island near Crom, there is an important heronry whose
big grey inmates occasionally accompany the boat with a great
flapping of wings. From the Share Centre, the B127 crosses Upper
Lough Erne via bridge-connected Trasna island, joining the main
Enniskillen road at **Derrylin** hamlet. Look out for Derrylin's weird
black-and-white stone man, with a pudding-basin hairdo, bow tie
and dinner jacket, next to Blake's public house. Craggy **Knockninny
Hill**, a striking feature on the upper lake, is 3 miles (5km) north of
Derrylin. The hill is a well known beauty spot and there is a view of
the islands from the top.

Two superb great houses near Enniskillen in National Trust care
are open to the public most afternoons from June to August. You can
visit in April, May and September, but only on weekend and bank
holiday afternoons. The magnificent neo-classical mansion at **Castle
Coole**, the most palatial of Ireland's late eighteenth-century houses,
is the more famous but the setting of **Florence Court** is memorably
dramatic. The house stands in a natural amphitheatre of mountains
— the hump of Benaughlin to the south, the long flat ridge of
Cuilcagh and the Leitrim hills to the south-west and west, and
Mount Belmore on the north side. Former seat of the earls of
Enniskillen, descendants of planter-constable William Cole, Florence Court is a three-storey early eighteenth-century house joined by
long arcades to small pavilions. Sumptuous rococo plasterwork
(1755) by the Dublin stuccodore, Robert West, is the most notable
feature of the interior.

The surrounding woodlands, now a forest park, shelter the original Irish Yew, progenitor of the columnar tree now found throughout the world (*taxus baccata fastigiata*). Discovered as a seedling on the
rocky slopes of Cuilcagh in the mid-eighteenth century, the tree can
be propagated only by cuttings. A great number of cuttings have
been taken from the old mother tree which stands, exhausted and

gaunt, at the edge of a clearing. Cuilcagh (2,188ft/667m) can be climbed from Florence Court, if you have seven hours or so to spare, and the right boots. The top is very steep and rugged.

The first big house at Castle Coole was a plantation castle which was destroyed in 1641. Two more houses, each bigger and better than the last, came and went before the present masterpiece was completed in 1798. Designed by James Wyatt for the Lowry-Corry family, earls of Belmore, it has a beautiful Palladian main front, 275ft (84m) long, with pillared colonnades and elegant pavilions at each end. Silver-coloured Portland stone, imported at great expense by boat and hauled here by ox-cart, was used for the façade. Art historians describe the splendid interior in tremulous tones of emotion. The garden front overlooks a lake, where a large breeding colony of greylag geese has lived since 1700, and the park has some noble beeches and a four-row avenue of ancient oaks. The stables and the head gardener's house were built in the 1820s by Richard Morrison. A young French emigré, the Chevalier de Latocnaye, who visited Castle Coole in 1796, declared that Lord Belmore's palace was rather too grand for a private individual. 'The temples should be left to the gods,' he said.

During his visit to Fermanagh the Chevalier went into the underground caves at **Marble Arch** and got lost when his candle blew out. Until structural engineering work was completed in 1985, only geologists, cavers and a few adventurous individuals went down into the caves. Now they are a big public attraction. The entrance is signposted up the Marlbank Loop road, just west of Florence Court. Apart from the usual stalagmites and stalactites there are underground lakes and rivers fed by surface streams rising in the Cuilcagh mountains. A subterranean boat trip across the lower lake is a highlight of the guided tour. The 'marble arch' — a detached limestone arch 30ft (9m) high — is above ground, at the lower entrance to the caves in a flowery glen where the Cladagh river rushes out from underground and flows beneath the arch.

The show caves are only a fraction of the extensive cave systems of County Fermanagh. Caves on the moors around Boho hamlet (due north of Marble Arch) include **Noon's Hole** which is the deepest pothole in Ireland. It is nearly 300ft (91m) to the bottom. **Knockmore Cliff**, a sheer reef of limestone 800ft (244m) high with a fine view from the top, has several visitable caves (north-west of Boho). Generally speaking, however, it is not advisable to go exploring round here without a guide. When leaving the Marble Arch carpark, turn right to complete the scenic run along the wild Cuilcagh plateau, passing first a small bridge where the Sruh Croppa river suddenly

The great Palladian mansion of Castle Coole

vanishes into a crevice called the Cat's Hole. After 2 miles (3km) the
loop rejoins the lower road. Two nearby lakes, the Macneans, are full
of heavyweight pike which fishermen come to do battle with. German and Swiss anglers are particularly partial to poached pike, in the
culinary sense.

Guesthouses and B&Bs with views over the lake punctuate the
shore route from Enniskillen to Belleek (A46). The road runs through
Ely Lodge Forest, especially pretty in autumn when the leaves turn.
Ely Lodge, the Irish seat of the Duke of Westminster, is on a
promontory beyond and visible from the lake. An earlier house on
the site was blown up by its owner, the fourth Marquis of Ely, to
celebrate his 21st birthday.

Turn inland to see **Monea Castle**, a fine ruined castle surrounded
by bog, overlooking a lake. Built in 1618 by Malcolm Hamilton, rector
of Devenish, later archbishop of Cashel, Monea has an impressive
entrance front — two glowering circular towers with square turrets
supported on Scottish-type corbels at the top. The 1641 insurgents
captured it (one wonders how) but the Hamiltons soon got it back.
The governor of Enniskillen, Gustavus Hamilton, who was one of
William III's generals at the Boyne, lived in the castle. After the battle,
and now raised to the peerage, the new Viscount Boyne moved out
of Monea and built a grand country residence not far from the

battleground in county Meath and called it after himself — Boyne House.

Derrygonnelly is an 1830s village with a harmonious main street lined with two-storey houses, shops and musical pubs such as Corrigan's, where the fiddle, the tin whistle and the *bodhran*, a small single-skin drum, can be heard for the price of a pint of Guinness. Just north of the village pause at an interesting church (ruined) that combines medieval and Renaissance features, built in 1627 by Sir John Dunbar. The Dunbar family arms are over the doorway. The B81 from Derrygonnelly runs north to Tully Bay where the ruin of a small castle overlooks Lower Lough Erne. Built in 1613 by Sir John Hume, **Tully Castle** was burnt by the ousted Maguires in 1641. The Maguires were in particularly vengeful mood. Though they spared the Humes they killed everyone else in the castle and, since the garrison was away, these were mostly women and children. A little formal herb garden, recreated by the Department of the Environment in seventeenth-century style with sweet briars, lavender and hyssop, is a poignant reminder of the domestic duties and pleasures of the household.

For a panorama of lakes and mountains, the viewpoint in **Lough Navar Forest** takes some beating. The forest is signposted east of Tully off the main shore road (A46). Entrance is opposite Correl Glen nature reserve and you can drive right up to the map table. It is right on the Ulster Way. The long-distance walkers who have toiled up a zigzag path from the lough shore 1,000ft (305m) below soon revive at the sight of all Lower Lough Erne spread out below, with the cone of Errigal (2,467ft/752m) north-north-west and Ben Bulben (1,730ft/527m) due west.

The border village of **Belleek** marks the end of the Erne navigation. The current at the low bridge opposite the pottery reaches six knots on occasion, and a sluice here controls the level of Lough Erne. Half a mile (1km) beyond are the dams of the Erne hydro-electric scheme, after which the river plunges down to meet the Atlantic at Ballyshannon. Part of Belleek is in Donegal but most of it is in Fermanagh. The village hosts an annual fiddle festival, the Fiddle Stone Festival (late June/early July) when fiddlers come from all over Ireland for a weekend of traditional music-making. Motor boats and rowing boats can be hired with the minimum of formalities and there are some attractive lakeside self-catering cottages.

The pottery at Belleek was started after local deposits of felspar were discovered at Castle Caldwell in 1857. Nowadays the felspar is imported. However, some delectable extravaganzas from the early

Strange species of trout bring anglers to remote Lough Melvin

days are on display in a small museum in the visitor centre. The porcelain is especially collected by Americans. Early pieces change hands for large sums. Cream coloured lattice-worked baskets, decorated with pink and yellow rosebuds, blue cornflowers or daisies, or possibly all of them, are characteristic of the Belleek style. These 'woven' baskets are definitely not for putting things in. One or two smaller factories nearby, but across the border, now make pottery rather similar in appearance to the Belleek product.

Lough Melvin a few miles to the south is one of the best wild trout fisheries in Europe. It has a fine spring run of salmon but the great attraction is the trout fishing, in particular three unusual subspecies: the sonaghan, a small trout with black spots that catches insects near the surface of the water; the gillaroo, a bigger, red-spotted fish that feeds on snails and larvae at the bottom of the lake; and thirdly, the ferox, a very big trout with strong jaws. This fierce (*ferox*) fish eats other fish and thoroughly deserves its name. Anglers stay in comfortable hostel and B&B accommodation in Garrison village at the east end of this remote peaty lake, or else on Roskit island nearby. There are plenty of boats, and boatmen who know their way around the islands. Only a bit of the lake is in Fermanagh, most of it is in Leitrim. The globe flower, a rare member of the buttercup family, grows in profusion on one island, and others have little-visited antiquities, such as MacClancy's Castle, Rosclogher, refuge of Armada survivors in 1588. The wild plateau east of Garrison is great bilberry country. On Bilberry Sunday at the end of July small armies of pickers come for the day from Enniskillen.

The nature reserve at Castle Caldwell estate, in the fork of a double-pronged peninsula, is still a popular haunt of birdwatchers though, as on Galloon island, the corncrake is a rare bird these days and the common scoter, a handsome shiny black diving sea duck, seems to have gone elsewhere recently. Old Castle Caldwell, first built in 1612, passed in 1662 to the Caldwell family. It is now very ruined and covered in ivy. At the entrance to the main forest (on A47) is a giant stone fiddle, 5ft (1.5m) high, inscribed with an obituary rhyme to Denis McCabe, an inebriated fiddler who was drowned when he fell off the Caldwells' barge in 1770. The Belleek fiddle festival commemorates his demise.

To see the Bronze Age stone circle at Drumskinny, take the Castlederg road north from the fishing village of Kesh for about 4 ½ miles (7km). Further west past Kesh, **Castle Archdale Country Park** is the departure point for the ferry to White Island. The exceedingly ruined old castle in the forest was built in 1615 by John Archdale, an English planter from Norfolk, and destroyed during the Williamite wars. The Georgian house known as 'New' Castle Archdale, now derelict, was used by the RAF and the Canadian Air Force from 1941 when this part of Lower Lough Erne was a base for flying boat squadrons. Catalinas — American 'lend-lease' twin-engined flying boats, and British Sunderlands, developed and built in Belfast — took off from Lower Lough Erne to hunt for U-boats in the Atlantic. A 16-mile (26km) air corridor over Leitrim and Donegal was the subject of a secret agreement between Britain and neutral Eire. Some Donegal headlands still bear the huge white-painted signs intended to stop Allied pilots from straying outside the corridor. The eighteenth-century stables at Castle Archdale have been converted to a youth hostel and there is a small Battle of the Atlantic exhibition, mostly pictures — no flying boats alas! Other relics of World War II are the outsize concrete ramps at the yacht club at Goblusk Bay, and the airfield at St Angelo nearby which was opened in 1941 and used by Dakotas.

Irvinestown is enlivened in summer by a 10-day carnival. A clock tower with pinnacled battlements is all that is left of the 1734 church of Dr Patrick Delany, then rector at Irvinestown, later dean of Down. His wife, Mrs Mary Delany (1700-88, née Granville), was a London literary and society hostess, confidante of Pope, Burke and Horace Walpole, and a favourite at court. Delany met her through his friend, Swift. After their marriage in 1743, Mrs Delany accompanied her husband all over Ireland, staying in all the great Anglo-Irish houses, and writing everything down. Her voluminous autobiography and correspondence, published in 1861-62, include spirited portraits of eighteenth-century Irish society.

Ireland's Last Gaelic Stronghold

North of Irvinestown lies the very large county of Tyrone. It stretches east-west across Ulster from huge Lough Neagh to within 10 miles (16km) of Donegal bay. There are places of historical interest and pretty river valleys but also barren stretches that challenge the inventiveness of tour guides. In the later sixteenth century this was the last Gaelic stronghold in Ireland, densely forested, a haunt of wolves, and lawless. The forests were cut down when Scots and English planters arrived, and the last Irish wolf was killed in 1786 but people in parts of Tyrone like to do things their own way even today.

The aim of England's sixteenth-century rulers was to substitute English administration and the rule of law for Irish feudal custom and tribal practice, and to turn the Gaelic chieftains and Anglo-Norman lords into peers under the Crown. They equated a hereditary nobility with a stable, manageable society, and the Irish elective system with instability and chaos. As for religion, it mattered rather little, so long as people did not transfer their loyalties. For 9 years Hugh (The Great) O'Neill, earl of Tyrone, held out. His resistance was so effective that when at last he submitted to Elizabeth I in 1603, the terms he got were quite favourable. However, they were not good enough to prevent land-grab and the advance of English administration into his territory. In 1607, together with Rory O'Donnell, earl of Tyrconnell, he boarded a boat in Lough Swilly and fled to Spain.

Those local Irish Catholic landowners who had managed to keep their estates following the Flight of the Earls forfeited them after the 1641 rebellion which started when Sir Phelim O'Neill seized Charlemont and Dungannon in Tyrone. The Irish wanted restitution of their lands and there was a great slaughter of Scots and English settlers. This was avenged 8 years later when Oliver Cromwell put the people of Drogheda to the sword.

The chief crowning place of the O'Neills, from the twelfth to the seventeenth century, was over in east Tyrone at **Tullahoge**, headquarters of the O'Hagans, chief justices of Tyrone. There is a fine view of the old kingdom of Tyrone from the top of the tree-ringed hill. The circular graveyard nearby, with a wall round it, was the O'Hagan burial place. During the ceremony the king-elect sat on a stone inauguration chair, new sandals were placed on his feet, the assembled chiefs chanted his name in unison 'amid the clang of bucklers and the music of a hundred harps', and he was then anointed and crowned by the primate of Armagh. The last king to sit on the chair was the Great O'Neill in 1593. The O'Hagan role as prominent law officers continued into modern times, and the first Lord O'Hagan (1812-85) was chancellor of Ireland. Tullahoge is 10 miles (16km) due north of the M1, junction 15, off the Cookstown road (A29).

The west Tyrone border town of **Strabane** looks across the Foyle to Lifford. James II made his base here in 1688-9 for the attack on Londonderry. Unlikely though it seems now, Strabane was an important printing and book publishing centre in the eighteenth century. The only relic of that humanistic tradition is a little shop with a Georgian front in Main Street, Gray's printing shop, rescued by the National Trust. Meetinghouse Street was the birthplace of John Dunlap (1747-1812) who printed the broadsheets of the American Declaration of Independence in July 1776 and founded the *Pennsylvania Packet*, which became America's first daily newspaper (1784). James Wilson, grandfather of Woodrow Wilson, US president 1913-21, was also a Strabane printer. The Wilson ancestral home, a thatched farmhouse at **Dergalt** signposted 2 miles (3km) down the Plumbridge road, is open all year. Wilsons live in the modern farmhouse next door and still work the farm.

The Foyle at Strabane is the confluence of two noted salmon rivers, the Finn which runs west through Ballybofey and on to Lough Finn, and the Mourne which descends from Sion Mills and Newtownstewart. **Sion Mills** was laid out as a model linen village by three god-fearing brothers, James, John and George Herdman. In 1835 they converted an old flour mill on the Mourne into a flax-spinning mill and built a bigger mill behind it in the 1850s. Their factory is still working. The village is an exotic mix of polychrome brick, black-and-white half-timbered buildings, and terraced millworkers' cottages, all set off by wide grassy verges and horse-chestnut trees. Nearly everything in Sion Mills except St Teresa's church was designed by James Herdman's son-in-law, the English architect William Unsworth. The village's big house is a half-timbered Elizabethan-style mansion with pepperpot chimneys, not in the least Irish. By contrast the Catholic church of St Teresa (1963) by Patrick Haughey has lots of straight lines, and a striking representation (by Oisin Kelly) of the *Last Supper* on the façade which is made of slate. The Sion Mills cricket team made headlines in 1969 when a West Indies touring team was defeated on the village ground.

There is good angling in the Mourne around Victoria Bridge and Douglas Bridge, blink-and-miss hamlets on either side of the river, each with its strong stone bridge. Douglas Bridge features in a ballad by the Irish-American poet, Francis Carlin:

'On Douglas Bridge I met a man
Who lived adjacent to Strabane,
Before the English hung him high
For riding with O'Hanlon.'

'Count' Redmond O'Hanlon, the highwayman who was slain at Hilltown in the Mournes in 1681, was the political heir of Sir Phelim O'Neill. Handsome many-arched eighteenth-century stone bridges are a striking feature of this otherwise unremarkable area. Newtownstewart town bridge and Ardstraw bridge on the B164 Castlederg road are two more.

James II came through Tyrone in 1689 on his way back to Dublin after the unsuccessful assault on Londonderry, and he spent the night at **Newtownstewart**. He got up next morning in a bad temper and ordered the Stewart castle, and the town, to be burnt down. A dramatic triple gable wall of the ruined castle still dominates the village main street. The Northern Bank building on the corner was the scene of a famous murder in 1871 when bank cashier William Glass was robbed of £1,600 and done to death. District Inspector Montgomery, of the Royal Irish Constabulary, who was in charge of the case, turned out to be the murderer.

Half a mile (1km) south-west of Newtownstewart, on a hill, are the massive D-shaped towers of **Harry Avery's Castle**, the ruined keep of a fourteenth-century stone castle associated with Henry Aimbreidh O'Neill (died 1392). Rather little is known about it or him but it is unusual to come upon a stone castle so far inside Gaelic Ulster. Here you are very close to Baronscourt, country seat of the Hamiltons, dukes of Abercorn. The mansion and Italianate gardens are private, although tourists staying at holiday cottages near the golf course can arrange pike fishing and water-skiing on the lakes. Visitors to the estate garden centre, which has a café, will notice the elegant agent's house, built in 1741 by James Martin, architect of Clogher cathedral.

The A5 from Newtownstewart runs south between two distinctive small hills, Bessie Bell and Mary Gray, and on to the Ulster-American Folk Park, near Omagh, a rewarding visit for anyone interested in the migrations of Irish people over the centuries.

At one time a narrow gauge railway ran from Victoria Bridge to the lively market town of **Castlederg**, full of little shops selling home-made cakes and jam, the remotest town in Tyrone. It has a very thoroughly ruined castle, built in 1619 by Sir John Davies and damaged beyond repair, though not captured, by Sir Phelim O'Neill in 1641. The Anglican church, with a good Classical doorway, dates from 1731. The town centre underwent a major improvement in 1993. However, though firmly within Northern Ireland, the parking habits of the Castledergians show signs of contamination from the neighbouring culture. Cars, tractors and vans can build up three deep from the pavement. Nothing moves, nobody hoots, gridlock. No one seems to mind. The border is 3 miles (5km) away and you can cross there. Although there are no road signs or visible placenames it does not much matter because there is only one road. At the end of it is **Castlefin**, a quiet Donegal village with a large sloping market-place.

There can be magical days when Donegal is serenely sunny while Ulster's eastern seaboard is wet and dull but this is certainly not to be counted on. The Atlantic clouds that drift in over Donegal all year round can hardly wait to dump their watery load on to the quartzite heights of Slieve League (1,972ft/601m), black Muckish (2,197ft/670m), Slieve Snaght (2,240ft/683m), and the shining cone of Errigal (2,467ft/752m). The famous Donegal light is at its most beautiful just after the rain has stopped. The more rocky the terrain, the more moisture is left to hang in the air, giving a soft, misty, almost dreamlike quality to the mountains, lakes, beaches and everything else. To plan offshore boat trips, to Tory Island for example, nothing less than a prolonged period of high pressure weather systems out in the Atlantic will do. Otherwise be ready to go at short notice.

From anywhere along the north bank of Lower Lough Erne, you can join the A35 to the border town of **Pettigo** in Donegal. It is not a particularly attractive introduction to the county, utterly unlike the north-west coastal region but typical of inland Donegal, and called the Donegal Highlands — a designation that sometimes confuses visitors. At Pettigo you are only 5 miles (8km) from **St Patrick's Purgatory**, a renowned pilgrimage centre on Station Island, an island in Lough Derg — not to be confused with Lough Derg, largest of the Shannon lakes, between Portumna and Killaloe; the Donegal

Handwoven tweeds and Aran knitwear can be bought at Ardara

Derg is a puddle by comparison. Pilgrims started coming here in about 1150 to undergo severe penitential exercises and the stream of the faithful has hardly faltered, despite the edicts of popes, bishops and monarchs who tried to put a stop to it. The pilgrimage was at first to Saint's Island, a larger island on the west side of the lake, where the focus of fascination was an underground cave. It is said the Celts believed this to be the door to the underworld. In the Middle Ages, after a travelling knight saw with his own eyes the flames of Purgatory darting from the cave, sinners came in large numbers to suffer the torments of hell.

The masochistic medieval excesses have long since ceased but at any one time during the main season (1 June-15 August) some 400 people without their shoes on are undergoing sleep deprivation and a self-inflicted diet of dry bread and black tea. Non-pilgrims should not try to get on to the island during this busy period. However, just to look at it from the bank is probably enough. The entire island is crowded with large ornate buildings as weird and wonderful as Kubla Khan's pleasure dome, until you look closer and see that it is twentieth-century neo-Romanesque. Other islands on the lake are thickly wooded, the water is dark, and the surrounding hills are brown and featureless. Statistics about the efficacy of the pilgrimage are not easily come by, though one anonymous seventeenth-century poet was disappointed: 'Truagh mo thuras go Loch Dearg' — 'In vain my visit to Lough Derg'.

Calm water at tiny Teelin

On to cheerful **Donegal** town where every other person in the Diamond (main square) seems to be wearing a chunky white woollen sweater and a tweed cap. Tweeds, in all those subtle colours that reflect something of Donegal's soft-textured light, are made locally and holiday visitors spend much time inspecting numerous tweedy articles before deciding what to buy. Donegal Castle on the Eske river bank is a well preserved ruin. In the Irish context this is not a contradiction in terms; most castles are ruined as are many historic churches. This castle has a large square tower, built by Red Hugh II O'Donnell in 1505 and it was the chief stronghold of the O'Donnells for 100 years. After the Flight of the Earls it was granted to Sir Basil Brooke and he added the fortified Jacobean manor house attached to the south side. The gables on the tower are Sir Basil's. He wanted it to match his new house.

The road west from Donegal runs along the north shore of Donegal Bay. As an alternative to continuing west at Killybegs, stay with the N56 when it turns due north at the T-junction up a scenic road to the sleepy town of **Ardara**. A centre for handwoven Donegal tweeds and Aran sweaters, Ardara does not bestir itself much before 10am, even on weekdays. It is a good place to stay for exploring the area from Loughros peninsula up to **Gweebarra Bay**, a stony, little-visited region with wonderful views in all directions. It is rich in early Christian pillar stones and cross-carved slabs and, at **Kilclooney**, there is a particularly appealing dolmen with a magnificent capstone. From Ardara a fine road through the Glengesh Pass continues down the bleak Crow valley to Meenaneary, there joining with the Glencolumbkille road.

A small straggly town with a rather pungent fish-processing industry, **Killybegs** has a natural harbour which, according to the Four Masters, was 'saved' by St Catherine, patron saint of Killybegs, in 1513. The most famous ship to have called here was the unlucky Armada vessel *Girona*, a Neapolitan galleass, which limped in, to a friendly reception from the pro-Spanish MacSweeneys, to repair a broken rudder in 1588. She offloaded most of her armaments to make room for Armada survivors and set sail again, only to be wrecked off the Giant's Causeway soon afterwards. There used to be a factory here that made the hand-tufted Killybegs carpets that grace the floors of palaces and stately homes across Europe. Few grand houses in Ireland were considered properly furnished unless they had a Killybegs carpet.

West of Killybegs is a Gaeltacht area, with several villages — Kilcar, Carrick, Teelin and Glencolumbkille — where Irish is the spoken language, along a scenic road (R263), past the massy lump of Slieve League which looks surprisingly unimpressive from this angle. The little holiday settlement of **Glencolumbkille** has a folk village of thatched cottages with period furnishings, a café serving delicious soups and bread from the kitchens of the rural co-operative, and an Irish language/culture centre with a music archive. The village and its glen are named after St Colmcille (Columba).

Saint Columba

Colmcille, Columcille, Columbkille, Colm, Columba and Columb are all that same saintly historical person, born in AD521, a prince of Tyrconnell, great-great-grandson of Niall of the Nine Hostages, founder of Derry and thirty-six other monasteries in Ireland, and founder of Iona, off the west coast of Scotland. Ireland certainly has many saints, but to know that these are variant spellings is to realise that there are rather fewer than one might imagine. Irish placenames, mountains, lakes and so on, also may have three or four variant spellings and even different names. It is all very inexact.

St Columba's Day (9 June) in Glencolumbkille is celebrated with a 3-mile (5km) pilgrim walk or *tura* around 15 'stations' in the valley. At almost every station is a prehistoric or early Christian monument of some kind, including ninth-century carved pillars, a perforated cross, some fine carved-cross slabs, and many cairns. The walk may

The folk village at Glencolumbkille

be made at any time, you do not have to wait until 9 June.

The big walk round here is along the knife-edge ridge of Slieve League (1,972ft/601m) which has a breathtaking ocean frontage. The popular approach is from Bunglass carpark. From up here is is possible to look down and see the letters EIRE fashioned out of small stones pressed into the slope. They have been there since 1941 when Eire's neutrality during World War II needed underlining.

For a scenic drive from Donegal town around the whole of the Bluestack mountains, take the N15 north-east out of town past **Lough Eske**, with a ruined tower on an island where the O'Donnells locked up their prisoners, and along the Lowerymore valley up to Barnesmore Gap. The Bluestacks are named for their bare slaty granite summits rising to over 2,000ft (610m). After Lough Mourne the road runs on to Ballybofey, where the R252 follows the course of the Finn river round the back of the Bluestacks up the valley to Fintown and Finn Lough, and thereafter (R250) into Glenties village, a hand knitwear centre.

Stranorlar and Ballybofey are twin settlements, hardly towns, on either side of the Finn. **Stranorlar** is the more genteel, with an old coaching inn to match. The founder of the Home Rule party, Isaac Butt (1813-79), is buried in the graveyard of the Anglican parish church. Butt was a professor, barrister, journalist, newspaper proprietor, committed nationalist and, at one time or another, MP for three parliamentary constituencies — Harwich in England, Youghal in Cork, and Limerick. In untidy **Ballybofey** the former village college fronts a mini-shopping mall across the road from the Isaac Butt Memorial Hall, and there is a somewhat brash but comfortable hotel.

From Fintown little roads go north-west through undemanding hamlets and crossroad settlements, past chunks of conifer forest, a region of many small reedy lakes, fishermen in waders, peat bee-hives, whispy haystacks, stone-walled fields and bungalows, domi-nated by the handsome dome of Slieve Snaght and the edge of the Derryveagh mountains. Beyond the Gweebarra river and the steep hairpins at Doocharry village, the rock-strewn landscape becomes more and more stony. Here and there a shockingly green crannog or patch of rhododendron or laurel catches the eye. Brown trout and sea trout fishing is on offer at Dunglow lake. It is useful around here to know that An Clocháin Léith means Dunglow or you might miss this steep little village, where the home bakery sells fresh dulse, edible seaweed, alongside the cakes and wheaten bread.

At **Burtonport**, a small port with a fishermen's co-operative, a plaque commemorates the occasion in 1798 when James Napper Tandy landed from the French cruiser *Anacreon*. Napper Tandy (1740-1803) was a rather ineffectual United Irishman who had a knack for turning up at the wrong time or in the wrong place. Nevertheless he impressed Napoleon enough for the emperor to obtain his extradition just when the British authorities were about to execute him. A notice at Burtonport quay suggests that the car ferry to Aranmore island leaves six times a day (five on Sunday), 20 minutes each way. Since low neap tides can affect this schedule it is as well to know that Burtonport is a good place for the consumption of fresh mussels, oysters and crab. **Aranmore** has good cliff scenery, some caves, and a hippy colony which, finding itself unpopular in Burtonport a few years ago, decamped to the island. The last time Aranmore made headlines was when a rare Snowy Owl, the first seen in Ireland for 25 years, was sighted there in summer 1993.

North and east from Burtonport the road signs are all in Gaelic. Bungalow blight is very noticeable in the area, reaching something of a crescendo at Braade and Annagary. Many of these houses have the most delightful front gardens crammed with bright flowers and, in a few cases, miniature cottages like large dolls' houses.

In summer there are excursion boats from Bunbeg around Gweedore Bay and the offshore islands, interesting for their cliff scenery. **Gola** is the largest. The war artist Henry Lamb (born, 1884) spent his summers on Gola as a young man and painted the local fishermen. A medical officer in Palestine with the Fifth Royal Inniskilling Fusiliers, he was a near contemporary of Stanley Spencer and a friend of Augustus John. His large powerful 'Irish troops surprised by a Turkish bombardment in the Judaean hills', painted in 1919 shows Spencer's influence. It is in the Imperial War Museum, London.

Bloody Foreland may or may not take its name from the colour of the rock which is especially vivid at sunset. The legend says that Balor of the Evil Eye, leader of the demonic Formorian people, was slain by his grandson Lugh on the slopes hereabouts and that the blood that came out of the eye gave the headland its name.

From Bunbeg go east to **Gweedore** village, pronounced 'Giddaw', a curious place where the highpoint of the year is Graveyard Sunday. Relatives of people buried here come from far and wide, including busloads from Glasgow, Scotland, to spend the day in the cemetery. The R251 (L82) from Gweedore passes a track (signposted right) to the Poisoned Glen. Instead continue along the north bank of Lough Nacung, past the Cung Barrier, past the youth hostel, stopping at the highest point on the road (picnic site). There is a tremendous view here of Dunlewy Lough and the dramatically steep-sided Poisoned Glen. People have forgotten why it is called that. Botanists think that a toxic plant, a kind of spurge, may have grown here once but they have not been able to find any. The glen gets narrower and narrower and finally disappears into a cleft in the buttresses of Slieve Snaght. Immediately below where you are standing is the black basalt ruin of Dunlewy Anglican church, hardly used since it was built in 1844 — one service per year was the norm — but roofless only since 1955. The graveyard appears to have only one gravestone in it. For walkers, the picnic site is the start for the ascent of Errigal and there are two waymarked paths to the summit, the highest point in Donegal. Technically speaking, this south side of Errigal is part of Glenveagh National Park, though isolated from it.

The disposition of these mountain ranges means that the roads mostly run south-west/north-east and so there are mountains on both sides of the R251 as it continues in a north-easterly direction. On one side are the shapely Aghlas, Aghla Mor (1,916ft/584m) being the larger. To approach them from here you would have to walk up through firebreaks in the forestry, not an appealing approach. The Aghlas and boggy Crocknalaragagh, with their various interspersed lakes, are part of the so-called 'Marathon' walk that starts at Muckish, the flat black mountain to the north-east (which has a great view all the way from Malin Head to Bloody Foreland), and ends on the top of Errigal. To continue the drive north-east along the R251, the barren Derryveagh mountain ridge on the right marks the north-west edge of **Glenveagh National Park**, 25,000 acres (10,000 hectares) of mountains, moors, peat bogs, lakes and woods, divided down the middle by a deep glen (Glenveagh) and a narrow lake 6 miles (10km) long (Lough Veagh). 'Veagh' seems to come from the Gaelic for 'birch tree'. Some 28 miles (45km) of fencing at the south-west end of the park keep the Glenveagh red deer from straying. Now 600 strong, the herd was introduced in Victorian times.

The entrance to the park is at the northern edge where there is a visitor centre with good facilities. Cars stop here. A regular shuttlebus runs up to Glenveagh Castle, a battlemented feudal-looking castle, built of rough-hewn granite, on a wooded promontory jutting out into the water halfway down the lake. It was built in 1870 by John George Adair, of Bellegrove, County Laois, a hard man. According to the visitor centre leaflet his greatest infamy was to evict all 254 tenants on his Glenveagh estate in the cold April of 1861. The gardens which were first laid out by Adair's widow were developed by Glenveagh's last owner, Henry McIlhenny of Philadelphia, a philanthropic American who gave the house and gardens to the state in 1981. Windbreaks of pine and rhododendron give protection from the rigours of Donegal's weather. There are rare and exotic shrubs, terraces, statuary, a formal pool near the lake, and a walled garden with a Gothic orangery.

The area between the north end of Glenveagh and Letterkenny has many associations with St Columba, particularly around Church Hill. He was born in AD521 at **Gartan** (Little Field) where there are now two tiny medieval ruins on an east-facing hill just north of Gartan Lough, with beautiful pastoral views. A flat stone slab called the Flagstone of Loneliness is, rather unscientifically, associated with the saint's birth. Lie down on the stone and your troubles will fall away. In the nineteenth century emigrants came to lie on the stone before they left, hoping that this would stop them from feeling homesick. It did not work very often. Nearby is a very big commemorative cross and Gartan has lately acquired a heritage centre that goes into the story of the saint's life and times.

Putting their sons and daughters out to be fostered was common practice among noble families in pagan Ireland. Columba's foster father, the priest Cruithnechan (the Pict), is said to have baptised the saintly infant with the name Colum, at Temple Douglas *(Tulach-Dubhglaise)* beside the Glashagh river (R251) 3 miles (5km) south-west of Gartan Bridge, where there is now a ruined church with a fine thirteenth-century lancet window in the east gable. Colum becomes Columba, the dove, in Latin, though by all accounts he was not dove-like. His secular name was Crimthann, the fox.

From Tory to Inishowen

The main attraction in **Church Hill**, a small angling resort on the R251, is a collection of some 300 paintings at Glebe House, a rather superior former rectory on the shore of Gartan Lough. It is open to the public as an art gallery and museum. Picasso, Bonnard, Kokoschka, Jack Yeats, Victor Pasmore and Basil Blackshaw are all represented, and there are works by the Tory Island fishermen-painters, including the primitive painter James Dixon (1887-1971).

Tory Island, 7 miles (11km) north of Bloody Foreland headland, takes some getting to. The mailboat from Bunbeg, 15 miles (24km) each way, operates all year round weather permitting. It is a 9-mile (14km) trip from Magheraroarty quay near Gortahork, the nearest mainland departure point, and there are day trips from Portnablagh and Downings in summer. Most of the 100 or so inhabitants of this treeless rock out in the Atlantic spend the winter on the Donegal mainland. The establishment of the school of painting, mostly in the naive style and using house paints, is the result of determined efforts to try to keep the community alive. Some of the paintings fetch good prices in London and Dublin.

St Columba is said to have come here by curragh for the purpose of founding a monastery. Certainly there were monks on Tory until 1595. By the landing pier at West Town — the island's other village is East Town — is a striking Tau Cross, 6½ft (2m) high, T-shaped, hewn from a single slab of mica slate, one of only two in Ireland. The other is in the Burren Centre, County Clare. Nearby is the impressive stump of an exceedingly old granite round tower, 42ft (13m) high and 52ft (16m) in circumference.

The name Tory has an interesting provenance. It comes from *toraidhe* meaning 'outlaw' and was first used to describe the dispossessed Irish who turned to highway robbery in the seventeenth century. Soon it was a derogatory nickname for supporters of the succession of James II to the English throne, and eventually it became attached to a parliamentary party.

Falcarragh, a Gaelic-speaking village, hosts large numbers of students who come here in the summer to learn Irish. It is also a good base for walkers who want to climb Muckish mountain. The road from Falcarragh through Muckish Gap passes at the mid-point over a small two-arch bridge known as *Droichead Na Caointe* (Bridge of

Sorrows). This was the long road out to the port at Londonderry some 40 miles (64km) away, the road the emigrants walked before the railway was built. Their friends and family walked with them as far as the bridge.

From **Dunfanaghy**, where there is a major outbreak of those hardy garden escapees, the orange-flowered, sword-leaved montbretias (*crocosmiiflora*), that grow wild on road verges and patches of rough grass, there is a 3-mile (5km) scenic drive around heathery Horn Head. At any time of the year, thousands of seabirds perching on the stacks and ledges of this tremendous headland make an impressive sight. The largest razorbill colony in Ireland lives in the cliffs here. From the cliff road, cormorants can be seen dashing about far below, diving and swimming at great speed under the water. When they catch a fish they beat it senseless on the surface. It makes it easier to swallow!

It is a 24-mile (39km) scenic drive up the west side of Lough Swilly to Fanad Head from **Ramelton**. People tend to linger in this most attractive town and so find they have run out of time. The railway might have come here but, fortunately, it went to Letterkenny instead. Ramelton is a planned seventeenth-century plantation settlement with fine old warehouses and Georgian houses on a mall facing the Lennon river where it broadens into a creek of Lough Swilly. An eighteenth-century fish house, where boats entered from the river, is a prominent feature.

Francis Makemie (1658-1708), who sailed to Virginia in 1682 and founded the first American Presbytery (1706), was born in Ramelton and preached at the (Old) Presbyterian meeting house (1680). Close to the building, now restored as a library and genealogy centre, are cottages and houses in the vernacular style surviving from the eighteenth-century community that grew round the meeting house.

Killydonnell Friary, where Shane 'the Proud' O'Neill captured Calvagh O'Donnell and his wife, Catherine MacLean, in 1559, is well signposted from Ramelton, along a pleasant inland road with many traditional stone round gate pillars, but the signs run out a mile (2km) short of your goal. Keep straight on, down to a very small carpark overlooking Lough Swilly and Inch Island. (You cannot see it from here but Inch is linked to Inishowen by a bridge). The friary was founded for the Franciscans in 1471 by the O'Donnells and suppressed in 1603. It is now an atmospheric ruin draped in ivy.

The front at **Rathmullan**, a small port and holiday resort, is dominated by the ruin of the Carmelite priory built in 1508 by Rory MacSweeney of Fanad. It was not a place of quiet contemplation for long. In 1595 it was plundered by troops under Bingham (fresh from destroying the Tory monastery) and by 1601 it was a barracks. Rather more appropriately, in 1618 Bishop Knox adapted it as a bishop's residence and moved in. By the time the Duke of Berwick's Jacobite troops came this way in 1689 it was a Williamite garrison and was damaged again. The view from here is of Inishowen across Lough Swilly, with the lump of Inch Island upstream and a large Irish coastguard vessel *Gray Seal* anchored at the end of Rathmullan pier. A battery fort at the top of the pier, one of six fortifications built around Lough Swilly in Napoleonic times, has been put to good use as a permanent home for an excellent historical exhibition centred on the Flight of the Earls, a mysterious event that was the final blow to the old Gaelic order. The exact circumstances of their abrupt departure from Rathmullan harbour on 14 September 1607, never to return, are still mysterious. The tale is as romantic and romanticised as that of Bonny Prince Charlie across the water in Scotland.

The present road from Ramelton to Letterkenny runs across the estuarial land where in 1567 the mailed and helmeted horsemen of Shane 'the Proud' O'Neill came galloping across the sands to attack Hugh O'Donnell, his nephew. Hugh had the support of three MacSweeney septs and Shane was repulsed at the battle of Farsetmore.

The Grianan of Aileach, a hilltop stone fort with wonderful views of the north Donegal coast, is one of Ireland's most impressive historic monuments

He fled back across the Swilly river but by the time his cavalry reached the sands the tide had come in and many of them were drowned. A sandbank here is still called Marcaghs Bed (*marcach* means horseman).

Beyond Letterkenny, a workaday town that suffers from blaring loudspeakers slung from lamp posts at holiday time, it is a fast (N13) 15 miles (24km) to the **Grianan of Aileach**, a huge stone fort crowning a high hill, one of the most impressive historic monuments in Ireland. Though the elevation is only 800ft (244m), it gives an unparalleled view of Lough Swilly and Lough Foyle. The astronomer/geographer Ptolemy noted this place in the second century AD. From the fifth to the twelfth century it was the seat of the O'Neills, kings of Ulster. Murtagh O'Brien, king of Munster, virtually dismantled it in a revenge attack in 1101. The dimensions of the fort, its large central space 77ft (23m) in diameter, the thick walls (13ft/4m at the bottom) and the traces of three ancient concentric walls surrounding it, are very remarkable. The height of the walls was raised from 6ft (2m) to 17ft (5m) in the 1870s and you can walk around the top.

A clockwise drive round the mountainous **Inishowen** peninsula via Buncrana, a popular seaside town, is signposted for visitors but you may not have time to drive the 100 miles (60km) suggested. However, apart from the lure of Malin Head, of shipping forecast fame, there are some interesting antiquities and natural features to see. The biggest rock on this rocky peninsula is Slieve Snaght (2,019ft/615m) — not to be confused with the other, higher (but not much) Slieve Snaght south of Errigal mountain (*snaght* means snow) — and the hilly ground extends from it in all directions. Despite the unpromising terrain, Inishowen has always had plenty of people living on it. At Fahan, where the Lough Swilly Yacht Club has its base, there is a superb eighth-century carved cross slab known as St Mura's Cross on the east side of the (modern) church. Its inscription is not very interesting: 'Glory and honour to the Father, Son and Holy Ghost'. What is unusual is that it is in Greek, the only Greek inscription known from early Christian Ireland.

After Buncrana stay with the coast road up to the gentle Urris Hills — which are such a pretty feature of the drive to Fanad Head after you leave Rathmullan — and through very steep Mamore Gap, and on to **Carndonagh** to see the eighth-century Donagh Cross and its carved flanking pillars beside the Anglican church. Between here and Moville there are a number of other antiquities, including crosses at Carrowmore. Ask at Carndonagh tourist office in Chapel Street for details and directions.

The seaside town of Buncrana on Lough Swilly's east bank

The R242 up from Carndonagh skirts Trawbreaga Bay and crosses a wide sandy creek on a 10-arch stone bridge. It is one of the longest bridges in Ireland but it cannot be going anywhere much because we are nearly at the extremity of the peninsula. But now straight ahead is a most delightful sight, a seventeenth-century triangular village green fringed with cherry trees, oaks and sycamores. This is **Malin**, a tiny plantation settlement, still unspoiled, the prettiest village in Donegal. Ranged round the triangle are a couple of dozen houses, a parish church with a tower, and the convivial Malin Head Hotel. Here begins a scenic road to Malin Head past some big sand dunes. The white church at Lagg was the first Roman Catholic church built (1784) on Inishowen after penal times.

'And finally **Malin Head**'. If it were not for the shipping forecast on the radio, Malin Head would be rather less famous. The last of the network of coastal weather stations around the British Isles, the headland is Ireland's most northerly point, well placed to give warning of Atlantic gales and with a fine view of its craggy neighbours. For all that, it is only a couple of hundred feet above the sea. On the highest point is a derelict signal station for Lloyd's, the London-based association of marine insurance underwriters. This five-sided lookout tower cannot have been a comfortable place to work but vital to the business: a message from the lookout that a particular ship had been seen and was safe, allowed Lloyd's immediately to switch insurance to another vessel. These days the shipping forecast from Malin Head comes from the radio station down in Ballyhillin village. On the headland is another 'EIRE' message to World War II pilots painted on stones pressed into the grass. To see it follow the Malin Head/Banba Crown signposts.

Leaving Inishowen by continuing eastwards you pass **Kinnego Bay** where the Spanish Armada warship *Trinidad Valencera* went down on the reefs on 16 September 1588. Most of the 360 men on board, soldiers and crew, were massacred when they came ashore. The wreck was discovered by chance in 1971 by members of the City of Derry Sub-Aqua Club. Clothing, ship's furniture and fittings and other substantial finds, giving a good picture of life on board, are preserved in the Ulster Museum, Belfast. From Greencastle, 2 miles (3km) north of the resort of Moville there is a striking view of Binevenagh mountain in County Londonderry, with Magilligan's curious triangular sandy strand extending across Lough Foyle to within a mile (2km) of the Donegal coast. In winter great flocks of geese come to feed on eel grass in the estuary.

Further Information
— The North West: Lakes & Mountains —

Places to Visit

Belleek
Co Fermanagh
Belleek Pottery Visitor Centre
Tours of the pottery all year.
☎ (01365) 658501

Church Hill
Co Donegal
Glenveagh National Park
Open: every day 10am-6.30pm April to October. Tours of castle July and August only.
☎ (074) 37088

Glebe House Gallery
Open: each day except Friday 11am-6.30pm April/May to September.
☎ (074) 37071

Enniskillen
Co Fermanagh
Enniskillen Castle
Castle Barracks
Open: Monday to Friday all year, plus weekends in summer. Hours vary.
☎ (01365) 325000

Castle Coole and Florence Court
Opening times (afternoons only) for these National Trust houses are complicated. Contact Fermanagh Tourist Information Office for details.
☎ (01365) 323110. The grounds are always open.

Lissadell House

Co Sligo
Near Carney (off N15 at Drumcliff)
Open: June to September, late
mornings and early afternoons except
Sunday.
☎ (071) 63150

Marble Arch Caves

Co Fermanagh
Marlbank Scenic Loop Road
Florence Court
Open: daily mid-March to September,
depending on weather. Telephone the
warden for subterranean weather
report ☎ (01365) 348855

Rathmullan

Co Donegal
Flight of the Earls Heritage Centre
Open: 10am-6pm Monday to Saturday
and Sunday from 12noon, spring to
end September.
☎ (074) 58178/58131/21160

Sligo

Co Sligo
Sligo County Museum and Art Gallery
Stephen Street
Open: Tuesday to Saturday 10.30am-
12.30pm and 2.30-4.30pm June to
September. Only open mornings in
April, May and October.
☎ (071) 42212

Strabane

Co Tyrone
Gray's Printing Press
49 Main Street
Open: April to September, afternoons
2-5.30pm, except Sunday and Thursday.
☎ (01504) 884094

Travel

Ferries to Lough Erne Islands

Ferries go to Devenish and White
Island in the main holiday season
every day except Monday (and not
Sunday morning) 10am-7pm. For
Devenish depart Trory off A32 north of
Enniskillen. For White Island depart
Castle Archdale marina, off B82, south
of Kesh.
Lower Lough Erne cruises from
Enniskillen (Round O quay) May to
September ☎ (01365) 322882.
Upper Lough Erne cruises from Share
Holiday Village in summer ☎ (013657)
22122/21892.

Boats to Tory Island

Donegal Coastal Cruises, Strand Road,
Middletown, Derrybeg ☎ (075) 31320.
Cruises are organised from June to
September, weather permitting. Ask
about access out of season.
Bunbeg pier office — ☎ (075) 31665.
Magheraroarty pier office — ☎ (074)
35061.

Tourist Information Offices

Open: all year.

Enniskillen

Co Fermanagh
Wellington Road
☎ (01365) 323110

Letterkenny

Co Donegal
Derry Road
☎ (074) 21160

Omagh

Co Tyrone
1 Market Street
☎ (01662) 247831

Sligo

Co Sligo
Aras Reddan
Temple Street
☎ (071) 61201

Strabane

Co Tyrone
Council Offices
47 Derry Road
☎ (01504) 382204

4 • Northern Ulster

Londonderry and the Sperrins, Antrim and the Glens

The city with two names, **Londonderry** and **Derry**, stands on a hill on the Foyle estuary, close to the open sea. It has been an important seaport for most of its history. From the end of the eighteenth century it was the main port for Irish emigration. In World War II it was designated 'Base One Europe' by the US navy. At the height of the battle of the Atlantic, Allied warships were jammed eight abreast across the Foyle river up as far as the Guildhall. Since the political tribulations of the 1970s a huge investment of cash, with more to come, has helped re-establish the city's credentials as the commercial and cultural centre of the north-west of Ireland. Textiles, shirt-making in particular, is a major industry. There can hardly be an Englishman, Scotsman, Welshman or Irishman without a few Derry-made shirts in the wardrobe.

In the popular imagination, however, the history of the city stopped around 1690. Certainly there are many memorials to that tumultuous period — most impressively, the sturdy seventeenth-century walls which encircle the historic centre. Completed by 1618 and still entire, with old cannon pointing over the ramparts, they are a most striking feature, well preserved as a historic monument by the Department of the Environment. Inside, four main streets radiate out from the Diamond, or square, to the four original gates, Bishop Gate, Butcher Gate, Shipquay Gate and Ferryquay Gate. Three more gates were let into the walls later.

St Columba founded his first monastery in AD546 on top of the hill which, at that time, was thickly wooded and surrounded by water. The city's older name, Derry, derives from the Gaelic *doire* which means oakwood or grove of oaks. Columba's monastery thrived and, despite attacks of various kinds, successive communities of Augustinians, Cistercians, Dominicans and Franciscans flourished here throughout the Middle Ages.

The English first came to Derry in 1566 after a revolt by Shane 'the Proud' O'Neill. They installed a garrison which was wiped out the

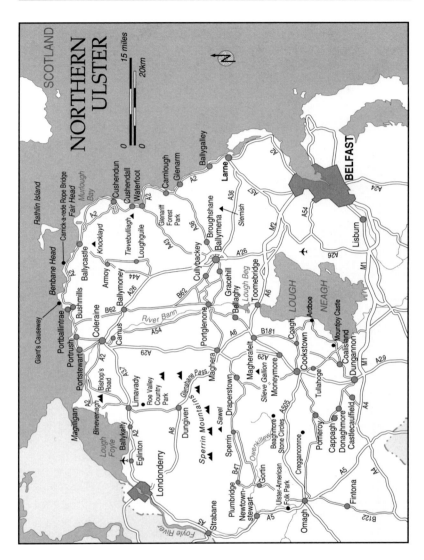

following year after the arsenal, located inside the great medieval church of Templemore, exploded accidentally. There was another revolt in 1600, and in 1608 the fortifications were over-run by the O'Dohertys, chiefs of Inishowen. To prevent future rebellions, James I gave the City of London responsibility for settling this whole region of Ulster. Accustomed to stumping up vast sums for the Crown, the City was on this occasion cajoled and bullied into an intimate and

Bishop Gate, one of the four original gates of Londonderry

permanent involvement — the plantation of Londonderry, rebuilding and fortifying the ruined medieval town, planning and building
dozens of smaller towns and villages, and supplying craftsmen to do
the work. The financial commitment was to last for hundreds of
years.

A new county, called Londonderry, was created by combining
Derry town with the lands of the troublesome O'Cahans in the old
county of Coleraine and adding various tracts of Tyrone and Antrim.
The City of London set up a special body, The Honourable The Irish
Society, to manage their lands, keeping direct control over three
strategic main towns — Derry, Coleraine and Limavady — and
parcelling out the rest of County Londonderry between the twelve
ancient London livery companies. A royal charter of 1613 contained
provision for a mayor and corporation and added London to the
town's name. It envisaged the new Londonderry as 'both a town of
war and a town of merchandise', and that is how it turned out.

A carpark near the Guildhall in Foyle Street close to Shipquay
Gate, is conveniently close for visitors wanting to walk on the walls.
A plaque below the fountain in Foyle Street marks the quay where
hundreds of thousands of emigrants embarked for America. The last
sailing ship to carry Irish emigrants across the Atlantic was a copper-
fastened wooden clipper, *Minnehaha*, owned by William McCorkell
& Co, a Londonderry shipping company. She could sail home in 15

Derry's characterful Guildhall

days but the new steamships could do better and she made her final passenger run to New York in 1873. The bosomy figurehead from *Minnehaha's* prow is preserved in a small museum behind the Guildhall in the Italianate Harbour Commissioners' Office. The handsome boardroom on the first floor has a magnificent handwoven Killybegs carpet with an oakleaf (*doire*) motif, made for the commissioners when the port was booming in the 1880s. In the Guildhall there are dozens of stained glass windows illustrating almost every episode of note in the city's history. The story flows up the staircase and floods all the chambers with light. The building was burnt out in 1908 and bombed in 1972. The City of London finished restoring the glass in 1984 — the year the city council, now with a nationalist majority, renamed itself Derry City Council.

The encircling city walls are punctuated at intervals with bastions and picturesque stone watch towers, and dozens of gunloops, small ones for muskets and large ones open at the top for cannon. It is possible to make a circuit of the old city by walking around the top of the walls, except for a short section above St Columb's cathedral, where you have to come down briefly at Bishop Gate. One of the cannon over Shipquay Gate was a gift from Elizabeth I in 1590. Four others were given to the city in 1642 by the Mercers, Grocers, Vintners and Merchant Taylors of London. Someone has had the solemn idea of installing some cast-iron moulded figures, like dummies used in car crash impact research, at various points along the circuit. Down at street level the scene is enlivened by buskers and stalls selling T-shirts, and a market on Saturdays but the fun does not seem to extend up here.

The first test of the walls came with a siege in 1641, and again in 1648, when supplies were brought in by sea, and lastly and most memorably, in the great siege of 1688-89 which lasted 105 days. Jacobite forces had devastated all the plantation lands in north-west Ulster and driven out the settlers, and now they crossed the Bann and advanced on Londonderry. Governor Robert Lundy was prepared to admit them because, he said, the city was not adequately garrisoned and resistance would be futile. But there were an estimated 30,000 panic-stricken Protestants inside who feared they would be massacred. As the soldiers approached the Ferry Gate, thirteen apprentice boys rushed out and raised the drawbridge. Having seized the keys from the guards, they locked all four of the city's gates. Civil administration was taken over by George Walker, a formidable Anglican clergyman from Donaghmore. The untrustworthy Colonel Lundy left in a hurry — he shinned up a pear tree growing against the wall at the bottom of Orchard Street — and is remembered still as a traitor: his effigy is severely dealt with at a 'closing of the gates' ceremony, a kind of Guy Fawkes ritual, on 18 December every year. The city thus declared for William of Orange and against King James II. James landed in Ireland in March 1689 and hurried north to restore his authority, arriving outside Bishop Gate on 18 April. Since his engineers were too few to scale the walls, he set up guns opposite Shipquay Gate and the siege began.

For the people inside, help was slow in coming. About 7,000 of them died of starvation and disease. Near the end cats and dogs were being sold in butchers' shops and even a rat cost a shilling. To stop supplies reaching the town, the besiegers had built a wooden barrier, a boom, across the river at the place where a Georgian villa with lovely gardens, Boom Hall, now stands. On 28 July 1689 a ship commanded by Captain Michael Browning, a native of Londonderry, sailed up the Foyle under artillery fire, broke through the boom and relieved the city.

Though far from the main theatre of Europe's power struggle, there was an important European dimension to the siege — Macaulay called it 'the most memorable in the annals of the British Isles' — because it gave William of Orange time to organise his army, paving the way to victory in 1690 at the Boyne. It was this battle which secured William as king of England and also damaged the prestige of Louis XIV in Europe.

There are two bridges over the Foyle that link the city with the county it administers. The very long modern bridge across the widening estuary downstream virtually bypasses the city. It came too late to save Derry from a beltway that separates the old city from the river and from its south and west suburbs. The Waterside district on the east bank, where most residents are Protestant, is linked to the city centre by Craigavon Bridge, an ungainly double-deck bridge of 1931 that dumps traffic unceremoniously off the top deck into Carlisle Square. The bottom deck was built originally to allow the lines of the various railway companies to interconnect. Nowadays there is just one railway and it stops on the east bank of the river.

On the west bank a couple of miles of 3ft narrow-gauge track is preserved as part of a railway centre that features steam locomotives and rolling stock of the old County Donegal Railway (CDR) and the Londonderry & Lough Swilly Railway (L&LSR). Beside the bridge is a large decaying redbrick block with mansarded roofs, the former shirt factory of Tillie & Henderson, built in 1857. In 1920 there were 18,000 people in the city, mostly women, cutting out shirts and running them up on little Singer sewing machines imported from America. The old T & H factory, opened in 1857, is cited by Karl Marx in *Das Kapital* (1867) as an example of the horrid capitalist practice of supplementing factory production by using outworkers — more modern examples being newspaper staffers and freelances, civil servants and management consultants. The old factory is a neglected piece of the city's industrial history.

A medieval-looking tower peering over the walls at Shipquay Gate is an agreeable fake on the site of Sir Cahir O'Doherty's long vanished castle. It is the Tower Museum, a rewarding visit for anyone interested in the city's past. Sir Cahir's beautiful two-handed sword, very long and elegant, is on display and some fine silver, including two huge cups and a silver tankard made in 1709 to mark the centenary of the start of the Ulster plantation. From the river the main thoroughfare, Shipquay Street, rises steeply to the war memorial in the Diamond, passing basement pubs and shops and the entrance to a modern craft village. In the basement of No. 8 Shipquay Street you can buy Irish linen, tweeds and woollens. Thomas Colby, (1784-1852) a lieutenant colonel in the Royal Engineers, who took charge of the Ordnance Survey's nineteenth-century mapping of Ireland, lodged in this house. The survey was based on a triangulation system. The first triangle was in the north at the Lough Foyle Base, a kind of huge spirit level established on the flat land of Magilligan strand. It was the first-ever mapping of a whole country on a large scale and produced the famous six-inch-to-one-mile maps that showed 'every road and track, every stone wall and hedge, every river and stream, every house and barn'. It also preserved the identity of the rural neighbourhoods known as 'townlands' by recording the name of each one, all 60,462 of them. The townland name is still a part of any rural Irish address, despite the post office's preference for postcodes. The herculean task took 22 years (1824-46) to accomplish. Its banausic purpose was for land valuation and taxation! No doubt it was of military value too.

At the Diamond is the flamboyant Edwardian baroque frontage of Austin's department store, opened in 1906. 'First store in Ireland,' says a notice. It has retained a polished wooden staircase with broad balustrades, and other original fittings. An old-style fast-moving escalator whisks customers up to a 150-seater restaurant on the third floor with good westerly views across the city. In this same room there is a Met. office with weather maps and reports. Continue up Bishop Street Within past the Irish Society's house (1764) and a classical courthouse (1813) across the road from the Regency-style former bishop's palace. Smaller roads in the shadow of the walls and church spires glimpsed beyond narrow side streets give some dramatic architectural perspectives.

Amply proportioned St Columb's Temperance Hall fits neatly into a steep site on Orchard Street and, like a number of other large old buildings in the city, shelters a motley collection of activities. A modern art gallery occupies the bottom end, and there are rooms of all shapes and sizes for cinema shows, theatrical performances, priests' weekend retreats, meetings of all kinds.

The most interesting church inside the walls, and the chief repository of the city's seventeenth-century memories, is St Columb's Anglican cathedral built in 1633. The London link is proclaimed on a date stone in the porch:

> 'If stones could speake then London's prayse should sound
> Who built this church and cittie from the grounde.'

Among scores of plaques and memorials ranged round the walls is a marble monument shared by Colonel Henry Baker, a city governor who died on the seventy-fourth day of the siege, and Captain Browning, killed by a shot after his ship broke the boom a month later. One window depicts St Columba's mission to Britain; another illustrates hymns written by Mrs C. F Alexander (1818-95), wife of a bishop of Derry. Her *Hymns for little children*, published in 1848, went into sixty-nine editions during her life. The three represented here are 'There is a green hill far away', 'Once in David's royal city', and

'The golden gates are lifted up'. An organ case over the west door is by the celebrated wood carver, Grinling Gibbons, whose commissions included Hampton Court and the choir of St Paul's Cathedral. A groyne near the organ is a likeness of George Walker, governor of Derry during the siege. Another looks distinctly like George Berkeley (1685-1753), the metaphysical philosopher who said that 'all reality is in the mind', or words to that effect. In fact it is Berkeley. He held the lucrative office of dean of Derry from 1724 until 1732. He came here, once, to have a look round.

Among treasures in the chapterhouse are the seventeenth-century locks and keys of the city gates, Lord Macaulay's manuscript account of the siege, interesting paintings, and a pair of duelling pistols belonging to Frederick Hervey (1730-1803), fourth Earl of Bristol and Bishop of Derry. This Byronic nobleman, a flamboyant character whose name is preserved in all the Bristol Hotels in Europe, acquired the rich bishopric of Derry in 1768 and immediately began building churches and improving old ones. He spent £1,000 on putting an enormous stone spire on St Columb's but it was too heavy and had to be dismantled. Active in the Volunteer movement and a supporter of emancipation, the Earl Bishop is also remembered for his support for the building of Roman Catholic and nonconformist churches.

One of Hervey's beneficiaries was the Long Tower Church, Derry's oldest Catholic church. It stands a few yards outside the walls, close to the site of the great cathedral church (Teampall Mór), built by the Augustinian abbot O'Broclain in 1164 and destroyed in the explosion of 1567, and now only a name on a seventeenth-century map. To see the Long Tower Church go past the space-age surveillance towers and through Bishop Gate (1789) into Bishop Street Without. When it was built in 1786 the church had only a mud floor and no seats but there was enough standing room for 2,000 people. The present interior is most attractive, with steeply stepped galleries and double-gabled transepts. The district and the church are named Long Tower after a twelfth-century round tower that survived near the ruined Teampall Mór until the mid-seventeenth century.

Returning towards Bishop Gate, take the path to the left to walk along the outside of the western city wall. Spread out down below are the acres of the 1960s Bogside housing estate, its 'Free Derry' monument and graffiti rendered less strident by the creation of an urban park spread grassily over the hillside. Beyond it, towards the north-west, rises the large Catholic cathedral, St Eugene's. Reaching Butcher Gate, turn right back into the walled city, emerging near the youth hostel, or else continue to Waterloo Street, with its classy fashion boutiques and pubs where traditional Irish music-making goes on most evenings. During the daytime you can turn right down steep, narrow Harvey Street in the direction, more or less, of the Bogside. A gate at the bottom (closed 11pm-7am) gives access to Pilot's Row community/arts centre where there are alternative art exhibitions in a newish gallery. It is a short walk from here to St Eugene's, or you may prefer to go back to collect your car and drive round via Strand Road (A2) which is also the road to Magee University College. Completed in 1873 to designs by J.J McCarthy, St Eugene's had to wait 30 years more for the spire. The east window, a memorial to the cathedral's builder, Bishop Francis Kelly, depicts the crucifixion and seven Irish saints. Three miles (5km) beyond Magee College, at **Ballyarnet Field**, a cottage exhibition centre commemorates the transatlantic flight in 1932 by Amelia Earhart, the first woman to fly the Atlantic solo. She landed in this field.

The polder appearance of the coastal strip between Londonderry and the mouth of the Roe is an unusual landscape to find in Ireland. Drivers along the A2 east from the city will not see it except by turning down side roads, but it is most striking from the train. Reclaimed from the sea in the nineteenth century for flax growing, these fertile polders — called 'levels' locally — are actually below sea level and are drained by pumping stations. The crops now are grain and vegetables, mostly potatoes. In between the polders are mudflats and deserted runways of old wartime aerodromes. The City of Derry airport at Eglinton, which has daily scheduled flights to Glasgow and Manchester, developed from one such aerodrome.

Plantation Towns of the London Companies

The village of **Eglinton** was created by the Grocers' Company in 1823-5 and has an elegant courthouse in the tree-lined main street. At the same time the Fishmongers' Company was busy developing a model farm at Ballykelly, recently turned into a retirement home, its green paddock destroyed. Plantation buildings in Ballykelly include the Presbyterian church, a school, and a dispensary (now Bridge House). These north coast plantation villages still manage to be extraordinarily appealing, despite the usual depredations of environmental delinquency found almost everywhere in Ireland, north and south. Bishop Hervey built the Anglican parish church (1795), with three-stage tower and a needle spire. Among the interesting funerary monuments inside is an elaborate marble memorial to Mrs Jane Hamilton (1672-1716) which looks uncannily like a famous Grinling Gibbon memorial to Mrs Mary Beaufoy (died 1705) in Westminster Abbey, London.

North of Ballykelly bridge Walworth House is a handsome eighteenth-century five-bay house with three impressive flanker towers preserved intact from the Fishmongers' early seventeenth-century bawn. The ruins of the Company's church of 1629 are opposite the house. At the roadside (still A2) on the edge of Farlow Wood a mile before Limavady, Sampson's Tower was erected in memory of an agent for the Fishmongers' estates. The large tree-fringed earthwork a few yards further on, on the other side of the road, is Rough Fort rath. At Broighter, north of here, a collection of prehistoric gold ornaments was discovered by a ploughman in the 1890s. It is now in the National Museum, Dublin. A hologram of the Broighter golden boat is in the Tower Museum, Londonderry.

The market town of **Limavady** on the Roe river has some attractive Georgian features. It was created by an energetic Welshman, Sir Thomas Phillips, who was the City of London's chief agent in Ulster

Roe Valley Country Park, near Limavady

from 1609. W.M Thackeray stopped for ale at the inn (demolished) in the main street in 1842 and wrote some doggerel verses about the barmaid, 'Sweet Peg of Limavady'. Number 51 Main Street was the home of Jane Ross (1810-79) who noted down the famous London-derry Air, 'Danny Boy', from an itinerant fiddler in 1851. She lived here with her three younger sisters, and a plaque commemorates her great service in preserving the best known of all Irish melodies. The Ross sisters are buried across the road at the eighteenth-century parish church, which has a collection of several hundred tapestry kneelers, each one different.

In the gorges of the **Roe Valley Country Park**, a mile (2km) south of Limavady, a hydro-electric plant, water mills and a weaving shed are among a tremendous collection of restored rural industrial buildings on the banks of the peaty red river. The park is popular for canoeing, camping and especially game fishing.

When the Four Citizens of London came to Ulster in 1609, their guide was under instructions from the Lord Deputy of Ireland not to show them the Sperrin mountains. As agents for the City of London merchant companies, the visitors were looking at the region's invest-ment potential, and the fear was that these rugged peaty hills would create a bad impression. Nowadays, the Sperrins are the haunt of trout fishermen, turf-cutters, and people panning for gold in the Foyle headwaters above the beautiful Owenkillew river. You may come across a backpacker walking the Ulster Way, or small parties on archaeological tramps. There are thousands of standing stones and chambered graves across the moors, mysterious testaments to the prehistoric Irish who lived up here.

Threaded by streams and small roads, the main expanse of the Sperrins is bounded by the towns of Strabane, Dungiven, Draperstown and Newtownstewart. A section of the range spills south towards Omagh over the Owenkillew, and the north-east fringe is bisected by the **Glenshane Pass** which has a friendly roadhouse at the highest point. There has been a pub at this lonesome place for over 200 years. It has mains electricity (since 1990). Water is drawn from the well. There are more hills further north, running along the east side of the Roe Valley, with craggy Binevenagh rearing 1,271ft (387m) over Lough Foyle. The highest peak, Sawel, is only 2,240ft but access to the landlocked settlements of Tyrone and County Londonderry was difficult until modern times. For the same reason, overland attacks on Derry city were rarely successful.

South of the Sperrins the main centres of population are Dungannon, Cookstown and Omagh. The M1 from Belfast ends around **Dungannon**, a manufacturing town with a glassware factory. It was an O'Neill stronghold from the fourteenth century until the plantation. The first Bible in Irish characters was produced here on a printing press established by Shane O'Neill in about 1567. All trace of the O'Neill castle on the hill has gone. The Royal School in Northland Row dates from the early seventeenth century. The bronze statue in front of the present eighteenth-century building is ex-pupil General John Nicholson, killed storming Delhi during the Indian Mutiny (1857). The statue stood at the Kashmir Gate in Delhi until 1960. This same general pops up again in the market place in his home town of Lisburn, though the Dungannon bronze is nicer.

Parkanaur, west of Dungannon, is a pretty forest park with an arboretum and a herd of white deer. Much history attaches to the fortified mansion and the church (of Donaghmore parish) at nearby **Castlecaulfield**. Sir Toby Caulfield, ancestor of the earls of Charlemont, was an Oxfordshire knight who commanded Charlemont Fort during Mountjoy's 1602 campaign. He built the Castlecaulfield mansion in 1619 on the site of a Donnelly fort. After being burnt in 1641, it was repaired and lived in by the Caulfield/Charlemont family until about 1670. The tolerant first Viscount Charlemont allowed the Catholic primate, Oliver Plunket, to use the courtyard for ordinations in 1670, and John Wesley preached here on at least four occasions. Now in ruins, and incongruously surrounded by a housing estate, the mansion retains a gatehouse with murder-holes, gunloops and the Caulfield arms over the top.

Outside the graveyard of the seventeenth-century parish church, a blue plaque commemorates the poet Charles Wolfe (1791-1823) who was curate of Donaghmore 1818-21. His famous lines on 'The burial of Sir John Moore after Corunna' were published in the *Newry Telegraph* in 1817.

'Not a drum was heard, not a funeral note,
As his corse to the rampart we hurried'

The High Crosses of County Tyrone

Rector of Donaghmore from 1674 was the Reverend George Walker, better known as governor of Londonderry during the great siege. He was killed at the Boyne in 1690 and is buried in the south transept. The gabled porch is carved with cherubs holding a Bible open at psalm 24. Various pieces inside the church, including the windows in the south nave, were brought from a vanished medieval church 2 miles (3km) north in **Donaghmore**, a village with a tenth-century high cross, 15ft (4m) tall and rather worn, at the top of the main street. Close to the site of an early monastery associated with St Patrick, it was damaged in the seventeenth century. The obvious join midway up the shaft suggests that bits from two separate crosses were used when it was put together in 1776. A pillar in the graveyard behind the cross is a modern memorial to Hugh O'Neill. A short distance down the Pomeroy road (B43) an old National School (1885) preserves townland maps, artefacts from vanished local industries, and runs a genealogical service.

The O'Neill inauguration stone at **Tullahoge**, near Cookstown, was broken by Lord Mountjoy in 1602 and when the leader of the 1641 rebellion, Phelim O'Neill, had himself inaugurated in 1641, he had to manage without it. Sir Phelim epitomised the political turmoil and shaky allegiances of the day: he was simultaneously a knight of the realm, premier prince of Ulster (as recognised by the pope), member of parliament for Dungannon and executioner of many of his English and Scottish constituents. He remained at large until 1653, when he was captured near Newmills, north-east of Dungannon, hiding on the crannog in Roughan Lough. He was taken to Dublin and hanged for treason. Ruined Roughan Castle, a fortress with stubby round towers near the lake, was built by Sir Andrew Stewart in 1618. The lake is popular with water-skiers.

The main street in **Cookstown** is very wide (130ft/40m) and very long (1¼ miles/2.2km) with a hump in the middle. It was part of an ambitious town plan by William Stewart of Killymoon, an eighteenth-century Tyrone landlord, but neither he nor his descendants ever got round to developing the town beyond this remarkable central avenue. Its great advantage, from the visitor's point of view, is convenient parking. The life and bustle of Cookstown, at the centre of good farming country, focuses wholly on the main street which has eight names, a new one every couple of hundred yards. Although the shops and houses are rather ordinary, the broad avenue has a certain theatrical appeal, with the bleak outline of Slieve Gallion (1,737ft/530m) rising up 8 miles (13km) directly north. Biggest building by far is Holy Trinity, a Catholic church halfway down the west side. Built in 1855 by J.J McCarthy, it has a massive tower and spire, visible from far off.

The linen industry was important here. The father of the botanist Augustine Henry was a Cookstown flax buyer, and there are old mills along the nearby Ballinderry river. The modern town is known for its sausages, made in the large bacon factory. **Killymoon Castle**, a Norman revival castle, was designed for the Stewarts in 1802 by the

English architect John Nash (1752-1835). South of the town is **Loughry Manor** (now an agricultural college), a plantation mansion which has associations with Dean Jonathan Swift. He stayed here as a guest of the Lindsay family, while writing *Gulliver's Travels* (published 1726). Portraits of 'Stella' (Esther Johnson, died 1728) and 'Vanessa' (Esther Vanhomrigh, died 1723) still hang in the Old Library. The Dean loved them both, and made them both miserable.

Ardboe high cross, 18ft (6m) tall, with twenty-two very weathered panels, stands inside a small railing on an early monastic site on a bleak stretch of Lough Neagh's western shore. It is about the same age as the Donaghmore cross. Old Testament scenes on the east side start at the bottom with Adam and Eve, with New Testament scenes up the west side. Nearby is the ruin of a seventeenth-century church. Lughnasa (Lammas) used to be celebrated at Ardboe, with praying at the cross and much washing in the lake. It is reckoned that eel fishing has gone on here for 5,000 years. The monks of the sixth-century monastery at Ardboe used eel oil in their lamps. The small farms around Ardboe are mostly owned by eel fishermen. From May onwards you can see them setting lines in sections up to 2 miles (3km) long. The catch is worth several millions of pounds a year.

The development of the Tyrone coalfields in the nineteenth century was not a success story. The coal is still there, waiting for someone to work out a way to extract it profitably. The countryside around **Coalisland**, where brickmaking is a local industry, is disfigured by large scale sand, gravel and clay extraction and the detritus of old coal mines. The village was briefly the inland port for the coalfields. Industrial archaeologists enthuse about the beehive kilns and old brickwork chimneys. A four-storey cornmill has been preserved as a museum. Take the B161 west from Coalisland to see on the left after 4 miles (6km), a little north of Washing Bay, the interesting ruin of **Mountjoy Castle**, a three-storey fort with four rectangular corner towers built in 1605 to command the south-west corner of Lough Neagh. In this unfriendly terrain (O'Neill country) attack could come from any direction and the fort is remarkable for the number of gun loops ranged round the ground floor to give fire-cover all round. Garrisoned during the Williamite wars, the fort has little seventeenth-century red bricks on the upper floors. Continue along this road to see the cross at Ardboe.

West of Cookstown, past Drum Manor Forest Park on the A505, a lane runs down to **Wellbrook** beetling mill in a pretty setting on the fast-flowing Ballinderry river. It started work in 1768 and was one of six beetling mills serving a local bleachworks. Beetling was the noisy process that gave sheen and smoothness to the linen cloth by pounding it with heavy wooden hammers, or beetles. The two-storey mill, big waterwheel and picturesque mill race have been restored by the National Trust. There are seven large engines inside, all in working order and there is an exhibition on linen making in the loft. If your idea of how a mill race works is vague, a walk along the path at the back is instructive.

There are many ancient monuments around here. Be sceptical of signposting. As in other parts of Tyrone, direction signs are frequently vandalised, though local people will go out of their way to help if you ask. The **Beaghmore** Stone Circles on the fringe of the Sperrins were discovered in the 1930s. Seven stone circles, three pairs and an odd one, and a dozen or so stone alignments and round cairns, have been cleared of peat. Most of the circle stones are small — no more than 2 to 3ft high. Many are barely a foot tall, and the tallest is only 4ft. The site dates from the middle of the Bronze Age. Other similar sets of circles and alignments have been found in the Sperrins, including Moymore near Lough Bracken, 2 miles (3km) from Pomeroy. The heathery windswept moors around Beaghmore are littered with the remains of other monuments which have been turned up by turf cutting.

Cregganconroe court grave, overlooking Cam Lough, is signposted off the main Cookstown-Omagh road (A505). It is typical of some 300 similar north Irish megalithic graves, where the narrow burial chamber is entered through a wider forecourt. A similar grave, on the west side of Lough Mallon at Creggandevesky, was excavated a few years ago. To be up here at twilight is an eery experience, even on a summer day.

A secondary road (B4) from Cookstown to Omagh runs through the upland village of **Pomeroy**, with a modern forestry school on the estate of the Reverend James Lowry who laid the village out in the eighteenth century. The Anglican church (1841) in the neat market square later acquired a belfry and spire which, according to an inscription, were added by John and Armar Lowry 'as a tribute of attachment to their birthplace'.

American connections in the area are interesting. James B Irwin, the Apollo 15 astronaut who drove a buggy across the moon in 1971, has family links with Pomeroy and his Irwin relatives still live here. James Shields, one of Lincoln's generals in the American Civil War, was born in 1806 near Cappagh, south of Pomeroy. A now derelict building in **Cappagh** village was the Shields' family bank, the Altmore Loan Fund, which flourished from 1852 to 1903. James

Omagh stands at the confluence of the Camowen and Drumragh rivers

Shields, who defeated the Confederate general, Stonewall Jackson, at Kernstown, Virginia, emigrated at the age of 20. Jackson's own ancestral home, The Birches, is just across the Tyrone/Armagh border. President James Buchanan's father emigrated from Deroran, south-east of Omagh, to Pennsylvania where the future president was born in 1791. Buchanan, president from 1857 to 1861, was one of the only three first-generation Americans ever to occupy the White House. All three of them were sons of Ulster emigrants.

Eclectic snippets like this, and the broader picture of Ulster emigrations to the north American continent, can be discovered at the **Ulster-American Folk Park** outside Omagh. The park developed round the cottage where Judge Thomas Mellon, founder of the fabulously rich Mellon dynasty, was born in 1813. Thomas was aged 5 when the family emigrated. Another Tyrone native, John Joseph Hughes, later archbishop of New York, left at the same time as the Mellons. His boyhood home, rebuilt stone by stone, has been moved into the park. Hughes was known as 'Dagger John' for his single-minded campaign to secure civic rights for Roman Catholic Irish emigrants. The centre also contains replicas of American log cabins and early farmsteads and has a large databank on Irish emigration based on tens of thousands of passenger lists from emigrant ships, including vessels bound for Australia, New Zealand and South Africa.

Principal market town of Tyrone, **Omagh** stands at the confluence of the Camowen and Drumragh rivers which form the wide, shallow Strule. The town centre is a hilly architectural muddle of nineteenth-century and later buildings, away from the pretty rivers down below. Despite this, and the frequent batterings which have made Omagh a security-conscious place, it has a cheerful atmosphere. Wildfowlers, and anglers fishing the remoter lakes to the west beyond Drumquin, tend to base themselves here and the local trout and salmon fishing, and pike and roach in the Strule and Fairy Water, bring others into town for bait and tackle. A lot of rather stolid Victorian churches jostle for space on top of the hill. The biggest, best-looking one, the Sacred Heart Catholic church (1893-99), is a prominent landmark. It has twin spires, unequal in height, and you may be able to go up the tower for the view. To see the Black Bell of Drumragh, said to be ninth century, ask at the sacristy (or call at 33 George's Street, to the right of the taller spire).

Playwright Brian Friel, author of *Philadelphia here I come* and *Translations*, was born in Omagh (1930) and so was the songwriter Jimmy Kennedy (1903-84) who wrote *'Teddy bears' picnic'* and *'South*

*A feature of the pretty river Glenelly, in the Sperrin mountains,
are the old stone bridges*

of the border'. West of Omagh, the Black Bog, a very old, deep bog, north-west of the A505/B46 crossroads, supplies refined peat for the local craft industry of ornaments made from compressed peat. **Fintona**, south of Omagh is a small town well equipped with public houses, among them the Poet's Pub, named in honour of the landlady's son, John Montague, the Ulster poet (born 1929). Game rearing (pheasant and partridge) at nearby Seskinore Forest, plus woodcock and rough game, attract field sportsmen to this area.

Going north towards the gorge of Gortin Glen Forest Park, the B48 runs past the **Ulster History Park** where an outsize twentieth-century dolmen stands beside a futuristic visitor centre. A Stone Age hut, a sixth-century crannog, a tenth-century round tower, an eleventh-century Norman motte, and other buildings up to and including the seventeenth-century plantation, have been constructed in the park, and some 9,000 years of built environment can be painlessly absorbed in 20 minutes.

This area is all very scenic and there are fine views up around Mullaghcarn mountain (1,778ft, 542m), Gortin, and on minor roads along the Owenkillew river. Further north the Glenelly river has carved a narrow gorge through the mountains. At the bottom of the valley hemmed in by crags is **Plumbridge** village, a sleepy place except on market days. In this wild region where spring is late and

The sheep fair at Draperstown

autumn comes early you might not expect to see large mature beech trees, but here they are, near the pink church. The region is subject to periodic attacks of gold rush fever though the locals say it takes weeks of laborious panning in the headwaters of the Foyle to find a few flecks. Pearls of gem quality have occasionally been found in freshwater mussels that live in certain small streams but the mussels themselves are now almost as rare as the pearls once were. An attractive drive is east from Gortin, then north through dramatic Barnes Gap to join the Plumbridge-Draperstown road (B47), running east along the Glenelly to **Sperrin/Mount Hamilton**, a hamlet with two names at the foot of Sawel mountain. If you have four hours or so to spare and the weather is clear, park at the nameless pub in Sperrin and stride out north. The pub is a landmark, by far the most substantial building hereabouts. Do not assume it will be open. After 2 miles (3km), leave the road and make for Sawel summit (2,240ft/683m), an hour's tramp, for views of Lough Neagh, the Foyle estuary and the Mournes. Dart mountain (2,040ft/622m) is a half-hour walk west along the ridge. Turn south to Cranagh hamlet and regain the road conveniently close to a heritage centre just below Dart. After

Beaghmore Stone Circles on the southern fringes of the Sperrins, County Tyrone (Chapter 4)

Ulster History Park, County Tyrone (Chapter 4)

The rural landscape around Limavady, County Londonderry (Chapter 4)

A pretty thatched cottage, County Antrim (Chapter 4)

Pony trekking at Watertop Open Farm near Ballycastle, County Antrim (Chapter 4)

refreshment at the café you will be in good shape to walk along the road back to your car at the pub with no name. Even at a lowly 570ft (174m) the B47 gives good views over the valley.

The vanished forest of Glenconkeyne north-west of Lough Neagh was chopped down early in the seventeenth century. The oaks and elms were floated down the Bann and used to build houses in Limavady and Coleraine. Many of the trees went for smelting the iron ore deposits found around Slieve Gallion. There are still reminders of the green gaiety of the ancient wood around **Springhill House**, a National Trust property near Moneymore towards Coagh (B18). A thicket of old yews has survived in the grounds of this fortified seventeenth-century house, which is surely the prettiest house in Ulster.

Moneymore is an unusually harmonious plantation town with attractive buildings along the wide main street. This was the Drapers' first settlement, and the first town in Ulster to have piped water (1615). Like so many such settlements, it was destroyed in 1641 and the present buildings, which include two market houses, two Presbyterian churches, a school and a dispensary, date from the Georgian period. Some other small towns and villages round here, laid out at the plantation, have been disfigured by haphazard development. Certainly they lack the charm of Moneymore but are not the less interesting for that.

The triangular green at **Draperstown**, a village that grew round a big livestock and linen market, is a lively place on market days. The market town of **Magherafelt** was part of the Salters' estates and has a large central square with wide roads leading off. **Castledawson** on the gravelly Moyola river which flows into Lough Neagh, retains a sturdy bridge and an unusually substantial, tall and handsome house, called 'The Gravel', in Main Street, a striking contrast to its neighbours. The wooded estate of Moyola Park nearby was the home of James Chichester-Clark, Lord Moyola, stop-gap prime minister of Northern Ireland 1969-71.

County Londonderry's Medieval Churches

Maghera at the foot of the Glenshane Pass was church property before the plantation and, quite unlike the settlers' towns, the streets are narrow. Its main interest is Maghera Old Church on the site of a sixth-century monastery founded by St Lurach. In the Middle Ages Maghera was the seat of a bishop. The twelfth-century west door has sculpted sloping jambs, decorated with animal and floral motifs, and a massive lintel carved with a crucifixion scene. The head on the inside of the door is semicircular in shape. In the seventeenth century the priest at Maghera lived in a modest little first-floor flat in the old tower. Unfortunately, an appalling mess of building, electrical sub-station and builder's yard has been allowed to develop round this historic site.

One of the finest medieval tombs in Ireland, the tomb of Cooey na Gall O'Cahan who died in 1385, is preserved at **Dungiven** in St Mary's Augustinian priory, signposted on the A6 on the east side of town. Until the plantation, when the place was granted to the Skinners' Company, Dungiven was an O'Cahan stronghold. Park at the top of the lane and walk down to the ruins, passing on the right a holy well — a bullaun stone surrounded by thorn bushes hung with rags. Cooey's sculptured effigy, wearing Irish armour, lies under a traceried canopy in the ruined thirteenth-century chancel. Six bare-legged warriors in kilts, standing in niches below the prone chieftain, were his foreign mercenaries, probably Scots, from whom he derived his nickname 'na Gall' meaning 'of foreigners'. The priory church dates from about 1150 and was remodelled in the seventeenth century when a fortified house was added. Access to the chancel is by arrangement. Back on the A6, the massive remains of the Skin-ners' bawn (1618) are incorporated into a Victorian battlemented mansion, Dungiven Castle, visible from the road.

Dungiven priory and Maghera church were built at about the same time as **Banagher**, founded in 1100 by St Muiredach O'Heney on a hill 2 miles (3km) south-west of Dungiven. It is signposted off the Dungiven-Feeny road (B74) but from Dungiven centre turn down unpromising New Street near the public lavatories, towards Turmeel. The nave at Banagher is the oldest part. It has an impressive square-headed lintelled west door, like Maghera but without the carvings, and a nave window closely resembling the one at Dungiven. On a sandhill close by is the saint's appealing little mortuary house, also about 1100. It is not the only mortuary house in the area — there is another at Bovevagh off the B192 north of Dungiven — but the Banagher one is in near-perfect condition and has a carving of an abbot on the gable end. 'Banagher sand' scraped from under St Muiredach's tomb is said to bring luck to all O'Heneys. The most famous bearer of that name hereabouts is the poet Seamus Heaney, born in 1939 south of Bellaghy on the family farm, Mossbawn, at **Tamniarin** off the A6. Heaney has written incomparably of the places of his Ulster childhood and the flat landscape of Lough Neagh's western shore recurs many times in his poems. The ruined bawn at **Bellaghy**, which the Vintners' Company built in 1619, is to be the repository of a permanent Heaney exhibition. The Department of the Environment has restored the bawn wall and a large flanker tower.

There is an interesting surviving example near here of the open-fields system of tenant farming that was widely practised in Ulster until the 1750s. Take the A54 north from Bellaghy for 2½ miles (4km) and turn east to the small settlements of Thornstown and Culbane at **Ballynease-MacPeake**. The system was based on the principle that each tenant should have a piece of every kind of land in the townland — meadow, arable, bog, rough grazing. The ladder pattern of fields enclosed by hedges is a distinctive feature of the Antrim glens but this little settlement tucked in between Portglenone forest and the Bann is somewhat different. Instead of a compact piece of land the tenant sometimes ended up with bits and pieces, or land of an irregular shape or, as at Culbane, a minute long thin strip on a steep slope plus a share of common land and various grazing rights. There are no walls or fences to protect these tiny crop-growing strips and they must have been vulnerable to trampling by stock. The tenants at Culbane all belonged to one family. Similarly the Thornstown tenants were a self-contained kin group. The custom was, perhaps still is, to take cattle along the lane — the 'booley' road — in summer to graze the Bann flood plain down as far as Mullagh strand. Not much seems to have changed in 200 years. If ever there was a backwater, this delightfully untidy spot is it.

The sluice gates at **Toomebridge** control the outflow of **Lough Neagh** to the Atlantic, and there is an eel co-operative where visitors can call in. Demand in Europe for Lough Neagh eels is insatiable. At the height of the fishing season every day seven tons of brown eels are flown to Holland from Belfast International. Elvers, baby eels that look like silver matchsticks, are a delicacy not appreciated in Ireland, and most of them are allowed to grow to maturity in the lough. Large quantities are collected at Coleraine and brought to Lough Neagh by lorry. Left to their own devices, elvers take a year to make their way up the Bann. Salmon, on the other hand, swim up in a month. If you take a trip along the Bann after 1 May, there are dramatic piscatorial scenes of anglers tussling with these beautiful fish at every lock and weir. However, there is no likelihood of anyone beating the record for salmon harvesting on the Bann. It was set in 1635 when 62 tons of salmon were taken at Coleraine on one extraordinary day, sacred in the annals of Ulster fishing.

Apart from Coleraine bridge, there was only one other bridge across the 35-mile-long (56km) Lower **Bann** until the mid-eighteenth century. The one at **Portglenone** was a drawbridge and it was pulled up at night to protect the settlement from 'tories', dispossessed Irish desperadoes lurking in the forests on the opposite bank. The pleasant elongated marketplace of Portglenone today is lined with small houses and shops. A plaque at the door of 48 Main Street, records that Timothy Eaton, who later emigrated to Toronto and made a fortune from retailing, learned the drapery business in this shop 1847-52. He worked 16 hours a day and slept under the counter.

Portglenone Forest is an appropriate place to find a memorial to the Tyrone-born botanist Augustine Henry (1857-1930) who introduced fast-growing American conifers like the sitka spruce and Douglas fir to the British Isles. It is a commercial forest with a big chunk of sitka spruce but it also preserves the old woods along the Bann and there are plenty of beech, oak and other deciduous trees. Northern Ireland has not suffered the excesses of the conifer profiteers who have blackened the hills of Scotland, Wales and northern England with blankets of birdless forest.

The settlers of **Ballymena**, largest town in County Antrim, came mostly from south-west Scotland. The Bard of Dunclug, David Herbison (1800-80), who was born in Mill Street, captured the lowland accent and intonation in his ballads and songs. People here still talk that way. The town's prosperity was based on linen which, with other textiles, continues in a small way but the region is now overwhelmingly agricultural. There are four weekly livestock markets in Ballymena, and the Saturday variety market has been going strong since 1626 when the Adair family obtained patents from Charles I. The love song *Robin Adair* was written by Lady Caroline Keppel whose parents tried to end her romance with Dr Robert Adair of Ballymena. They did eventually marry and lived happy ever after.

The local building material is the black basalt which covers most of the Antrim plateau. The banks are solidly built and the churches are sober-looking. Ballymena Academy (emblem: the industrious ant) has produced judges, doctors, and outstanding athletes such as Mary Peters, pentathlon gold medallist in the 1972 Olympics in Munich, and Willie John McBride, Irish international and captain of the British Lions rugby team. The name of the academy's best known pupil, Roger Casement, does not appear on the school roll.

The centre of **Gracehill**, west of Ballymena, is much as it was in the eighteenth century when a small band of Moravians settled here. The village is built round a green, with separate houses for the brothers and sisters who lived by making clocks and lace. The church (1765) contains interesting stained glass windows and a central pulpit. A long path down the middle of the grassy cemetery separates the graves of men from those of women, a burial custom which is still observed.

Industrious Ulstermen

On the A43 north of Ballymena watch for a small outbreak of brown signage and blue plaquery, indicating the birthplaces of two industrious Ulstermen, Timothy Eaton (1834-1907) founder of the Canadian chainstore (30 Killyfleugh Road, Clogher), and Sir Samuel McCaughey (1835-1919) the Australian sheep king (146 Cloughwater Road, Tullynewey). The brown signs cease as soon as you leave the main road and so finding either of these farmhouses, both private homes, is a challenge. The thought that blue plaques are more suited to an urban setting is entirely inappropriate. Round here one whitewashed farmhouse is much like the next. You are looking for the one with the blue plaque.

The flat landscape around **Broughshane** is relieved by **Slemish**, a small extinct volcano (1,437ft/438m) which can be seen from a great distance. Evidence from St Patrick's *Confession* suggests that this solitary hill is where he herded swine as a boy slave. Captured on the coast of Britain by pirates, Patrick was brought to the north of Ireland where he worked for 6 years for Miluic, chieftain at Slemish, before making his escape. He returned to Ireland in AD432 to convert the Irish. From the top of Slemish — a scramble of less than 700ft (213m) from the carpark — the ruin of old Skerry Church on a hill where Miluic's fort once stood, is clearly visible to the north. Several well known daffodil breeders have lived at Broughshane and rare bulbs descended from Broughshane hybrids can be obtained from the Carncairn nursery. The parish church graveyard contains a copy of the famous tenth-century Monasterboice high cross. It marks the grave of the naturalist and collector John Grainger, whose private collection of 60,000 objects started the Ulster Museum's collection. As rector of Broughshane 1869-91, he had a roomy rectory. He needed every inch of space to put his things in.

A signpost at **Cullybackey** on the Portglenone road (B96) indicates that the ancestral home of Chester Alan Arthur, US president 1881-85, is up a lane through potato fields, an awkward sharp turn. Arthur's father emigrated from Cullybackey to Vermont in 1816. Crochet and quilt-making is demonstrated in the thatched cottage in summer.

Binevenagh mountain is a northern outlier of the Sperrin range. Bishop Hervey built a road right across it to improve access to

The weir and locks at The Cutts, Coleraine

Limavady from his palatial house at Downhill. If you approach the mountain from the south, take the B201 off the A2. The scenic Bishop's Road is signposted after a mile. After 5 miles (8km) stop at the Bishop's View for the panorama over the plain. You may see hang-gliders jumping off the mountain around here. A 7-mile (11km) golden strand sweeps round to the martello tower at **Magilligan Point** at the approach to Lough Foyle. There is a gliding club at **Bellarena** nearby. Swirling air currents around the point can waft sailplanes up to 20,000ft (6,097m). Beyond the Bishop's View, the road swoops down to join the A2 at **Downhill**. At the roadside a neo-classical gateway marks the entrance to Downhill demesne where you can walk up the glen to the windswept headland.

Bishop Hervey's huge uncomfortable Downhill mansion was never much lived in. Used as a military billet during the 1939-45 war and partly dismantled afterwards, it is now very ruined, a landmark for walkers on the Ulster Way. Visitors come up the leafy glen to look at the Mussenden Temple, a small domed rotunda which the bishop used as his summer library and which is looked after by the National Trust. Perched on the cliff edge, it shudders a little whenever a train rushes past on the narrow ledge below the cliff. In the days of the liberal Hervey, the basement was lent to the local Roman Catholic priest to celebrate mass. An Epicurean quotation from Lucretius on the frieze round the dome translates, rather disconcertingly: 'It is agreeable to watch, from land, someone else involved in a great struggle while winds whip up the waves out at sea.' The temple was named as a compliment and memorial to Mrs Frideswide Mussenden, the bishop's cousin, though she died aged 22 before it was completed in 1785.

Downhill strand is popular for surf fishing, especially bass. The view east from the Mussenden Temple embraces the beach and sandhills at the resort of **Castlerock** and the first of a string of fine golflinks stretching eastwards along the coast. On the A2 at Liffock crossroads a mile (2km) south of Castlerock, **Hezlett House** is a long low thatched rectory of 'cruck' construction dating from 1690 — an exceptionally old house in Irish terms. The building method involved standing naturally curved timbers, or crucks, in pairs to form a series of uprights and arches and then building the house round this frame. There are no foundations — the frame stands on the bare rock. The National Trust restored the house after a fire in 1986.

Coleraine, a sedate market town and boating centre above the Bann estuary, is linked to Belfast and Londonderry by rail and has a university campus on the outskirts. It was an important place in the early days of the London plantation and held out against the Irish in 1641, though the fortifications here never amounted to much more than earthen ramparts. A number of functional office blocks and factories are evidence of the town's present administrative and manufacturing interests. Apart from a handsome town hall, the centre is unexceptional. However, the river aspect is lively. There is a pretty weir and locks at The Cutts upstream, an imposing old town bridge, a quay where coasters load potatoes in exchange for coal, trains swooping across the river on a railway viaduct, a large boating marina downstream and, out at the estuary, waders and wildfowl busy in the reed beds.

Mountsandel, on the east bank of the river a mile (2km) south of Coleraine (signposted from the A26/A29 roundabout) is said to be the earliest known inhabited place in Ireland. It is an oval mound,

200ft (61m) high, and according to the scientists, post holes of a wooden dwelling found here are 9,000 years old. More interesting than these ancient holes, however, is the position of the mound overlooking the Bann, particularly striking seen from the river.

St Comgall of Bangor founded a monastery at **Camus** 2 miles (3km) upstream from Mountsandel, on the west bank of the river (separated from it now by the A54). The only trace of this foundation is a small graveyard with part of the carved shaft of a red sandstone high cross and a bullaun, a large stone with a deep hole in the centre, of the kind found all over Ireland. These stones may have started as mortars, used with a pestle to grind things up, but they are often found near a church or graveyard and were commonly used as fonts or for cures. In Ireland, there is always rainwater in a bullaun.

The Giant's Causeway

The north Antrim coast became an instant tourist attraction after a description of the **Giant's Causeway** was published in 1693 by the Royal Society. Ever since, people have flocked to look at and sit on and clamber over the amazing geological phenomenon, and have their photograph taken against its tall colonnades. The dramatic beauty of this whole coast, where craggy headlands give way to sandy bays and small harbours lasts for the whole of the 60-mile (97km) coastal drive from Portrush round to Larne.

The artist Susanna Drury, who was painting from about 1733 to 1770, helped make the Causeway famous in Europe. A pair of her pictures, one showing the east, and the other the west prospect, painted on vellum in about 1740 (now in the Ulster Museum, Belfast), were engraved and circulated widely on the continent. The origins of the columnar structures excited speculation by two rival groups of scientists. The Neptunists said the columns were sedimentary rocks, formed by chemical precipitation in the water. The Vulcanists said they were igneous — the result of volcanic action. By the nineteenth century the Vulcanists were acknowledged to be correct. The cliffs all the way along the north Antrim coast are still of interest to geologists. Flows of molten lava buried a whole series of older rocks which jut out as many-coloured cliffs along the edge of the plateau — red sandstone, chalk, coal, blue clay, iron ore, black basalt. Fair Head, a 626ft (191m) cliff at the east end, has 16 different strata.

The Causeway proper is a mass of basalt columns packed tightly together. The tops of the columns form stepping stones leading from the cliff foot and disappearing under the sea. Altogether there are about 40,000 of these strangely symmetrical columns, mostly six-sided but some with four or five, and others with seven or eight sides.

The tallest are about 40ft (12m) high, and the solidified lava in the cliffs is 90ft (27m) thick in places.

The ancient Irish must have wondered at the Causeway. This was clearly giants' work and, more particularly, the work of the giant Finn McCool, the Ulster warrior and commander of the king of Ireland's armies. When he fell in love with a lady giant on Staffa off the Scottish coast — the island of Fingal's Cave — Finn built this commodious highway to bring her across to Ulster. Fingal is Finn, of course, and there are similar rock formations on Staffa. Like Mrs Drury's paintings, Thackeray's description in his *Irish Sketch Book* (1842) conveys a sense of the fantastic:

'When the world was...fashioned out of formless chaos, this must have been the bit over — a remnant of chaos ...'.

Early visitors arrived on horseback or by boat. Later the train from Belfast brought people to Portrush where they transferred to jaunting cars. In 1883 the Giant's Causeway Tramway opened, the first hydro-electric tram in Europe. Its toast-rack carriages ran on a narrow gauge railway from Portrush to the Causeway until 1949. One of them is in the visitor centre but do not let this detain you: hurry on down to see the real thing.

A 5-mile (8km) circular walk goes down to the Grand Causeway and along a narrow path past majestic amphitheatres and rock formations, with names like the Organ and the Harp, past Port na Spaniagh where gold treasure from the Armada galleass *Girona* was recovered at Lacada Point by divers in 1968, and up a wooden staircase to Benbane Head, returning along the cliff top. A 2-mile (3km) circular walk is via the Shepherd's Path. A minibus shuttles between the visitor centre and the Grand Causeway.

Back at the carpark, you may notice a white-washed Austrian Tyrolean church — a 1915 conceit by Clough Williams-Ellis, architect of Portmeirion in Wales. It was built as a National School and now contains a 1920s classroom, with inkwells and splodgy pens. The louvred bell tower is not the only eccentric rooftop round here: the profile of the visitor centre mimics the malt-house roofs of the whiskey distillery at Bushmills 2 miles (3km) away.

The resort of **Portstewart** with a small sheltered harbour, smart houses along the promenade, and 3-mile (5km) strand stretching to the Bann mouth, always had more pretensions than Portrush next door. The railway company was obliged to build the station a decent but inconvenient distance away for fear of bringing vulgar people to the town. Visitors came the last mile by steam tram. The 'North West 200' motorcycle race now held here each May, with bikes roaring along the roads around Portstewart, would surely have appalled

The sheltered harbour at Portstewart

that genteel nineteenth-century society. The motorcar, on the other hand, was tolerated. Unreconstructed motorists still claim a traditional right to take their cars down to the sea and drive along the beautiful firm sand, though the strand's new owners, the National Trust, make sure they pay for the pleasure. In summer there are boat trips to the Causeway from both Portstewart and Portrush.

Portrush has a fine position on Ramore Head peninsula jutting out into the Atlantic, with sandy beaches running east and west, and picture-postcard seaside terraces above the harbour. When the wind blows from the north-west, any time from late summer the grassy clifftop at the end of the promontory is crawling with ornithologists who have humped their tripods and telescopes up here to watch a ceaseless flypast of gulls and gannets. The resort has the usual seaside amenities, including several large all-weather entertainment centres, and summer theatre shows in the redbrick town hall, a bulbous and jolly Victorian pile.

A 2-mile (3km) strand east of the town is backed by the sand dunes of Royal Portrush Golf Club, scene of many Irish golf championships. The British Open has also been held here. The strand ends at the **White Rocks**, limestone cliffs weathered into caves and arches. There is a steep path from the road to the Cathedral Cave which is 180ft (55m) deep with two huge limestone columns supporting the roof at the seaward entrance. The carpark near here is a good place

Dunluce Castle teeters on the brink of an isolated crag

to stop for lunch. The view is splendid. The Skerries, a chain of small grassy islands a couple of miles offshore, can be inspected at close quarters by excursion boats from Portrush.

The romantic ruin of **Dunluce Castle** teeters on the edge of an isolated crag. Some of it actually fell off during a storm in 1639, carrying away the kitchens, the cooks and all the pots. In the thirteenth century Richard de Burgh built a Norman castle on this desirable site. Defenders could come and go through the large sea cave that slopes up into the castle precincts, and a drawbridge lay across the deep chasm now spanned by a wooden footbridge. In the late sixteenth century the MacDonnells, Lords of the Isles, ruled all the north-east corner of Ulster from their stronghold at Dunluce. Sir John Perrott came up from Dublin in 1584 and ejected Sorley Boy MacDonnell after pounding the castle with artillery. As soon as Perrott returned south, leaving an English garrison in situ, Sorley Boy regained possession after one of his men, employed in the castle, hauled various MacDonnells up the crag in a basket. The garrison was wiped out and the constable hanged over the wall.

Sorley's antecedents are clear from his name: *somhairle* is from the Norse for 'summer soldier' or Viking, *buidhe* is 'yellow' in Gaelic. The Scots were in the habit of leading raiding parties against both the Irish and English and many, like the MacDonnells, stayed on. This yellow-haired summer soldier was soon able to repair the damaged castle with proceeds from the wreck of the *Girona* which sank off the Causeway in October 1588. The pitifully few survivors, five out of 1,300, were put up at Dunluce and sent home via Scotland.

The castle fell into decay after Sorley's descendants, the earls of Antrim, moved to more comfortable accommodation at Glenarm in the glens. The extensive ruins include two thirteenth-century towers, a Scottish-style gatehouse (about 1600), and the remains of a seventeenth-century house built inside the defences. From the windows there is a view through the limestone arches of the White Rocks. In a flat calm the cave underneath Dunluce can be visited with care by boat. It is one of many narrow sea caves along this coast.

The small port and beach resort of **Portballintrae** is down a loop road off the A2. Beyond the half-moon bay is Bushfoot Strand and the western end of the Causeway cliffs. The Bush is a great salmon and trout river, with good stretches from Bushmills village up to Ballymoney. **Bushmills** was the last stop for carriages from Belfast before the final push to the Causeway. Travellers restored themselves with a few glasses of whiskey from the Old Bushmills Distillery. Its charter of 1608 making it the world's oldest legal whiskey distillery. Its last private owners sold to the giant Irish Distillers which was bought out in 1989 by Pernod Ricard. All Irish whiskey is now owned by the French. It is a sobering thought. The village has an attractive square with solidly built houses, a traditional inn and a Victorian clock tower vaguely resembling an Irish round tower.

Anyone walking from the Giant's Causeway to Benbane Head can continue along the cliff path to the pear-shaped crag of **Dunseverick Castle** where the path almost converges with the road (B146). It must be said that the very ruinous sixteenth-century gatehouse is a poor thing. Nevertheless, the human history of this impressive crag is long and interesting. Dunseverick, the capital of the ancient kingdom of Dalriada, was the terminal of one of Ireland's five great highways from Tara, near Drogheda, and a main jumping-off point for Scotland. Irishmen from Dalriada had established a colony on the Argyll coast by the fifth century — the colony which St Columba joined and from which he established Iona. Dunseverick is also featured in Ireland's oldest love story, the ninth-century *Longas mac n-Usnig* (The Fate of the Children of Uisneach), as the legendary landing place of Deirdre of the Sorrows and the sons of Uisneach. Deirdre, the intended bride of King Conor, falls in love with his bodyguard, Noisi. To escape the king's wrath they flee to Scotland, together with Noisi's two brothers. Fergus, another of Conor's warriors, in good faith persuades them that the king has

The pleasant resort of Portballintrae

forgiven them and that it is safe to come back. They land at Dunseverick and take the road south to Conor's court at Emain Macha (Navan Fort) at Armagh. But the vengeful king kills the brothers and takes Deirdre for himself, whereupon she dashes her head against a stone and dies. Outraged by Conor's treachery, the noble Fergus destroys the palace.

Another ruined gatehouse with a spectacular position is **Kinbane Castle** on a long white promontory, built in 1544 by Colla Dubh MacDonnell. It is signposted off the B15 2 miles (3km) east of Carrick-a-rede. There are fine views of Fair Head and Rathlin Island from the path leading down to the castle from the cliff-top carpark. Watch out for erosion and steep drops. A profusion of wild flowers, including orchids, grows beside the path in early summer. A cave that goes right through the promontory is accessible only by boat in a flat calm.

Crescent-shaped **Whitepark Bay**, with a youth hostel and a mile (2km) of sand backed by grassy dunes, is in National Trust care. At the west end is the picturesque hamlet of **Portbraddan**. An odd slate-roofed church squeezed in next to a private house measures only 12ft by 6½ft (4m x 2m). The smallest church in Ireland, it is privately owned. Neolithic flints have been found in the caves at the raised beach at the other end of the bay. A footpath leads round to **Ballintoy** harbour, a sturdy limestone harbour set among rocks, lively with small boats and people having tea in the café. **Sheep Island**, a perpendicular stack with a flat grassy top offshore, is a bird sanctuary and has an enormous cormorant colony. The rats that killed off the island's puffins have themselves been routed and puffins have started coming back.

The switchback road down to the harbour passes a pretty white church in a meadow. Its tapered square tower has pinnacles at the corners and very small windows. In 1641 the Earl of Antrim rescued local Protestants who had taken refuge inside the original church on the site and were being besieged. There used to be a castle at Ballintoy. When it was demolished in 1795, the staircase and oak panelling were carefully preserved, taken to England and installed in Downing College, Cambridge.

Crossing the rope bridge at **Carrick-a-rede** is quite scary. Swinging 80ft (24m) above the sea and made of planks strung between wires, it starts bouncing up and down as soon as you step on it. There is no safety netting on the sides and a large notice warns of the risks of crossing. Despite this, or perhaps because of it, there is a steady stream of visitors keen to cross the 60ft (18m) wide chasm to the island on the other side. The bridge gives access to the commercial salmon fishery on the south-east side of the island. It is removed in September at the end of the fishing season and put up again in April.

Dunseverick, capital of the ancient kingdom of Dalriada

Early spring in the Glens of Antrim

Carrick-a-rede means 'Rock in the Road' — the road taken by Atlantic salmon returning to spawn in the rivers. The tidal conditions and the deep water are ideal for salmon netting and the fishery has been here for a long time. An engraving of 1790 shows a rope bridge at the rock. A cunning system of nets intercepts the fish as they move westwards, keeping close to the shore searching for their ancestral waters. Until recently a steep path from the main road ran down to the bridge across a field. Now the approach is via a path along ½ mile (1km) of cliff top from Larrybane carpark where there is a National Trust information centre; campers can pitch a tent for the night here. A lime kiln on chalky Larrybane Head is a remnant of past quarrying operations.

A memorial near the harbour at Ballycastle recalls the experimental wireless link which Marconi and his assistant, George Kemp, established in 1898 between Ballycastle and **Rathlin Island**, a 50-minute boat trip across the sound. Signals were transmitted over a distance of 6 miles (10km) between a mast erected near the island's east lighthouse and a house on the cliff at Ballycastle.

Across the Sound to Rathlin

Rathlin is a boomerang shape with a lighthouse at each of its three points, and high white cliffs round most of the coast. In the angle the sheltered modern harbour at Church Bay is a staging post for yachts heading for the Hebrides — the Mull of Kintyre is only 12 miles (19km) away. Birdwatchers, botanists and divers (scoobies) drape themselves around the quay at Ballycastle, waiting for a boat to transport them and their gear across the sound. About 100 people live on the island, making a living from fishing, farming and tourism.

Bear in mind that crossings are dependent on weather conditions. However, a passenger ferry to the island leaves from Ballycastle every a day all year, more frequently in July and August. You can also make your own arrangements with local boatmen. The ferrymen like to direct your attention to Slough-na-Mor, 'Swallow of the Sea', a whirlpool where St Columba was nearly drowned en route to Iona in the sixth century, and they point out the site of *HMS Drake*, torpedoed in 1917 and lying in 50ft (15m) of water in Church Bay, one of more than 200 known wrecks around the island. The first recorded mishap in the sound was when Brecain, son of Niall of the Nine Hostages, and his fleet of fifty curraghs were lost in a great tide rip in AD440. However, scoobie interest tends to focus on more recent wrecks, like *Drake* and *Loch Garry*, sitting upright 100ft (30m) down near Rue Point since 1942. The long, very deep underwater cliffs on the north-west side of the island are also popular scoobie haunts. The islanders' efforts to promote activity holidays were helped after they rescued Richard Branson, the Virgin tycoon, when his transatlantic air balloon fell into the sea off Rathlin. The grateful millionaire underwrote an activity centre at Church Bay.

The ownership of **Rathlin** was disputed between Ireland and Scotland for centuries. It was settled, in Ireland's favour, in a famous seventeenth-century court case. The island's history before that was regularly punctuated by battles and massacres. The Vikings raided it, perhaps as early as the eighth century. Sir Francis Drake landed guns on Rathlin in 1575 when his commander, the Earl of Essex, massacred the MacDonnell population while Sorley Boy MacDonnell looked on helplessly from the mainland. The MacDonnells were again massacred in 1642, this time on the orders of Archibald Campbell, earl of Argyll. It should be said that the MacDonnells did their own massacring when the need arose.

Walking is the best way to get around. The most distant place, the Kebble nature reserve at the west end, is less than 5 miles (8km) from the harbour. In summer there is an unofficial, somewhat unpredictable minibus service. Scattered ruined cottages, with pairs of big gate pillars, indicate a much larger population in the past. One deserted house was the birthplace of the father of the folk singer Mary Black. You can still see patterns of small arable fields criss-crossed with lazy

The amazing
geological
structure of the
Giant's Causeway,
County Antrim
(Chapter 4)

The famous
rope bridge at
Carrick-a-rede
swings 80 feet
above the sea,
County Antrim
(Chapter 4)

The limestone White Rocks near the lovely Royal Portrush golflinks, County Antrim (Chapter 4)

beds, particularly noticeable on land behind the harbour at the east end. The flowery meadows and rough grassy places shelter ground-nesting birds, among them until recently the corncrake which has almost gone from Ireland. Corncrakes nest in long grass for cover. Mechanised agriculture has destroyed much of their habitat and they freeze in terror at the noise of the combine harvester. When meadows were cut by hand once a year for hay, the birds had a chance.

Some 6,000 years ago a neolithic axe factory on Rathlin was producing distinctive axe heads of porcellanite which have been found all over Ireland and in parts of England. It was one of three main axe factories in the British Isles. The others were at Tievebulliagh in the Antrim glens, and at Langdale in the Pennines. Stone Age men discovered a small outcrop of this rare, very hard, fine-grained blue stone in Brockley townland on the west side of the island. North of Brockley at Doonmore is an ancient rath with some very thick stone walls on the top. At Knockans, south-east of Brockley, there is a stone sweat house, a kind of early sauna. Mrs Catherine Gage, a local historian, writing in 1851, records that girls employed in the dirty business of kelp (seaweed) burning would resort to these beehive sweat houses after work to clear their complexions before going to dance the night away at Ballycastle.

Rathlin's cliffs are home to vast numbers of seabirds. The ledges and rock stacks of the cliffs on the north side and the huge cliff towering 100ft (30m) over the west lighthouse above Bull Point are crowded with them, tens of thousands, guillemots, kittiwakes, razorbills, and puffins standing on grassy mounds outside their burrows. The lighthouse light is actually at the foot of a square four-storey tower which has chimney pots and sash windows. It was completed in 1919. From here you can see clear across to Inishowen.

Most Rathlin caves can be visited only by boat in a flat calm. The high caves before Bull Point are jammed to the roof with iron girders, steel plates and chunks of engines from ancient wrecks, wrenched from the seabed by Atlantic storms — a reminder, on a sunny day, of the ferocious winter storms that lash these parts. Bruce's Cave, below the east lighthouse at the other end of the island, is where Robert the Bruce hid in 1306 after his defeat by the English at Perth. It was a Rathlin spider whose arachnoid energies gave the despondent warrior new heart and sent him back to Scotland to win the battle of Bannockburn. Some of the cliff formations at this end of the island have similarities with the Giant's Causeway.

The track from the harbour to the east lighthouse passes

Knocknascreedin, or 'Hill of Screaming'. The Gaelic sobriquet was acquired after 1642 when the MacDonnell women watched the massacre of their menfolk from this place. Some of them suffered the same fate soon afterwards and were thrown off the cliff into the sea. The east lighthouse, looking, one feels, as a lighthouse ought to look — a tall confident black-and-white cylinder — was erected in 1856. Concrete slabs in the grass are marked 'Lloyds'. They are the remains of the Marconi wireless mast of 1898. The lighthouse keeper does not live here any more. All Rathlin's lighthouses are now automatic.

The small Anglican parish church, which was rebuilt in 1815, has a lovely position close to the water, backed by whin-covered slopes. Inside is a memorial to the Reverend John Martin, who was rector here in 1723-40, and monuments to members of the Gage family, resident landlords of Rathlin from the eighteenth century. The historian Mrs Gage, who died in 1862, is commemorated by two shapely maidens in diaphanous gowns of gleaming white marble. The Gages have gone now but they built the long low manor house that extends along the waterfront at Church Bay. A short distance back up the track is a Catholic church (1865), Rathlin's main place of worship, next to the priest's house. It has a pretty grotto in the garden.

Salty winds rake the island all year round and stop trees from growing more than a few feet; the landscape is virtually treeless. Electricity is generated by three giant wind turbines on Kilpatrick hill, the highest point, with a central diesel/battery facility at the harbour, ready to cut in when the wind drops. The turbines and the overhead cables are not a pretty sight, but Rathliners consider it a small price to pay for twentieth-century comforts — freezers, washing machines, tumble driers and microwaves. Until the 'mains' came in 1992, it was bottled gas and diesel. Many islanders still get their water straight from a well or stream. For people round Church Bay it is pumped from Craigmacagan Lough, along miles of plastic tubing lying around on the ground. The first car on the island arrived in 1955 for the district nurse's use, though now there are a number of cars, vans and minibuses jolting over the rough tracks. Quite reasonably, the islanders are exempted from paying road fund tax.

For the visitor, the island's delightful primitiveness is more apparent than real. There is hostel accommodation at the manor house, a guesthouse at the harbour, a licensed restaurant, a pub and two shops, all of which remove any imperative to do the round trip in a day.

Bonamargy Friary, where the Black Nun lies in eternal humility

There is a great disparity in standard between Rathlin's modern harbour and the poor state of the harbour at Ballycastle which has silted up. This is a source of much exasperation locally. Cattle sold at auction on the island, for example, have to be ferried to the mainland in small boats since Ballycastle cannot cope with anything larger. Once the problem is solved, however, some of the island's allure for the visitor will surely be lost.

The tidy town of **Ballycastle**, above the harbour, is the social and business centre for the people of the glens and the setting for Ireland's oldest popular fair, the Ould Lammas Fair, held here since the MacDonnells first obtained a charter in 1606. In its heyday the fair lasted a week. Now a 2-day event at the end of August, it has sheep and pony sales and several hundred stalls crammed into the Diamond and down Fairhill Street. The Diamond is lined with some agreeable houses, with Holy Trinity parish church (1756) a little to one side. The church has an octagonal spire and a square tower with a very big clock face, big enough to read from a long way off, out of all proportion to the tower. Inside is a star-spangled blue ceiling and memorials to the Boyd family who developed the town. The red sandstone memorial with pink marble columns in front of the church was erected to a nineteenth-century benefactor. A plaque over a newsagent's shop at 21 Ann Street recalls that here John McAuley, a Ballycastle woodcarver, wrote the popular song which asks:

'Did you treat your Mary Ann
To dulse and Yellow Man
At the Ould Lammas Fair in Ballycastle-O?'

Dulse is an edible seaweed, something of an acquired taste. Yellow Man is a rock-like bright yellow toffee so hard that it has to be broken with a hammer. It is best to suck a small piece, slowly.

On steep Castle Street the former courthouse is now a museum with a view of Fair Head from the door. Among exhibits is a old milestone: 'Ballycastle ⅛ mile, Belfast 65'. An Irish mile, at 2,240 yards, is 480 yards longer than an English mile, putting Ballycastle about 83 English miles from Belfast — or about 30 miles longer than the quickest route today. Lower down the street McDonnell's pub (est. 1744) invites any visiting singer or instrumentalist to step inside — a reminder that this is one of the best places in Ireland to hear traditional Irish music, particularly in June when the town hosts a 3-day Irish music and dance festival, the Fleadh Amhran agus Rince. At the bottom is the Antrim Arms, the hostelry where Marconi stayed in 1898.

In 1988 this whole area — the coast, the glens and the bleak peaty plateau — was designated an area of outstanding natural beauty (AONB) which gives it some protection, especially from bungalow blight. Outside the AONB, between the A44 and the western edge of the Antrim plateau, is an interesting area of small trout streams and quiet country lanes rarely seen by visitors. In general tourists stay with the coastal strip and are not much encouraged to turn inland.

Leave Ballycastle by the A44 and, just before Armoy, take the Loughguile road, so straight you would think the Romans built it, passing after ½ mile (1km) the ivy-clad stump of **Armoy** round tower in a graveyard on the right; on then past a distinctive roadside motte to **Magherahoney** to visit St MacNissi's Roman Catholic church with its striking stations of the cross, some by the Ulster artist Cherith McKinstry. MacNissi, who made a pilgrimage to Jerusalem in the late fifth century and returned with his bag full of holy relics, is much associated with this part of county Antrim; on again to **Loughguile** (2½ miles/4km) where you may be able to see inside All Saints', an Anglican church which has a beautiful triptych window with glass by Mayer from the original Munich factory. You can drive along the south shore of lovely Loughguile lake for a glimpse of a very large and exotic cottage beyond the lake on the fringe of a wooded estate (private). The estate was the seat of the first and last Earl Macartney (1737-1806). He started building a mansion, Lisanoure Castle, in 1770 but he was away governing the colonies too long to make much headway. His heirs gave up trying to finish it after an accident with gunpowder in 1847. When you hit the A44, you are very close to the impressive castle mound (motte) of Knockaholet built inside a ring fort.

US president William McKinley's ancestor, James McKinley, emigrated to America from this area in the 1740s. The McKinley family home was west of Armoy near **Dervock** (where there is a small safari park with lions roaming about). James's nephew, Francis McKinley, was hanged as a United Irishman and the family house was burned down as a reprisal by the local yeomanry. A painting in the Giant's Causeway visitor centre shows the house in flames. It was commissioned for a St Louis, Missouri, exhibition after president McKinley's assassination in 1901.

An early seventeenth-century MacDonnell castle at the Diamond in Ballycastle has vanished completely but the bones of Sorley Boy, who died in 1590 aged 85, are preserved in a sealed vault at the ruined friary of **Bonamargy**, ½ mile (1km) outside the town on the A2 to Cushendall. Sorley's descendants, the first earls of Antrim, are also buried here. Inscriptions on the tomb of Randal MacDonnell, the second earl, who died in 1682, are in Gaelic as well as the more usual Latin and English. The Gaelic inscription translates with typical Celtic gloom: 'Every seventh year a calamity befalls the Irish. Now that the Marquis has departed, it will happen every year'. The tombs are not accessible to the public. Founded for the Franciscans by Rory MacQuillan in about 1500, the friary's survival for 150 years after the dissolution of the monasteries (1537) is something of a puzzle. The east range of the monastery was the residential wing. The friars slept in their dormitory on the first floor and came downstairs to the workshops underneath. A flat stone incised with a cross just inside the main entrance to the church marks the grave of Julia MacQuillan, a seventeenth-century recluse known as the Black Nun. Her choice of burial place ensured that worshippers would walk on her when entering the church, thus perpetuating her perfect humility. Sailors lost at sea in the two world wars and washed on to this treacherous coast are buried in a plot with a large cross in the graveyard corner. They include crewmen from *HMS Drake*. A bit of Ballycastle golf course seems to have jumped across the A2 and comes right up against the graveyard. Raise your eyes to the south-west and the rounded mountain of **Knocklayd** (1,695ft/517m). This mountain

*The curfew tower at
Cushendall*

was used in an elaborate geologists' hoax in 1788 when, according to
the Dublin newspapers, it erupted and engulfed the neighbourhood
in boiling lava.

Fair Head and the Nine Glens

From Bonamargy the A2 runs east across the Antrim plateau, past
the forest of Ballypatrick, past Watertop Farm — an 'open farm' —
and across one end of the 'vanishing lake' of Loughareema, before
dropping down to Cushendall. After heavy rain the lake can flood
the road and then it suddenly runs completely dry. The water drains
away rapidly through porous chalk under the mud and the lake
vanishes. In the nineteenth century, when this inland road was just
a track, it was not unknown for coach horses to gallop into a watery
grave at Loughareema, taking the passengers with them.

To experience the exhilarating heights of **Fair Head**, turn left off
the A2 3 miles (5km) from Ballycastle and follow the lane up to a

carpark, stopping on the way to look at **Lough na Cranagh** on the left, largest of three lakes in the vicinity. The exquisite oval-shaped island in the middle is in fact an artificial lake dwelling, a crannog, with a stone revetment 6ft (2m) above the water level. It is believed to have been a royal residence of the Dalriada kingdom, and connected to Dunseverick. From the carpark, the cliff top is about a mile walk north across heathery boggy scrub. You can follow the National Trust's yellow circle markings for a bit but after ½ mile (1km) their route swerves to the east, away from the cliff edge. Buzzards, kestrels and peregrine falcons patrol the desolate tableland in search of rock doves, and you may see small flocks of red-legged choughs. This mighty headland which marks off Ulster's north-east corner is only 3 miles (5km) from Rue Point on Rathlin, and there is a superlative view of the hills and islands of Scotland, very close indeed across the narrow North Channel. At the cliff edge Grey Man's Path, plunging down a steep gully, is a short cut for wild goats foraging on the cliffs. These are real wild goats, with long hairy coats. The billy goats have big horns. Similar feisty beasts are found on Slieve Gullion near Newry and on Knockmore in Fermanagh. Where there are young conifers, they can do damage, but here the soil is sour and treeless. Mostly they are on the scree at the bottom where there is good cover among the rocks. The descent of the Grey Man's Path is actually less difficult to negotiate than it looks, though inexperienced walkers should give it a miss.

Murlough Bay, the loveliest of all the bays along the Antrim coast, is in the lee of this great headland. Unless you want to walk to it, you should return to the carpark and drive round via Ballylucan where the turning is well signposted. The contrast between the scrubby top of Fair Head and this lush green place is most striking. Below the chalk escarpment, buttercup meadows and trees run nearly to the water's edge, with sheep and a few cows grazing the slopes. The main carpark is up above the bay but there is a smaller one on a hairpin bend further down, past the stone cross memorial to Sir Roger Casement, executed for treason in 1916.

Regarded by Irish nationalists as a martyr, Casement had a brilliant career in the British colonial civil service; in particular, he reported on labour conditions in the Belgian Congo and Peru. In 1911 he accepted a knighthood. However, he reckoned that war with Germany offered an opportunity for a successful Irish rebellion, and he went to Berlin to negotiate for military aid against Britain. At the height of the war he came back with a shipload of armaments and landed from a German submarine on the Kerry coast. The plan did not go well, he was arrested and hanged at Pentonville. Despite persistent rumours about his unsavoury personal sexual life his remains were taken to Dublin in 1965 after representations by the Irish Government, and buried alongside O'Connell, Parnell and other heroes at Glasnevin. The Murlough Bay memorial was erected by his cousin, Mrs Parry of Cushendun.

A scenic road, very steep and winding, runs from Murlough Bay past **Torr Head**, where a modern Celtic cross commemorates Shane 'the Proud' O'Neill who was killed by the MacDonnells in 1567 shortly after his defeat at Farsetmore by Hugh O'Donnell. Like other Ulster clans at that time, the MacDonnells had had enough of his bullying. The road wriggling down to the National Trust village of Cushendun is hedged with wild fuchsia and honeysuckle.

Two of the 'nine glens' of Antrim, Glentaisie and Glenshesk, cut north to the bay at Ballycastle. Better known, however, are the glens running west to east, bisecting the mountainous region all the way from Cushendun down to Larne. The physical isolation of the small communities of farmers and fishermen, which has left the glens with a wealth of myth and legend, was alleviated in 1834 when a Scottish engineer, William Bald, blasted a road out of the chalky cliffs for a distance of some 28 miles (45km) up the eastern seaboard, passing by the foot of each of the glens. The road was later extended to Ballycastle. Names of the traditional nine glens with their popular translations are, from north to south: **Glentaisie**, Taisie's glen — Princess Taisie, daughter of the king of Rathlin, who escaped being kidnapped by a Norwegian king when her fiancé, 'Long Nails' Congal, beat off the invaders and scuppered their boats off Rathlin in 200BC; **Glenshesk**, Sedgy glen; **Glendun**, brown glen; **Glencorp**, glen of the slaughter; **Glenaan**, glen of rush lights; **Glenballyeamon**, Eamonn's townland glen; **Glenariff**, ploughman's glen; **Glencloy**, glen of hedges; and **Glenarm**, meaning — apparently — glen of the army.

Cushendun, once a highly fashionable watering place, is admired for the quaint Cornish architecture which Ronald McNeill, first (and last) Lord Cushendun, and his Cornish wife, Maud, commissioned from Clough Williams-Ellis (1883-1977). The square with small white-washed terraces is approached through large gate pillars. It was built in 1912. A row of cottages with hanging slates on the upper storey, facing the sea, was erected in memory of Maud in 1925. Williams-Ellis also designed Lord Cushendun's large neo-Georgian house, Glenmona Lodge, set among trees in the middle of the bay. Now a home for the elderly, it has an eccentric five-arch arcade at the front. The white Georgian house at the north end of the beach,

Rockport Lodge, was the home of a local poetaster, Moira O'Neill, whose real name, Nesta Higginson, suited her verses much better than the romantic alias she adopted. The ivy-covered ruins of a MacDonnell castle above Rockport House off the Torr Head road was where Shane 'the Proud' was killed and his head sent to be spiked at Dublin Castle. Cave House, another substantial Cushendun mansion, occupies a completely secluded position in an amphitheatre of cliffs at the end of a red sandstone cave 60ft (18m) long. The only approach is through this cave. John Masefield (1878-1967), the poet (and poet laureate from 1930) who wrote *Sea Fever* ('I must go down to the sea again . . .') and *Cargoes* ('Dirty British coaster with a salt-caked smokestack . . .') knew the house well. He married a daughter of the Crommelin family who built the house in 1820. It is now a religious retreat.

Beautiful **Craigagh Wood**, west of the village, conceals a rock where mass was said in the eighteenth century. It is carved with a crucifixion scene and is said to have been brought here from Iona. The Gloonan Stone nearby, opposite the Catholic church, has two hollows made, they say, by St Patrick's knees. The name is from the Gaelic *gluire* meaning 'knees'. An immense red stone viaduct with three arches, built by Charles Lanyon in 1839, carries the A2 over the tawny-coloured Glendun river. This glen has the wildest scenery of all the Antrim glens, and the walk up to the waterfalls is memorable. The B92 from Cushendun rejoins the A2 to Cushendall south of the viaduct.

Ossian's Grave, on the north-east slopes of the pointed mountain of **Tievebulliagh** (1,320ft/402m) is signposted to the right (west) a mile (2km) before Cushendall. There is a carpark behind a house about ½ mile (1km) up the lane from where a short walk brings you to a small grassy enclosure with Ossian's Grave — actually a neolithic court grave — in the middle and a memorial cairn to the Antrim glens poet John Hewitt (1907-87). The site of Tievebulliagh's ancient porcellanite axe factory is near the summit. From Ossian's Grave there are lovely views to Glendun, Glenaan and Scotland, and to the south-west is **Trostan** (1,817ft/554m), highest mountain on the plateau. The warrior-bard who gave his name to the tales known as the 'Ossianic Cycle' was the son of Finn McCool. The legends about Finn and his warrior band, the Fianna, originate from the third century. James Macpherson (1736-96), who translated and popularised them in the 1760s, added quite a few elements of his own but the tales are none the worse for that. Ossian is said to have returned from the fabulous kingdom of Tir na nOg, 'Land of the Ever-young', to

Tieveragh Hill, linked with the supernatural

find St Patrick preaching to the Celts. Despite the saint's best efforts, Ossian preferred the old gods and died unconverted. He thought Christianity was too strict for the Celts.

Three glens converge at **Cushendall** where the river meanders past a golf course into the bay. The red sandstone curfew tower on the corner of Mill Street was built in 1809 by Francis Turnly, a nabob of the East India Company, as 'a place of confinement for idlers and rioters'. North of the village, **Tieveragh Hill** is a small curiously rounded volcanic plug which is one of the best known 'gentle' or supernatural places in the glens, a haunt of the 'wee folk'. A cliff path north from the beach leads after a mile (2km) to the appealing ruin of thirteenth-century **Layde Old Church**. It was rebuilt at least three times and served as a parish church until 1790. Fine stones in the graveyard include a cross in memory of Dr James MacDonnell, a pioneer in the use of chloroform for surgical operations. He was one of the organisers of the famous Belfast festival of Irish harpers in 1792.

Going south, flat-topped **Lurigethan** (1,153ft/351m) looms on the right. Passing under Red Arch, notice the fragmentary walls of a sixteenth-century castle on the cliff side above. Red Bay boatyard, which builds wooden boats, has fishing boats and tackle for hire. Iron ore was mined in upper Glenariff until the end of the nineteenth century and was loaded at Red Bay. The shell-strewn sand on the beach here has a noticeable red tinge to it. Between Red Bay pier and Waterfoot village are several interesting caves. The biggest one, **Nanny's Cave**, is 40ft (12m) long and was inhabited by Ann Murray who was aged 100 when she died in 1847. She supported herself by spinning and knitting and was known to the revenue men for selling poteen. In the eighteenth century the children of Red Bay learned reading and writing at a 'hedge school' inside another of these caves. Hedge schools were unlicensed Irish schools run by unlicensed schoolmasters or itinerant priests, in the open air if necessary, from the late seventeenth century. They were replaced by the National School system after Catholic Emancipation (1829). The 'school' cave can be entered just beyond Red Arch. **Waterfoot** village, which is also known as **Glenariff** village, hosts the Feis na nGleann, one of the lively *feisanna* — competitive festivals of Irish sport and culture. The waterfalls and woodlands of Glenariff, best known of all the Antrim glens, should not be missed. In spring and early summer the upper glen is luxuriant with wild flowers, and there is a superb view from the café in the visitor centre.

The A2 now follows every indentation of the coast round Garron Point, where there is a marked change in the rock from red sandstone to limestone. After the chalky White Lady formation, watch out at a bend in the road for a large limestone rock with a bronze inscription, a rather dreadful poem, by Frances Anne Vane Tempest, marchioness of Londonderry (1800-65). Immediately round the point a lane winds up to Garron Tower, a castellated blackstone mansion overlooking the sea, where she entertained on a grand scale. An inscription at the front door was written by, and about, the marchioness. The house is now a boarding school.

The quarries above **Carnlough** village are worked out now but until the 1960s the white bridge over the main road carried a railway which brought limestone down to the harbour. The bridge, an adjacent clock tower and old courthouse, all made of large squared blocks of limestone, were built by the Londonderrys in 1854. The marchioness was not able to resist having a few words about herself inscribed on a plaque which is set into the bridge on the south side, to be seen and read from the carriages passing underneath. The Londonderry Arms hotel, built about the same time, was briefly owned by Winston Churchill who came on a visit while he was Chancellor of the Exchequer. Flatfish spearing is advertised on the main road. Carnlough has a nice sandy beach, a tourist office in the post office, an art nouveau pub of 1912 (McAuley's) and, like most of the villages down this coast, caravan parks.

Carnlough, where Winston Churchill once owned a hotel

Glenarm, which exports limestone and powdered chalk from the harbour, developed after Randal MacDonnell built a hunting lodge in the glen in 1603. When Dunluce on the north coast was abandoned, the lodge was enlarged and Glenarm became the principal seat of the earls of Antrim. To view Glenarm Castle, a theatrical pile of turrets and cupolas, go through the stone arch at the top of the village street (parking beyond). The castle is clearly visible across the river. There was a major rebuilding around 1750, and the Tudor parts are nineteenth century. The main entrance to the private demesne is a barbican archway with fake portcullis slits and boiling oil holes. A stone crest dated 1636, from the original castle, is set in the front. The lower glen is planted with Forest Service conifers but the woodlands of the upper glen, covenanted to the National Trust in 1980, are pleasant enough. The village itself has a self-possessed air, an interesting place to explore on foot. At the shop on the pier you can buy superior farmed salmon, grown in a natural way in the strong tides in Glenarm bay. Entirely chemical free, it is said to be the best farmed salmon available to the London market. At Glenarm you have the option here of turning inland to see something of the mid-Antrim region. The road joins with the A42 running across the Braid river valley, through Broughshane and on to Ballymena.

South of Glenarm, the road hugs the shore past a tumbled heap of limestone known as the Madman's Window, and on down past Ballygally Castle, an engaging plantation castle which is now a hotel. Apart from sash windows, it is unchanged since it was built in 1625. After a view of the Maidens' lighthouses out to sea at Drain's Bay — the name is a corruption of *draighean*, Gaelic for 'blackthorn' — the road snakes through Blackcave Tunnel, towards the ro-ro traffic rumbling off the ferries at Larne.

Further Information
— Northern Ulster —

Places to Visit

Londonderry/Derry:
Co Londonderry
In summer guided tours of the old walled city start from the tourist information centre in Bishop Street.

Harbour Museum
Behind Guildhall
Open: Monday to Friday 10am-1pm and 2-5pm.
☎ (01504) 365151

Guildhall
Please telephone the superintendent for a guided tour Monday to Friday 9am-4pm.
☎ (01504) 365151

Tower Museum
Union Hall Place
Open: Tuesday to Saturday 10am-5pm (longer hours in summer).
☎ (01504) 372411

Foyle Valley Railway Centre
Near Craigavon Bridge (west bank).
Open: Tuesday to Saturday 10am-5pm, and also on Sunday afternoons (2-6pm) from May to September.
☎ (01504) 265234

Earhart Centre
Ballyarna Field, 1½ miles beyond Foyle Bridge, off B194. Site always accessible. Cottage open every day in summer but not Friday afternoons.
☎ (01504) 354040

Ballycastle
Co Antrim
Ballycastle Museum
59 Castle Street
Open: in the afternoon from July to September. To visit at other times contact: ☎ (012657) 62024.

Coalisland
Co Tyrone
Coalisland Cornmill
Open: all year on weekdays, and Saturday and Sunday afternoon, April to October.
☎ (018687) 48532

Cullybackey
Co Antrim
Arthur Ancestral Home
Dreen, Cullybackey
Open: every day except Sunday, May to October.
☎ (01266) 44111

Donaghmore
Co Tyrone
Donaghmore Heritage Centre
Open: until 4pm on weekdays, and on
Saturdays in summer.
☎ (01868) 767039

Dungiven
Co Londonderry
Dungiven Priory
For access to the chancel call at the last
house in the approach lane (keyholder)
or ☎ (01232) 235000 in advance.

Dunluce Castle
Co Antrim
3 miles (5km) east of Portrush,
Access to precincts/visitor centre
Monday to Saturday 10am-7pm and
Sunday 2-7pm. In winter closed
Monday and shorter hours.

Giant's Causeway Centre
At the Causeway, Co Antrim
Open: every day except 24-26 December. Tourist information on the whole
north coast region is available at the
centre. Film show, mini-museum
(geology, legends, history), bookshop,
teashop.

Glenarm
Co Antrim
Glenarm Salmon Farm
☎ (01574) 841691

Liffock
Co Londonderry
Hezlett House
National Trust house — so complicated
opening times (but never open on
Tuesday).
☎ (0265) 848567 or ask at the nearest TIC.

Maghera
Co Londonderry
Maghera Old Church
Key from recreation centre reception,
St Lurach's Road, off Bank Square.

Moneymore
Co Londonderry
Springhill House
Opening times (afternoons only, and
never on Thursday) for this National
Trust house are complicated. Ask at the
nearest tourist information centre (see
below) or ☎ (016487) 48210.

Roe Valley Country Park
Limavady, Co Londonderry
Well signposted off B192. The restored
industrial buildings and visitor centre
are open 11am-4pm every day, with
much longer hours in July and August.
☎ (015047) 22074

Sperrin Heritage Centre
Co Tyrone
274 Glenelly Road
Cranagh, Omagh
Open: Easter to September every day
except Sunday mornings.
☎ (016626) 48142

Ulster-American Folk Park
Co Tyrone
3 miles (5km) north of Omagh
Open: every day from April to
September 11am-5pm, longer hours in
high season, plus weekdays in winter.
☎ (01662) 243292

Ulster History Park
Co Tyrone
Signposted on B48 north of Omagh
Similar hours to Folk Park.
☎ (016626) 48188

Wellbrook Beetling Mill
Co Tyrone
4 miles west of Cookstown off A505
Open: summer afternoons, and
weekend afternoons in April, May,
June and September.
☎ (016487) 51735

Tourist Information Offices

Open: all year.

Londonderry/Derry
Co Londonderry
8 Bishop Street
☎ (01504) 267284

Ballycastle
Co Antrim
Sheskburn House
7 Mary Street
☎ (012657) 62024

Ballymena
Co Antrim
Morrow's Shop
17 Bridge Street
☎ (01266) 653663

Coleraine
Co Londonderry
Railway Road
☎ (01265) 44723

Cookstown
Co Tyrone
Cookstown Council Offices
Burn Road
☎ (016487) 66727

Dungannon
Co Tyrone
Dungannon Council Offices
Circular Road
☎ (01868) 725311

Giant's Causeway
Co Antrim
Giant's Causeway Centre
Open long hours
☎ (012657) 31855

Limavady
Co Londonderry
Limavady Council Offices
Benevenegh Drive
☎ (015047) 22226

Omagh
Co Tyrone
1 Market Street
☎ (01662) 247831

Travel

Getting to Rathlin
Year-round passenger ferry leaves
daily from Ballycastle harbour,
weather permitting, at 10.30am.
The returning ferry leaves Church
Bay, Rathlin at 4pm (3pm in winter).
In July and August there are addi-
tional sailings in each direction. More
details from Ballycastle Tourist
Information Office (see above).
For access to the West Light platform
at Kebble National Nature Reserve
contact Royal Society for the
Preservation of Birds (RSPB) warden
in advance: ☎ (012657) 63935.

5 • Belfast & Environs

The City and the Country

In a country where cities are the size of small English towns and many towns are hardly larger than an English village, Belfast stands out as a true metropolis, with half a million people living within 10 miles (16km) of the City Hall. The absence in the culture of the habit of conservation plus the handiwork of bombers over the past 25 years surely should combine to guarantee Belfast the wooden spoon in any built environment contest. Be that as it may, the city, when you walk round it, seems distinctly more prosperous than economic and political commentators suggest it ought to be.

The centre has been redeveloped, with new hotels and covered shopping arcades and a 2,500-seat conference centre has risen up on the bank of the Lagan estuary. A busty statue of Queen Victoria in front of the City Hall gazes regally down Donegall Place into the main shopping area. Many of the chainstore names are familiar to visitors from Britain, and you might at first believe yourself in Manchester or Liverpool. Like those breezy cities across the Irish Sea, Belfast was a phenomenon of the Industrial Revolution.

In a century when Ireland's population was cut by half through emigration and famine, Belfast grew from 20,000 in 1800 to a linen boom town of 387,000 by 1911. By 1939 it was 438,000, bigger than Dublin. The pattern thereafter was for the city's traditional industries, textiles, shipbuilding, rope-making and tobacco, to decline, though the giant cranes of Harland & Wolff preside over what is still the United Kingdom's largest shipyard, with a dry dock taking ships up to 200,000 tons, and an innovatory engineering yard. The firm's order books for new tonnage are said to be in good shape.

Like other industrial cities built on rivers Belfast has recently rediscovered its waterfront. A new weir across the Lagan has raised the water level, allowing navigation on the river. A new bridge, Belfast's seventh, carries traffic and trains across the Lagan above the SeaCat ferry terminal, nineteenth-century maritime buildings have been conserved and the atmospheric old fish market has been rescued.

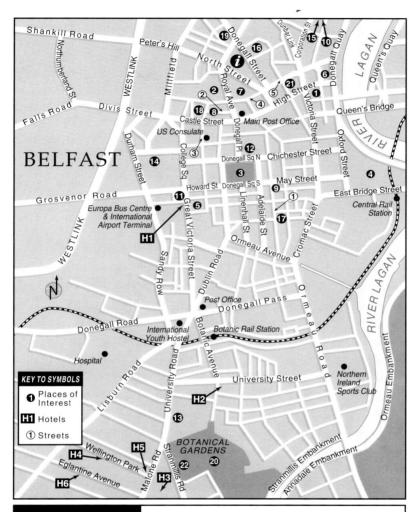

KEY TO MAP

Places of Interest

1 Albert Memorial Clock Tower
2 Castlecourt Shopping Centre
3 City Hall
4 Conference Centre
5 Crown Liquor Saloon
6 Custom House
7 First Presbyterian Church
8 Kelly's Cellars
9 May Str Presbyterian Church
10 Harbour Office
11 Opera House
12 Linen Warehouse *(M&S)*

13 Queen's University
14 Royal Belfast Academical Institution
15 Sinclair Seamen's Church
16 St Anne's Cathedral
17 St Malachy's
18 St Mary's
19 'The Front Page' Pub
20 Tropical Ravine
21 Ulster Bank
22 Ulster Museum

Hotels

1 Europa Hotel
2 Dukes Hotel

3 Stranmillis Lodge
4 Camera House
5 Pearl Court House
6 The George

Streets

1 Alfred Street
2 Bank Street
3 Queen Street
4 Rosemary Street
5 Waring Street

Visitors interested in Belfast's seafaring history — only London and Liverpool were larger ports in the nineteenth century — may be able to see inside the handsome old **Harbour Office**, completed in 1895, and now the most historic feature of the regenerated waterfront. Its long colonnaded public room has a vaulted ceiling and heraldic stained glass. A repository of the city's maritime history, with a collection of pictures, sculptures and bronzes assembled by the harbour commissioners over the past 150 years, the building and its contents give a stronger sense of culture and tradition than anywhere else in the city. There are nineteenth-century Belfast landscapes, many portraits and a large painting of the battle of Ballynahinch by Thomas Robinson painted in 1798 the year it happened.

Across the river is the frenetically busy Belfast City Airport on a

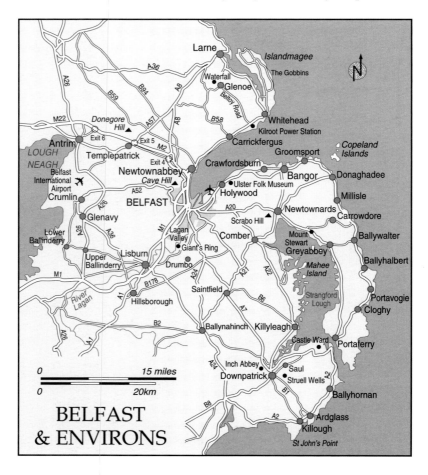

BELFAST & ENVIRONS

*The University area
provides a pleasant
introduction to Belfast*

congested site adjoining Shorts' aircraft works. Not to be confused with Belfast International 20 miles (32km) up the M2, the city centre airport is based on the airstrip where Short Brothers have tested their aircraft for the past 50 years. The Sunderland flying boat was developed here, and the first vertical take-off jet, the SCI. The company, which also makes weapons systems and is now owned by Bombardier of Montreal, is best known for its commuter aircraft.

A walk round the city centre and a visit to the university and museum area provide a good introduction to Belfast for first-time visitors who are touring by car and have only limited time. First find a carpark. There are plenty around the central shopping area which is pedestrianised, except for buses. Quite large areas in the middle of Belfast are designated no-parking control zones indicated by strongly worded pink signs at the curb. There are a limited number of parking meters but not in the areas where visitors tend to go, except near St Anne's cathedral.

The rather splendid **City Hall** was intended to dominate Donegall Square and so it does. Built of white Portland stone, the main façade is 300ft (91m) long with a copper dome rising 173ft (53m) above the traffic. After Belfast was declared a city in 1888 the city fathers set about demolishing the White Linen Hall of 1784 to build a city hall worthy of the new civic status. The architect, Brumwell Thomas, was knighted on its completion in 1906 but he had to sue the corporation to get his fees. Behind the railings is a statue of Sir Edward Harland (died 1895) who came to Belfast from Yorkshire as a young marine engineer in the 1850s. Just behind him — rather uncomfortably close! — a marble figure commemorates the loss in 1912 of the *Titanic* built at Harland's yard. *Titanic* was the biggest of many huge ships built

The ceiling of the Grand Opera House, Belfast

here around that time, including *Olympic* (1910) and *Brittanic* (1914). The dashing nobleman with handlebar moustaches and cocked hat in the little temple on the west side is the first marquis of Dufferin who, among other things, was governor of Canada, ambassador to Moscow and viceroy of India. The statue was unveiled in 1906. Together with the City Hall itself, it says much about Belfast's past imperial pretensions.

The City Hall interior features colourful Italian marble, an oak-panelled banqueting hall, a large industrial mural, and an enormous crimson Smyrna carpet in the Great Hall. The hall, 120ft (36m) long, was destroyed in the 1941 blitz when 1,000 Belfast citizens were killed. At that time fire engines came north from neutral Dublin to help put out the fires; this is still remembered by a few people. The damaged City Hall was repaired in time for Queen Elizabeth II's visit in Coronation year (1953).

Like Dublin, Belfast has a radial bus system. Getting across the city always involves changing buses at the City Hall so the area is always bustling with people. Most of Donegall Square West is occupied by the massive Scottish Provident building, decorated with lion's heads, queens, dolphins, sphinxes, and sculptures representing the industries that made Belfast prosperous — a loom, a ship, ropes and a spinning wheel. There are many other exuberant Victorian and

Edwardian buildings with elaborate sculptures over doors and windows. Gods and poets, scientists, kings and queens peer down from the high ledges of banks and old linen warehouses. The pink front of the linen warehouse on Donegall Square North offers no clues to its occupants, Marks & Spencer.

The **Grand Opera House**, Great Victoria Street, was designed by Frank Matcham (1854-1920), the celebrated theatre-architect who built the London Palladium and the Coliseum. It has a particularly gorgeous interior and comfortable seats. Its reopening after restoration in 1980 signalled a revival of evening entertainment in the city after the 'troubles' of the 1970s. At about that time the arts scene in Belfast, particularly theatre and music, began to emerge as a life-enhancing force in a resilient city. Next door is the brash 200-room four-star Europa Hotel, with a nightclub on the top floor. Across the road is a pub much admired by John Betjeman, the **Crown Liquor Saloon**. Its stained and painted glass and panelled snugs lit by the original gas lamps have been restored by the National Trust. Other cosy atmospheric pubs are to be found in the narrow passageways called 'entries' in the High Street area east of the Albert Memorial Clock Tower. **White's Tavern** in three-cornered Wine Cellar Entry is the city's oldest pub. Off Castle Street there was an even narrower entry, which has now disappeared, called Squeeze-Gut Entry. Before St Mary's (1784) opened in Chapel Street, Catholics gathered there to celebrate mass. **Kelly's Cellars**, Bank Street, a haunt of the United Irishmen who rebelled in 1798, has traditional music sessions at night. Some of the players, and the fiddle and tin-whistle buskers standing outside Castlecourt shopping centre, are graduates of the Francis McPeake Saturday night music 'academy' off the Falls Road. Young people come to learn to play any one of half a dozen instruments including the flute, fiddle, whistle and the harp.

Some of the city's grandest buildings are banks. The one on the corner of Waring Street, close to the North Street Tourist Information Centre, is the earliest public building surviving in Belfast. Built in 1769 as a market house, it was the venue in 1792 for a famous assembly of Irish harpers. The interior of the Ulster Bank (1860), also in Waring Street, resembles nothing so much as a Venetian palace.

Belfast's oldest church is **Knockbreda** parish church (1737), dark and bawn-like, a little outside the city but clearly visible on a hill (right) on the A24 driving south, just before the ring road. Its architect, Richard Cassels, designed many notable Dublin houses, including Leinster House where the Irish parliament has met since 1923. The chancel has a starry blue ceiling. The Duke of Wellington's mother, Lady Anne Hill, worshipped here, and it was a fashionable place in which to be buried. The churchyard contains some late eighteenth-century tombs big enough to live in.

Churches in the city centre to note include **St Malachy's** in Alfred Street, a Catholic church of 1844, with a fan-vaulted ceiling and romantic turrets overlooking the neat terraces of the Upper Markets 'village' built by the Housing Executive, Northern Ireland's (one and

Belfast's Anglican cathedral, St Anne's, faces across a trim urban park

only) public housing authority. The nearby May Street Presbyterian church (1829) was designed for the Reverend Henry Cooke, a formidable Victorian who campaigned against the theological errors of the time. Cooke's statue stands at the top of Wellington Place in front of the **Royal Belfast Academical Institution** ('Inst') where Lord Kelvin's father taught mathematics. Kelvin (1824-1907) invented the absolute scale of thermodynamics (the Kelvin Scale). He also made a fortune from his submarine cable patents. A statue of the great man stands inside the gates of the Botanic Gardens. 'Inst' opened in 1814 as an interdenominational school. The poet-physician William Drennan (1754-1820) saw the school as a place 'where the youth of Ireland might sit together on these benches and learn to love and esteem one another'. Son of a Presbyterian minister, Drennan helped found the United Irishmen Society and was inspired by the spirit of free thought sweeping through Europe. He was the first to call Ireland the 'emerald isle'.

Occasional lunchtime concerts are held at the **First Presbyterian Church**, Rosemary Street, completed 1783 and praised by John Wesley for its elliptical interior. Less accessible is **Sinclair Seamen's Church** (1857), Corporation Square, which is got up like a ship inside. The organ has port and starboard lights and the pulpit is a ship's prow. The church (though not the interior) was designed by Charles Lanyon who was also architect of the E-shaped Custom House, opened the same year. Fronting St Anne's, the large spacious Anglican cathedral in Donegall Street, is one of Belfast's rather few open spaces, a tiny urban park. Two of Northern Ireland's three main newspapers are produced near here: the evening *Belfast Telegraph* (Thomson Group) and, opposite 'The Front Page' pub, the Nationalist/Catholic *Irish News*, a morning newspaper. Production of the other morning paper, the venerable *News Letter*, founded in 1737 and Unionist/Protestant in outlook, has moved away but its old buildings (Nos. 49-67) lend character to Donegall Street. The number of shops selling religious books in Belfast, a city with rather few good bookshops, is striking.

The area around **Queen's University** is good for inexpensive eating places, restaurants, art galleries and theatre. The main college building, revived Tudor style in mellow brick, with cloisters and an entrance tower paraphrased from Magdalen, Oxford, was designed by Lanyon in 1849 and stands at the centre of charming little mid-Victorian terraces with magnolia trees in their front gardens. The university's arts and law faculties occupy most of the houses.

For a free steam bath step into the Tropical Ravine in the **Botanic**

Gardens. There is a view from the balcony down into a sunken glen of exotic plants. The pride of the gardens js a magnificent palm house, an early example (1839-52) of curvilinear glass and cast-iron, the work of the Dublin iron founder Richard Turner. The **Ulster Museum** faces into the gardens. It has international collections too, but its Irish exhibits are of especial interest to tourists. There is a permanent 'Made in Belfast' exhibition and some huge industrial steam engines and linen-making machines on the ground floor. Antiquities include the Spanish treasure from the Armada ship *Girona* which sank in 1588 off the Giant's Causeway. Gold and silver jewellery and much else was salvaged in 1967-68 by Belgian divers. Among paintings by Irish artists in the museum's art gallery are works by Sir John Lavery, Andrew Nicholl and William Conor, all Belfast-born, plus pictures by Paul Henry, Jack Yeats and George Russell (*AE*). There is good Irish silver, glass, pottery, furniture,

The Crown Liquor Saloon, Great Victoria Street, Belfast

Castlecourt Shopping Centre, a favourite pitch for Belfast's traditional street musicians

some grandfather clocks made in Ulster and the harp belonging to the blind bard Art O'Neill (1737-1818).

To see something of the so-called seismic part of the city, it does not take long to drive up the loyalist (Protestant) Shankill Road and down the nationalist (Catholic) Falls Road because they are immediately west of the centre and very close together. In fact they are linked by a small cross road (Northumberland Road) with a yellow barrier at one end which may or may not be closed. The names of these two rundown roads are also the names of the areas behind them and the resonance which they undoubtedly have derives from the sectarian tensions between adjacent housing estates. Protestant estates in the west of the city include: Woodvale, Springmartin and Suffolk. Catholic areas include: Whiterock, Turf Lodge, Ardoyne and Twinbrook. Mixed housing areas in Belfast are middle class areas. This complete segregation of working class housing on religious lines is baffling to visitors, but then so is the schools system. Protestant children attend the state schools and Catholic children opt out, or are opted out.

Go to **Belfast Castle**, a Scottish baronial pile on the lower slopes of Cave Hill, for the restaurants and the view. There is an ever-flowing stream of brides and wedding cakes into other parts of the castle but it is capacious enough to cope. **Cave Hill** itself is popular for walks and picnics in summer. The caves near the top are man-made, carved out in the Stone Age and used as shelter by hundreds of later generations. At **McArt's Fort** on the summit, Wolfe Tone, Henry Joy McCracken and other United Irishmen in 1795 plotted rebellion for two heady days and nights and pledged themselves to the cause of Irish independence.

Here, you are at 1,200ft (366m) and it is a good spot from which to appreciate Belfast's fine setting, ringed by hills rising to nearly 1,600ft/488m (Divis mountain), a deep sea lough and the valley of the Lagan river. A plan to erect a 'wind farm' along the tops of the hills, including Cave Hill itself, may prove irresistible: Ulster has a surfeit of high winds and, with no natural gas on tap, energy is expensive. Golf courses and parks on the city's outskirts are now visible, including the rolling parklands around the former parliament building at **Stormont** over to the east. The green sward even at this distance is clearly divided by an impressive avenue, nearly a mile (2km) long, running up to a white portico. It is a splendid hilltop site. Completed in 1932, the building is not generally open to the public though visitors can stroll in the immaculately kept grounds and take pictures. Six miles (10km) from the city centre, it has never been very busy. The old parliament — suspended in 1972 when the British government introduced direct rule — apparently sat only for 3 months of the year, 3 days a week, 3 hours a day. Also on Cave Hill, **Belfast Zoo** faces over the city. It is a real mountain zoo, getting steeper and steeper as you penetrate further. Once past the flamingoes on the lake, with a crannog (an artificial island) in the middle, and heading for the polar bears, you are literally moving up the side of the mountain.

Southside: the Leafy Lagan Valley

The towpath along the Lagan from Belfast to Lisburn starts in the university area near the Belfast boat club. Joggers, birdwatchers, anglers, painters and boys on bikes are not quite so numerous as people out for a stroll. Even so, it must be the most crowded bit of the whole of the Ulster Way, a 600-mile (966km) footpath running all round Northern Ireland. The 9 miles (14km) of old locks and lock houses are the industrial archaeology of the Lagan Navigation that

The fan-vaulted ceiling in St Malachy's Church, Alfred Street, Belfast

ran from Belfast to the shores of Lough Neagh where coal had been discovered. The Lagan was made navigable as far as Lisburn in the 1760s. In the 1790s the whole route was open. Its heyday was comparatively brief. Paradoxically, the canal provided the chief means of distributing coal imported through Belfast rather than moving Tyrone coal eastwards. It closed in 1958 and much of the waterway has disappeared under the huge rhubarb leaves of *gunnera manicata* and the pink and white flowers of wild balsam.

If time is short, the carpark at Shaw's Bridge on the ring road is a convenient place to join the towpath, 3 miles (5km) from the start. A wooden bridge was thrown across the river here to transport the guns of Cromwell's army in 1655. The present picturesque bridge with five arches was built in 1709. Close by, too close, a concrete bridge carries ring road traffic.

The nearby former mill village of **Edenderry** is hidden away in a bend on the river, a beautiful setting. Take the side road at the bridge (signposted) and turn right after 200 yards to Minnowburn Beeches carpark. A pleasant 1½-mile (2km) walk along the bank will bring

The river Lagan at Drumbridge

you into the village, wedged between the river and the hillside, but you can drive to the same place — small terraces with slate roofs, tall red chimneys, footscrapers and minuscule front gardens. Two twelve-house terraces front the quay where barges once delivered coal to a weaving factory famous for damask linen. Two other terraces lead to a tiny gospel hall. The area becomes animated on Orangeman's Day, 12 July, when thousands of marchers from Belfast come this way with bands and banners to listen to religious and political speeches in an open field near the village.

Orangemen are members of the Orange Order, a Protestant society that has a high profile in Northern Ireland. On 12 July they celebrate the victory of William of Orange (William III) at the Boyne in 1690 which established the Protestant succession in Britain. This particular parade, in Belfast, is the largest of many similar parades on 'the Twelfth' which is a general holiday in the province. The marchers wear an orange sash, good walking shoes and, if they own them, a bowler hat and white gloves. Standards of dress have slipped in recent times. Trainers and even jeans are not unknown. Some of the parades have a few 'lambegs', giant drums with painted goatskins and hoops, weighing over 30lb, and their 'blattering' can be heard for miles across the countryside. The lambeg drummers do their loudest

The neat terrace houses of Edenderry, a former mill village on the Lagan

drumming at Sandy Row, the main assembly point in Belfast, before the parade moves off for the field 7 miles (11km) away. After the speeches or often, during them, the marchers flop out on the grass for a picnic. Then they change their socks in readiness for the long walk back to Belfast.

There are some 2,000 parades in the province every year, some very small, a kind of practice run for the mega-parades like 12 July and another big one at the end of August. The Feast of the Assumption (15 August) sees the Hibernians donning their finery to walk in similar processions with bands and painted banners. They are also in evidence in parades on St Patrick's Day, 17 March. The Hibernians' sashes are green, the banners bear different images but some of the tunes are the same and the style closely resembles the Orangemen's. The bands are very important. Sometimes, if there is a shortage, you may find that a band that has played in an Orange parade one week may turn out for a Hibernian one the next. An onlooker can find it all rather confusing.

From Edenderry a circular enclosure known as the **Giant's Ring** is a short walk away across the open meadow. The enclosure is nearly 200 yards across, with an earthen bank 20ft (6m) wide and 12ft (4m) high, and a sort of dolmen in the middle. Rather little is known about it. In the eighteenth century it was used for horse racing. A 2-mile (3km) race was six circuits and the punters stood on the ramparts. In 2,000BC it must have been a place for rituals too. If you insist on driving, go via Ballynahatty Road. It is well signposted and there is a carpark.

To continue the towpath walk, the halfway point is reached around **Drumbridge** where a lock-keeper's house dated 1757 has been well restored. Or drive there via the Upper Malone Road (B103), parking just beyond the entrance to grandly named Sir Thomas and Lady Dixon Park, where the roses attract huge crowds in summer. Hidden below the level of the bridge, the keeper's house was built to designs by Thomas Omer, the Lagan Canal engineer. Opposite the carpark is **Drumbeg** church with a pretty lychgate and tombs of founders of the city. The church tower (1798) has a seventeenth-century bell.

At **Drumbo** village to the south-west is the stump of a twelfth-century round tower (*druim* means ridge) but its parish church, also eighteenth century, is 2 miles (3km) away, at **Ballylesson**. In the graveyard a huge tomb contains the remains of a local worthy who rejoiced in the name Narcissus Batt. He was 16 years old when he helped form the Belfast chamber of commerce in 1783. The fifty-nine founder-members were not stuffy city-suited gents. Many were active in the Volunteers, the liberal movement in Ireland at the end of the eighteenth century. Their first president was commander of the Belfast Volunteers, and some were United Irishmen. Several went to prison and the grandson of one founder was leader of the United Irishmen, and went to the scaffold (Henry Joy McCracken). Narcissus Batt, more fortunate, died in his bed, rich and influential. Historically interesting, leafy and peaceful, this little backwater is only 6 miles (10km) from central Belfast.

Northside: Carrickfergus and the Islandmagee Witches

The road north to Carrickfergus and Larne runs through a quite different landscape. A ten-lane strip of motorway between the crag of Cave Hill and Belfast Lough soon narrows and turns towards the north-west and the international airport. Traffic volume seems

The fine Palm House in Belfast's Botanic Gardens

scarcely to warrant such a highway but if you are driving into the city, it is a pleasant approach with striking views of Belfast Lough and Cave Hill.

Carrickfergus grew up round the massive castle built by John de Courcy in 1180 to guard the approach to Belfast Lough. Shaped to fit the rocky spur on which it stands, it was crucially important to the Anglo-Norman toehold on Ulster. Infilling around the rock has detracted from the visual impact the castle must once have made, and the wide A2 road cuts it off from the town. In June 1690 William of Orange landed on the pier beneath the castle walls on his way to the battle of the Boyne. A plaque at the end of the quay marks the spot. His commander in chief, the Duke of Schomberg (1615-90) had been here already. In fact he had bombarded the castle into a wreck the previous year in order oust a Jacobite garrison.

Around the time of the old Irish quarterly festival of Lughnasa

(1 August), the castle fills up with archers, minstrels, wrestlers, and 'monks' tending braziers, and there are banquets, medieval ones, to help bring in the tourists. In 1760 this fine example of medieval military architecture was easily captured by a French squadron which appeared in the lough. Fortunately, it was recaptured soon afterwards. In 1778 the American privateer Paul Jones sailed past the castle and carried off *HMS Drake* in what turned out to be America's first naval victory. It is said that Belfast citizens ran to the shore to cheer the attackers. Ulster Protestants were generally sympathetic to the American revolution though the French one was not at all to their liking.

More than half the early seventeenth-century defensive town wall is still standing at its full original height. A section beyond **St Nicholas parish church** was excavated in the 1970s by a young archaeologist, Thomas Delaney, who is commemorated by a stone in front of Gill's almshouses. The church, which stands above the market place, is contemporary with the castle, with late twelfth-century pillars in the nave. The chancel was finished in 1305 and is out of alignment with the nave, an unusual feature. It was damaged and burnt many times down the years and much restored in 1614. The north transept contains the kneeling figures of Sir Arthur Chichester, his wife and infant son in a marble and alabaster monument. Chichester was governor of Carrickfergus and, from 1605, Lord Deputy of Ireland. He was also the landlord of Belfast. A small effigy of his brother, Sir John, is part of the same monument. In 1597 Sir John was ambushed at Glynn, a small village near Larne, by the MacDonnells and they cut off his head. The Chichesters were the earls of Donegall, a name which besprinkles the Belfast street directory. Their eventual bankruptcy coincided with the end of the great famine and allowed their tenants to become freeholders, a disaster for the Chichesters but a boon for the citizens of Belfast. Four stained windows are by Irish artists and the nave contains sixteenth-century glass.

In High Street a seventeenth-century hostelry, still a hotel, and a market house of 1755, now a bank, are noteworthy, and some of the town's numerous antique shops occupy attractive old buildings. A monorail time-trip centre, is tucked away behind the handsome Georgian town hall, formerly the courthouse. In 1710 a mass trial of witches took place in this building. Eight young women, including five named Janet, were sentenced to a year in jail, plus four sessions in the public stocks during which one poor witch had an eye knocked out. Among their crimes was persecuting a clergyman's widow by occult means.

Literary associations with Carrickfergus are numerous. The father of William Congreve, the Restoration dramatist, was a soldier and the boy came to live in the castle in 1678. He was 8 years old and Carrickfergus was a busy port 'filled with English sailors, rough and jovial fellows'. He put one of them, Sailor Ben, into *Love for Love* (1695). Jonathan Swift's first living was at nearby Kilroot where he wrote *Tale of a Tub* between 1694 and 1696. Though born in Belfast, 'between the mountain and the gantries' as he put it, the poet Louis MacNeice (1907-63) spent his boyhood here. His father was rector of St Nicholas' and the family lived in North Road at the rectory (demolished 1986, plaque at entrance). The town's most famous international connection is with Andrew Jackson, the American 'People's President' (1829-37), born in South Carolina in 1767. His Scotch-Irish parents emigrated from Carrickfergus in 1765. The Andrew Jackson Centre, a reconstruction of an eighteenth-century thatched cottage containing a little museum, stands near the site of their original home. Memorabilia of the US Rangers, the American equivalent of the Commandos, have also found a home in the centre. The first battalion of the Rangers, the US Army's most decorated unit, was raised in Carrickfergus in 1942. The juxtaposition is not inappropriate. Jackson was a soldier before he was a president. He was idolised by the American people for his victory over the British at New Orleans in 1815 and for seizing Florida from Spain in 1818. Scholars may argue about his spots and blemishes but certainly Jackson was the embodiment of the self-made man ideal. Committed to democracy and equality, he was the most dynamic force in American politics in the first half of the nineteenth century.

Whitehead, a small resort with a pebbly beach and long promenade, is the base of the Railway Preservation Society of Ireland. The *Portrush Flyer*, a famous steam express, puffs out of the excursion station at holiday times. The port of **Larne** is best viewed from a distance. To join a scenic road just outside Carrickfergus, turn left off the A2 opposite the chimney of Kilroot power station (Beltoy Road). At the top turn left (sharp turn) to go up to Glenoe waterfalls but turn right, along the old Carrickfergus road, for a bird's-eye view of shapely Larne Lough with a lighthouse on the tip of the peninsula. The three chimneys of Ballylumford power station, necklace-like Swan Island further up the lough, and the dark shape of Olderfleet Castle, a sixteenth-century tower house near a cluttered boatyard, are prominent features. A small ferry boat dashes across to Ballylumford on Islandmagee every hour or so, and the hoots of the roll-on roll-off ferries float up the ridge. The port handles over half-a-million vehicles a year on the short sea crossing to Scotland.

Islandmagee is not an island but a 7-mile-long (11km) peninsula. Even so, it has a distinctive separate feeling about it. Four of the wicked witches jailed in 1711 were from Islandmagee. On the east side, wild basalt cliffs called the Gobbins were the scene of a gruesome incident in 1641 when soldiers from the Carrickfergus garrison threw the inhabitants into the sea. The sea-level path cut in the face of the rock is dangerous in places. To reach the peninsula turn left off the A2 going back towards Belfast, and drive up the west side along the B90. There is not much traffic, lots of churches, signposts pointing to still more inland, some (spotless) public toilets, and good places for picnics or camping. The church at Kilcoan is of ancient foundation. They say St Patrick must have come to Kilcoan and blessed the ferryman since there is no record of any ferryman having drowned in fifteen centuries. Look out on the left for the Ballylumford dolmen, sitting for the past 4,000 years overlooking Larne Lough and now

Cave Hill, where Wolfe Tone plotted rebellion in 1795,
has a superb view over Belfast

incorporated into the front garden of No. 91 Ballylumford Road. The front door of the house is so close to the monument that the occupants find it more convenient to use a side entrance. The view across the lough is filled by container ships and ferries that dwarf the harbour buildings and a modern folly that looks like an Irish round tower. Fuel, groceries and fishing tackle are sold above the sandy beaches at Brown's Bay and other beauty spots. The outline of steep sharp Ailsa Craig is visible from Brown's Bay. The coast here is hilly, with windswept palm trees towards Muck Island, and a fine coastguard watch house on a promontory down the switchback road to Portmuck harbour.

The old county town of **Antrim** has trebled in population over the past 15 years and you need to plan your visit to avoid its housing estates and shopping centres. A tenth-century round tower stands in Steeple Park, a mile (2km) from the centre, on the site of an important sixth-century monastery called *Aentrobh*, abandoned in 1147. Though over 90ft (27m) high, it is rather obscured in summer by even taller trees. Over the lintel is an unusual cross-carved stone. At the base lies a giant bullaun with two holes. A sentry monk on watch at the high windows could sound his handbell if strangers approached, and a rope ladder to the raised doorway, 7ft (2m) off the ground, could be pulled up and the door slammed shut. It is one of the finest intact round towers in Ireland.

One of several famous battles fought around Antrim was in 1798 when royal forces fought off and defeated 3,500 United Irishmen. The plantation castle (1662) built by Sir John Clotworthy (Lord Massereene) was burnt down in 1922, leaving only a tall black basalt tower which has been carefully conserved, prominent seen from the road. Opposite the courthouse (1726) in Market Square, the estate's Tudor-style gateway leads to magnificent gardens. Now a public park, they were first laid out at the end of the seventeenth and restored in the nineteenth century. Features include long ornamental fishponds flanked by high hedges, straight avenues converging on a round pool, a Norman mound with a hedged spiral path to the top, memorial urns to departed Massereenes, inscribed stones to favour-ite dogs and horses, and a stone bridge over the Sixmilewater river. The stables and coach house are now used as an arts centre (Clotworthy House) with an open-air theatre in the yard.

An atmospheric corner of the town is Pogue's Entry, a tiny cobbled cul-de-sac off Church Street with an eighteenth-century cottage, birthplace of Alexander Irvine (1863-1941), a newspaper boy who became a missionary in the New York Bowery and is remembered as the author of *My Lady of the Chimney Corner*, a shamelessly sentimental tale about his parents. He and they are buried in the churchyard of All Saints parish church which contains some Renaissance stained glass and many Massereene monuments. The steeple was erected in 1816 though the church dates from 1596. In summer boats leave from Sixmilewater marina for cruises on Lough Neagh.

Lough Neagh: Ulster's Inland Sea

The level of this inland sea, some 150 square miles (389sq km) of fresh water, was lowered in 1846 and twice since, the last time in 1959, but drainage round the edge is still too marshy for arable farming. Together with little Lough Beg, **Lough Neagh** is a wetland of international significance, designated a Ramsar site. In winter there are enormous rafts of ducks and swans, as many as 100,000 birds. Flowering rushes and Irish Lady's Tresses, a delicate white orchid, flourish on the shores of Lough Beg. Passing through this small shallow lake, your eye is drawn to a solitary tower on Church Island. Now slightly lopsided, it was built in 1788 by Bishop Hervey of Derry to enliven the landscape.

Lough Neagh is fished commercially for freshwater herring (pollan), and a huge salmon-trout called dollaghan is caught around Washing Bay but its biggest harvest by far is eels. The elvers swim up the Bann from the Atlantic but an estimated 20 million lucky ones are saved the trouble. They are trapped at Coleraine and brought here by tanker to grow to maturity. In spring and early summer there can be as many as 200 boats line-fishing for eels. Chironomid midges, which have a spectacular emergence at certain times in spring and summer, can be a nuisance on windless days. Though harmless they descend in clouds and get into everything. The bang of the Lough Neagh 'water guns', mysterious daytime booming sounds that are sometimes muffled but sometimes loud enough to frighten feeding waterfowl into the air, can be heard when the atmospherics are right.

At the south end of Lough Neagh a large colony of great-crested grebe nest in the reeds at Oxford Island and there is a heronry on Raughlan peninsula. To get a boat to explore this southern shore or to get to Coney Island where there is an ancient keep and holy well, ask at the Lough Neagh Discovery Centre, Oxford Island.

Pieces of petrified wood, altered by silica salts, are sometimes washed up on the shore. Belfast street hawkers used to sell them as knife sharpeners with the cry

'Lough Neagh hones! Lough Neagh hones!
'You put them in sticks, and you take them out stones!'

The historic manor house of Castle Upton at **Templepatrick** is not open to the public but there is access to the estate's splendid Robert Adam stable block of 1789. The triumphal arch of the adjacent Templeton Mausoleum, which is looked after by the National Trust and is always accessible directly from the A57, was also built to Adam's design but not completed. John Knox's grandson, Josias Welsh, who was chaplain at Castle Upton, is buried in this graveyard. The Trust has another property in Templepatrick — Patterson's Mill, a water-driven spade mill, now the only one left in Ireland.

Donegore Hill and its man-made medieval castle mound, a prominent feature of the landscape north of the M2, is reached from the motorway by taking exit 6 on to the A508, or exit 4 to the A57/A6 Templepatrick roundabout where Donegore is signposted. Now topped by a modern garden centre, the hill has been inhabited since the Stone Age. Some people think that when the kings of Ulster were defeated at Emain Macha (Navan Fort) in AD332, they retrenched around Donegore. Until about 1920 May Day in Donegore was celebrated with dancing round a maypole on the mound. There is a view of six counties from the top though you need a local person to point them out to you! To climb it the best approach is via a small gate near the church and up a made-up path. In 1798 Henry Joy McCracken tried to rally his men on the hill after the retreat from Antrim and waited for reinforcements which never came. The church, St John's, dates from 1659. To the right of the path is the grave of the poet and antiquarian Sir Samuel Ferguson (1810-86) though the inscription makes no mention of his literary achievements. Admired by Yeats, he was an important figure in the Irish literary revival. The subject of his translations and long poems often derived from Gaelic legend but he is remembered mostly for his ballads and songs like 'the lark in the clear air'. He got his knighthood for reorganising the public records of Ireland. A curious stone vault with a turfed roof in the graveyard was built in the early 1800s as a watch-keeper's house in response to the ghoulish trade of resurrectionists, body snatchers. Corpses had to be guarded until they passed the sell-by date and so of no use for dissection.

Interesting small settlements on the east shore of Lough Neagh include **Crumlin** village, where an eighteenth-century walled garden provides an sanctuary for sick and injured birds and a natural habitat for many small native species. **Glenavy** village which has a lovely three-arch bridge spanning the river beside St Aidan's parish church. The village war memorial commemorates all the Glenavy men who fought in the two world wars (and the Falklands War), carefully listing the dead and all the survivors too. The birthplace (1839) of John Ballance, a pioneer of the welfare state and prime minister of New Zealand in the 1890s, is at Ballypitmave townland 2 miles (3km) along the A30. A display of Maori objects is among exhibits in the house. His mother's family (MacNeice) owned long thin Ram's Island on Lough Neagh. Sunderland and Catalina flying boats used the island during World War II. A small wartime centre at Langford Lodge recalls the days 50 years ago when this was the main USAAF repair base in Europe. A private airfield nearby is used for testing Martin Baker ejector seats for aircraft.

South-west of Glenavy are the two Ballinderrys, a couple of miles apart on a quiet little river of the same name. **Lower Ballinderry** has a Moravian church and manse under one roof, church at one end, manse (with chimneys) at the other. At **Upper Ballinderry** is a barn church with bull's-eye glass in the windows, built in 1666 for Jeremy Taylor, a famous bishop of Down and Connor who was one of the great prose writers of the seventeenth century. His ancestor, Dr Rowland Taylor, was burnt at the stake by Queen Mary. Theological tussles with local Presbyterians apparently made Taylor's bishopric 'a place of torment'. He died, aged 54, a year before the Ballinderry church was consecrated and is buried in Dromore cathedral. Antiques are sold from a large rambling warehouse at Upper Ballinderry, an Aladdin's cave of furniture, objets d'art and baskets, including a few locally made osier baskets.

On the Lagan upstream from Belfast, **Lisburn** is a modern commercial and industrial town, with a sloping triangular market square and some good shops. Few buildings survived a devastating fire in 1707. One that did was the assembly rooms, now a museum with an adjoining linen exhibition centre which occupies the top half of the market square. Below it is a bronze statue of General John Nicholson with a pistol in one hand and a sword in the other. He was killed in the attack on Delhi during the Indian Mutiny (1857).

The exhibition centre traces the development of the Irish linen industry. Lisburn was at the centre of the Linen Triangle (Belfast-Armagh-Dungannon), source of half Ulster's whole linen output in the eighteenth and nineteenth centuries. Yarn from all over Ireland was brought to the bleach greens along the banks of the Lagan, a river with a good head of water in summer (necessary for the bleaching process) and with access to export markets via Belfast port. The first bleach green in Ulster was established before 1626 at Lambeg 1 mile (2km) downstream, an attractive hamlet that gave its name to the big drums which came to Ireland from Holland with the army of William of Orange.

Louis Crommelin, appointed linen overseer of Ireland by William, also came from Holland. He found Lisburn an ideal headquarters. After the revocation of the Edict of Nantes in 1685, Huguenot families from Holland and France came to Ulster at Crommelin's invitation. Sewing thread, made by twisting together two or more strands of yarn, is still made in the Barbour Campbell Threads factory at Hilden where John Barbour set up Ulster's first hand-twisting mill in 1784. By 1840 the firm employed 5,000 people and although only about 10 per cent of that number work there today, it is still the largest employer in the borough.

Louis Crommelin and other Huguenots who helped develop the industry are buried at Christ Church cathedral, Lisburn. Built in 1623 and raised to cathedral status in 1662, it is only the size of a parish church. The slender octagonal spire was added to the tower in 1804. The interior contains some significant tablets and monuments. How squeezed it all is! The cathedral is almost invisible from the street and the grave of Crommelin, who brought such prosperity to the town, is outside, squashed into a churchyard no bigger than a pocket handkerchief.

The village of **Hillsborough** 10 miles (16km) south of Belfast, is something of a showpiece. Many of the small terraced houses along the steep main street are craft and antique shops. Across the square with its charming market house (about 1760) and Georgian townhouses, the mansion visible through a pair of beautiful wrought-iron gates is Hillsborough Castle, formerly the residence of the governor of Northern Ireland, now used for visiting VIPs and occasional royal garden parties. The Anglo-Irish Agreement was announced here by the two governments in 1985. Signs like that on the front of Belfast City Hall — 'Belfast says no' (to the Agreement) — were erected on many town halls in the province at about that time. Some are still there. The gates and screen (1745) at Hillsborough came from Richhill Castle in County Armagh in 1936. On the other side of the square, beyond an oval lawn, **Hillsborough Fort** was built by Colonel Arthur Hill in 1650 to command the road from Dublin to Carrickfergus. The first Hill arrived in Ireland in the army of the Earl of Essex sent by Elizabeth I to subdue the O'Neills. He founded one of Ireland's most powerful plantation families. According to a stone in the gateway, William of Orange stayed there for 4 days en route to the Boyne in June 1690.

Sir Hamilton Harty, called the 'Irish Toscanini' (1879-1941), was born in Ballynahinch Street and is buried in the parish church graveyard. His father was church organist for 40 years. Side streets

*The castle at Carrickfergus was built by the Normans to guard
the approach to Belfast Lough*

to explore include Arthur Street with its terraces of 1½-storey slate-roofed houses in the cottage orné style (about 1850). A lane behind the Shambles art gallery leads to an artificial lake. A prominent feature of the east and south approaches to Hillsborough is a 5-mile (8km) wall surrounding this lake and its adjoining forest. Built in 1841 by the third marquis of Downshire, the wall has since acquired a utilitarian concrete capping in parts. On a hill overlooking the town, an immense Doric column and statue of the marquis appears to sprout from a cluster of bungalows. On the base is the inscription 'Per deum et ferrum obtinuit'.

The Ards Peninsula

When St Patrick came to Ireland in AD432 strong currents swept his boat through the tidal narrows of Strangford Lough and he landed on the Down mainland.

The **Ards Peninsula** stretches 23 miles (37km) from Bangor to Ballyquintin Point and varies in width from 3 to 5 miles (5-8km). Crossing west to east at the narrowest place, from Grey Abbey to the breezy beach at Ballywalter, you see how effectively the peninsula shelters the lough. The people in the fishing villages along the seashore, and in farms among the low hills, are mostly of Scottish descent. The accession of James VI of Scotland to the English throne coincided with the first phase of the plantation of Ulster, and some of his countrymen were quick off the mark to take advantage. Elizabeth I had previously granted land patents on the Ards to Sir Thomas Smith, an Englishman, but he seems to have been tricked out of them. In 1605 the king divided a big chunk of north Down into three lots — one stayed with the original landowner, Con O'Neill of Clandeboye, and two entrepreneurial Scotsmen, Hugh Montgomery and James Hamilton, got one lot each. The Scottish adventurers quickly divested Con of his share, and soon control of 'the whole Great Ardes' was split between Montgomery, later Viscount Ards, and Hamilton, created Lord Clandeboye in 1622, who owned the land on the west side of the lough down to Killyleagh.

Hamilton brought men from Ayrshire to build the town of **Bangor** where St Comgall had founded a famous missionary abbey in 558. Today Bangor is a commuter town efficiently linked by road and rail to Belfast 12 miles (19km) away. Its Scottish character has been diluted and it hardly seems part of the Ards. Bangor Abbey parish church, which was altered in 1960, has kept its fifteenth-century tower and octagonal spire dated 1693. Memorials inside include a marble statue and cameo-busts of John Hamilton (died 1693) and his wife, Sophia Mordaunt, made in 1760 by Scheemakers.

Nothing remains of Comgall's abbey, nor of two twelfth-century monasteries, except possibly a fragment of wall near the church and the early sundial outside Bangor Castle. The sixth-century foundation was very influential. Comgall's pupil, Columbanus (AD543-AD615) who founded Luxeuil in France and Bobbio in Italy, had gone from *Banchor* (White Choir) to evangelise the tribes of central Europe; another missionary monk, St Gall, established the foundation of St Gallen, Switzerland. The 'Bangor Antiphonary', compiled at Bangor in the AD680s is preserved in the Ambrosian Library, Milan.

Most other buildings of any substance are Victorian — like Bangor Castle which has an enjoyable heritage centre, with recordings of panpipes and lyre music, a picture of St Columbanus and St Gall crossing Lake Constance in Germany (from an illustration of 1452). A jolly clock tower with four faces on the front was put up during World War I and paid for by Mr McKee, the borough's rates collector. Across the road behind a large coastguard building, tourist information is dispensed from a ruined tower house with Scottish corbelling, built as a customs house in 1637. Redevelopment has made a hash of the seafront at Bangor. Somewhere beyond the carparks and the clutter is the sea.

The train from Belfast to Bangor stops here and there to deposit commuters in the evening, at **Holywood** for instance. Holywood has high house prices and good delicatessens. The clock tower of its priory, dating from the thirteenth century, is floodlit at night. An abbey founded in woods (Sanctus Boscus) here in AD620 by St Laiseran was connected with Bangor Abbey. A Franciscan monastery was established in the sixteenth century but it did not last long. Together with Bangor Abbey, Grey Abbey and Movilla at Newtownards, it was burned in 1572 by Sir Brian O'Neill to prevent English troops from garrisoning them. At the bottom of Church Street is a 70ft (21m) mast with a weathervane at the top which, although it does not look like one, is known locally as 'the maypole'. Similar masts have stood here at least since a Dutch ship went aground nearby on the eve of May Day in 1700. In High Street, a bronze statue of a boy playing an accordion, 'Johnny the Jig', is by Rosamund Praeger (1867-1954). A Gothic mansion out on the main road (A2) used to be the bishop of Down's palace. It is now a hotel (Culloden).

Some trains stop at Cultra Halt for the **Ulster Folk and Transport Museum**. It has been growing bigger and better over the past 30 years and deserves an extended visit. Many of the buildings dotted around the park have been removed stone by stone from the Ulster countryside and re-erected in a setting as close as possible to the original landscape. There are two main areas in the folk section: a countryside area and a large village. The rural part has isolated farmhouses and rural industrial buildings, including a flax mill brought from Tyrone, a blacksmith's forge from Fermanagh, and a County Down bleach green watch tower — a conical stone hut where the watchman sat with his musket, guarding linen laid out to bleach in the sun. The village has whole urban terraces, a school, a court-house, a rectory and a church — all looking as if they have always been there. The houses from Tea Lane off Sandy Row in Belfast represent the oldest surviving terrace housing in the city. They were built in the 1820s. The parish church stood in Kilmore, County Down, from 1792 until it was dismantled and reassembled here in 1976. You can picnic anywhere in the open-air part, or go to the tea room in Cultra Manor, one building that started life in the right place.

The Irish Railway Collection is excellently presented in the transport section, connected by a road bridge across the Belfast-Bangor road. Among the exhibits is a full-scale model of the monoplane that Harry Ferguson flew across his father's farm near Hillsborough in 1909. Ferguson is more famous for his tractors but he was also the first man in Ireland to fly.

The part-thatched Old Inn at **Crawfordsburn**, there since 1614, was the main hostelry on an ancient track from Holywood to Bangor Abbey. The sandy beach here, and the one at Helen's Bay, are part of Crawfordsburn country park where a glen walk under a five-arch railway viaduct (carrying the Belfast train) leads up to a waterfall.

Inland, the demesne of **Clandeboye**, seat of the late, last marquis of Dufferin and Ava, is the venue for a field sports fair in June. At the far end of the estate on a hilltop, three-storey **Helen's Tower** (about 1858) was erected in honour of Helen, Lady Dufferin, composer of the popular ballad *The Irish Emigrant*. She was Sheridan's grand-daughter. In 1915 and 1916 the 36th (Ulster) Division was camped at Clandeboye and drilled in sight of this tower. A sad replica, called the Ulster Memorial Tower, was later erected on the Somme battle-field at Thiepval where 6,000 Ulstermen were killed or injured in July 1916. A reconstruction of features of the battlefield, including trenches, has recently been opened. *Helen's Tower*, a biography of the first marquis by his nephew, Harold Nicolson, is one of the tower's numerous literary connections. Nicolson (1886-1968) belonged to the Bloomsbury Group.

On a hill 3 miles (5km) across the valley, and twice as tall as Helen's Tower, **Scrabo Tower** was built at about the same time in memory of the third marquis of Londonderry. It has 122 steps up to a good view of Strangford Lough and beyond (open in summer).

Newtownards, a manufacturing and market garden town with a lively commercial radio station (Downtown), a bit inland from the head of the lough, dates from the thirteenth century when a Dominican priory was founded by Walter de Burgh. The nave of his church survives in Court Square within later ruins which include a seventeenth-century square tower. The family vault of the Londonderrys, successors to the Montgomerys as landlords of Newtownards, is in a corner. The market cross at the end of High Street was smashed in 1653 but repaired soon after, though left somewhat shorter. It was practical as well as decorative. The small chamber inside was useful for locking up rowdies. The handsome market house (1765), now the town hall, has an outsize market square (Conway Square) with a Saturday market. A harvest fair (September) has been going strong since about 1613. Many of Belfast's vegetables come from around Newtownards and the horticultural firm of Dickson's (established in 1836) is famous for its roses. The mayor's chain of office is fashioned from twenty-six gold medals won by the Dickson nurseries.

The name of Comber is synonymous with early potatoes, mollycoddled in the rich soil around here. In a mild spring they are in the shops in April. A monument in the middle of the town commemorates a swashbuckling soldier, Sir Robert Rollo Gillespie. He was a native of Comber. Killed in action in Nepal, he died enunciating the words inscribed on the column: 'One last shot for the honour of Down.'

At **Groomsport**, where Marshal Schomberg landed with 10,000 Williamite soldiers in 1689, the harbour has a sandy beach on either side. Two eighteenth-century cottages on Cockle Row are used as an art gallery. You can buy the paintings propped along the wall outside. Excursion boats go to the Copeland islands in summer. Proximity to Bangor, 3 miles (5km) west, may account for the modern bungalow developments, and caravan sites. Some brightly painted wooden prefabs with posh names at Fort Hill are holiday homes.

At a time when the only life insurance available on the Irish Sea crossing was said to be 'a bottle of claret to put the want of insurance out of your head', the shortest route — the 21 miles (34km) from Portpatrick to Donaghadee — was the most popular. Up until the nineteenth century **Donaghadee** offered the only safe refuge from the treacherous reefs on this coast. In the expectation that the town would remain the mail packet station for Scotland, the harbour was greatly enlarged in 1820 but the service was switched to the Stranraer-Larne route in 1849. Local fishermen kept an unofficial ferry service going long afterwards. On a calm day you could get yourself rowed across to Scotland. At low tide, dulse-gatherers

Whitehead, last town before Islandmagee, on the east Antrim coast

armed with small scythes go out in boats to cut at the purply fronds of this edible seaweed. It is léft lying on the slope at the back of the harbour, shrinking and drying in the sun. Fresh dulse turns green when fried in bacon fat. Mostly it is dried and sold in little paper bags for eating raw, though sales are said to have dropped off because of worries about pollution from Sellafield nuclear power station across the water.

Donaghadee lighthouse is the work of Sir John Rennie and David Logan, of Eddystone fame. It had an identical twin, the Portpatrick lighthouse. Donaghadee people on long-haul holidays blink when they see the lighthouse in Colombo, Sri Lanka. It is Portpatrick lighthouse, dismantled and reassembled.

Famous visitors landing here from Portpatrick were legion. James Boswell came in 1769, Keats came in 1818 to walk to the Giant's Causeway but it was too far. Daniel Defoe was acquainted with the town's hospitality, and so was Franz Liszt, who had a piano in his baggage, and was stuck here for 3 days in bad weather. The elderly Wordsworth made his cautious way back home via Donaghadee after a grand tour of Ireland in 1829. Grace Neill's Inn in High Street, now a pub, has been in business since 1611. A persistent claim on behalf of the old inn is that Peter the Great stayed there during his tour of Western Europe (1697-98) to learn shipbuilding and other technical matters. It is a story Brendan Behan would have heard during his stay in the town. After World War II, the Commissioners for Irish Lights gave Behan the job of painting Donaghadee lighthouse.

Biggest of the three **Copeland** islands to the north-east is, appropriately, Big Isle. Beyond it is **Cross**, or Lighthouse Island where there was once a rogue lighthouse — a beacon that burned 1½ tons of coal a night. It was suspected of actually contributing to some of the many wrecks in these waters. The present lighthouse is on Mew, the outermost island. Cross Island is now an RSPB bird observatory visitable with National Trust permission. Garden herbs growing there are thought to have been part of a kitchen garden established by monks from Bangor Abbey. On Big Isle in the eighteenth century the thriving fishing and farming community of 'god-fearing Presbyterians' rowed across every Sunday to attend church in Donaghadee. By the 1860s the population was down to forty but they had a church and a schoolroom. The new teacher had to sleep in the schoolroom until people got to know him. Then he lodged with each family in turn, a month at a time. The last islanders moved to Donaghadee in the 1940s. Sheep graze Big Isle now, narcissus, roses and fuchsia grow wild and the empty houses are used by weekenders. There are swimming races across the one-mile (2km) strait, and excursion boats in summer from several places on the coast.

Windmill stumps are a familiar sight in County Down, especially around the Ards. There used to be over 100 windmills in the county. The tower-type cornmill at **Ballycopeland**, built in about 1790, stands on a drumlin a mile (2km) inland from **Millisle**, an unpretentious fish-and-chips resort with acres of caravan sites. Ballycopeland windmill has a movable cap turned by an automatic fantail so that the sails always face into the wind. It was in use up until 1915 and is said to be in working order, though visitors mostly have to be content with an electrically operated model in the miller's house which has been well restored.

South from Millisle the A2 runs along the coast through a succession of shore villages. At Cloghy it slants inland towards Portaferry. To visit **Kearney**, a perfect little nineteenth-century fishing village in National Trust care, stay with the coast by leaving the A2 at Cloghy. Though distances here are small, there are inconveniently few places of refreshment on the Ards, so plan your journey accordingly. After Kearney the road takes you quickly to Portaferry.

North-west of **Ballywalter** village are the fragmentary ruins of medieval **Templefinn** (White Church) parish church. Three Norman grave slabs lie at the east gable. Ballywalter Park is a magnificent Italianate palazzo by Lanyon built in the 1840s for Andrew Mulholland, a Belfast textile tycoon. It has an open day only very occasionally. **Burr Point** at **Ballyhalbert** is the most easterly place in Ireland, though perhaps Burial Island offshore where seals bask on the reefs, ought to count as being even more easterly!

Most evenings at **Portavogie** there is a fish auction on the quay. The village has a substantial fishing fleet, a modern harbour and boat-building yards. Giant prawns, already peeled, are sold in the village. There is intensive farming round here and at harvest time everyone has to pitch in. The secondary school closes while the children help get in the potato crop.

At the north end of pebbly Cloghy Bay, near the golf course, **Kirkistown Castle** is a tower house, one of the fortified private homes built from the fifteenth to the early sevententh century by local landlords, often as a protection from each other. This one was built by Roland Savage in 1622 and has the remains of a bawn round it. The Savage family were the Norman landlords of the 'Little Ardes' and they built many of these small castles. **Portaferry Castle** is an earlier one of theirs, erected in 1500.

Around Strangford Lough

Portaferry has a beautiful site on the east side of the entrance to **Strangford Lough**. The long low waterfront is best seen from the car ferry which takes you crabwise across the narrows to **Strangford** village in a few minutes. The Vikings called the lough 'violent fjord' — Strang-ford. Four hundred million tons of water rush through the gap twice a day. It is a pity the crossing is so short since the views up and down are worth savouring. Before the famines of the 1840s Portaferry was a busy coastal town with lively industries. Now it is a centre for yachting and sea angling — deep sea fishing outside the narrows and inshore fishing in the lough. Underwater photography, diving, and wreck fishing for big conger eels and wrasse are popular. The lough is a national nature reserve and a wetland of international importance, supporting up to 100,000 wildfowl and waders, with great skeins of pale-bellied brent geese arriving in autumn. Queen's University, Belfast, has had a marine biology station here for the last 50 years, occupying two Georgian houses opposite the ferry slipway. A large marine aquarium attracts many visitors. There is an all-round view of the lough and the land from the top of Windmill Hill, east of the town centre. Several small castles on the far shore are prominent landmarks.

The drumlins, small rounded hills that cover north Down, extend into the lough. Dozens of drowned drumlins pop up here and there, mostly near the shore. These islands give Strangford the appearance of a freshwater lake, especially at the sheltered north end. The word, from *druim* meaning 'ridge', was coined in 1833 to describe 'low ridges of superficial debris in the North of Ireland'. There are thousands of these streamlined hillocks across north-central Ireland, from Down to Sligo, with more north of Lough Neagh, and in Donegal, east Mayo and east Clare, extending seawards into Clew Bay and Bantry Bay.

Of the four Cistercian monasteries in medieval County Down, three were built round Strangford — Grey Abbey, Inch Abbey and Comber. A stone in the parish church is all that is left of Comber's abbey but Inch (1180) and Grey Abbey (1193) have substantial remains. All three foundations had filial connections with England, and for nearly 400 years the monks carried corn, wheat, flour, fish and salt in their sixty-oared galleys to the beleaguered English abbeys in Cumbria and Lancashire.

Turning north up the sheltered loughside road, pause a while at **Kircubbin,** a boating and fishing village where you can gather clean mussels and cockles on the shore. There are usually a couple of fishermen digging for lugworm. **Grey Abbey** ruins are further up the lough, on the edge of Greyabbey village. Founded by Affreca, daughter of the king of Man and wife of John de Courcy, Grey Abbey was a daughter house of Holm Cultram in Cumbria. Affreca brought her monks from England, the usual Norman practice. The Irish Church's links with clan chiefs made it untrustworthy. The abbey was burned in 1572 but the Montgomerys repaired the church and used it (interesting memorials) until they built another nearby in 1778 (above the carpark). The ruins of the abbey, in sheltered grounds with lawns and a physick garden, have triple lancet windows in the chancel and a west door, looking much like one from a twelfth-century English cathedral.

The National Trust property, **Mount Stewart**, on this same scenic loughside road (A20), is best known for its gardens, ranked in the Trust's top six UK gardens, and created by Edith, Lady Londonderry, from 1921. It includes almost every style of gardening, and some of the inspiration of Gertrude Jekyll. The stone figures of dodos, dinosaurs, griffins, platypuses and other mythological creatures on the terraces, were made for the amusement of Lady Londonderry's children. An Irish harp is among the garden's imaginative topiary art. Special gardens include a Spanish garden, Italian garden, sunken garden, and a paved shamrock garden surrounding a 'Red Hand' of Ulster (red-leaved plants). An octagonal garden building, the Temple of the Winds, was designed by 'Athenian' Stuart (1780).

More historically interesting, Mount Stewart was the Irish home of Robert Stewart, Lord Castlereagh (1769-1822), foreign secretary of England during the Napoleonic Wars. Many treasures in the house, like the painting of the racehorse Hambletonian by George Stubbs, were accumulated later but you can see some of Castlereagh's personal possessions, portraits of his political contemporaries, and objects connected with the great happenings in Europe during his brilliant career. These include the twenty-two original Empire chairs used by the plenipotentiaries at the Congress of Vienna (1814-15) which, after the defeat of Napoleon, established the 'balance of power' principle in international politics. They were brought from Vienna by the English ambassador, Castlereagh's half-brother, Charles.

Though Presbyterian, Castlereagh was educated under the auspices of the established church, at the Royal School, Armagh, a prudent choice since dissenters were still barred from military and civil office. He was a model landlord. He endowed schools, built a chapel, houses for his tenants, and a pier in front of the house for local fishing boats. However, he had an enigmatic and chilly personality and, despite his good works, hardly anyone seems to have liked him. As a politician, and an Irishman, who helped destroy the Irish parliament (the Grattan Parliament) and who brought about the Act of Union (1800) he made himself one of the most disliked men in Irish history. Eighteen months after succeeding his father as second marquis of Londonderry he committed suicide after a minor sexual indiscretion, a 'back to basics' victim.

North-east of Mount Stewart, in the churchyard at **Carrowdore**, is the grave of the poet Louis MacNeice (1907-63). The village main street is closed off in September for a motorcycle race. The Northern Irish have a penchant for racing on their public roads. Apart from major occasions, like the Circuit of Ireland car rally, Ulster Grand Prix motorcycle race and other big events, there are half-a-dozen small motorcycle races like the Carrowdore one. The road surfaces in the host towns are said to be especially well maintained.

The west shore of Strangford, south of Comber, is a mass of small islands, submerged drumlins. The primitive monastic site of **Nendrum** is on **Mahee Island** at the end of a twisting causeway linking several islands. St Mochaoi was its fifth-century founder-abbot. Three concentric stone walls (cashels) on top of the hill were excavated and restored in the 1920s. Finds from the digs, now in the Ulster Museum, Belfast, give a glimpse of life in a tenth-century Irish monastery. The inner wall contains a ruined church with a twelfth-century chancel built by Benedictine monks, brought from Cumbria by John de Courcy. Leave your car at Nendrum carpark and walk back along the road to inspect Captain Brown's Castle, a fifteenth-century tower house. The water level has changed since the days when the owners kept their boat locked up in a bay on the ground floor.

South of here, on **Sketrick Island**, the scanty ruins of a much bigger tower house also has a secure boat bay. Good reasons for going to Sketrick include the pub-restaurant behind the castle, and the Hen Island race, a quaint competition in October when a fleet of oil drums, crates and home-made rafts are paddled between Sketrick and tiny Hen Island.

Going south on the A22 to **Killyleagh** a skyline of romantic turrets comes into view just before the village. Killyleagh Castle, home of the Hamilton family since the plantation, acquired its fairytale silhouette in the 1850s when the turrets were added, but it is mostly the same castle that the second earl of Clanbrassil rebuilt in 1666. In a lurid intrigue over ownership, involving a bad wife and a burnt will, the earl was poisoned in 1675. One of the towers is Norman. The castle has a massive fortified outer wall (bawn) and a Victorian gatehouse. You can stay in it, self-catering. A stone at the gatehouse commemorates Killyleagh's most famous son, Sir Hans Sloane (1660-1753), physician to George II and founder of both the British Museum and Kew Gardens.

Sloane was a native of Killyleagh and, encouraged by the soon-to-be-poisoned earl, educated himself in the castle library. His collection of 50,000 books, 3,560 manuscripts and cabinet of curiosities was the nucleus of the British Museum. Sloane settled in Chelsea in 1712. He gave his name to a Circle Line station on the London Underground as well as to Sloane Square and Hans Place.

The Lecale region between Strangford and Dundrum Bay is often called St Patrick's Country. The A25 from Strangford village to Downpatrick is close to a number of sites connected with the saint. However, there are other places of interest on the route. The tower house that overlooks the small double harbour and ferry landing in Strangford shared with Portaferry Castle the task of policing traffic on the lough. South of the village is an early 'gatehouse' tower house, **Kilclief Castle**, which was the summer home of John Cely, bishop of Down from 1413 until he was sacked in 1443 for living adulterously in the castle with one Lettice Savage, a married woman. No such colourful story attaches to three other tower houses nearby — Walshestown (private), Audley's, and Old Castle Ward standing in the farmyard on the National Trust estate of Castle Ward. There are more tower houses down the coast at Ardglass.

The designer of **Castle Ward** is unknown. Whoever he was, he did as he was told. The house was built after 1762 by Bernard Ward, later the first Lord Bangor, and his wife Anne, daughter of Lord Darnley. He favoured the Palladian style of architecture, Lady Anne preferred the Strawberry Hill gothic which was fashionable at the time. The result is a compromise. The entrance front is in the classical idiom, with a pillared pedimented portico, and the garden front facing Strangford Lough is gothic, with seven bays of pointed windows and urns on the battlements. Inside, each style keeps strictly to its own side of the house — the exception being the staircase, in the middle. Mr Ward got that and so it is classical. His rooms have Doric columns and restrained panelling, hers have quatrefoils, pointed doorways and extravagant plaster fan vaulting in the boudoir. The Wards continued not seeing eye to eye and later separated.

St Patrick was probably born in Scotland or Wales, the son of a

Roman centurion, and was taken to Ulster (Slemish) as a boy slave. He escaped and returned years later to preach the Gospel after studying with Martin of Tours in Gaul. The Slaney river where he is said to have landed in the fifth century is now a rivulet near the townland of Ringbane north of Saul in the district known as Lecale. The chieftain of Lecale at that time was Dichu who was apparently quickly converted and gave Patrick a barn (*sabhal* in Gaelic, pronounced 'saul') for holding services. In the 30 years up to AD461 when he died in the abbey at Saul, he preached in many parts of Ireland. Other bishops came to Ireland before St Patrick but he became the most important because he was a writer, and copies of his writings have survived. According to the eighth-century *Hymn of St Fiacc*, St Patrick received his last communion from St Tassach. The slight ruins of St Tassach's church, one of Ireland's earliest Christian buildings, are behind an isolated row of houses at Raholp.

At **Saul** itself, a Celtic revival Anglican church (with a round tower adjoining the chancel) on the site of a twelfth-century monastery is where St Patrick's abbey is thought to have been. In the churchyard is an early Christian mortuary house. Built in 1932 by the Church of Ireland to commemorate the fifteenth centenary of the saint's landfall, the church contains a thirteenth-century font basin and an informative permanent exhibition. The statue of St Patrick prominent on a hill across the valley, was designed by Francis Doyle-Jones for the Catholic church. It too was erected in 1932. A 10-minute walk up to the statue to examine the bronze panels round the base has the bonus of a fine view over Strangford's islands.

According to the precious *Book of Armagh* (AD802), now in Trinity College Library, Patrick is buried on the great hill at **Downpatrick**. The reputed grave is in the churchyard at Down cathedral beside a weeping elm tree. So much earth was scooped up from the grave and carried away that a granite monolith was put on the top in 1901 to protect it. Pilgrims strew daffodils on the stone on St Patrick's Day (17 March). John de Courcy claimed to have dug up the remains of Ireland's other two great saints, Columba (died Iona AD597) and Brigid (died Kildare AD523), and to have put them in St Patrick's grave.

Downpatrick takes its name from the dun (fort) where a sixth-century monastery, an Augustinian church, a Benedictine church and several versions of Down cathedral, were built — not to be confused with the other great earthworks called the Mound of Down on the edge of the Quoile marshes. The strong association with St Patrick brought many medieval religious orders to Downpatrick and the monasteries established here grew into the regional capital which, by extension, gave its name to County Down.

As was the norm in Ireland, the cathedral was pillaged, burnt and rebuilt on several occasions. An earthquake damaged it in 1245 and, in 1538, Lord Deputy Grey used it as stables — a sacrilege that counted towards his execution not long afterwards. The chancel was restored 1790-1818 and a tower added in 1829. The interior has undulating pews and a tall elegant Georgian organ case. The organ was given to the cathedral in 1802 by George III. Some of the carved capitals are fourteenth or fifteenth century, others are eighteenth-century restorations. The coats of arms of the county's leading families, post-plantation, are ranged round the upper walls. There is a slab in the porch to the governor of Lecale, Lord Edward Cromwell, and his grandson Oliver Cromwell. These Cromwells, ennobled to earls of Ardglass, were direct descendants of Thomas Cromwell, secretary to Henry VIII and chief architect of the Disso-lution of the Monasteries. The Lecale Cromwells were Royalists. Oliver Cromwell, Lord Protector of England, was distantly related to Secretary Cromwell.

Outside the cathedral a worn tenth-century high cross faces into English Street which runs down the hill to meet Scotch Street and Irish Street at the bottom. This enclosed and hilly town has some interesting Georgian buildings. In English Street the former gaol, built 1789-96, is now Down County Museum. The United Irishman Thomas Russell was hanged at the entrance. Russell had survived the 1798 uprising but was implicated in the Emmet conspiracy in 1803. The inscribed stone over his grave, in the churchyard of the parish church (1737) lower down the street, was put there by Mary Ann McCracken. The redbrick almshouse and school of the Southwell Charity opposite the museum was established in 1733 to support six old men and six old women and to educate ten poor boys and ten poor girls. Now used as flats for elderly people, the buildings are rather spoilt by the high level of the road, raised 15ft (5m) in 1790. Denvir's Hotel (1642) at the bottom of English Street had a sanctuary for debtors in the back yard and also in the recess at the front. Creditors had to wait outside. One Georgian building is now used as club rooms by the Downe Hunt, the oldest hunt club in the British Isles. The T-shaped non-subscribing Presbyterian church of 1710, Stream Street, has preserved its original pews and high pulpit intact.

North of Downpatrick the ruins of **Inch Abbey** overlook the Quoile river. The monastery here was plundered in 1001 by Vikings, destroyed again in 1149 and founded as a Cistercian abbey by John de Courcy in 1180. The whole of the foundations have been excavated. The most striking feature still standing is the tall triple east window. Traces of a hospital and a bakery, with a well, lie between the church and the river. A nature reserve known as **Quoile Pondage** runs along the river banks from Quoile Bridge to a flood-control barrage. Built in 1957 the barrage has artificially converted the saltwater estuary to a slow-moving freshwater lake which has resulted in some unusually rich colonisations by insects, fish and vegetation.

Taking the Ardglass road (B1) south from the city, past the enormous red-and-yellow hospital (1834), **Struell Wells** is signposted. The healing powers of the water in this rocky valley, where yellow whin grows in ridges, were first mentioned in written records of 1306. The wells are built along the course of an underground stream. The roofed men's bath house has an anteroom with seats and a sunken bath. The women's house, a bit smaller and minus its roof, is near a large sycamore tree. There is a drinking well and, in the centre of the enclosure, an eye well with a pyramid roof. Pilgrims carry the magic away in bottles.

West of Struell **Ballyhornan** village faces **Guns Island**, which you can get to at low tide. Rare seaside and lime-loving plants, including the bee orchid and eight other orchid species, grow at **Killard Point**, a National Nature Reserve north of the village. To the south, on the A2, the little Chapeltown Catholic church of 1791 has a life-size pre-Reformation statue of the Virgin and Child in a niche in the east gable.

Once the busiest seaport in Ulster, **Ardglass** has a deep double harbour and is still an important fishing port. What is most striking is the way castles pop up everywhere. Between the fifteenth and sixteenth century a ring of tower houses and fortified warehouses were built to protect the harbour. Jordan's Castle in the middle of the town was besieged in about 1600 but held out for 3 years. It was bought and repaired in 1911 by a Belfast solicitor and antiquarian, F.J Bigger, who filled it with country antiques and left it to the government in his will. It was Mr Bigger who put the granite slab over St Patrick's Grave. A curious row of fortified warehouses, now used as a golf clubhouse, has a tiny tower house (Cowd Castle) at the end. Other well kept fortified buildings include a circular battlemented tower on top of a small tower house (No. 7, Green Road) and two nineteenth-century castellated structures, Isabella's Tower and King's Castle.

Killough is a quiet backwater. The main street, unbroken façades of single and two-storey early Victorian houses, is lined with sycamore trees. The village has a pretty parish church on the wall of the silted-up harbour and almshouses built by Lanyon, Lynn & Lanyon in 1868. There is little work here since the brickworks closed. You could park past the windmill stump near the coastguard station, and take the rather rough coastal path to the lighthouse and a ruined tenth-century church at St John's Point. Or drive to the point, and then walk towards the beaches of Minerstown and Tyrella Strand along the edge of Dundrum Bay for ever-improving views of the Mournes.

Further Information
— Belfast & Environs —

Places to Visit in Belfast

The tourist information centre in North Street, Belfast is open 7 days a week all year and has access information for all places of interest is described in this chapter. The Centre, run by the Northern Ireland Tourist Board, provides the same level of information for all parts of Northern Ireland.
Guided walks of old Belfast town leave the centre at weekends in summer.
☎ (01232) 246609.
Belfast city 'hopper' tours: get on and off the bus where you like.
Long (3½ hours) tours of Belfast leave from Castle Place, near the main post office, at 2pm on Tuesday, Wednesday and Thursday. Both these bus services operate in summer only.
☎ (01232) 246485

Belfast Castle
The Cave Hill Heritage Centre on the upper floors is open 9am-9.30pm every day (until 5.30pm on Sunday).
☎ (01232) 776925

Belfast City Hall
Tour every Wednesday at 10.30am.
To book ☎ (01232) 320202

Belfast Harbour Office
Access at present is limited. Telephone or write for information.
Harbour Commissioners, Harbour Office, Corporation Street, Belfast 1
☎ (01232) 234422

Belfast Zoo
Open: every day 10am-5pm. In winter closes at 3.30pm (2.30pm on Friday).
☎ (01232) 776277

Sinclair Seamen's Church
Corporation Square.
Open on Sunday at service times:
11.30am and 7pm.

Ulster Museum
Botanic Gardens.
Open: Monday to Friday 10am-5pm, Saturday 1-5pm, Sunday 2-5pm.
☎ (01232) 381251
There is access to the palm house/ tropical ravine during these hours. The gardens are open until dusk every day.

Other Places to Visit

Antrim
Co Antrim
Pogue's Entry
Church Street
Open: Monday to Friday 10am-5pm,
Saturday 10am-2pm.
☎ (01849) 428331

Ardglass
Co Down
Jordan's Castle
Open: July and August only 10am-
7pm. Tuesday to Saturday and Sunday
afternoon.

Bangor
Co Down
Bangor Castle
The heritage centre in the castle is open
Tuesday to Saturday 10.30am-4.30pm
and Sunday 2-4.30pm. In July and
August it stays open an extra hour, and
also opens on Mondays.
☎ (01247) 271200

Ulster Folk & Transport Museum
Co Down
Signposted on Bangor-Belfast road
(A2), near Holywood
Open: daily all year. Closed Sunday
morning, and Saturday morning in
winter.
☎ (01232) 428428 .

Carrickfergus
Co Antrim
Carrickfergus Castle
Open: Monday to Saturday 10am-6pm,
Sunday 2-6pm. Winter, closes 4pm.
☎ (01960) 351273. Longer hours for
Knightride monorail Centre
☎ (01960) 366455

Andrew Jackson Centre
Open: Monday to Friday 10am-6pm
and weekend afternoons, May to
October. Closed 1-2pm.
☎ (01960) 364972

Downpatrick
Co Down
Down County Museum
English Street
Open: weekdays and weekend
afternoons. Closed on Sunday and
Monday from mid-September until
June. For hours/other openings.
☎ (01396) 615218

Glenavy
Co Antrim
Ballance House
Signposted on Lisburn-Glenavy road
(A30).
Open: Tuesday-Sunday afternoons
April to September.
☎ (01846) 648492

Hillsborough
Co Down
Hillsborough Fort
Open: Tuesday to Saturday 10am-4pm,
Sunday 2-4pm, and until 7pm in
summer.
☎ (01846) 683285

Inch Abbey, Grey Abbey and Nendrum
On-site facilities at these historic
monuments in state care are available
April to September — same hours as
Ballycopeland.

Islandmagee
Co Antrim
Ford Farm Park
8 Low Road (on B90)
Family farm/museum.
Open: daily 2-6pm.
☎ (01960) 353264

Lisburn
Co Antrim
Lisburn Museum/Irish Linen Centre
☎ (01846) 663377

Millisle
Co Down
Ballycopeland Windmill
Open: Tuesday to Saturday 10am-7pm
and Sunday 2-7pm April to September.
Only open weekends (until 4pm) in
winter.
☎ (01247) 861413

Newtownards
Co Down
Mount Stewart
National Trust property. Gardens open
daily April to September and weekends
in October. House opens each
afternoon except Tuesday May to
September. For hours/other openings:
☎ (0124 77) 88387/88487

Somme Heritage Centre
Bangor Road, Conlig
Open: 10am-6pm Tuesday to Saturday
and from 11am on Sunday. In winter
the centre closes at 5pm.
☎ (01247) 823202

Oxford Island
Co Armagh
Lough Neagh Discovery Centre
Take exit 10 from M1
Open: April to September 10am-7pm
daily. For winter opening hours:
☎ (01762) 322205

Portaferry
Co Down
Exploris Aquarium
Open: Monday to Saturday 10am-6pm,
Sunday 1-6pm.
☎ (0124 77) 28062

Strangford
Co Down
Castle Ward
National Trust property. The house is
open 1-6pm daily except Thursday
May to September. For other openings.
☎ (01396) 881204

Templepatrick
Co Antrim
Patterson's Spade Mill
Open: every afternoon except Tuesday
in June, July and August. Plus weekend
and bank holiday afternoons in April.
May and September. (National Trust).
☎ (01849) 433619

Travel
Strangford Lough Car Ferry:
Every 30 minutes. Last boat from
Strangford 10.30pm, last boat from
Portaferry 10.45pm. Saturday night
revellers get an extra hour but do not
cut it too fine or you risk 50-mile
(80km) round trip by road. No service
Christmas Day.

Tourist Information Offices
Open: all year.

Belfast
59 North Street, Belfast city centre
☎ (01232) 246609
Belfast City Airport
☎ (01232) 457745
Belfast International Airport
☎ (01849) 422888

Antrim
Co Antrim
Council Offices, The Steeple
☎ (01849) 463113

Bangor
Co Down
34 Quay Street, Bangor
☎ (01247) 270069

Carrickfergus
Co Antrim
Antrim Street
☎ (01960) 366455

Downpatrick
Co Down
74 Market Street
☎ (01396) 612233

Larne
Co Antrim
Narrow Gauge Road
☎ (01574) 260088

6 • From the Mournes to the Boyne

South Down, Armagh, Monaghan, Louth and Meath

Deciding which route to take through the Mourne mountains can present something of a dilemma. They are beautiful from every direction, and so compact — only 15 miles (24km) long and 8 miles (13km) across — that it does not much matter where you come back down to main roads. Of the sixty or so individual summits about a dozen rise above 2,000ft (610m) but there is not a Munro among them: at 2,796ft (852m), Slieve Donard is the highest. The ancient Kingdom of Mourne is hidden away behind the bare eastern summits which, from the north, appear as an unbroken line of steep and shapely hills. South Down is dominated by these much painted, much walked mountains and whichever route you take south from Belfast, they are there in front of you.

The National Trust's gardens at **Rowallane** (A7) near Saintfield are best known for their spectacular massed plantings of rhododendrons and azaleas. The garden is on a windy ridge 200ft (61m) above sea level encircled by a windbreak of Australian laurels, hollies, pines and beech trees. The protected yet open meadowy setting inside the windbreak makes the rhododendrons flower profusely. The more light, the more blooms.

Saintfield was the scene of a battle in the 1798 rebellion. A local minister, the Reverend T.L Birch, was active in the United Irishmen Society, founded in Belfast in 1791 to win religious equality and parliamentary reform, and he established a branch in the town. The rebels held Saintfield for a few days but were defeated at Ballynahinch soon afterwards. The long grassy graveyard of Mr Birch's church contains the headstones of his slain parishioners and a memorial plaque (First Presbyterian church, Main Street). Ballynahinch was laid out in about 1640 by the earls of Moira. From the stump on Windmill Hill you can look across the valley to their former seat, the wooded demesne of Montalto. The last and biggest battle of the United Irishmen's rebellion was fought in this valley.

An impressive Norman motte — an artificial mound with a flat top — and a modest Anglican cathedral testify to the historical

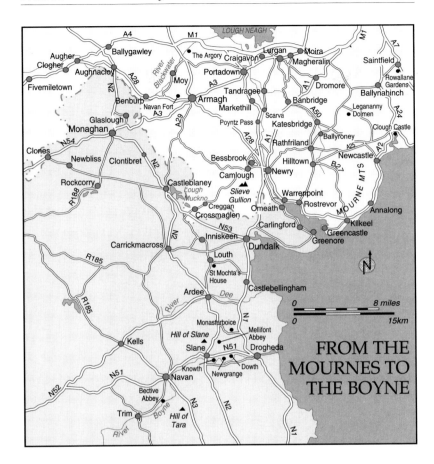

FROM THE
MOURNES TO
THE BOYNE

importance of **Dromore**, a market town on the Lagan. St Colman founded an abbey at Dromore in the sixth century. If the cathedral is locked apply to the rectory for access. The town was devastated in 1641 and the only relics of the early times are a Celtic cross in the graveyard boundary wall and a single stone (St Colman's Pillow) in the south wall of the chancel. Two men of great literary distinction, Jeremy Taylor (1613-67) and Thomas Percy (1729-1811), who were both bishops of Dromore, are buried here. Taylor, author of *Holy Living; Holy Dying* , one of the best seventeenth-century prose works in the English language, rebuilt the cathedral in the 1660s. Percy, who enlarged it, is remembered for his *Reliques* of ancient English poetry — a collection of ballads that influenced the poetic revival signalled by Wordsworth's *Lyrical Ballads* (1798). The local running club holds races on the third Saturday in August in memory of Sam Ferris who

The National Trust gardens at Rowallane, near Saintfield

ran in three Olympic marathons but did not come anywhere. Dromore's contribution to Irish gastronomy is delectable crumbly Drumiller cheese, made from ewes' milk.

Banbridge is the industrial centre of the district. Now bypassed by the A1, it was an important stop on the Dublin-Belfast road. The underpass in the middle of the broad, very steep, main street was cut out in 1834 to assist Royal Mail coaches to go through the town centre. Ironically the coach inn had to be demolished to make room for the coach underpass. In Church Square the statue of Captain Francis Crozier RN, who discovered the North-West Passage in 1848, is flanked by four large and friendly looking polar bears. A blue plaque on a house nearby records that this was his birthplace in 1796. Hymn writer and benefactor of Port Hope, Ontario, Joseph Scriven (1819-1886), was born at 91 Dromore Road. He wrote 'What a friend we have in Jesus'.

Clough Castle, just yards off the A24/A25 crossroads (always accessible), is a good example of a late thirteenth-century Norman motte-and-bailey fortification, small compared with the one at Dromore, but with more to look at because it has a stone keep on top. To appreciate mottes and baileys (big mounds and lesser mounds) you must concentrate on the grassy mounds, even when the stone buildings on top look rather more interesting. The motte, with a ditch round it and a wooden tower on top, had a lower level enclosure (bailey) as the first line of defence. The bailey at Clough is a kidney-shaped mound, the one at Dromore is oblong. If the fort came under attack, the defenders on the motte could pull up the ladder across the ditch and cut themselves off from the bailey, and then see off the attackers with a hail of arrows from the tower. In Down and Antrim alone there are more than 100 of these mottes, built in a hurry by the early Normans. The invaders did not bother much with the Mournes,

Saintfield in full bloom

though there is a motte at Hilltown — one of a string of mottes from Belfast down to the Crown Mound near Newry (access from Sheeptown Road).

The Normans soon abandoned mottes in favour of decent stone castles like **Dundrum** 3 miles (5km) away, the very model of a modern Norman castle — a massive circular keep, with spiral staircase, integrated bathroom (latrines), a rock-cut ditch and a supremely strategic position on a high rock above the bay. King John captured it in 1210, the Magennises occupied it in the fourteenth century, and it was damaged by Cromwellians in 1652. It is one of a line of castles that controlled this coast from Carrickfergus to Carlingford. The waders and the wildfowl, and the seals sunning themselves on the point, seem unperturbed by the popping from a nearby rifle range across the narrow channel at Ballykinler. About 1½ miles (2km) beyond Dundrum village, the **Slidderyford** dolmen is signposted off the A2. Keep a lookout for the sign and you should be able to see it from the main road. The sand dunes of Murlough nature reserve (after 200yd) were farmed as a rabbit warren by the Normans.

Approached from Dundrum, the resort of **Newcastle** seems quite spacious. At the south end it squeezes on to a ledge up against the mountain. The caravan sites and also the championship courses of the Royal County Down golf club are all at the 'fat' end, invisible from the promenade which stretches from an outsize redbrick Victorian hotel round to the harbour. The blue mountains are a backcloth to a curved raised beach where horse-riders come for a morning canter on the sands. There is no resort in Ireland with a more attractive setting. Percy French (1854-1920) celebrated Newcastle 'where the mountains of Mourne sweep down to the sea' in a popular song and the grateful town built him a memorial fountain in the promenade gardens. A stone in the promenade wall commemorates Harry Ferguson's flight in a home-made monoplane along the beach in 1910. The town council gave him £100 as a reward. Ferguson invented the four-wheel drive system, and he sued the Ford Motor Company for $250 million for patent infringements of his most famous invention, the modern tractor. Evening entertainment and plenty of restaurants help make this a lively place.

Many prehistoric and early Christian monuments in the Mournes have vanished as the granite was hacked out to pave the streets of Liverpool, but there are still numerous stone-walled cashels in the rocky uplands including, near Lough Island Reavy at **Drumena**, a well preserved oval-shaped cashel with a souterrain you can go inside. It is signposted off the A25 to Rathfriland, 2 miles (3km) from **Castlewellan**, a small spacious town laid out in the 1750s which has two market houses and two squares. The lower square is the venue

Banbridge, once an important stop on the old Dublin-Belfast road

The Norman castle at Dundrum, captured by King John in 1210

for a traditional horse fair on May Day. The outstanding feature of Castlewellan Forest Park is the national arboretum dating from 1740. Nearby **Tollymore**, originally a Magennis estate which passed by inheritance to the earls of Roden in 1798, is also a forest park (open until dusk). Both parks are popular for camping and have good facilities for touring caravans. The Roden mansion at Tollymore has been demolished but the demesne is full of entertaining follies, gateways, bridges and other extraordinary garden architecture. You drive in at the Barbican Gate, with chunky round castellated turrets and quatrefoil loopholes, and drive out through the Gothic arch, pinnacles and flying buttresses of Bryansford Gate. Extravaganzas inside include a gateway with stone acorns and strange bobbles like buns (or baps) on top, a pair of immense gate pillars with spires and baps, a melancholy grotto or hermitage, and bridges studded with large stone bobbles, beside waterfalls and over rivulets. A Gothic church turns out to be a barn with a café inside. Himalayan cedars, a 100ft (30m) Wellingtonia, a Monterey pine, silver firs and beeches are among outstanding trees. Most of the modern conifer forests are away on the other side of the river. The Mournes mountain rescue service operates from a log-cabined centre on the Hilltown road.

Tollymore is a convenient departure point for walks into the high Mournes, and there are marked paths to follow. The footpath west

The small, spacious town of Castlewellan

joins up with the Hare's Gap, the path south-west follows the course of the Spinkwee river up to Slievenaglogh and the Diamond Rocks. Up there you can see smoky quartz and black mica crystals in cavities in the granite. Silver jewellery set with semi-precious Mourne stones, and ornaments made from polished granite, are sold locally.

Coastguard lookout points from Newcastle to Carlingford are an indication of the area's smuggling traditions. Wines and spirits, tobacco, tea, silk and soap used to be brought across from the Isle of Man in small boats, landed at lonely beaches and carried on ponies through the mountains along the Brandy Pad, an old smugglers' trail, to Hilltown in the western foothills, the main distribution centre.

The Kingdom of Mourne

The Kingdom of Mourne has very precise limits, marked on the three main roads through it. It comprises the southern uplands and the coastal plain of south-facing farms with potato fields enclosed in dry-stone walls, centred on the market town and fishing port of Kilkeel. One 'welcome' sign is on the B27 from Hilltown towards Kilkeel, another is at Cassy Water on the A2 5 miles (8km) west of Kilkeel. A third sign is 2 miles (3km) south of Newcastle, before Maggie's Leap. St Patrick is said not to have ventured beyond a small stream here.

Belfast city centre, from the City Hall, County Antrim (Chapter 5)

Fun on stilts around the City Hall, Belfast (Chapter 5)

The resort of Newcastle with the Mournes beyond and (below) a friendly farmer above Annalong in the Kingdom of Mourne, County Down (Chapter 6)

The task of making Christians out of the men of Mourne was left to St Donard (died AD506) who lived inside a stone cell on top of the mountain named after him. **Bloody Bridge** carpark, just inside the kingdom boundary, is a convenient place from which to climb Slieve Donard, although this is not the most attractive route to the summit, because of quarrying. Scene of a massacre by the Magennises in 1641, Bloody Bridge is where the Brandy Pad begins, running up the side of the river.

The water authority allows vehicle access to the south end of the Silent Valley reservoir, two artificial lakes which supply Belfast's water, 30 million gallons of 'soft' water a day — Belfast's kettles never need descaling. Erosion damage by pounding boots ended the annual Mourne Wall Walk which used to bring thousands of walkers to walk the length of the 22-mile (35km) wall surrounding the reservoir. The huge wall of rough stone runs up and down fifteen mountains and provided work for unemployed men in the Mournes from 1910 to 1922. Quickest access is up the B27 from Kilkeel and right (Head Road) after 4 miles (6km) to the water commissioners' big red gates.

Ribbon development mars the approach to the fishing village of **Annalong** but from a restored cornmill overlooking the harbour there is a panoramic view of the Mournes. Craggy Slieve Binnian and the patchwork of small fields that cover its lower slopes running up the mountain slopes appears in thousands of landscape paintings. You can walk up Binnian by following the course of the Annalong river, keeping to the west bank. The harbour was enlarged in the 1880s in response to demand for Mourne granite exports. The fishing skiffs are no longer crowded out by coasters off-loading English coal and taking on potatoes and Mourne granite, but the place bestirs itself in the herring season (mid-September to late October) when the Annalong skiffs head off in the early evening to lay their nets. A stone dressing yard, fishermen's cottages with flowery gardens, a pub and a fish smokery are all part of the harbour scene. Visitors to the cornmill come away having learned that wheat only needs one grinding. Oats are harder work. Being two-husked, they need two grindings.

South now to **Kilkeel**, a lively country town with the largest fishing fleet in Ulster, busiest at auction time when fish, including herring, is sold on the quay. There are fish processing factories around the port and miles of lobster pots along the coast. The town has winding streets, terraced shops and houses with stepped pavements, and a bend in the middle round the ruins of the medieval Old

The fishing village of Annalong has a restored cornmill at the harbour

Church, site of a sixth-century foundation from which the town took its name — *cill caol* (church at the narrows). The water in the granite bullaun in the churchyard will only cure a wart if you first drop a pin in it.

The megalithic tomb of Dunnaman, a court tomb with a long gallery, is on the A2 west of Kilkeel at **Massforth**, behind St Colman's church. An unobtrusive sign on the parochial house indicates the path between clipped hedges. St Colman's is typical of the large nineteenth-century Roman Catholic churches, with acres of adjacent carparking, which occupy sites on the edge of towns or out in the country miles from anywhere. Designed by O'Neill and Byrne of Belfast, St Colman's serves the people of Upper Mourne. It needed to be big since, when it opened in 1879, it had 5,000 parishioners. From 1540, when the Catholic priests of Kilkeel Old Church were expelled, until the relaxation of the penal code in the 1770s, the Catholic clergy ministered to their flocks in private houses or out in the open at mass rocks. Even in the mid-nineteenth century there were so few Catholic churches in Ireland that an average congregation was 3,000. Nonconformists were also subject to the penal laws though to a lesser extent, and they too had few churches — for example, in 1834 there was one church for every 1,500 Presbyterians. Since then all of them have made up for lost time. Gothic-style St Colman's is built from squared

Mourne granite blocks, with pinnacles. The church at **Attical** (1890) in the mountains is its small sister.

About 3½ miles (6km) west of Kilkeel, **Kilfeaghan** dolmen (signposted off the A2) is at the end of a narrow ½ mile (1km) track. Park near the farm. Access is beyond a pair of round pillars, then through gates in the dry-stone walls.

It is a 4-mile (6km) run from Kilkeel to the ruined royal fortress of **Greencastle**, with a formidable jagged rock-cut ditch. Across the narrows is another Norman pile guarding the opposite shore of Carlingford Lough. Greencastle had a famous Ram Fair until about 1880 but, unlike Carlingford, the village was never more than a handful of scattered farms, and after 1495 both castles were controlled by the same constable. The remains of a medieval church are in a field between the massive ruins and a motte behind the coastguard station. There are wide views from three enormous sixteenth-century windows in the great hall. Cranfield Point lighthouse, thick and graceless, is a reminder that lighthouses, even small ones, can be ugly. **Cranfield** itself is a popular swimming place, with a fine sandy beach where the water is said to be the least cold in Ulster.

Stop for the view at the carpark above the **Spelga Dam**, which supplies water to Banbridge and the Craigavon area. The B27 south of the dam, runs close to **Pigeon Rock Mountain**, where there is a popular rock climb called The Thing. A mile (2km) west of Kinnahalla, a few yards from the road at **Bush Town**, is the largest fairy thorn in Ulster, an ancient sprawling tree, immune from the axe. Farmers are careful to plough round sacred thorns, a familiar feature of the Irish countryside, standing alone in potato fields. To cut one down invariably brings bad luck, and they are a potent image in Irish myth and magic. Samuel Ferguson wrote a poem *The Fairy Thorn* about a group of young girls going at twilight to dance round one of these trees. Overcome by the intensity of the experience, they are seduced by the fairy folk:

> 'Soft o'er their bosoms' beating — the only human sound,
> They hear the silky footsteps of the silent fairy crowd,
> Like a river in the air. . .'.

At the T-junction the ruins of **Clonduff** church contain a Magennis gravestone.

The many pubs of **Hilltown** are a legacy from eighteenth-century smugglers who shared out their contraband here. The village has a livestock market on alternate Saturdays and a sheep fair and festival ('booley' fair) in early July. The Georgian market house opposite St

John's parish church (1766) adjoins the Downshire Arms, an old hostelry which is now a pub/restaurant with self-catering holiday apartments in the courtyard. The weathervane on the cupola is a fish, a reminder of the good fishing in the Bann and its tributaries. The more recent of the two Roman Catholic churches was built in 1844 on land given by Hilltown's Protestant landlord. Such gifts, which some recipients may have considered more as restitution, were not uncommon after emancipation. To visit the **Goward** dolmen, cross Eight Mile Bridge where Redmond O'Hanlon, a famous highwayman, was slain in 1681, and take the B8 east. The dolmen is signposted on the right after 2 miles (3km). The track ends after ¾ mile at a carpark close to the dolmen — called locally Pat Kearney's Big Stone.

From the square at **Rathfriland** on top of a hill, five streets with stepped terraces fall away sharply on all sides. Before the combustion engine, to spare the horses people climbed down from their traps and carts and walked home. The all-round views from such a position are likely to be good, and so they are. The town has a midweek variety market in the square and three livestock sale days a week. During the potato famine, the market house (1770) was used as a soup kitchen, though Rathfriland escaped the worst deprivations, since cereals as well as potatoes were cultivated in this area. Four substantial Presbyterian churches are testimony to past differences of opinion. The old Quaker meeting house is now a scout hall, and the small shop with pointed windows on the first floor was originally the town's Methodist chapel. Andrew 'Captain Moonlight' Scott, born in 1842, the son of a nineteenth-century rector of Rathfriland, brought shame to his family when he was arrested and hanged as a bushranger in Sydney in 1880. A prominent funnel-shaped water tower occupies the high point in the riverless town, near the site of a sixteenth-century Magennis castle, now vanished.

The area has distinguished connections with pioneer Canada. The intrepid Catherine O'Hare, mother of the first European child born west of the Rockies (delivered by Indian midwives in 1862), was herself born in Rathfriland in 1835. She and her husband, Augustus Schubert, joined 200 Overlanders who went west in search of gold, and blazed the trail for the Canadian Pacific Railway. The city park in Kamloops, British Columbia, is named after her and Armstrong also has a monument. Rathfriland has not yet erected a memorial to this remarkable woman.

The Dromara road (B7) from Rathfriland passes **Drumballyroney** parish church and school. Patrick Prunty was a schoolmaster here before he went to England, became a clergyman, refined his name and, having settled in the sombre moors of the West Riding of Yorkshire, fathered the novelists Charlotte, Emily and Anne Brontë. Their brother Branwell's stories, set in an imaginary country called Angria where half the people have Irish names, make explicit the Irish influences which, it is claimed, tinge the wild landscapes of Emily's *Wuthering Heights*. A signposted 10-mile (16km) trail (unconvincingly labelled 'Brontë homeland drive') links several other places connected with the Prunty family. These include ruined Magherally Old Church which, however, is more interesting as the burial place of the scholar and author Helen Waddell (1889-1965). Now remembered for her novel *Peter Abelard*, Waddell's contemporary reputation was built on some passionate renderings in English of medieval secular Latin lyrics.

The nobly proportioned, many-arched bridge at **Katesbridge** is said to have withstood the weight of several Churchill tanks during the 1939-45 war. It is a popular spot for fishing — salmon, trout and pike. The blacksmith beside the bridge keeps his old forge and handbellows in good repair in case there is a power cut while he is shoeing. There are various mottes around **Ballyroney** village, an enormous Presbyterian church, a lough with an island in the centre and, signposted on the right, a side road to the **Legananny dolmen**, an elegant tripod with star quality. Theatrically positioned on the

Katesbridge on the Upper Bann, a popular spot for salmon, trout and pike fishing

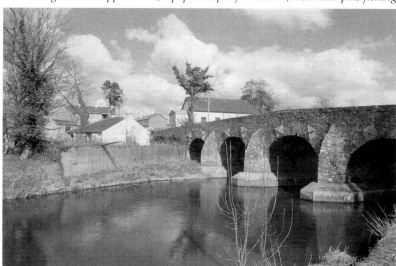

southern slope of Slieve Croob, the dolmen has very tall and slender uprights. However, the miserably small piece of ground surrounding it ensures that your photographs will include barbed wire and fence posts. Continuing along the B7, St Michael's church, at a kink in the road at **Finnis**, is next to a mass house of 1760 (now an outhouse of the parochial house) which this large Roman Catholic church replaced in the 1830s. The architect, Thomas Duff, also designed Newry cathedral which was started the same year, though St Michael's took a decade to complete. There are many old mass sites in the area where a small tributary runs into the infant Lagan, only 2 miles (3km) from its source on Slieve Croob. A mile (2km) north is the village of Dromara with nice hump bridges over the broadening river. The scenic road from **Dromara** to Castlewellan gives views across Dundrum Bay to the Mournes.

The M1 from Belfast bypasses the comparatively industrialised Lurgan/Portadown area. If the numerous signposts to **Craigavon** intrigue you, take exit 11 for a look at a New Town that never happened. A civic centre and other isolated buildings stand in a landscape of roundabouts and bridges at the end of a stumpy little motorway (M12). The plan was for the existing towns, Lurgan and Portadown, to grow towards each other, taking overspill from Belfast to create a small city of 180,000. Designated in 1965, the town is still waiting for the people to arrive.

The Vernacular Architecture of Mid-Down

Unassuming **Lurgan** town was granted to the Brownlows of Nottingham after 1607. It became prosperous with the introduction of linen-damask weaving at the end of the century. Textiles and clothing manufacturers are still important here. You can see well preserved weavers' cottages, with pot-bellied front parlours built to accommodate the loom, if you go looking for them around Bownes Lane. Distinguished locals include the poet and painter George Russell (*AE*), born in Lurgan in 1867, and James Logan (1674-1751) who was president of Pennsylvania's first state council. A blue plaque on a pillar in High Street marks his birthplace. Logan's father was a schoolmaster here, at Ireland's first Quaker meeting house (1653). The top dog in Lurgan is Master McGrath, a coursing greyhound who won the Waterloo Cup three times between 1868 and 1871. He has a memorial window in the eighteenth-century parish church and appears on the town's coat of arms. A statue of the noble hound was put up in 1993, but you have to go out to Craigavon civic centre to see it.

The leggy Legananny dolmen stands on Slieve Croob's southern slope

In **Portadown**, carpet-making is a now somewhat remote link with the town's linen past. The name of Sir Robert Hart (1835-1911), creator of China's post office and founder of that country's lighthouse service, appears in street and school names and there is a memorial in St Mark's vestry. The house in Woodhouse Street where he was born has been knocked down in favour of a supermarket but since he was in China for 54 years, he cannot have spent much time in it. One of Hart's less well known achievements was to introduce the Chinese to the music of the brass band — a fitting service from a native of Portadown, because this town goes in for bands in a big way, not only in the 'marching season' (around 'the Twelfth'), and it has a good male voice choir.

Between Dromore and Lough Neagh, the Lagan meanders down through meadows, under eighteenth-century whinstone bridges and past small country towns founded in the plantation period. Particular features of the area are yeoman planters' houses, and massive round gate pillars with conical tops marking the entrance to farms and fields. Taking the B2 west from Dromore for 5½ miles (9km), a white late eighteenth-century slated farmhouse stands at the B9 crossroads. From here you are 1½ miles (2km) from each of three villages. Go south for Donaghcloney, straight on for Waringstown, north for Magheralin.

The former factory village of **Donaghcloney**, where kerbs and bridge parapets are painted red, white and blue, has a solid redbrick parish church with a war memorial in front. It is an odd combination of church and house — net curtains at the windows and a TV aerial on the roof. Half a mile (1km) west of the B2/B9 crossroads, the turning to Waringstown is marked by a pair of gate pillars at a thatched yeoman's house of about 1680. A second pair flanks the farmyard. The founder of **Waringstown** built himself a two-storey Jacobean-style gentleman's house, one of the first unfortified houses in Ireland (1667). A third storey was added later. A handsome pink-painted mansion with tall Tudor-Revival chimneys, it looks solid enough but is actually built of mud and rubble. Across the road are seven curious terraces in sets of three and four houses, with scalloped garden walls and railings — some of Mr Waring's seventeenth-century cottages rebuilt 1930s' style. The Waring fortune was founded on linen, and Dutch-style houses were built along the main street for the weavers, most of whom came from Flanders. A yeoman's house (built 1698, now a restaurant) stands on a high bend in the road. Waringstown cricket club, founded 1851, fields a strong team (as does Donaghcloney). The big house and the parish church

(1681) had the same designer, James Robb, chief mason of the king's works in Ireland. The church's Jacobean interior is largely of ancient oak — roof, panelling, choir screen and a notable pulpit.

Big trees, meadows, planters' houses and old cornmills along the B9 make this an attractive approach to blink-and-miss **Magheralin**. Stained glass artists created the scenes from the lives of Irish saints in the parish church. The eighteenth-century memorials came from a church of 1657 up the road, used until 1845, now ruined but well tended. To see the stained glass, ask at the rectory opposite. It can be a pleasurable task, and not difficult, to track down church key-holders in Ireland. You will usually find one nearby. John Macoun, naturalist and explorer of the Rockies, was born in Magheralin in 1831. He was the surveyor for the Canadian Pacific Railway.

Moira is a proper village, small, smart and smug, like all the best villages the world over. The main street is lined with red-berried rowans and eighteenth-century blackstone houses flanked by carriage archways. Many Moira residents were dealers in linen, prosperous middle-men, rather than mere weavers, and it remains a desirable place to live. A frequent winner of *ententes florales* competitions, the village is decorated for most of the year with hanging baskets, flowering shrubs, roses, and masses of flowers squeezed on to traffic islands, verges, any little corner where a corm, a bulb or an Easiplug can be trowelled in. Sausage connoisseurs travel from far afield to buy from a Moira master butcher who has to open his shop at 8am — 7am on Saturday — to cope with customers wanting his prize bangers and black puddings. On the northern edge of town, a long grassy avenue terminates in Moira parish church, a top-heavy but appealing building of 1723 where William Butler Yeats, grandfather of the poet, was curate in the 1830s. The wood-and-copper spire is a replacement for a ponderous stone steeple which fell down. Seen from the church door, the lawns give the illusion of running smoothly down into a dip and up again on the far side into the forested estate of Moira's founder, Sir Arthur Rawdon. But in the dip is the busy A3 trunk road. The road opposite Station Road leads to Berwick Hall, a picturesque yeoman's house of 1700 with a straw thatch. Moira was the scene of a victory in AD637 by the king of Tara over the Ulster king, Comgall.

For unusual peaty landscapes visit **Peatlands Park** where wooded drumlins stick up through the flat bog of cut-over peat and there is a narrow gauge railway with locomotives once used for peat extraction (M1 exit 13). The Birches, 4 miles (6km) east (or M1 exit 12), was the ancestral home of Stonewall Jackson, the great Confederate general killed in 1863 at Chancellorsville in the American civil war. A blue plaque in the pretty courtyard of Waugh's farm records the connection.

Small settlements benefiting from the construction in the 1730s of the 18-mile (29km) Newry canal included Scarva, Poyntz Pass and Jerrettspass. These sleepy places are heavy with history. An annual fixture for at least 200 years has been a curious pageant at Scarva on the Upper Bann river. On 13 July thousands of 'Blackmen' (cousins to the 'Orangemen') converge on this picturesque village for a symbolic re-enactment of the battle of the Boyne in 1690. Highlight of the day is a joust (the Sham Fight) between two horsemen in period costume representing James II and William III. 'James' always obliges by falling off his horse. However, the importance of **Scarva** is of much greater antiquity. It was a part of the defensive earthworks and ditches known as the Black Pig's Dyke, sometimes called the Dorsey and, sometimes, the Dane's Caste. A section of these earthen defences, built in the fourth century BC by the Ulster kings after their retreat east from Emain Macha near Armagh, is clearly visible in the grounds of Scarva House, a two-storey house of about 1717 with a charming courtyard. The large raths, or forts, of Lisnagade (1¼ miles/2km east of Scarva village) and Lisnavaragh (½ mile/1km west of Lisnagade on a bend in the road) are believed to mark the north end of the defensive frontier.

On now to **Newry** town, named from a yew tree said to have been planted by St Patrick, and strategically placed at the head of the 'Gap of the North', a pass between two ranges of hills. In the days of the Fianna legends the men of Ulster surged through the Gap to harry the tribes of Leinster. Sometimes the action was in the other direction. The settlement at Newry always came in for a battering. The barricaded public buildings today are a dismaying sight. At the security checkpoint on the A1 south of Newry there is an astonishing array of soaring concrete barriers, prestressed megaliths, and look-out towers on the bare hills above. Visitors coming north, waiting at the red stop light for permission to proceed, have time to reflect on the drama of the legends.

An abbey on the bank of the Clanrye river at Newry was colonised by Cistercians in 1153. A granite slab inscribed with a plain Celtic cross belonging to the abbey can be inspected in Arthur McCann's bakery on Castle Street. This bakery, incidentally, produces the most appetising shiny barmbracks, and moist fruit cakes spiked with whiskey and Guinness. Ireland's first post-Reformation (ie Protestant) church, built by Sir Nicholas Bagenal in 1578 and still with its

The historic Newry canal, constructed in the 1730s, is a venue for angling competitions

old tower, stands on a high hill on the east side of town. There is a good view of the church from the garden of the Poor Clares' pink convent in steep High Street. The convent garden almost encircles the burial ground of Newry's first Presbyterian (Unitarian) congregation, established in 1650, where John Mitchel (1815-75), a famous republican, is buried. Transported for the offence of treason-felony he came back to Ireland 28 years later and was elected MP for Tipperary. There is a statue of him in the pedestrianised shopping centre. If the graveyard is locked, ask at the convent about access. Mitchel wrote a nineteenth-century bestseller, *Jail Journal*, a classic of Anglophobia but quite readable. The A1 slices through the east side of Newry, over the site of the abbey, separating this historical hilly quarter from the rest of town.

The earliest inland canal in the British Isles, the Newry canal was built between 1730 and 1742 and extended down to Carlingford Lough as a ship canal in 1761. It has fourteen locks, some of them recently restored, and a single carefully preserved swing-bridge surviving at the bottom of Monaghan Street. The last vessel passed through the locks in the 1930s. To reopen the waterway the modern concrete road bridges would have to be removed — either that, or build another lock. The town's mercantile past is reflected in names

Rostrevor, on the north shore of Carlingford Lough, is noted for its mild climate

A panoramic view from Slievemartin

like Buttercrane Quay, Sugar Island and Sugarhouse Quay, and tall warehouses line the quays. The main downstream (export) traffic was linen, Tyrone coal, Mourne granite, farm produce and early emigrants who bought passage on American flaxseed ships. By the 1840s, however, canal trade had declined.

Atmospheric faded corners of old Newry include River Street, a row of tiny houses with eagles over the doors, and Ballybot (Poor Town) beyond the former cattle market. At one time the universal roofing material was slate from the North Wales quarries, and many houses in the town are still roofed with 'Bangor blues'.

Warrenpoint and Rostrevor are small resorts on the sheltered north shore of Carlingford Lough. The port at **Warrenpoint** has a regular direct shipping service to the west coast of France and handles substantial tonnages of coal, timber, paper and grain. When Newry port closed in the 1970s, this harbour was enlarged, and the town has an animated waterfront and a spacious square. A passenger ferry plies between Warrenpoint and Omeath in summer. The road into Rostrevor winds past a tall granite obelisk to Robert Ross (1766-1814), commander of a small British force which captured Washington in 1814 after unexpectedly defeating the Americans at Bladensburg.

Palm trees and mimosa flourish in the mild climate of **Rostrevor** and natural oakwoods make a fine show in autumn when the leaves turn. Behind the town on the slopes of Slievemartin a glacial erratic boulder called the Cloghmore (Great Stone) is a geological curiosity. Follow the forest drive to the carpark, then walk to the viewpoint (½ mile/1km) beyond the pines and on up to the stone. The bronze bell of Rostrevor's Catholic church was rescued from the ruins of Kilbroney church a mile (2km) up the mountain road (B25) where St Bronach, patron saint of seafarers, founded a monastery in the sixth century. A granite cross survives from the early foundation.

The Ring of Gullion and South Armagh

The southern end of **Slieve Gullion** is a forest park, with a steep drive up almost to the top. Wild goats move along the ridges and a neolithic passage grave crowns the south summit (1,894ft/577m). The water of a small lake on the bare north summit makes excellent tea and is also said to cure toothache. From the top of Slieve Gullion the whole of the **Ring of Gullion** is laid out below — a ring dyke of wild and rugged hills, of an unusual shape and colour, about 7 miles (11km) in diameter. The strange circle, rising to over 1,000ft (305m), has an untamed and thrilling aspect, as compelling in its way as the Giant's Causeway. It is not practicable to take to the hills because the area is militarised, with observation posts on some of the prominent hills of the ring dyke but the view from the forest park is worth the 8-mile (13km) drive. The entrance to the park and visitor centre is 5 miles (8km) south-east of Newry on the Forkhill road (B113). Slieve Gullion dominates the Gap of the North and like Emain Macha (Navan Fort), it features in the prose epic *Táin Bó Cuailnge* (The Cattle Raid of Cooley) which dates from the fourth century. The *Táin* and other sagas were written down after writing was introduced to Ireland in St Patrick's time, probably in the eighth century. The region's vanishing folklore is also well documented. Just in time, it found a popular chronicler, Michael J Murphy (born 1913), who collected enough Irish folk stories and superstitions (pisthogues) to fill 300 volumes.

The **Killevy** churches, on Gullion's south-east slope, signposted on the B113 a mile (2km) before the forest park, are the back-to-back ruins of two medieval rectangular churches, perfectly aligned east-west and possibly built 300 years apart. They are joined together but with no way through from one to the other. The most striking feature is the massive lintelled door of the earlier, tenth-century church (west side). The pointed window of the thirteenth-century church dates from the fifteenth century. Killevy is the site of an important fifth-century nunnery founded by St Monenna, also called St Blinne who (like St Bronach) was a patron saint of sailors. A granite slab in the graveyard is traditionally this lady saint's grave, and a holy well associated with her is further up the mountain, marked by a white cross visible from the west doorway. The Vikings raided the nunnery in AD923 but it was in use as a convent of Augustinian nuns up until the dissolution (1542). The many O'Hanlon graves around the churches are a reminder that Armagh was the country of the O'Hanlons for hundreds of years.

Well signposted prehistoric cairns and dolmens around Gullion include **Ballymacdermot** cairn, a court grave near **Bernish** viewpoint, which was slightly damaged when an American tank bumped into it in World War II; **Ballykeel** dolmen, a portal tomb with a huge capstone, between Slieve Gullion and Camlough; and the eighth-century pillar stone of **Kilnasaggart**, made of granite and over 7ft (2m) high, about a mile south of Jonesborough. It stands on the line of the early Christian highway from Tara, near Drogheda, to Dunseverick on the north Antrim coast. **Moyry Castle**, a ruined tower on a rocky height nearby, was built by the English in 1601 to control the pass below. The pillar has thirteen carved crosses and a long Irish inscription which can be studied in comfort by visitors to the museum in Dundalk (Jocelyn Street) which has a fibreglass copy on display.

The A25 runs across the north end of Camlough, a ribbony lake which supplies the taps of Newry. The south Armagh hills peter out at the border in small rock-strewn, stone-ditched fields fringed with yellow whin, beyond the ramparts of the Dorsey — the name means 'gates'. The Dorsey is thought to be one of the Iron Age gates of Ulster, a pre-Christian defensive earthworks contemporary with Navan Fort. A little further along the road is **Crossmaglen**. This remote village has an exceptionally large market square adjoined by an army base, and a reputation for, among other things, horse breeding and handmade lace (Carrickmacross lace). There is a market in Crossmaglen on alternate Saturdays, but browsing among the stalls in the din and draught from an overhead helicopter is an unusual shopping experience.

The graveyard at **Creggan** parish church, outside Crossmaglen, was an O'Neill burying place from about 1450 when Hugh 'of the Fews' O'Neill came from Tyrone (Tír Eoghain) to settle in south Armagh. Other O'Neills were on the move at that time. One branch settled in Antrim (the Clandeboye O'Neills). Among all the warring tribes of Ireland, the Ulster O'Neills were the fiercest. They took their name from Niall Glundubh (Black-Knee), a high king of Ireland killed fighting the Norsemen in AD919. Their chess sets were said to be carved from the bones of Leinster warriors slain in battle, and the

Red Hand of Ulster is part of their arms. There is a deep underground O'Neill vault at Creggan, close to the wall of the church. Nearby are some interesting tablet-memorials to eighteenth-century Irish bards, Art McCooey (1738-73), Patrick MacAlinden (died 1733) and the bandit-poet Seamus Mór MacMurphy (1720-50).

Bessbrook was among the earliest of the model villages associated with the Industrial Revolution. It was founded in 1845 by John Grubb Richardson, a Quaker linen manufacturer, to house workers at his flax mill. Earlier than Saltaire in Yorkshire (1852) and Port Sunlight in Cheshire (1888), Bessbrook was the inspiration for the Cadbury garden village of Bournville near Birmingham. Granite houses with slate roofs are ranged in terraces round two squares linked by a broad parade. Both squares have a green in the middle. Community life revolved around the village hall, the schools and the churches. There was no pub — a terrible deprivation in Ireland. However, thirsty mill workers could walk to the neighbouring well-pubbed village of Camlough. The linens of the Bessbrook Spinning Company were world famous; the big mill, which worked until 1972, its pond, weirs and sluices, are an interesting part of Ulster's industrial archaeology. Bessbrook itself is something of a museum today. With no work, young people have moved away, and a large security base has been established in the village. An eighteen-arch viaduct, built in 1851, still carries the Belfast-Dublin railway, but not many trains stop at the small station between here and Newry.

Derrymore House, an eighteenth-century thatched cottage-orné manor house just outside the village, was built by Isaac Corry (1755-1813), MP for Newry and last chancellor of the Irish Exchequer. As chancellor, he imposed the window tax and supported union between Ireland and Britain. He was a friend of Lord Castlereagh, and the Act of Union was drafted in the pretty drawing room in 1800. The house is in National Trust care, but currently closed to the public.

Gosford Forest Park near Markethill was formerly the estate of the Achesons, earls of Gosford, who built a large mock-Norman castle in the middle. The first Norman revival castle in the British Isles, Gosford (1819) was designed by Thomas Hopper who later built Penrhyn Castle in Wales. It is a huge sprawling building with a square keep, round tower with a circular drawing room, and extremely thick walls. The fourth earl sold the furniture in 1921 to pay his debts. In World War II the castle was in military use (writer Anthony Powell was billeted here) and at one time it housed a circus, including the lions. The forest park is used by caravanners and campers all year round. It has some fine walnut trees and a walled cherry garden.

The heritage town of Trim on the south bank of the Boyne river, County Meath (Chapter 6)

The magnificent classical architecture of the Four Courts beside the Liffey in Dublin (Chapter 7)

Georgian doorway, Merrion Street, south of Dublin (Chapter 7)

Dun Laoghaire harbour, south of Dublin (Chapter 7)

The castle replaced a manor house where Jonathan Swift spent many months as a guest of the Achesons, his friends, between 1728 and 1730. Several of the nature walks round the estate were devised by him. Dean Swift's Chair, a half-moon seat hedged with yew in the arboretum, is where Swift sat in fine weather composing poems, some of them about Markethill. The Achesons were indulgent hosts but Sir Arthur Acheson was greatly offended when Swift instructed staff, in Sir Arthur's absence, to cut down a fairy tree outside the main gate. Swift's poem, 'On cutting down the old thorn at Markethill', explains why he did it. Below a bridge with a waterfall is Dean Swift's Well. There is no suggestion that the well is holy but even so this may be carrying the association too far. The dean was a man of robust and rational faith. The main street at **Tandragee**, on the Cusher river, curves up the steep hill to a baronial-style castle built in about 1837 by the sixth duke of Manchester. In the 1950s it became a potato crisp factory. A tour of the factory provides an opportunity to see the inner courtyards and to learn something about the potato, Ireland's staple food from the mid-seventeenth century. An earlier O'Hanlon castle on the site was confiscated at the plantation of Ulster, but the O'Hanlons recaptured and destroyed it in 1641. Outlawed Redmond O'Hanlon, killed at Hilltown in 1681, is buried at Terryhoogan graveyard, 2 miles (3km) south-east of Tandragee on the A27. The ninth-century Bell of Armagh, now in the National Museum, Dublin, was discovered near his grave, left of the gate, in the eighteenth century.

Ancient Armagh – Seat of Ireland's Archbishops

Spiritual capital of Ireland for 1,500 years, **Armagh** has preserved an air of quiet dignity and refinement against considerable odds. This small city is the seat of both the Anglican and the Roman Catholic archbishops of Ireland. The twin-spired Catholic cathedral is on a hill north-west of the city. Two marble archbishops standing on plinths outside the entrance look mildly across to the Anglican cathedral on top of the ancient rath where St Patrick built his stone church in AD445. Steep streets, climbing and intersecting, follow the curve of the ditches and banks which ringed the rath and its church. Parking around the Anglican cathedral is not feasible but down the hill there is usually space on the beautiful tree-lined Mall, where cricket is played in summer.

The Mall used to be the city's racecourse, and many of the Georgian townhouses facing each other across the green have large balconied first-floor reception rooms which would have given a good view of the starting and finishing posts. Archbishop Richard Robinson (1709-94) ejected the bookies and turned the course into an urban park. The moving spirit behind the eighteenth-century city, Archbishop Robinson was patron of the celebrated Francis Johnston (1761-1829), who left his mark on his native Armagh and, later, on Georgian Dublin.

The local building stone, used to good effect, is warm-coloured carboniferous limestone. The buildings in Charlemont Place, Johnston's fine classical courthouse at the north end of the Mall, and the house called Patrick's Fold (36 Scotch Street) are good examples. The colour varies from grey to pink, yellow and red. The brighter stone, from quarries south of the city and called 'Armagh marble', was polished and used for pavements, doorsteps and mantelpieces. No. 36 Scotch Street, set back from the present building line, was designed for the Dobbin family by Johnston in 1812. It is reputed to be the site of a church built by St Patrick in AD444, the year before he obtained the prime site up on the hill.

On the east side Armagh County Museum, in an Ionic school-house of 1833 with a small lawn of its own, is a most rewarding visit. Its art gallery, natural history and folk collections and library are especially notable. Self-portraits and other works by *AE* (George Russell, 1867-1935) and James Sleator (born in Armagh 1889) are on display. Characters from Irish legend — 'Deirdre at the door of her dun', 'Cuchula at the ford' are examples here — provided much of *AE*'s subject matter.

Since AD447, when St Patrick said that his church in Armagh should have pre-eminence over all the churches of Ireland, about eighteen successive churches have occupied the hill top. The Anglican cathedral of St Patrick has a medieval core, and was restored in 1765 by Archbishop Robinson. However, its present sandstone exterior is more recent. The cathedral was brand new when Thackeray visited it in 1842 and admired the eighteenth-century monuments inside. These include a statue of Sir Thomas Molyneux by Roubiliac, one of Dean Drelincourt by the Flemish sculptor Rysbrack, and a bust of Archbishop Robinson by Nollekens. Notice a fine kneeling figure of Primate William Stuart by Chantrey, a brass tablet to the archaeologist and historian Bishop Reeves and a collection of pagan stone figures in the north transept (chapterhouse) where seventeenth-century memorials to the earls of Charlemont are set in the west wall. The Royal Irish Fusiliers' chapel is in the south transept.

Outside, a door at the east end leads to Archbishop Patrick O'Scanail's thirteenth-century crypt. Note grotesque medieval stone heads high up round the exterior walls and a sundial of 1706. A slab in the north transept west wall marks the position of the grave of Brian Boru, high king of Ireland, who defeated the Norsemen at Clontarf in 1014. Brian, aged 73, and his son Murchard were killed in the battle and their bodies brought to Armagh for burial. A scion of the Munster house of O'Brien, Brian Boru was considered a usurper of the Irish throne. Because of this, no northern contingents helped him at Clontarf but he still won. His victory was said to have ended two centuries of Viking supremacy in Ireland, though recent ring-dating of a Dublin-built Viking warship, found scuttled in a Danish fjord, suggests the Norsemen hung on in Ireland until about 1060.

The Robinson Library (1771) was the first public library in Ireland outside Dublin. It contains a copy of *Gulliver's Travels* corrected in Swift's hand and the Claims of the Innocents (pleas to Oliver Cromwell). The registers of archbishops of Armagh from 1361 are in the Public Record Office, Belfast. James Ussher, who was primate from 1624, is remembered for a statement in his 1650 diary that the world was created on 23 October in 4004BC. He calculated this by adding up the ages of the patriarchs. An adjacent infirmary, also founded by Robinson, is still in out-patient use. Stones from an early twelfth-century Augustinian abbey (Saints Peter and Paul) on this site were used for the Presbyterian church (1722) lower down Abbey Street. Dean Swift passed the church during construction and observed stone masons 'chipping the popery out of the stones'. If Swift were to walk to the interpretive centre on English Street today, he would discover a giant Lemuel Gulliver pinioned in the 'Land of Lilliput' and also a lifesize (5ft) figure of John Wesley, the evangelical preacher who made twenty one visits to Ireland, the first in 1747. He travelled all over the island, with a pair of candlesticks and a rosary — he was of course an Anglican before he was a Methodist.

The terrace known as Vicar's Hill, opposite the cathedral's west door, was built for cathedral choimen and the widows of Church of Ireland clergy. Numbers 1 to 4, the earliest in the row, with tiny windows, date from 1720. The end house, No. 11, was the birthplace of Charles Wood (1866-1926), composer of organ music, string quartets and anthems. Early eighteenth-century terraced houses in Castle Street were demolished by the Housing Executive (the public housing authority) and replaced by some modern terraces which curve round the south-east side of the ancient hill fort.

The Catholic cathedral, also dedicated to St Patrick, was begun in 1840. Building stopped during the great famine. For many years the walls stayed at a mere 15ft (5m) and the outside was not finished until

Armagh Observatory was founded in 1790 by Archbishop Robinson

1873. The best views of the twin spires are from the city's west and north-west approaches. The pope and many of Europe's royal families helped with the builders' bills but mostly the cash was raised through collections, bazaars and raffles. A grandfather clock, a prize in the 1865 bazaar, is still waiting in the sacristy for the lucky winner to collect it. The archbishops whose statues flank a long flight of steps up to the grand entrance, were the incumbents under whom building began, Primate Crolly, and ended, Primate McGettigan. Cardinal Logue later beautified the interior, a dazzle of mosaic, painting, stained glass and marble.

Armagh Observatory was founded in 1790 by Archbishop Robinson as part of his plan for a university. The building, by Johnston, was not finished until 1825. It has astronomical books and instruments of great interest. Some of these are on public display in the adjacent planetarium and include a Herschel Newtonian mirror and Gregorian telescope by Adams, and a 20-inch radius quadrant belonging to George III which were presented to the observatory by Queen Victoria in 1840. The planetarium has star shows in a domed theatre and original equipment used by American astronauts. Opened in 1968, its first director was Patrick (Sky at Night) Moore. Across the road (A3) from the planetarium are the red castellations of the Royal School, founded by James I in 1608 and rebuilt by Robinson in 1774.

The old Irish game of road bowls, so popular in Cork, is also played in Armagh all summer long. In fact County Armagh, which has about ten clubs as against Cork's 300, is the only other place in Ireland where the game is established. Competitions are held on particular 2-mile (3km) stretches of winding country roads, though a course can be spoilt by road-straightening schemes. Players spin small solid metal balls round corners or sky them over hedges to land on the road beyond, completing the course in as few throws as possible. Corkmen do a complete 360-degree arm swing, the Armagh players have a low underarm throw and a longer run-up. It is a strenuous game and betting is brisk. Indeed some of the bets are huge. The all-Ireland finals alternate between Armagh (end of July) and Cork (early August). Strictly, the game is illegal as it obstructs roads, and so is the betting but no one is arrested these days. The all-Ireland winner in 1985 was a policeman from County Cork.

To visit the remains of the longest friary church in Ireland (163ft/ 50m), you have to cross the A28. The ruins are just beyond the gates of the former bishop's palace demesne and are all that survives of a

The Argory, a fine house in National Trust care

Franciscan friary established in 1263 by Archbishop O'Scanail. From here, you can see a tall obelisk raised by Archbishop Robinson, and looking back towards the city, the bawn-like modern St Malachy's church (Roman Catholic). St Malachy was born in Armagh and was archbishop in 1129-48. The Anglican archbishop's palace was built in 1770 by Cooley. It is used as council offices. No council could be more splendidly accommodated. Johnston added a third storey in 1786 and also designed the beautiful interior of the primate's chapel, a detached Ionic temple to the right of the main door. Among interesting paintings in the palace's chandeliered hall are portraits of George III and Queen Charlotte, painted in 1762 by Allan Ramsay (1713-84) who was the king's court painter. A large reception room contains portraits of George I, George II and other heavy jowled Hanoverians. Armagh ceased officially to be a city in 1840. It tried several times to get its status restored and at last succeeded in 1994.

Navan Fort (Emain Macha) is signposted off the Caledon-Killylea road (A28) 1½ miles (2km) west of Armagh. This great earthwork was the chief stronghold of the Celtic kings of Ulster from about 700BC until its destruction in AD332. Queen Macha's palace crowned the summit, and her hospital ('house of sorrow') sheltered the sick; Deirdre of the Sorrows first encountered her lover, Noisi, on the ramparts; Cuchulain practised feats of arms below the palace, and the deeds of the Red Branch knights, a hereditary order of chivalry, were celebrated in song. Later a huge Celtic temple, 120ft (37m) wide and 40ft (12m) high, was erected on the top and ritually burnt down in 94BC.

Long before the coming of Christianity, the House of the Red Branch ruled all Ulster (Uladh) from Navan Fort, which appears as *Isamnium* in Ptolemy's second-century world atlas. Irish vernacular literature, the oldest and richest north of the Alps, had its greatest flowering in this part of Ireland. St Patrick made Armagh the centre of his mission in Ireland in the fifth century. He might have built his church among the ruins of Emain Macha but he settled for a high hill 2 miles (3km) east.

The fall of Emain Macha was quickly followed by the rise of Christian Armagh but the site retained political and religious significance for at least 1,000 years. Brian Boru camped at Emain Macha in 1005 and a fourteenth-century O'Neill entertained the scholars of Ireland at his house here. All that remains of this fabulous kingdom is a grassy enclosure 250yd across, with a large mound inside, and some prehistoric sacrificial lakes. The area is protected as an archaeological park and has a modern interpretive centre concealed, or nearly concealed, on the south side of the enclosure. Prehistoric weapons, tools and jewellery found at Emain Macha are on display. The most important finds were four bronze trumpets, 2,000 years old, now in the National Museum, Dublin. From the breezy top of the mound, beyond a limestone quarry, is a fine view of the cathedrals of Armagh.

The big house with curvilinear Dutch gables at **Richhill** was built after 1664. Its magnificent wrought-iron gates, made in 1745 by the Thornberry brothers of Armagh, were moved to Hillsborough Castle in 1936. A mile (2km) south-east at **Aghory** (B131) the Presbyterian church commemorates the father-and-son founders of the Disciples of Christ, an indigenous American fundamentalist church which has over 1½ million adherents. Thomas Campbell had a bible teaching school here. He emigrated from Richhill to the Pennsylvanian backwoods, followed shortly (1809) by his son Alexander, known as the 'Sage of Bethany'. The tower and memorial window at Aghory were a gift from American church members. Another interesting church near here is at **Kilmore** where a medieval spiral staircase is built in to a square tower.

This area, north-east of Armagh, is Ireland's apple orchard country. The bulk of the crop is the tangy Bramley Seedling cooker, harvested in October and sold on the fresh market in Belfast and Dublin. The seventeenth-century settlers, from Worcestershire, laid out the orchards on the same pattern as the orchards of the Vale of Evesham. Round-roofed houses dotted about are mushroom production units. Soft fruit growing has declined though Armagh strawberries are still sold at the roadside in summer. **Loughgall** is surrounded by thousands of acres of apple orchards, a lovely sight in May and early June.

Ardress House and the Argory are two National Trust properties barely 3 miles (5km) apart, and it is easy to see both houses in an afternoon if you plan carefully and check opening days. Ardress House has a long imposing front, with urns on the parapets and a pedimented porch. It was a modest seventeenth-century farmhouse until its architect-owner, George Ensor, enlarged it in about 1770, adding a wing at one end and, for balance, a wall with fake windows at the other. The decoration of the drawing room, with exquisite plaques representing the Four Seasons, is by Michael Stapleton, the Dublin stuccodore, the leading plasterer of the time. Behind the house is an eighteenth-century cobbled farmyard with piggery (real pigs), smithy, chicken houses, and a well in the middle. The **Argory**, a large neo-classical house of about 1820, overlooks the Blackwater river. Its owners, the McGeough-Bonds, were much preoccupied with heating and lighting. A cast-iron stove in the front hall heated the middle of the house, and in 1906 the family installed an acetylene gas plant for lighting. On the first floor is an unusual cabinet barrel organ (1824). The house has a cheerful lived-in feeling, full of furniture, pictures and bric-à-brac. The gas plant, one of very few surviving in the British Isles, can be inspected in the laundry yard. Piped to the light fixtures, the gas gives a warm yellow light.

At the B28/A29 junction, south of the Argory, is ruined **Charlemont Fort** (not signposted) built in 1602 by Charles Blount, Lord Deputy Mountjoy, who had orders to crush O'Neill once and for all. Right on the Armagh/Tyrone border, the fort faced across the Blackwater into the territory of Hugh O'Neill. In 1598 he had beaten the English at Yellow Ford, a few miles from Charlemont, and his power had increased. The gatehouse entrance is visible from the road (B28) at the end of a short avenue of trees. Go through the adjacent farm gate to see the star-shaped ramparts stretching down towards the river (take care not to dislodge masonry). The main accommodation inside was in thatched cottages. One wonders how well the garrison slept in this dangerous place, so close to Tyrone territory. The people across the river had good reason to hate and fear Mountjoy, Elizabeth's toughest and most effective general. The Lord Deputy campaigned all year round. He swept off the cattle, burnt crops, destroyed the peasants' looms and distaffs, and starved O'Neill into submission in 1603. Another approach to the fort, which was finally burnt down in 1921, is via stone steps on Moy bridge.

On the west bank, across the massive stone bridge, it is a surprise to come suddenly on an eighteenth-century village market place, a formal rectangle of lawns and horse-chestnut trees. This is **Moy**, sometimes referred to by local people as 'The Moy'. Its plan was inspired by the square at Marengo in Lombardy, admired by the arty young earl of Charlemont, James Caulfield, during a grand tour of Europe. Houses round the sides mostly date from the 1760s though all the four churches are later. St John's (1819) used to open on to the market place but the front door was walled up, allegedly after a Charlemont lady complained of a draught in her pew, and the church has a peculiar blind look about it. Down towards the river the entrance to the family's estate is marked by a set of magnificent cast-iron white-painted gates, curved screens and pillars with red dragons on top, made by Richard Turner, the Dublin iron-founder who also made the palm house in Belfast's botanic gardens. Beyond the gates there used to be a huge Grand Hotel-style mansion, facing across to Charlemont Fort, but it too was burnt in 1921.

A local riding school is the last vestige of the days of the famous Moy horse fair, which supplied the best cavalry and carriage horses in the British Isles for more than a century. The village had stabling for 2,500 horses. The World War I records of one Moy dealer are an indication of the scale of the operation: a standing weekly order from the Army for 100 troopers and chargers, plus one horse which had to weigh one imperial ton. These noble beasts were destined to pull gun carriages across the battlefields of Europe. In the 1920s the fair dwindled to a 2-day event and ceased altogether by 1950. Ulster poet Paul Muldoon, who grew up here, has written memorably about the fair at 'The Moy'. The local library has a small permanent exhibition on the explorer John King, the only survivor of the 1860 Burke Wills expedition across Australia. He was born near Moy in 1838.

Byways of the Clogher Valley

This understated part of County Tyrone is easily bypassed via the M1 and the A4 linking Belfast and the Fermanagh lakes. Some attempts have been made to market part of the area as the Clogher Valley but the quiet villages along the meandering Blackwater are still largely undiscovered by tourists.

The centre of **Benburb** is dominated by the precincts of a large Victorian redbrick mansion, which has been a Servite priory since 1948. The ballroom is now a chapel and the stable block is a shop. You can see here a stone replica of the O'Neill inauguration stone ceremonially broken at Tullahoge by Mountjoy in 1602. The monks have built a turbine on the Blackwater which generates their electricity. There is a fine view from the priory lawns down the gorge to ruined Benburb castle standing on a rock high above the river where canoeists ride the fast rapids. Sir Richard Wingfield built the castle in 1615 on the site of a Shane O'Neill fort. The monks still call the place 'Shane O'Neill's Castle'. Inside the bawn is a small house with a TV aerial and burglar alarm on the chimney. One of the bawn flanker towers was filled with reinforced concrete in World War II when the mansion was an American army hospital, to serve some now mysterious purpose. The concrete is still there. Another flanker contains an informative display on the Blackwater Valley. A map locates seventeenth-century churches and Celtic crosses, including the massive Clonfeacle cross in the yard of the Catholic church **Clonfeacle** 1½ miles (2km) from Benburb (Blackwatertown direction) and Eglish cross, off Milltown Road, Benburb. Continue along Milltown Road to see a former nineteenth-century weaving factory (now called Benburb Valley Heritage Centre) which preserves an array of linen-making equipment. It has an idyllic setting in the valley beside the old Ulster Canal which may, one day, be linked once again to Lough Erne. It is possible to walk back to Benburb village along the bank, though the path may be overgrown.

In Benburb village street, tiny cottages used for years as apple-peeling sheds have been repaired. They date from the seventeenth century. In the same street, outside the priory gates, is St Patrick's Anglican parish church (confusingly called Clonfeacle parish church), one of the oldest (1618) churches in regular use in Ulster. For access ask at the redbrick rectory opposite. Basically a hall — the belfry tower was added in 1892 — the church has a seventeenth-century font and bell, and a monument to Captain James Hamilton. Hamilton was one of 3,000 Lowland Scots blue bonnets and Protestant Ulstermen killed at the battle of Benburb in 1646. Led by Major General Robert Monroe, the Scots were routed in a disastrous encounter with Owen Roe O'Neill, charismatic nephew of Hugh O'Neill. The Irish are said to have lost only forty men.

The tidy village of **Caledon** takes its name from the earls of Caledon. Their mansion, designed by Thomas Cooley (1779) and enlarged by John Nash (1810), is the fourth great house to be built here. The fourth earl — he was the father of Earl Alexander of Tunis (1891-1969), the World War II field marshal — kept black bears in the park. On the estate is a ruined folly made from the knuckle bones of cattle. It was built in the eighteenth century by Lord Orrery who hoped, he said, to 'strike the Caledonians with wonder and amazement'. The butchers and tanners of Tyrone supplied the bones, though their opinions of the 'bone house' are not recorded. The village street has some attractive buildings and an eighteenth-century Anglican church built by Archbishop Robinson.

Caledon was one of thirty-six villages and halts which were joined by the Clogher Valley Railway. The CVR line was 37 miles (60km) long and ran from Tynan in County Armagh to Maguiresbridge in Fermanagh. It closed in 1941. The railway stations were well built and have been turned into private houses. Some are used as shops and offices. The one at **Augher** is a teashop, and **Aughnacloy** station house is a masonic hall and carefully maintained. Aughnacloy has two eighteenth-century churches, and a row of pretty gabled almshouses. Built with a £10,000 endowment from a Dublin doctor, they are in good condition. This is more than can be said for many of the tall houses, old hotels and faded shop fronts — 'Medical Hall', 'Georgian Hall of Antiques' — lining the wide main street. A numbering system marked on the road is for the benefit of stall holders at the traditional street market held here on the first and third Wednesday of each month. Despite a rather derelict air, the village has a fine position on a high ridge, with good views of Slieve Beagh. However, so long as there is a fortified security checkpoint more or less in the middle of the village, there is little risk of Aughnacloy becoming gentrified.

The ancestral home of American president Ulysses Simpson Grant has been rebuilt and is signposted off the A4 east of Ballygawley. Commander of the victorious Federal armies in the American civil war. Grant took the surrender of Robert E Lee and his Confederate forces on the Appomattox river, Virginia, in 1865. John Simpson, Grant's maternal great-grandfather, left for America in the eighteenth century. He was born in the thatched cottage in 1738.

The romantic castle of Spur Royal across the lake at Augher, visible from the A4, incorporates part of a seventeeth-century bawn. A preserved cottage at **Springtown**, a mile (2km) south of Augher, was the childhood home of William Carleton (1794-1869), author of many stories of Irish peasant life. *Traits and stories of the Irish peasantry* was followed by numerous popular novels, including a bleak tale of the potato famine *Black Prophet* (1847). Youngest son of a small tenant farmer, Carleton went to a hedge school (unlicensed open-air school) and became a hedge schoolmaster himself briefly. Intended for the church, he was put off by a visit to Lough Derg, and soon escaped to a literary life in Dublin. The cottage where he and his thirteen brothers and sisters grew up is down a winding track shaded by trees (ample turning space at the house, where there is a plaque). His parents are buried in the graveyard of St MacCartan's Catholic church in **Ballynagurragh** townland a short distance away. The church has a memorial window to John Joseph Hughes, first archbishop of New York, baptised here in 1797. Hughes worked as a gardener on Favour Royal estate nearby before emigrating in 1817. Carleton's cottage and St MacCartan's church are both signposted from the A4.

Knockmany Hill, 2 miles (3km) north-west of Augher, is topped by a large passage grave with stones incised with swirling patterns similar to those at Newgrange. A cairn, an ugly one, was built over the top in 1959 to protect the grave, which appears above ground in old photographs. You can see the stones through an iron grid. The mythological mother goddess, Ainé, loved by the warrior Finn McCool, is traditionally buried on top of this hill.

Clogher was the fifth-century see of the diocese of Clogher, the oldest bishopric in Ireland, and gives its name to two dioceses,

Protestant and Catholic. The diocese corresponds roughly with Monaghan, Fermanagh and south Tyrone. The first bishop here was St MacCartan (died AD506), a disciple of St Patrick. In medieval times there were endless power struggles between the bishops of Clogher and the vicars general of the deanery of Lough Erne. Pope Sixtus IV made several appointments to the see but the bishop was rarely able to take possession. When the Blessed Oliver Plunket, primate of Armagh, visited Clogher in 1671 he inspected the old diocesan register which catalogued all the bishops. These included Bishop Eoghan (died 1515) who lost a finger on his left hand 'in defence of his church'. The first Protestant bishop, Myler Magrath, who was appointed in 1570 by Elizabeth I, had been appointed bishop of Down and Connor three years earlier — by the pope!

The little Anglican cathedral is tiny. It looks like an English parish church. Rebuilt in purply blue stone in 1744, it preserves an eighth-century sundial, an early sculptured slab cross, good stained glass and a gallery of portraits of long-dead bishops of Clogher. The tower gives a view right down the Clogher Valley. Ask at the rectory for access. In the churchyard are seventeenth-century monuments and two high crosses as well as some sad memorials of Ulster's more recent past. An impressive earthworks in the park behind the cathedral was the seat of the old kings of Oriel, ancestors of the Maguires. Driving south from the village, you cannot avoid seeing, on the left, a tall nineteenth-century tower known as Brackenridge's Folly. The local squirearchy of the time refused to admit George Brackenridge to their number. He remedied the injustice by building the tower as his own mausoleum, thus obliging the county bigwigs who looked down on the living Mr Brackenridge to look up to him when dead. The locals are still amiably rude about him. Sepulchral humour of this kind is not untypical of Northern Ireland.

Blessingbourne House, outside **Fivemiletown**, is an 1870s' Elizabethan-style manor looking on to a small round lake. It has a small carriage and costumes museum (ask at the library in the village). The stable yard is divided into holiday flats popular with pike fishermen. Fivemiletown is five (Irish) miles from the villages of Clogher, Brookeborough and Tempo. Its parish church was built in the same year as St James's in Aughnacloy (1736). Photographs in the library show the Clogher Valley Railway line running down the middle of the main street. Ask the librarian for directions to homes in the area where lace is made, a local cottage industry.

County town and site of an early monastery, **Monaghan's** centre comprises three squares: first, the Diamond, a sloping market square with a pedimented market house of 1792 (now used as the tourist office and for exhibitions), the county museum, the Westenra Hotel, and a large Victorian drinking fountain; next, Old Cross Square which has a peculiar-looking sundial/market cross — part of it is upside down — and a Presbyterian church, rather dour; third, Church Square, with St Patrick's (Anglican) church, the courthouse, and a Crimean War hero's obelisk. These symbols of gravity and orderliness preside over frequent scenes of parking delinquency and traffic jams and there is no point at all in being in a hurry to get out of town. The cathedral of the Roman Catholic diocese of Clogher, St Macartan's, occupies high ground just outside the town and its Gothic Revival outline is visible from a long way off. It was designed mostly by J.J McCarthy, one of his best cathedrals, but he died before it was finished.

The Cross of Clogher

Monaghan County Museum occupies two restored Georgian townhouses, with an adjoining art gallery at the back. It has a large collection of artefacts recovered from the site of lake dwellings (crannogs) common in this part of Ireland, and some fine early examples of nineteenth-century lace, a craft that was developed in Carrickmacross and Clones. Lace-making has recently enjoyed a revival and there is a workshop run on a commercial basis in Carrickmacross itself. The museum's great treasure, however, is the bronze-clad oaken Cross of Clogher, finely decorated with saints and scholars and red enamelwork on the arms. Experts cannot agree on its age — anything from the twelfth to the fourteenth-century.

A crannog in the Convent Lake at the St Louis convent was a stronghold of the MacMahons, who succeeded the O'Carrolls in the thirteenth century as kings of Oriel, a territory approximating to counties Monaghan and Louth. Heber MacMahon (1600-50) was the bishop of Clogher who was adviser to Owen Roe O'Neill. He took over as commander of the Ulster army of the Catholic confederacy after Owen Roe's mysterious death but he had no military training and was soon captured and beheaded. At least seven Macmahons were bishops of Clogher, and three became archbishops of Armagh. The convent's visitor centre traces the development of this French order of nuns which came to post-famine Ireland in 1859 and opened a reformatory for wayward Catholic girls. The order withered away in France but flourishes in all parts of Ireland. The Monaghan convent is the mother-house.

Sir Charles Gavan Duffy (1816-1903), 'Young Irelander' national-

A rector's wife started lace-making at Carrickmacross in the 1820s

ist and Australian statesman, was born in Dublin Street (plaque). He was founder-editor in 1842 of the weekly journal *The Nation* which proclaimed national unity and emancipation, and had a brilliant editorial team, though it lost direction after a disagreement with O'Connell. In 1855 Duffy went to Australia, having lost patience with the slow pace of land reform in Ireland. He became prime minister of Victoria in 1871 and was knighted soon after. He is more famous than another Monaghan-born Duffy — James Duffy (1809-71) — a hedge school-educated bookseller who published some of William Carleton's stories and pioneered cheap books with his Popular Sixpenny Library.

At **Glaslough**, 7 miles (11km) from Monaghan (R185), the house and gardens of Castle Leslie, in a beautiful setting beside a 'green lake' (*glas*, green), are open in summer. The house is a large Victorian mansion, by Lanyon, Lynn & Lanyon, with an unusual cloister joining the house to a billiard room and library. The interior is particularly interesting for its associations with fashionable Edwardian society. The Leslie family have lived here continuously since 1664 and run an equestrian centre on the estate. Glaslough village, built by the Leslies and dependent on the big estate as was the pattern, has a clearly defined architectural expression, with sturdy stone-built houses. At **Donagh** a mile (2km) away, a seventeenth-century ringed high cross, rescued from the bog nearby, has been erected in the old graveyard.

South-west from Monaghan to **Rockcorry** the countryside is strikingly drumlin country. Rockcorry was the birthplace of John Gregg (1867-1948), inventor of Gregg shorthand. His system, easier than Pitman, is still widely used in the US. A few miles west of Rockcorry, near **Newbliss**, the Tyrone Guthrie Centre is an artists' retreat. Sir Tyrone Guthrie (1900-71) directed at all the top theatres in the English-speaking world, founded the Festival Theatre at Stratford, Ontario, and had a theatre in Minneapolis, Minnesota, named in his honour. He left his home, Annaghmakerrig House, to the government to be used as a retreat for artists and writers from anywhere in Ireland and from abroad. Artists have the run of the large Victorian house which overlooks a wooded lake and is surrounded by 400 acres (160 hectares) of peace and quiet. His philanthropy was not confined to the arts: in 1962 he helped start a jam factory (closed 1971) in Newbliss to stem the emigration of people from County Monaghan. Visitors are welcome to walk in the estate at Annaghmakerrig.

Like so many small inland places in Ireland, **Clones** lost first its waterway link and then its railway. The Ulster Canal was abandoned in 1931, and the railway closed in 1959. More recently the road link to Enniskillen in Fermanagh, 24 miles (39km) away, was cut when the British security forces blew up the road bridge to discourage terrorist incursions from here into Northern Ireland. This now thoroughly dislocated town, built on top of a hill, with rather too many roads converging on it, has a wealth of old railway and canal buildings. With a mighty injection of money, they could be turned into heritage centres, museums, waterside pubs and restaurants. In fact some of the buildings along the derelict canal have been purchased by local tourism interests against the distant day when Lough Erne may again be linked to Lough Neagh, bringing tourists floating into town. In the meantime there is rather little to detain the visitor — a tall round tower (no cap) and a stone shrine known as St Tighernach's Grave in Abbey Street, a worn high cross in the market square (Diamond) with a big shaft joined to a too-small head, and a Norman motte. Also in the Diamond is a gallery exhibition of handmade Clones crochet lace. The craft was introduced in Clones in 1847 as a famine relief measure and employed several thousand women at one time. St Tighernach was a sixth-century saint who founded a monastery in Clones. His particular forte was bringing the dead back to life.

The road from Monaghan to Castleblaney (N2) passes **Clontibret** village, scene of Hugh O'Neill's attack in 1595 on Sir Henry Bagenal's forces as they marched home to Newry after routine garrison duties in Monaghan. It was the first proper battle of O'Neill's rebellion. He had been loyal to Queen Elizabeth for 25 years and helped put down a rebellion in Munster in 1569, and Bagenal was his own brother-in-law. But now he realised that Gaelic Ulster would not be allowed to keep its local independence, and so he rebelled. His soldiers had been trained by English captains and some of them even wore the same uniform — red coats. The boggy uneven ground was ideal for the skirmishing style of the Irish and they seem to have won easily. Both sides had muskets, a new weapon then. The English ran out of ammunition and Bagenal had to melt down his pewter plates overnight to make bullets. Clontibret was by way of a practice run for O'Neill's victory at the Yellow Ford in 1598, a success that he was not allowed to repeat. The site of the main battle is about 800yd northeast of the R184/N2 crossroads church.

The entrance to the fine public park at **Castleblaney** is right in the town centre. Residents can stroll from the sloping market square straight into the wooded demesne of a seventeenth-century estate. The town was founded at the north end of **Lough Muckno** by Sir Edward Blayney, governor of County Monaghan under James I. Blayney Castle, renamed Hope Castle, is a Georgian mansion close to the site of Blayney's plantation castle, and is used as a restaurant and community centre. The last (twelfth) Lord Blayney sold it in the 1850s to Henry Hope of the Scottish-Dutch banking family, famous as the owners of the Hope Diamond, largest blue diamond in the world, guaranteed to bring calamity to whoever possessed it. In his will Lord Blayney (died 1874) provided for the building of the town's row of little redbrick almshouses. There are angling competitions on Lough Muckno, a well known coarse fishing water, and international waterskiing. Youth groups bent on canoeing and windsurfing stay in the restored nineteenth-century coach house behind the mansion. Short waymarked trails through Black Island Forest, starting from the mansion, are a less strenuous option.

Approaching **Carrickmacross** from Castleblaney, a prominent wooded mound on the east side of the N2 is the great motte of Donaghmoyne (Manaan Castle), with a ruined stone castle of 1244 on the top. Once a Pipard stronghold, it was abandoned in the fifteenth century. Lace-making in Carrickmacross started in the 1820s, an initiative by Mrs Grace Porter, the rector's wife. It was revived in the hungry 1840s when the technique of tracing designs on cambric was copied from pieces of Belgian guipure lace, and revived again in 1898. Today there is a lace-making co-operative based in a former tollhouse, supported by the nuns of the St Louis convent, and there is a shop. The style is distinctive, appliqué harps and shamrocks on tulle, very labour intensive. St Joseph's church on the edge of the town contains stained glass designed by Harry Clarke (1889-1931) though executed mostly by his studio. On the road from Carrickmacross to Inniskeen, you might stop just before the village

The Cross of Clogher, Monaghan County Museum

to visit a striking modern Catholic church in the shape of a cockle-shell.

The bard of **Inniskeen**, the bohemian Patrick Kavanagh (1904-67) is buried in the cemetery of this little village on the Fane river. Born at Mucker, a mile (2km) from the village, Kavanagh was a farmer's son. He worked on the farm and as a shoemaker and published several books before leaving to earn a precarious literary living in Dublin. A long epic poem, *The Great Hunger* (1942), explores the relationship between the pastoral stereotype and the bleak reality of life for a peasant trapped in toil and poverty, dominated by his old

Hope Castle on the shores of Lough Muckno. The mansion is used as a community centre by the people of Castleblaney, and there is a restaurant

mother and frustrated in every possible way. Kavanagh's interest in archetypes and stereotypes, caricature and stage-Irishness, often pops up in his writings, and he seemed himself to become the embodiment of the coarse, hard-drinking Irish poet. One of his most anthologised lyrical poems *Shancoduff* describes the view from Inniskeen:

> 'My black hills have never seen the sun rising.
> Eternally they look north towards Armagh.'

A disused church near the 40ft (12m) stump of Inniskeen's round tower, makes an atmospheric local museum for memorabilia of the poet, including a death mask. The name of a periodical, *Kavanagh's Weekly*, produced in 1952 with his brother Peter, now attaches to an annual Kavanagh festival held in November. The round tower stump is evidence that there was at one time an important monastic settlement here. The saintly founder was a celebrated sixth-century metalworker, St Daigh. He seems to have spent years in the workshops at Clonmacnois, beating out sacred bells, croziers and umpteen gospel shrines before coming to Inniskeen. The last Inniskeen monk died in 1085 and only the round tower stump remains from that period.

Carlingford and the Cooley Peninsula

Leaving Newry, a scenic route to the Cooley peninsula via Flagstaff viewpoint is indicated immediately south of the town, to the right (Omeath road), and you should take it. The route not only avoids the border checkpoint but cuts out a bit of the truly bad A1/N1 trunk road. There cannot be many major routes in Western Europe where travelling on an unmodernised train is infinitely more civilised than going by road but the Belfast-Dublin route is one such, 100 miles (161km) of stressful driving. The tedium starts north of Newry and continues right into Dublin. The route is littered with broken promises of bypasses and improvements, and hoardings brazenly announcing long-past completion dates, and all underwritten by the 'EEC'. By contrast the Cooley road runs alongside the brimming Newry ship canal, then hugs the shore as far as Carlingford village, and snakes right round the peninsula to rejoin the N1 north of Dundalk. From the picnic site on Flagstaff hill there is a fine view of Carlingford Lough, with Narrow Water Castle on a rock jutting into the estuary on the north bank, prominent even at this distance. It was built in about 1560 to guard the entrance to the Clanrye river. The army of that nasty medieval monarch, King John, crossed the lough by pontoon bridge in 1210 a little further downstream where the dark mound of a Norman motte is visible on the land side of the A2. The king was on his way to confront the troublesome Norman barons at Carrickfergus. Beyond the motte you can see the Red Star ferry plying betweeen Omeath and Warrenpoint.

In an episode in the Ulster Cycle, Cuchulain harried Queen Maeve round the Cooley peninsula. According to the legend she took a short cut up through the Windy Gap at Long Woman's Grave and went back to Connaught, having failed to conquer Ulster or to seize the great Brown Bull of Cooley, a kind of Celtic holy grail. The heathery top of the Cooley mountains around the Windy Gap is the venue for an annual hurling competition — the Poc Fada (Big Hit). Boulders splashed with yellow paint mark out the course. A version of the ferocious ball-and-stick game, a cross between hockey and baseball with a few golf-like rules, can be identified in the *Táin* as played by Cuchulain. An early name for hurling was, in translation 'war games'. The aim is to complete a rugged 3-mile (5km) course in the fewest shots.

Backpackers on the boat from Warrenpoint are likely to be heading for the youth hostel at Omeath. In summer jaunting cars operate between the strand and an open-air stations of the cross in the grounds of a nearby monastery.

The village of **Carlingford**, which once had thirty-two tower houses, has retained its medieval layout, with narrow winding streets and a strongly fortified appearance. Behind it, almost like another natural fortification is Carlingford's highest mountain, Slieve Foy (1,935ft/590m). The main road follows the line of an old railway cutting and runs under the entrance to King John's Castle, an impressive Norman ruin on a rock overlooking the harbour. The castle gateway on the west side was constructed so that only one horseman at a time could pass through. The Protestant church, now an exhibition and heritage centre, was built against the town's fortifications so that the church's medieval tower is actually a part of the wall. Taaffe's Castle in the main street is a fortified town house with a square keep which had a boathouse in the basement that filled up when the tide was in. A picturesque building which forms an arch over the narrow street — just wide enough for a car to pass through — was originally a town gate and was much taller. Called the Tholsel (Parliament), it was where the sovereign and burgesses of Carlingford met. Later it was downgraded to a lockup for rowdies, not too congenial for people living in the adjacent houses, which still have thatched roofs. On the other side of the Tholsel is a fifteenth-century fortified house known as the Mint, though it never was a mint, which has some unusual window carvings. The ruined Dominican abbey with a square central tower dates from 1305. The monks were driven out in 1536 but came back in 1678. In their absence Franciscans had moved in and it took papal pressure to get them out. The narrow streets are filled with holidaymakers in summer, especially during the August oyster festival.

On to **Greenore**, a neat freight port set near the mouth of the sea lough, with the amphitheatre of the Mournes across the narrow channel. Like Carlingford, Greenore, with its golf club and Scotch pines, is extremely tidy, an immaculately-kept corner of Ireland. On the less sheltered south side of the peninsula, past the turning to Grange, which has a little church of 1762, is the small grey harbour and caravan park of Gyles Quay, with a neat terrace of B&B cottages. Before joining the traffic moving sluggishly along the N1, turn in to the estate of Ballymascanlon House hotel to inspect the **Proleek** dolmen, signposted along a path from the hotel carpark. There cannot be many dolmen capstones in Ireland whose precise weight is known: 46.74 tonnes. Someone must have weighed it in modern metric times.

Beer and cigarettes are manufactured in **Dundalk**, the county town of Louth. An austere Greek revival courthouse, its portico

Carlingford Lough, from the viewpoint on Flagstaff Hill

drawn from the Theseum in Athens, faces into the market square where some modern fountains have been installed to enliven the dispiriting town centre. A fledgling museum occupies a building in Jocelyn Street. Otherwise there is little reason to linger in Dundalk unless you want to visit the cigarette factory.

A twelfth-century motte 2 miles (3km) west of Dundalk, called **Dún Dealgan**, was thrown up by the de Verdons, the local Norman rulers. It was the site of the original settlement. Now overgrown with beech trees, it is a prominent landmark on the south side of the N53. The building on the top is an eighteenth-century folly. Continue along this road and turn left after 3 miles (5km) to see the impressive ruins of **Castle Roche**, the de Verdons' most ambitious building project, a guardian of the medieval English (Anglo-Norman) Pale. Standing on a high rock that rears up from the surrounding country-side, the thirteenth-century castle had a commanding view of the unfriendly Gaelic territory to the north. It marked the northern extent of the Pale — the part of Ireland which was under English jurisdiction, controlled from Dublin. The area varied from time to time but roughly speaking it stretched from Dundalk down as far as the Wicklow hills. Everywhere else was literally 'beyond the Pale'.

An agreeable pit-stop on the N1 is **Castlebellingham**, 8 miles (13km) south of Dundalk, where there is a kink in the road to accommodate the old demesne of the Bellingham estate. The first big house, owned by Colonel Thomas Bellingham, was burnt by King James's soldiers before the battle of the Boyne when the colonel was away fighting for King William. The house of 1690-1700, which had

*The huge entrance stone at Newgrange with its impressive spiral ornamentation.
Behind this is the entrance to the tomb itself*

a steeply pitched roof, was described in approving terms by Mrs Delany in 1745. Much altered since, the castle is now a hotel. The village has two small triangular greens, and a famous seventeenth-century physician is buried in the churchyard: Dr Thomas Guither, who is said to have introduced frogs into Ireland. The profusion of wild flowers on verges and beside paths in otherwise unpromising areas reminds visitors, from Great Britain at least, where industrialised farming methods have all but wiped out wild flowers, that they are in Ireland. At the end of April, for instance, this little place on the N1 is full of cow parsley, flowering wild garlic and snowbells — *allium triquetrum* — garlic masquerading as white bluebells.

A mile (2km) south of Dundalk on the N52, where the main road makes a 90-degree turn, take the road to Louth (R171) to see **St Mochta's House**, a twelfth-century church in the tiny village from which the county takes its name. St Mochta (died AD534) was a companion of St Patrick. According to the legend the first church here was built in a single night to give shelter to St Mochta who, for some reason, had been frozen out of his original church at Omeath. He moved inland to Louth, laid out a cemetery and lit a fire. After local druids tried but failed to put the fire out, the saint was able to get on with his work. The monastery he founded here produced 100 bishops and 300 priests. The present medieval church is a good example of double-roof construction: the great weight of the steeply pitched stone roof is supported by a vaulted arch. The upper storey has a small window and is reached from below by a narrow staircase. Inside the church there is a broken sundial. It is always accessible.

The thirteenth-century castle at **Ardee** is contemporary with Castle Roche and is a prominent feature seen from the N2 which goes through the middle of the town. You may be able to get inside Ardee castle if you ask the town clerk, but Ardee's other castle, Hatch's Castle in Market Street, is not accessible. Ardee was an important outpost of the Pale and levied tolls to pay for the walling of the town. The walls do not seem ever to have been very substantial and have vanished except for a minuscule fragment, not marked on the town's map, known as Cappock's Gate some way off the main street, past a memorial to an Ardee IRA man killed in 1920. A notice set into the town bridge is a reminder of another Cuchulain exploit described in the *Táin* when the Ulster hero slew Ferdia, champion of Connaught at a river ford, a place called thereafter Áth Phirdia, 'Ford of Ferdia'. There is a pleasant walk along the bank of the Dee towards the purported scene of the action.

The Celtic cross at **Monasterboice** known as Muiredach's Cross is

The monastic remains at Monasterboice

one of the finest in Ireland. So called because of the inscription on the base which says Muiredach erected it, the cross is made from one piece of rock and stands nearly 18ft (5m) high. The scenes are still marvellously clear more than 1,000 years after they were created (AD920). New Testament scenes appear on the west side, and Old Testament scenes on the east. On the top is a house with a steeply pitched, tiled roof. The monastic remains at Monasterboice, all inside the cemetery, consist of two churches, three crosses, a ninth-century round tower 95ft (29m) high but without a cap, a sundial and two early cross-carved grave slabs. Founded by St Buite (died AD521) the monastery was influential and wealthy. A second, more worn cross, called the West Cross or Tall Cross, is 21ft and 6 inches high, but is made up from several sections.

Trains started running between Dublin and Belfast when the last bit of the line, the viaduct over the Boyne at **Drogheda**, was finished in 1855. Today the express from Belfast rushes past the town but the stopping trains slow down on this spectacular Victorian viaduct before entering Drogheda station, giving a great view on both sides. To the right you see the steepness of the old town, its quays, bridges and huddle of austere grey churches and historic buildings on the north bank and, on the left side, the long narrow estuary and the port which handles most of the Republic's newsprint, coming in from Scandinavia.

The town walls, which were started in 1234, have more or less disappeared, with the exception of the St Lawrence Gate barbican, a splendid survivor from the thirteenth century, now in need of restoration. Francis Johnston designed the little Tholsel, now a bank, and the courthouse, which has an unusual weathervane, and also the tower and spire of the Anglican church of St Peter. Magdalene Tower, part of a Dominican friary church, is visible from all over the town. The Catholic church, another St Peter's, preserves the embalmed head of Oliver Plunkett, hanged at Tyburn in 1681 and canonised in 1975. It is a gruesome and pathetic sight.

Millmount hill, a large Norman mound on the south side of the river is topped by some eighteenth-century military barracks and a martello-type tower. There is a view over the whole town from up here. The tower still bears the scars of a battering by a pro-Treaty force in 1922 during the civil war. The old officers' quarters have been refurbished to house the town's museum, the Millmount museum, which has an outstanding collection of painted guild banners. The notorious massacre by Cromwell of the defenders of Drogheda during his Irish campaign of 1649-50 began on this hill. When the town wall was breached, the defenders, led by the royalist Sir Arthur Aston, were forced back to the Millmount. After they surrendered Cromwell ordered them to be put to death and, by his own reckoning, 2,000 men were summarily executed.

The historic battle of the Boyne when Protestant William of Orange defeated the exiled Catholic English king James, was fought about 4 miles (6km) upstream from Drogheda. The Boyne valley is good farming land and there is a lush greenness along its banks. On the day of the battle, 12 July 1690 (1 July in the old calendar), the countryside was all open cornfields. The leafy place called **King William's Glen** on the north bank at Oldbridge is signposted and there is a battlefield viewpoint above the carpark, but the area is mostly delightfully untamed, with the kind of vegetation associated with derelict canals. In fact the river at this point is canalised and there are two locks at Oldbridge, part of the 19-mile (31km) Boyne navigation abandoned in 1924. The earlier of the two locks was engineered in 1750 by Thomas Steers, an Englishman who had fought here as a young Williamite soldier 60 years before.

Treasures of the Historic Boyne Valley

A little further upstream are the great passage-tomb mounds of Newgrange, Knowth and Dowth, the three most impressive of some twenty-six collective passage tombs in a vast neolithic cemetery ranged along the Boyne valley. The largest is **Newgrange** which, from a distance, looks like a flying saucer. A constant stream of visitors, disgorged from the tourist coaches, flows through the site, examining the swirling geometric decorations carved on large stones and queueing to see inside the cruciform central chamber which has perfect solar alignment: it is illuminated for just 17 minutes at the winter solstice when the rising sun penetrates the length of the 60ft (18m) passageway. Both Knowth and Dowth are visible from Newgrange. The great mound at **Knowth** has two passage tombs inside, and seventeen smaller ones surrounding it. Excavations have been going on for more than 30 years. There is still no public access to the interior but there is a viewing platform, accessible all year, and guided tours of the site. When Knowth is fully opened perhaps there will be less pressure on Newgrange. Dowth is still unexcavated but you can look around the grounds.

There is a wealth of early and medieval Christian history to be explored along the valley of the Boyne. The following two places are particularly notable: firstly, the ruins of **Mellifont Abbey**, the 'honey fountain', Ireland's first and most influential Cistercian house, founded in 1142 by St Malachy who came here with monks from Clairvaux. It has an unusual two-storey lavabo. Access is north off the N51 west of Drogheda. Secondly, **Bective Abbey**, which was founded 5 years later by the king of Meath, also for the Cistercians, has a fine fifteenth-century cloister. It is 5 miles (8km) south of Navan, county town of Meath, in an area of arable farming and bloodstock farms, and where there seem to be many travelling people on the move in summer.

A mile (1km) north of Slane village is the **Hill of Slane** where St Patrick lit the first Paschal Fire in AD434 as a direct challenge to King Laoghaire's fire on the **Hill of Tara** south of here. Anyone setting a fire that was visible from Tara was meant to be put to death. Accordingly, Patrick was taken before the king and tried to convert him, calling on the spirit of Cuchulain to help him. Although Laoghaire decided against punishing the saint, he was not sufficiently impressed to change to the new religion from his own pagan beliefs. Today there is a statue of St Patrick standing on the top of the Hill of Tara. King Laoghaire is, one might say, nowhere. A redundant Anglican church on the site has been converted to a visitor centre. It is a pleasant surprise to find a two-light stained glass window by Evie Hone, made in 1936, in the church. **Slane** itself is a pretty village where four tall and elegant Georgian townhouses are built round an octagonal 'square' at the crossroads. Slane Castle, in a beautiful position above the Boyne, is the Irish estate of Lord Henry Mountcharles who holds megasonic international rock concerts in the grounds in summer.

The lyric poet Francis Ledwidge (c1891-1917) was born in a roadside cottage ½ mile (1km) down the Drogheda road. The eighth child of poor parents, Ledwidge was a farm labourer, then a road overseer, before going to Flanders in the ranks of the Inniskillings to fight, he said 'for the green fields along the Boyne'. He was killed at Ypres. The first collection of his poems *Songs of the fields* was published in 1916, a second in 1917 and a third in 1918. Exhibits include first drafts of some of his poems, and letters to Lord Dunsany, the prominent Irish revival figure, who saw in Ledwidge the promise of an authentic Irish rural voice. Dunsany wrote introductions to each of the three volumes.

The N2 from Slane to Ardee is roughly parallel with the N1 further east and is a much pleasanter way to cover the distance. The road runs through a deep green valley where small nimble cattle graze the steep meadows, so steep that one farmer uses not a dog but a sure-footed billygoat to herd his animals. Further north is **Collon** village, with a monster of an Anglican church that looks like King's College Chapel, Cambridge, England, dominating a deep valley. An adjoining domestic garden, but no house, suggests that until recently a clergyman's house stood here, surely inoffensive compared with the church. At Ardree you could continue north via Louth and St Mochta's House instead of taking the direct road to Dundalk.

The road from Ardee to **Kells** is 20 miles (32km) of bad N52 but the ancient town is a rewarding visit. Do not try to sightsee by car. Park tall round tower which, though minus its cap, is nearly 100ft (30m) high and has five windows round the top (a claimant to the high kingship of Ireland was murdered in the tower in 1076); a large ornately carved high cross (South Cross) near the tower dating from the ninth century; a tall stump of a cross covered in decorations; an unfinished cross with a plain back and shaft but beautfully carved on the front; a medieval belfry, standing alone, has some cross-carved grave slabs incorporated into it. Inside the modern church is a display of photographs showing various items connected with the monastery, including pages from the illuminated Latin manuscript of the four gospels, the Book of Kells, the monastery's greatest treasure which is now in Trinity College, Dublin. Outside the churchyard, turn up Market Street. The houses at the lower end are two-storey, but as you climb the hill they become single-storey cottages

St Columba's House, Kells, is thought to date from the early ninth century

Trim has the most extensive Norman castle in Ireland

arranged in short terraces, hugging the contour of the ancient hill. Right at the top, opposite Kells Handball Club, is St Columba's House contemporary with St Mochta's House at Louth, with the same double-roof construction, though the lower part of the walls may be as early as the ninth century.

One of the main strongholds of the medieval English Pale, **Trim** has more buildings dating from that period than most towns, but they have not been generally well looked after. Trim could be trimmer. Now officially designated a 'heritage town' it may become so. Admirably positioned on the south bank of the Boyne river, Trim Castle is the most extensive Norman castle in Ireland, with an outer wall almost 500yd long and D-shaped towers set into it at intervals, an awful lot of wall to have to defend. It used to be surrounded by a moat that could be filled with water diverted from the Boyne whenever the garrison deemed it necessary. Founded by Hugh de Lacy in about 1173, its first royal guest seems to have been King John who came here in 1210 during his feud with the Norman barons, and confiscated the castle. By the time of Richard II's visit of 1399 — the last visit to Ireland by a king of England until James II landed 300 years later — the castle was in poor shape.

Across the river on higher ground is a fine fourteenth-century bell tower known as the Yellow Steeple, 125ft (38m) high, built over an Augustinian monastery. The tower is the chief monument to the communities of Augustinian, Dominican and Franciscan friars who once flourished here. One wonders what the brothers would make of modern Trim's 'Nun Run', a Monty Python-like event devised by a Trim headmaster to raise school funds. Nun-jockeys up on Vatican Calling, Chastity's Delight (for example) race along the river bank. The old town bridge is part-medieval and the tower of the Anglican cathedral dates from 1449. The town walls have gone except for a little two-storey tower called Sheep Gate, one of the original five gates of the town. Near the Yellow Steeple, on the site of St Mary's Abbey, is Talbot's Castle, dating from the fifteenth century, which was converted into the diocesan school attended by Arthur Wellesley, Duke of Wellington. There is a statue of him in Patrick Street, on yop of a lofty column, where he had lodgings. In 1717 Talbot's Castle figured in a successful property speculation deal when Esther Johnson (Dean Swift's 'Stella') bought it and quickly sold it, to Swift. He promptly sold it in a rising market!

Further Information
— From the Mournes to the Boyne —

Places to Visit

Annalong
Co Down
Annalong Cornmill
Guided tours June to September 2-6pm.

Ardee
Co Louth
Contact: Ardee Town Clerk
☎ (041) 53555

Ardress House
Co Armagh
Annaghmore
National Trust property
Open: April to September but not Tuesday.
☎ (01762) 851236

The Argory
Co Armagh
Signposted at Moy
National Trust property. Open: April to September but not Thursday.
☎ (0186 87) 84753

Armagh
Robinson Library
Open: Monday to Friday 10am-1pm, 2-4pm.
☎ (01861) 523142

Armagh County Museum
Open: Monday to Saturday 10am-5pm.
☎ (01861) 523070

Armagh Planetarium
Open: 11.30am-5pm except Saturday/ Sunday mornings. Observatory grounds self-guided tours: April to September Monday to Friday 9.30am-4.30pm.
☎ (01861) 523689

Palace Stables
Archbishop's Palace
Heritage centre and estate buildings.
Open: daily 10am-7pm (until 5pm in winter).
☎ (01861) 522722
A second heritage centre, *St Patrick's Trian*, is behind the Tourist Information Office in English Street. Same hours as Stables.

Benburb
Co Tyrone
Benburb Valley Heritage Centre
Milltown Road
Open: Easter to September Tuesday to
Saturday 10am-5pm, and Sunday
afternoon.
☎ (01861) 549752

Carlingford
Co Louth
Holy Trinity Heritage Centre
Open: most days, guided tours of the
town.
☎ (042) 73454

Carrickmacross
Co Monaghan
Carrickmacross Lace Gallery
Open: May to October 9am-12.30pm,
1.30-5pm daily except Friday and
Sunday.

Castlewellan
Co Down
National Arboretum
Castlewellan Forest Park
Main Street
Open: Monday to Friday 8am-8pm,
Saturday and Sunday 10am-8pm,
closes 4pm in winter.
☎ (013967) 786664

Drogheda
Co Louth
Millmount Museum
Millmount
Open: 2-6pm Tuesday to Sunday in
summer, 3-5pm Wednesday, Saturday
and Sunday in winter.

Drumiller Cheese
Co Down
15 Leapoges Road
Dromore
☎ (01846) 692211

Drumballyroney School
Co Down
(Brontë Homeland Centre)
Near Rathfriland (B7)
Open: March to September 10am-6pm.
☎ (018206) 62991

Dundalk
Co Louth
Dundalk Museum
Jocelyn Street
Open: Tuesday to Saturday 10am-5pm,
Sunday 2-6pm.
☎ (042) 26579

Dundrum Castle
Co Down
Open: Tuesday to Saturday 10am-7pm,
Sunday 2-7pm (until 4pm in winter).

Fivemiletown
Co Tyrone
Blessingbourne Carriage Museum
Open: Easter to September.
☎ (013656) 21221

Fivemiletown Library
☎ (013655) 21409. Open: Monday,
Tuesday, Friday, Saturday 11am-5pm,
and Thursday 2-8pm.

Glaslough
Co Monaghan
Castle Leslie Estate and Gardens
Open: 12noon-7pm weekends and
holidays Easter to end October, and
every day June to August.
☎ (047) 88109

Gosford Forest Park
Co Armagh
Markethill (B28)
Open: 10am to dusk.
The castle is not open.
☎ (01861) 551277

Greencastle
Co Down
Greencastle Castle
On-site guide: April to September all
day except Mondays and Sunday
morning.

Hill of Tara
Co Meath
This site is always accessible. The
visitor centre, with audio visual and
guided tours, is open: May to end
October 9.30am-6pm.
☎ (046) 25903

Inniskeen
Inniskeen Folk Museum
Co Monaghan
☎ (042) 78102

Knowth
Co Meath
Open: May to end October 10am-5pm,
longer hours in summer. Guided tour
on request.
☎ (041) 24488

Mellifont Abbey
Co Louth
Guided tours May to September
9.30am-6.30pm but not on Sunday
morning, or Monday in spring.
☎ (041) 24488

Monaghan
Monaghan County Museum
Hill Street
Open: Tuesday to Saturday 11am-1pm,
2-5pm.
☎ (047) 82928

St Louis Convent Heritage Centre
Open: Monday, Tuesday, Thursday,
Friday 10am-12noon, 2-4pm, and
weekend afternoons.
☎ (047) 83529

Mullaghbawn
Co Armagh (on B30)
Mullaghbawn Folk Museum
Open: Monday to Saturday 11am-5pm,
Sunday 2-6pm May to September. In winter it is only open Sunday afternoon.
☎ (0693) 8882878/838762

Navan Fort (Emain Macha)
Co Armagh
Signposted off A28
Access always to the great mound.
Interpretative centre open Monday to
Saturday 10am-7pm (until 5pm in
winter) and Sunday from 11.30am.
☎ (01861) 525550

Newbliss
Co Monaghan
Tyrone Guthrie Centre
Annaghmakerrig House
☎ (047) 54003

Newgrange
Co Meath
Passage-tomb mound
Tours every day all year except
Monday in winter and 25-26 December.
Advance booking advised in summer.
☎ (041) 24488

Newry
Co Down
Newry Museum
Bank Parade
Open: Monday to Friday 11am-5pm
and Saturday morning.
☎ (01693) 66232

McCann's Bakery
Castle Street
☎ (01693) 2076

Peatlands Park
Co Armagh
M1 exit 13
Open: 9am to dusk. Railway: weekend
afternoons Easter to September.
☎ (01762) 851102

Silent Valley
Co Down
Head Road, off B27 from Kilkeel
Open: daily 10am-6.30pm, closes
4.30pm in winter.
☎ (01232) 746581

Saintfield
Co Down
Rowallane Gardens
Open: April to October 10.30am-6pm
weekdays and weekend afternoons. In
winter the gardens are not open at the
weekend.
☎ (01238) 510131

Slane
Slane Castle
Co Meath
Enquiries about guided tours: ☎ (041)
24207

Francis Ledwidge Cottage Museum
Slane
Open: daily. Closed Sunday mornings
and winter Saturdays.
☎ (041) 24285

Tandragee
Co Armagh
Tayto Potato Crisp Factory
☎ (01762) 840249

Trim
Co Meath
Trim Castle is accessible all year round.
Guided walking tours of the town
(June to September) leave from the
tourist office in Mill Street.
☎ (046) 37111 (summer). In the same
street is a heritage/exhibition centre.
☎ (046) 37227 or (off season) ☎ (046)
31238

Ulysses S Grant Ancestral Home
Co Tyrone
Watch for signposts on A4 east of
Ballygawley
Open: April to September Monday to
Saturday 10am-5pm and Sunday
afternoon.
☎ (01662) 527133

Travel
Carlingford Lough Boat
(Warrenpoint-Omeath)
Red Star passenger ferry departs every
20 minutes 1-6pm, June to September.
Marine Parade, Warrenpoint.
☎ (016937) 72001/72682

Tourist Information Offices
Open: all year.
Armagh
Co Armagh
40 English Street
☎ (01861) 527808

Banbridge
Co Down
Newry Road (A1)
☎ (018206) 23322

Dundalk
Co Louth
Market Square
☎ (042) 35484

Kilkeel
Co Down
6 Newcastle Street
☎ (016937) 62525

Lurgan
Co Armagh
Lurgan Town Hall
☎ (01762) 323757

Monaghan
Co Monaghan
Market House
☎ (047) 81122

Newcastle
Co Down
10 Central Promenade
☎ (013967) 22222

Portadown
Co Armagh
Portadown Town Hall
☎ (01762) 353260

7 • Dublin & Environs

The allure of the coastal areas north and south of Dublin presents the first-time visitor with some hard choices about what to see in the city itself. If you have only a few hours, spend them walking about in the centre. A whistle-stop car tour is not advised. For one thing, the understated charms of this still obsessively Anglophile city tend to elude the visitor in a hurry. For another, you are bound to get stuck in the traffic.

Numerous small residential districts tucked away here and there give parts of central Dublin the intimacy of a village. Even round the imposing Four Courts, the tell-tale scent of turf fills the air and sure enough, behind the courthouse is a mini-village. Opposite the deanery of St Patrick's cathedral a pocket of public housing with a tiny park has been built on the site of the disused Capuchin/Huguenot cemetery known locally as 'The Cabbage Patch'.

The south bank of the Liffey has a large proportion of the more interesting buildings, including the city's two cathedrals (both Anglican, some people are surprised to discover), the main museums, art galleries, Dublin Castle, Trinity College, Leinster House (parliament), and the better kept residential Georgian squares and streets. You will not need seven-league boots since all these are inside a 1-mile x ¾-mile rectangle fronted by the river.

The **Custom House** and the **Four Courts**, the two great classical architectural set pieces on the north bank, are best viewed from the quays on the south side. The Custom House has recently been superbly restored, mostly with money from the national lottery, and despite an intrusive railway bridge nearby, there is no more handsome waterfront façade in Europe. Like the Four Courts upstream, the interior was destroyed in the 1920s. The original 'four courts' were the courts of Chancery, King's Bench, Exchequer and Common Pleas which opened off a circular hall. Whenever the courts are working you can poke your head into the tumult of the central hall, an animated sea of bobbing wigs. Both these buildings were the work

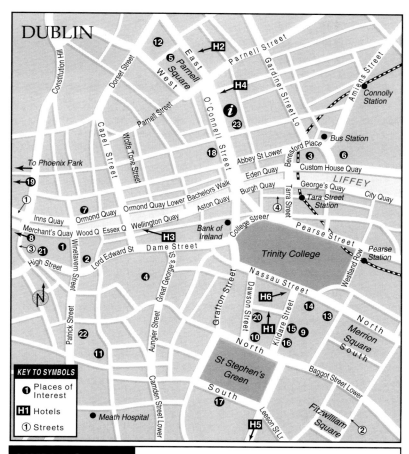

DUBLIN

H2

12
6 East Parnell Square West

H4

O'Connell Street
Parnell Street

i

23

Constitution Hill
Dorset Street
Capel Street
Wolfe Tone Street
Parnell Street

Amiens Street
Connolly Station

18

Abbey St Lower

Bus Station

To Phoenix Park

Eden Quay

3

6

Custom House Quay

19

Burgh Quay

George's Quay
LIFFEY
City Quay

1

Ormond Quay
Ormond Quay Lower
Bachelors Walk
Aston Quay

Tara Street Station
Tara Street

7

Inns Quay
Wellington Quay
College Street

4

Merchant's Quay Wood Q Essex Q
Bank of Ireland

Pearse Street
Pearse Station

8

H3

Dame Street

3 21 1

Lord Edward St
Great George's St

Winetavern Street

High Street

Trinity College

4

Nassau Street

Westland Row

N

Patrick Street

H6

Grafton Street
Dawson Street
Kildare Street

14

13

North Merrion Square South

22

20

H1

15 9

10

16

11

North

South

KEY TO SYMBOLS

1 Places of Interest

H1 Hotels

1 Streets

St Stephen's Green

Baggot Street Lower

Meath Hospital

17

South

Camden Street Lower

Leeson St Lr

Fitzwilliam Square

2

H5

KEY TO MAP

Places of Interest

1 'Adam & Eve' church
2 Christ Church Cathedral
3 Custom House
4 Dublin Castle
5 Dublin Writers Museum
6 Financial Centre
7 Four Courts
8 Kilmainham Royal Hospital
9 Leinster House
10 Mansion House
11 Marsh's Library
12 Municipal Gallery of Modern Art
13 National Gallery

14 National Library
15 National Museum
16 Natural History Museum
17 Newman House
18 Post Office
19 President's Residence
20 Royal Irish Academy
21 St Audeon's Church
22 St Patrick's Cathedral
23 St Mary's Pro-Cathedral

Hotels

1 Buswells
2 Castle Hotel
3 Clarence Hotel
4 Gresham Hotel
5 Kilronan House
6 Power's Hotel

Streets

1 Arran Quay
2 Fitzwilliam Street
3 Lower Bridge Street
4 Poolbeg Street

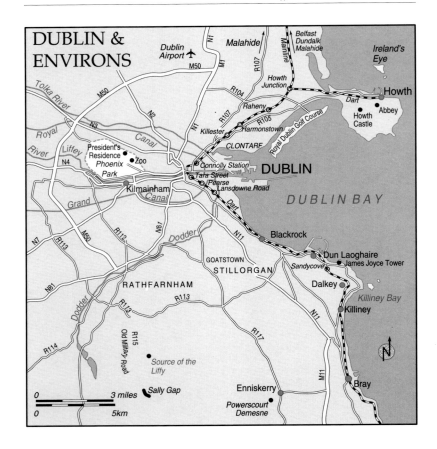

of the English Huguenot James Gandon (1743-1823) who also designed **O'Connell Bridge** — not that he would recognise the eight-
lane vehicle-laden highway it has become. This most essential bridge
appears even wider than it is: the traffic pours straight down O'Connell
Street, Dublin's brash and noisy central thoroughfare, and, once
across the river, must somehow dissipate itself through narrower
roads on the south side. The only direction it cannot go is straight on.

Just upstream in marked contrast is the elegant **Halfpenny Bridge**,
a cast-iron footbridge built across the river in 1816. Ragged beggar
children monitor both ends of the bridge, accosting pedestrians
hurrying to and from Merchant's Arch. Do they know, one wonders,
that this used to be a toll bridge? Unlikely; they turn out to be junior
detachments of the city's sizeable army of vagrants, which surprises
by its boldness and high visibility.

Next to the gleaming Portland stone of the Custom House, on the edge of Dublin's dockland, is something completely different: a huge power-dressed green glass office complex straight out of downtown Pittsburgh. It is Dublin's International Financial Services Centre (IFSC), occupied by banks and insurance companies. Dubliners do not know quite what to make of this self-assured newcomer to the banks of the Liffey.

Second-hand books and bric à brac are sold from the ground floor of often dilapidated buildings along the quays which have a distinctly neglected look, accentuated by rather too many unkempt hairy trees. Notable exceptions are the blue-and-gold painted fronts of the Dublin Woollen Mills shops facing each other across the river, the agreeable old-fashioned Clarence Hotel and, off Merchant's Quay, a domed Franciscan church called 'Adam and Eve' after a tavern which served as the church in the days before Catholic emancipation. Walk quickly past Dublin Corporation's unlovely civic offices on Wood Quay, and go up Winetavern Street. Just below an office block with a Lady of Shallot turret, turn right to **St Audoen's Arch**, the sole surviving gateway of the old walled city, with a bit of thirteenth-century wall attached. Crammed in on a steep incline behind the gateway is Dublin's last remaining medieval parish church. It has a twelfth-century bell tower and west door. The interesting architectural perspectives of this odd little corner vanish as you emerge on to High Street.

Dublin's Custom House, gutted by fire in the 1920s, splendidly retored in the 1990s

Up here at street level St Audeon has another church dedicated to him, a large Victorian church that has been saved from decay by a local priest, Father Fitzpatrick. He runs a coffee shop and travel agency in the church. There is a stereophonic multi-visual presentation of pre-Viking Ireland going full blast in the nave, every day except Sunday. The shows are timed to avoid mass.

Christ Church Cathedral and **St Patrick's Cathedral** both have an even direr need to raise money. In Victorian times they were rescued by wealthy drinks magnates — Sir Benjamin Guinness (beer) who funded the restoration of St Patrick's, and Sir Henry Roe (whiskey) who did the same for Christ Church. Nowadays both cathedrals are obliged to make a modest entrance charge. Founded in 1038 by Sitric, a Christianised king of the Danes of Dublin, Christ Church still has its original Danish crypt, though almost everything else you see now is Sir Henry's restoration. A Bridge of Sighs arch across the road links the cathedral with its synod hall. Instead of the soft shoe-shuffle of bishops hurrying to meetings, the building has adjusted itself to occupation by a historical audio-visual drama in the Great Hall and reconstructions of medieval Dublin streets. The National Museum has loaned some artefacts from the city's Viking period which were found during excavations at Wood Quay.

Richard de Clare, second earl of Pembroke, who enlarged the cathedral is better known as 'Strongbow', the invader of Ireland

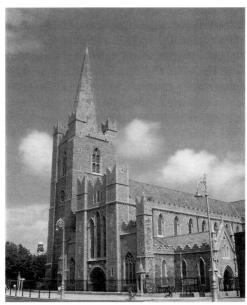

St Patrick's, the larger of Dublin's two Anglican cathedrals, is in the residential area known as the Liberties

The river Liffey, Dublin

(1169). He spoke French but most of his soldiers were Welsh. Names like Hughes, Price and Ellis, which sound so Welsh, are common Irish surnames. Visitors to the cathedral make a beeline for 'Strongbow's tomb' which, so it is said, contains only his intestines. A realistic heart-shaped casket with a large thick bolt on it, also attracts close attention. Inside is the heart of St Laurence O'Toole, a twelfth-century archbishop of Dublin.

The much bigger cathedral of St Patrick is a short walk away through a historically interesting but rundown residential area known as the Liberties. Many of the redbrick Victorian tenements were built by the philanthropist Edward Cecil Guinness (1847-1927), first earl of Iveagh. In fact, this whole area is Guinness country, with beery breezes wafting from the huge breweries just west of here.

St Patrick's is famous for its satirical eighteenth-century dean, Jonathan Swift (1667-1745), who gave a large part of his income to charities. He was idolised by the Liberties people. His grave and the grave of Esther Johnson ('Stella') in the south aisle, are on every literary pilgrim's itinerary. Inscribed above the door of the robing room is his own famous epitaph: 'ubi saeva indignatio ulterius cor lacerare nequit' — [here he lies] 'where fierce indignation can no longer tear his heart'.

In the north choir aisle is the sombre grave of Frederick, Duke of

Leinster House, the seat of the Irish Parliament, Dublin

Schomberg who was killed at the Boyne in 1690, aged 75. There was no memorial until, over 40 years later, Swift installed and paid for this tomb and wrote a sarcastic inscription reproaching the duke's neglectful family. A veteran of the Thirty Years' War Schomberg had been a Marshal of France under Louis XIV until the Huguenots were expelled at the Revocation of the Edict of Nantes (1685). Instead of retiring gracefully, he signed up with William of Orange. Turlough O'Carolan (1670-1738), last of the Irish bards, is also commemorated here, and so is the Irish painter Samuel Lover (1797-1868) — both of whom had trouble with their eyes. As Lover's sight deteriorated, he turned his hand to entertainment, writing and performing songs and sketches, the Percy French of his time. Handel gave an organ recital in the cathedral in 1742, the same year that the *Messiah* was first performed in Dublin.

Close to the cathedral, **Marsh's Library** opened in 1701 as the first public library in Ireland. The charming dark oak interior houses some 25,000 rare sixteenth- to eighteenth-century books bequeathed by scholarly theologians. Nearby is the cathedral choir school, founded 1432. The choirs of Dublin's two cathedrals sang in the chorus at the *Messiah* premiere.

The city's main Catholic church is **St Mary's Pro-Cathedral**, on the north side of the river off O'Connell Street. Started in 1816 as St

The National Gallery has an outstanding collection of Irish paintings, Dublin

Mary's Metropolitan Catholic Chapel, its Doric style is characteristic of Roman Catholic church buildings of the period. The Greek struggle for independence in the early nineteenth century was seen to have a parallel in Ireland.

Leinster House, the parliament building in Kildare Street, is flanked by the National Museum and the National Library, a nearly matching pair of buildings with rotunda entrances. The other façade, beyond a lawn on the Merrion Square side, is similarly flanked by the **National Gallery** and the **Natural History Museum**. None of these places opens until 10am. However, visitors who enjoy a surfeit of museums and galleries should note that the Gallery, which in addition to the national collections of Irish paintings and portraits, has a large collection of seventeenth-century European masters, is open 7 days a week. Leinster House itself is open to the public when parliament is not sitting. When it is sitting, you may be able to get into the public gallery of the Dáil (Lower House).

The **National Museum**'s superb collection of Celtic and early Christian Irish antiquities was created largely by the Royal Irish Academy (founded 1785) and transferred here from the Academy's premises in 1891. The collections have outgrown the premises and the lack of space is acute but you should be able to see some if not all of the following outstanding exhibits: the Tara Brooch and the

The Natural History Museum, Dublin

Ardagh Chalice, both exquisite eighth-century treasures, the twelfth-century Shrine of St Patrick's Bell, numerous other fine shrines and altar vessels, processional crosses and crucifixes. Notable pre-Christian treasures are the first-century BC Broighter Hoard found in County Londonderry, which includes a gold model boat with oars and a mast; and the seventh-century BC ornaments from County Clare known as the Feakle Treasure. Also on view are Irish harps, uilleann pipes and other musical instruments, Irish glass and silver, and more Wood Quay Viking finds.

Among the books and manuscripts in the **National Library** are first editions of works of Irish writers which are preserved in the Reading Room. To see the *Book of Kells* and some other important early illuminated manuscripts you must visit **Trinity College, Dublin** (often called TCD) round the corner. This beautifully ornamented manuscript of the four Gospels, written in Latin on vellum in about AD800, and the precious Books of Durrow, Dimma, and Armagh, were all conserved and rebound in the 1950s by the bookbinder Roger Powell (died 1990) and are on view in the Treasury. The Book of Armagh, which contains the complete New Testament and the Confession of St Patrick, dates from about AD807.

Founded by Elizabeth I in 1592, TCD was a great institution of the Reformation, an Anglican preserve until the eighteenth century. In front of the main façade on College Green are statues of Edmund

Trinity College, Dublin, was founded by Elizabeth I in 1592

Burke (1729-97) and Oliver Goldsmith (1728-74), scholars of TCD. Other past students include William Congreve, Jonathan Swift, Thomas Moore, Henry Brooke, Oscar Wilde, Samuel Beckett, Bram Stoker who wrote *Dracula*, and James Ussher (1581-1656), the archbishop of Armagh who calculated that the world was created on 23 October 4004BC. Ussher left all his books and manuscripts to the college. He had been one of its first scholars, at the tender age of 13. Nowadays, as one of the six copyright libraries in the British Isles, Trinity College Library receives books by the thousand. Like the university libraries of Oxford, Cambridge, Scotland (Edinburgh) and Wales (Aberystwyth) and the British Library in London, it is entitled to a copy of every book published in Britain and Ireland.

Long after all religious restrictions were removed (1873), Trinity's intellectual liberalism was regarded with suspicion by the Catholic hierarchy, and until quite recently any member of its flock wanting to study at TCD had to get permission from the archbishop of Dublin.

Some of Ireland's finest early manuscripts are in the custody of the **Royal Irish Academy** which occupies 19 Dawson Street. They include part of the *Cathach* (the Battler) — a psalter reputedly penned by St Columba (AD560), the *Book of the Dun Cow* (eleventh or twelfth century), and the seventeenth-century *Annals of the Four Masters*. Next door is the Mansion House, official residence of the Mayor of Dublin, and scene of many famous public meetings. Cheers and shouts from these worldly gatherings often penetrate the learned walls of No. 19.

Facing TCD across College Green is the elegant former parliament house, begun in 1729 and added to over the years by leading architects. After the Act of Union in 1800, when the independent Irish parliament was abolished, the building was bought by the **Bank of Ireland** and converted into a bank by Francis Johnston. The handsome interior retains some of its original eighteenth-century fittings and tapestries. The decline in Dublin's prestige and prosperity dates from this time, when the aristocracy and gentry followed the parliament to London.

The residence of the lord deputies of Ireland from 1565, **Dublin Castle** was a symbol of English power and the official seat of the lord lieutenant until 1922. Now it is largely used for ceremonial occasions. George V stayed in 1911 and John F Kennedy received the freedom of the city here in 1963. Neither of them can have been impressed by the condition of the building. There are tours of the state apartments 7 days a week. You may find it equally interesting to walk round the so-called red light area west of College Green known as **Temple Bar**, a characterful area of cobbled streets, seedy little shops, rock band rehearsal rooms, cheap restaurants, alternative art galleries, a brothel, the product of prolonged planning blight.

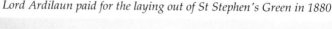

Lord Ardilaun paid for the laying out of St Stephen's Green in 1880

O'Connell Street is Dublin's main thoroughfare

Among numerous eighteenth-century buildings which have been restored recently is the grandest house on **St Stephen's Green**, No. 86, five bays wide with a magnificent interior, on the south side of this enormous public park. It was built in 1765 by Richard Chapell Whaley (nicknamed 'burn-Chapel' for his priest-hunting proclivities), MP for County Wicklow and father of the notorious rake, Buck Whaley. The Catholic Church later acquired the house, and the one next door, for conversion into a university. Called **Newman House** (after the cardinal, founder of University College, Dublin), it has sumptuous rococo plasterwork on wall panels and ceilings. In one huge room yet to be restored, naked goddesses frolic across the stucco ceiling. You cannot help noticing that someone has tried to cover up these wanton deities with swimming costumes. James Joyce attended university here, and the Jesuit poet Gerard Manley Hopkins had a study on the top floor where he worked himself to death marking student essays in 1889. In the basement a smart restaurant gives on to extensive gardens.

Sculptures on St Stephen's Green include a Henry Moore memorial to W.B Yeats, and a statue to Lord Ardilaun (a Guinness) at whose expense the park was laid out in 1880. There used to be a fine equestrian statue of George II by Van Nost the Elder but, like numerous other statues which failed the political correctness test, it was blown up.

A walk round **Merrion Square**, the most interesting of Dublin's residential Georgian squares, started in 1762, can be done in ten minutes. Ignore, please, the nameplates of the accountants, loss adjustors and estate agents now occupying many of the Georgian mansions that line three sides of the square, and you are in brilliant, if departed company right from No. 1, home of Sir William (1815-1876) and 'Speranza' Wilde, parents of Oscar Wilde. A plaque on the house details Sir William's accomplishments: 'aural and ophthalmic surgeon, archaeologist, ethnologist, antiquarian, biographer, statistician, naturalist, topographer, historian and folklorist'. Daniel O'Connell, 'the Liberator' (1775-1847) lived at No. 58, Sheridan Le Fanu (1814-73) at No. 70, Andrew O'Connor, the American sculptor (1874-1941) at No. 77, W.B Yeats (1865-1939) at No. 82, George Russell (*AE*) (1867-1935) at No. 84. The British Embassy used to be at No. 39 but was burnt out in 1972. The central gardens were used as a soup kitchen during the great famine of the late 1840s.

The much smaller **Fitzwilliam Square** nearby, occupied by well heeled doctors now, was the last (1825) Georgian square to be built in Dublin. William Dargan (1799-1867), the engineer and entrepreneur who constructed Ireland's first railway, from Dublin to Dun Laoghaire, lived at No. 2. In Lower Fitzwilliam Street, you can walk in off the street to No. 29 which has been restored as an elegant upper middle-class house typical of the 1790-1820 period.

The splendid state of preservation of the southside squares is in contrast with the decayed condition of that other once-elegant Georgian square across the river, Mountjoy Square. The small Dublin Writers Museum devoted entirely to Irish writers, happens to be in another Georgian square, Parnell Square, also on the north side of the city. The **Municipal Gallery of Modern** Art is close by. To get there, take a stroll up **O'Connell Street**.

Though the street is utterly changed from the handsome mall it once was the statues of nineteenth-century heroes and local worthies who peer out from behind ragged top-heavy trees along the central walkway, provide a potted history lesson on the founding of the state. Halfway up is the one building of architectural merit: the **General Post Office**, headquarters of the Irish Volunteers during the 1916 rising. Most of the original structure was destroyed in the fighting but the façade with its dignified Ionic portico survives. It still has bullet holes in it.

Step inside the main hall with the form-filling, stamp-licking customers. In the centre of the room is a curious bronze figure whose mien and stricken attitude suggests, perhaps, an early Christian martyr. But no, closer inspection shows it to be a representation of the death of the legendary Ulster warrior, Cuchulain, made in the 1930s.

Cuchulain, who was called 'the Hound of Ulster', defended Ulster single-handed against the invading armies of Connaught which had been sent to seize and carry off the great Bull of Cooley. A hero of epic proportions, Cuchulain had a war whoop 100 times louder and more terrifying than anyone else's. Armed with his fearsome javelin, the *gae bolga*, he could slay 500 warriors at one go. Often he would smite off the heads of a whole phalanx of warriors with a single sweep of his shield, which had a rim specially sharpened for the purpose. In each of his seven-fingered claw-hands he could hold aloft ten severed human heads, shaking them at the enemy. Not surprisingly, the men of Connaught were soon routed and Ulster was saved.

The story predates St Patrick's arrival in Ireland in the fifth century. It is the central action of the eighth-century Ulster Cycle of epic tales which are suffused with that same tremendous joy in battle that runs through the great Norse sagas. After yet another ferocious affray which leaves Cuchulain mortally wounded, he ties himself to a stone pillar in order to die standing up, still fighting. His enemies dare not approach until a crow alighting on his shoulder intimates that the hero is indeed dead — and even after that his sword manages a final venomous twitch and hacks off one last enemy hand. . . .

The effete figure in 'The Death of Cuchulain' in the post office cannot be Cuchulain, surely. In any case, what is he doing in O'Connell Street, far from his northern fastness? In fact, the sculpture is a memorial to Patrick Pearse, a leader of the 1916 rising and a political idealist. He was attracted by the myth of Cuchulain, most particularly his death. It was Pearse who proclaimed an Irish republic on the steps of the GPO on Easter Monday 1916 and who, before the week was out, surrendered on the same spot. His death wish was realised 4 days later when he was executed by firing squad at Kilmainham jail.

There are numerous other cases, you will find, of Irish heroes and giants popping up here and there, pressed into service in support of present-day causes, both political and cultural. Most of them are drawn from the ancient Ulster cycle and from the medieval Ossianic/ Fenian cycle of ballads about Finn McCool, a kind of Celtic Robin Hood, more sociable than Cuchulain.

Visitors passing the GPO in the evening may notice a very large number of wagtails in the plane trees outside. This city centre site has been a communal roost for pied wagtails for at least the past 60 years, with numbers reaching several thousand in cold winters. Not even the dynamiting and subsequent demolition of Nelson's Pillar nearby kept the birds away. The 134ft (41m) column, a little shorter than the one in London, and with a statue of the admiral on top, was erected shortly after the Battle of Trafalgar. No one thought of blowing up this imperial relic until 1966.

The **Dublin Writers Museum** is at 18 Parnell Square, one of a pair of restored eighteenth-century residences in this once-fashionable northside area. The museum and the writers' centre next door celebrate Ireland's strong literary tradition. Take your reading spectacles to tackle the fact-packed panels. Objects on display include Brendan Behan's painters and decorators union card, Patrick Kavanagh's death mask and Joyce's piano. If you insist on examining Joyce's guitar, take a trip on the DART — the Dublin Area Rapid Transit, an overground train service, to the **Joyce museum** at Sandycove.

Dublin is an intensely literary city with a self-absorbed contemporary cultural scene. In addition to the Joyce museum, literary treasures in the National Library and so on, other celebrations of the twentieth-century Irish literary revival include a small museum at 33 Synge Street (Shaw Birthplace) devoted to G.B.S. and then there's 'Bloomsday', 16 June — the day on which all the events in *Ulysses* take place — which is seriously threatening to displace St Patrick's Day in the affections of Dublin literati. Literary walks (and pub crawls) and summer schools abound, and there are torrents of new books with local imprints about literary Dublin and Dubliners each year. The agreeable bookshops around Trinity College are full of such books and visiting browsers should not allow themselves to be nonplussed by their somewhat allusive style. They will not provide you with a practical guide to the city.

Some Dublin Pubs

Take Dublin pubs as an example. Students of twentieth-century Irish literature are shaken to learn that despite its bibulous literary tradition, Dublin is severely under-pubbed. At the last count there were fewer than 700 pubs in Dublin — about one per 1,500 Dubliners, compared with one pub per 200 adults in the rest of the Republic. Even so, you cannot avoid encountering numerous atmospheric pubs in the city centre, among which are (going from east to west) the following hostelries. South of Leinster House there's the appealing

Doheny & Nesbitt's, Lower Baggot Street. **Doyle's** is an intimate little pub in College Street close to TCD. Nearby, **Mulligan's** in Poolbeg Street between Trinity and the river is exceptionally civilised. Two splendid glitzy gin palaces, very central, are **The Long Hall,** South Great Georges Street, and the **Stag's Head** in Dame Court, another delightful Victorian emporium. **Parliament Inn,** Parliament Street, is one of scores of ordinary pubs where the 'crack' (conversation) is likely to be good. The big central square bar in **O'Shea's,** Lower Bridge Street, is more comfortable because less crowded than the fashionable **Brazen Head** across the street: this latter pub has historical connections with the 1798 United Irishmen uprising, and a Northern equivalent in Kelly's Cellars, Belfast. **Boss Croker's Inn** on Arran Quay, west of the Four Courts, is an airy, friendly pub and, continuing west, just beyond Wolfe Tone Quay, poke your head into **Ryan's,** a Gay Nineties confection in Parkgate Street near Phoenix Park.

Many Dublin pubs have undergone serious 'improvements'. The rise of the lounge bar in the 1960s and the creation of large open drinking areas — rudely but accurately called 'boozeramas' — changed many of them for the worse. Some of the wood panelling and brass fittings that were ripped out have been replaced, after a fashion: the wood is polyurethane-varnished, the brass has no mellow gleam. Others are dispiritingly modern kitsch. Two Duke Street pubs that have been spoilt in this way are **Davy Byrne's** (which is featured in *Ulysses*) and the **Bailey,** which claims Brendan Behan, Patrick Kavanagh and J.P Donleavy as ex-regulars. Instead you could try **McDaid's,** yet another literary drinking hole, in Harry Street, on the other side of Grafton Street.

Visitors penetrating the south Dublin suburbs might call in at the **Stillorgan Orchard,** a remarkable reed-thatched pub, and, for something quite different, **The Goat** at Goatstown, very weird.

To visit **Kilmainham Royal Hospital** near Heuston Station, take a bus going west. A glorious seventeenth-century building erected by order of Charles II for war veterans, it was the first of a number of hospitals and charitable institutions built on this side of the city in the late seventeenth and early eighteenth century. Kilmainham was inspired by Les Invalides in Paris and was a precursor of Wren's Royal Hospital, Chelsea, and was used from 1684 until the 1920s when all the remaining pensioners left for Chelsea. It now houses the **Irish Museum of Modern Art.** It would be hard for any art, ancient or modern, to compete with the lavishness of the grandest rooms, the dining room and the baroque chapel, with its richly carved east window. The walls of the dining room are still lined with large full-length portraits of Charles II and his court, though the doorway is minus its coat of arms which was taken off to Chelsea with the pensioners (the Irish would like it back). The chapel ceiling is so ornately decorated that the heavy plaster pomegranates had to be replaced by papier maché ones to avoid injury to people struck by falling fruit. From the hospital a gate interconnects with Kilmainham gaol, one of the shrines of traditional Irish nationalism.

Across the river is the vast expanse of **Phoenix Park**, conceived on a magnificent scale (1,750acres/700 hectares), so big that Dublin zoo, the Garda Síochána HQ, the Irish Ordnance Survey HQ, the US ambassador's residence, a hospital and the Irish President's official residence are all hidden away behind great avenues of horse-chestnut trees. Curiosity brings visitors to hover around the president's gate in Main Road, and in larger numbers since the election of Ireland's first woman president, Mary Robinson. This restful spot, with fine views of the Wicklow hills to the south, was the scene of the Phoenix Park murders in 1882 when chief secretary, Lord Frederick Cavendish, and his under-secretary, Thomas Burke, were stabbed to death as they strolled along Main Road.

Environs of Dublin

To see places a little further out, go into Connolly Station (or Pearse Station immediately behind Trinity College), and hop on the DART which serves the east side of this sprawling city that extends more than 20 miles (32km) from north to south. You can see plenty without actually getting off the train.

Going north, the DART passes through Killester, Harmonstown and Raheny and then, after the tower blocks of Kilbarrack, veers east at Howth Junction to end at the breezy well set-up town of **Howth** on the peninsula. People come out from the city to buy fish from the shops along the west pier at Howth. There is a smoked (real) salmon stall, several fish restaurants on the front and, at the end of the pier, the agreeable St Lawrence Hotel, good for lunch. The name is associated not with the third-century deacon who was roasted alive on a gridiron but with the Norman family of St Lawrence, earls of Howth. Buildings on the seafront rather obscure the view of **Ireland's Eye**, a tiny offshore island or rather, a large quartzite rock, which is easily reached by boat. Beyond is **Lambay Island**. It was off Lambay, formerly called Rechru Island, that the very first sinister heavy square sail of a Viking ship was sighted in AD795. Within 20 years the Vikings had overrun all of Ireland's coasts, north, south, east and west.

Howth harbour is full of fishing boats, with a forest of leisure boat masts in the adjoining marina. Climb the steps from the promenade to the ruined abbey church founded in the eleventh century by Sitric, the Danish king of Dublin (founder of Christ Church cathedral). Near the south-east corner is the tomb of Christopher St Lawrence (died 1430) and his wife. To see the romantic towers and turrets of Howth Castle return to the railway station and continue west for a short distance. The castle itself is private but the magnificent gardens are open to visitors during daylight hours. Laid out in about 1720, the gardens have huge beech hedges, spectacular plantings of rhododendrons and azaleas, and an early eighteenth-century canal. You can get a bus up to the top of Howth Head for fine views of Dublin Bay and beyond, or better, take the cliff-top footpath.

A little north of Howth, and accessible by some (not all) trains from Howth Junction, is **Malahide Castle**, home of the Talbot family almost continuously from 1185 until the death in 1973 of the last Lord Talbot. Much of the contents were dispersed at that time but the castle is still packed with interesting furniture and paintings that include portraits of Richard Steele, founder of the *Tatler*, Thomas Sheridan, father of the dramatist, Frederick Hervey, Earl Bishop of Derry, and General Ginkel who captured Athlone for William III in 1691. The castle's botanic gardens contain some ten species of magnolia and many plants from Australia and New Zealand.

Going south from Dublin, the DART passes right under the stands of the rugby ground at Lansdowne Road and after Ballsbridge the track runs along the seaside to the leafy Victorian suburb of Blackrock, on to Dun Laoghaire where the ferry boats from Holyhead, in Wales, come in, and then to Sandycove. These fashionable places south of the city are good places to eat. After Sandycove, you trundle along a rocky ledge, on through Glenageary, arty Dalkey and Killiney, tunnelling through the massive granite outcrops of the **Wicklow mountains**. How high they are and how close to Dublin.

By car, the most direct way from Dublin to the high Wicklows is to shoot straight up the R115 from Rathfarnham to the **Sally Gap**, the highest mountain pass in Ireland. The R115 is part of the great 'Military Road' built by the British after the 1798 rising, and remains the only north-south route through the Wicklows. Alternatively go via the leafy, well-heeled village of Enniskerry and up a winding road past Powerscourt House demesne.

Further Information
— Dublin & Environs —

Places to Visit

Please note that opening times given below are subject to change. Check with Dublin Tourism ☎ (01) 2844768 for the latest information.

Dublin Castle
Open: all year except Christmas and Good Friday.
☎ (01) 6777129

Dublinia
Christ Church, Synod Hall
Open: daily 10am-5pm, slightly shorter hours in winter.
☎ (01) 6794611

Dublin Writers Museum
18-19 Parnell Square
Open: daily 10am-5pm
☎ (01) 8722077

Marsh's Library
Open: weekdays (except Tuesday) 10am-5pm and on Saturday morning.
☎ (01) 4543511

Municipal Gallery of Modern Art
Open: 9.30am-6pm Tues to Fri, until 5pm on Saturday, 11am-5pm on Sunday.
☎ (01) 8741903

National Gallery
Open: 10am-6pm Monday-Saturday, until 9pm on Thursday, 2-5pm on Sunday.

National Library
Open: until 9pm on Wed and Thurs but closes Fri and Sat afternoons.

National Museum and Natural History Museum
Open: Tuesday to Saturday until 5pm and on Sunday afternoon.

Newman House
St Stephen's Green
Open: June to September every day except Monday, hours vary.
☎ (01) 4757255

29 Lower Fitzwilliam Street
Open: Tues to Sat 10am-5pm and Sun afternoons except around Christmas.
☎ (01) 7026165

Shaw Birthplace
33 Synge Street
Open: 10am-5pm every day (until 6pm on Sunday).
☎ (01) 4750854

Trinity College
(Book of Kells)
Open: from 9.30am except Sunday.

Irish Museum of Modern Art
Kilmainham
Royal Hospital, Dublin 8
Open: Tues to Sat 10am-5.30pm, and Sun 12noon-5.30pm. Guided tours of the historic building on Sun afternoons.
☎ (01) 6718666

Kilmainham Gaol
Dublin 8
Open: daily 11am-6pm June to September, but only on Wednesday and Sunday afternoons rest of the year.
☎ (01) 4535984

Other Places to Visit

James Joyce Tower
Sandyccove, Co Dublin
Open: 10am-5pm Mon to Sat and Sun 2-6pm May to Sept and weekdays in April and Sept
☎ (01) 2809265.

Malahide Castle
Co Dublin
Malahide
Open: all year, 10am-5pm weekdays, hours on Sat and Sun vary. On winter weekends it is open afternoons only.
☎ (01) 8452655 Gardens are open all year
☎ (01) 8450940

Tourist Information Offices
Open: all year.

Dublin
14 Upper O'Connell Street
☎ (01) 2844768

Dublin Airport ☎ (01) 8376387

Dun Laoghaire
Co Dublin
St Michael's Wharf ☎ (01) 2806984

8 • The South
Wexford to Cork City

Including Wicklow, Carlow, Kildare, Laois, Kilkenny, Tipperary and Waterford

Well fed and rested, tourists landing in Ireland from the car ferries at **Rosslare** tend to scoot through County Wexford in a hurry to get to somewhere else. You can find yourself in the lush foothills of the Wicklows or across the Barrow river into Waterford without much noticing the unremarkable terrain in between. The Wexfordians know this. They would like people to stay longer, and their heritage centres, heritage parks and seafood festivals are intended to encourage you to do so. More attractive than any of these, however, is the climate. Wexford is the sunniest, warmest, mildest place in Ireland, and the sandy beaches on the east coast attract some genuine sunbathers. There is a soft fruits research station at Clonroche, 7 miles (11km) from Enniscorthy on the N79, and the strawberry and gooseberry vendors begin at Rosslare. Despite the benign weather, even in high summer the fragrant scent from peat-burning grates rises from the chimneys of roadside bungalows and elderly thatched cottages.

Wexford, Wicklow and Waterford, the three counties forming the south-east corner of Ireland were all Danish Viking foundations — the initial 'W' is a reminder of that — and the area was colonised in the twelfth century by Normans from South Wales. It seems that English was spoken here earlier than anywhere else in Ireland. All the invaders passed through **Wexford** town, including Cromwell who destroyed most of the churches and slew the garrison in 1649. A memorial to the Wexford pikemen of the 1798 rebellion stands in the Bull Ring, one of Wexford's two market places, this one used for bull-baiting in Norman times. The bronze figure is of a sturdy country boy, perhaps a farm worker, armed with a pike, the pikehead mounted on a long wooden stave. Determined though they were, the Wexford insurgents were for the most part untrained, poorly equipped and badly led, no match for the well armed professional

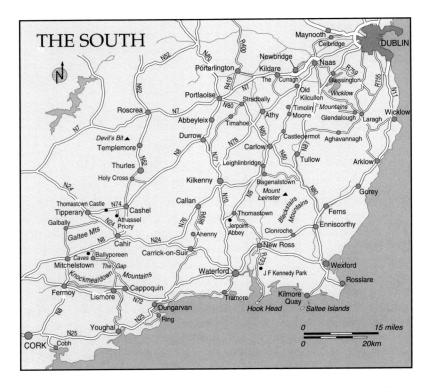

THE SOUTH

soldiers they challenged. There is a bewildering number of little plaques and notices about episodes and individuals from the town's past, stuck up here and there. In October the narrow streets fill with opera fans, here for the 2-week opera festival.

Fringe activities of the festival, which started in 1951, occupy every possible venue in the town, including an atmospheric old coaching inn in Main Street, now cleverly concealing a large modern hotel, White's, behind its 1820s' façade. First opened in 1779 as a lodging house for the local militia, the inn was the birthplace in 1807 of the Arctic explorer Robert McClure who discovered Barings Island and stumbled upon the North-West Passage in 1852 while looking for a lost expeditionary party. Between 1848 and 1854 fifteen British expeditions were despatched to find the passage linking the Atlantic and the Pacific round the top of north America. The earlier party, which included Francis Crozier of Banbridge, County Down, had found the passage but all its members perished on the way home.

Tom Codd, maternal grandfather of the poet Thomas Moore (1779-1852) kept an inn in Cornmarket, the town's other market-place, and there is a plaque on the house where Moore's mother lived and where Moore, by then old and very mad, stayed the year before his death. Moore wrote many patriotic and nostalgic songs such as 'The last rose of summer', 'The minstrel boy' and 'The harp that once through Tara's halls', published as Irish Melodies in dribs and drabs between 1807 and 1834. His novel, *Lalla Rookh* (1817) is a series of oriental tales in verse linked by a prose narrative. Immensely popular in England, it was reprinted twenty times by 1840. Moore is also remembered, with fury by English Literature scholars, as the man who burnt the manuscript of Byron's *Memoirs*.

Only one of the town's original five fortified gateways survives. Close to it are a fragmentary church nave and a square battlemented tower, the fourteenth and fifteenth-century remains of St Selskar's abbey. Repair work on these historic monuments seems to have been crudely executed. The main thoroughfare of Wexford is a long straggle of quays running in parallel with the Slaney estuary. It is lined by bars and singing pubs which are not in full voice until some time after 9pm. Upstream at **Ferrycarrig** the river flows through a large history park. Downstream at Castlebridge there are old warehouses, grain lofts and water mills overlooking Wexford's inner harbour, relics of the corn trade. Following land reclamation on a large scale, the landscape hereabouts has a poldery look. The Wexford slobs, mudflats at the river estuary, are busiest in autumn and early winter when birders come to study huge flocks of geese arriving from Arctic Canada and Greenland to overwinter. Other birders make for **Kilmore Quay**, south of Wexford, a lively pretty village with a maritime museum and a sandy beach, where sea anglers meet up to swap tall stories about giant sea bass. Kilmore is the jumping-off point for the **Saltee islands**, home to large colonies of gannets, guillemots and kittiwakes, and you can usually join a daytrip boat to the islands in summer.

At lunchtime, teatime and dinner time, river cruises for foodies leave from the waterfront at **New Ross**. The river aspect, with a Victorian swing-bridge across the Barrow, is an agreeable feature of this small port which has rather slight reminders of its medieval past apart from the narrowness of its steep streets.

A modern arboretum and park named after US president Kennedy near New Ross, is basically an enormous scientific plant collection with plants laid out on a grid system, well marshalled and well labelled. The eucalypts grown here are served up to the koala bears in Dublin zoo. The estate covers more than 600 acres (240 hectares) on a hill overlooking the ruined cottage at Dunganstown which Kennedy's great grandfather left for Boston in 1848. At **Grange** 3 miles (5km) south (R733) the road bowlers are out in force on summer evenings, and anglers and scuba divers make their way down to Hook Head, their gear piled on the car roof. The lighthouse off the head has been erected on top of a circular stone keep, 100ft (30m) high, built in about 1170 and operated by monks who kept a fire going at the top. At **Tacumshane** a delightful thatched windmill is one of only two complete windmills remaining in Ireland — the other is on the Ards peninsula.

An uneventful drive up the south-east coast takes in the little grey towns of Enniscorthy, Gorey and Arklow. If a signpost suggesting, for example, 'Enniscorthy 18' is followed immediately by another indicating 'Enniscorthy 10', you are not necessarily eating up the miles: the implementation of the government's metrication policy is a slow process. At **Enniscorthy** the Blackstairs and Mount Leinster begin to dominate the view to the west. A sprawly, hilly town, Enniscorthy is the place to come in early July for the county strawberry fair. With a cathedral, a museum and a large four-storey castle keep sporting prominent corner towers, the town has rather more pretensions than might at first appear. Sir Henry Wallop rebuilt the Norman castle in about 1590, in good time for Cromwell in person to

The Bull Ring, Wexford. The bronze statue of a Wexford pikeman commemorates the 1798 rebellion

capture it 50 years later. It owes its present neat appearance to a nineteenth-century restoration by the earl of Portsmouth, an ennobled Wallop descendant. The county folk museum inside the keep has plenty to say about the United Irishmen uprising and the Wexford rebels' last big battle on Vinegar Hill which rises above the Slaney river across the valley. The rebels were finally overwhelmed on 21 June 1789 after frightful atrocities on both sides. On the hill an old windmill stump, a rebel command post, has been carefully preserved. There is a good view of it from the corner of Castle Street. The uprising in Wexford seems to have had a strongly sectarian character, with murderous animosities between Protestants and Catholics, not 'united' at all.

Continuing towards Arklow via Gorey, the road goes through **Ferns** where a Celtic-style cross in the village centre is a memorial to John Murphy, a local priest who led the men of north Wexford in the uprising. Ferns was the capital of the kingdom of Leinster and has extensive medieval remains, ruined churches, a castle and other buildings, all very derelict, spread over a wide area. It figured in a historic episode in the twelfth century which Thomas Moore described as 'an event of most melancholy importance to Ireland' because it was the immediate cause of the Anglo-Norman invasion.

In 1152 Dervorgilla, wife of Tiernan O'Rourke, prince of Breffny, ran off with Dermot MacMurrough, king of Leinster, who brought her to Ferns. She went home a year later but vengeful O'Rourke attacked Ferns and Dermot was forced to flee. He submitted himself to Henry II, invited Strongbow to Ireland to fight O'Rourke and offered his daughter, Eva, in marriage to cement the pact. Strongbow duly landed in Ireland with a Welsh army (1169), captured Dublin and married Eva in Waterford cathedral soon after. Dermot's name has been mud ever since.

The **Wicklows** stretch for 40 miles (64km) south from Dublin, an impassive mass of rounded, granite mountains rising to 3,039ft (927m) at Lugnaquillia. The most extensive area of uplands in Ireland, they are bleak and inhospitable. For centuries they were the haunt of bandits and refugees, and raiding parties of the dispossessed O'Byrnes and O'Tooles were accustomed to swoop down on the Pale to harry the English. Red Hugh O'Donnell spent the bitter winter of 1591-92 in the Wicklows after escaping from Dublin Castle on Christmas night. He had to have both his big toes amputated when he got home to Donegal. Nowadays one might expect these mountains to be rather empty and unvisited, and that may be so in winter but in summer they are swarming with people. There are

Wexford harbour

walkers in twos and threes, and sometimes in big groups, ambling along the Wicklow Way long-distance footpath, posses of cyclists freewheeling down to Glendalough, minibuses laden with rock-climbing gear and Dubliners heaving plastic bags of peat into vans and beat-up old cars. Hostel accommodation is plentiful and backpackers can explore the region without wondering too much about where they will sleep. The spectacular glen of Glendalough, with an outstanding group of monastic ruins, and historic gardens at Mount Usher and, most notably, at **Powerscourt Demesne** which also has a spectacular waterfall — Ireland's highest at 400ft (122m), attract many visitors in high season.

There is a 40-mile (64km) scenic drive along the route of the old Military Road, built through the mountains after the 1798 uprising to control the area. From Aghavannagh, a desolate mountain valley with a convenient youth hostel, the road runs spectacularly to Laragh, passing east of Glendalough, then up Glenmacnass, with its thundering waterfall, to the Sally Gap which is the highest mountain pass (1,657ft/505m) in Ireland, across Liffey Head Bridge close to where the river rises, and down the R115 to the Dublin suburb of Rathfarnham. The Wicklow Way runs further east, roughly in parallel. Road and path and they converge briefly at Laragh before the walkers head off into Glendalough. Lorry traffic on the main road from Arklow into the mountains is heavy, especially around a large

The Wicklows are the most extensive area of uplands in Ireland

fertiliser factory after 3 miles (5km) and also sand extraction operations just before the rather touristy village of **Avoca**, where two rivers meet. A minuscule, cherubic bust of Thomas Moore, who wrote a sentimental song called 'The meeting of the waters' after visiting Avoca in 1807, stands close to 'Tom Moore's Tree', a thoroughly dead tree inartistically surrounded by concrete to preserve it from souvenir-hunters.

At **Glendalough** where St Kevin founded a famous religious centre in the sixth century, the interest of the settlement — virtually a whole town scattered around the shores of two lakes — is matched by the beauty of the steep-sided glen. It broadens to a flat-bottomed valley, filled with a lake (upper lake), then narrows to a sharp defile and rises dramatically towards the top of the pass. Some of the hills beyond are heavily wooded, some are green and others are rocky.

The main complex is through a double stone archway close to the visitor centre, where there is a hotel and a pub and, consequently, many people. A less congested approach is accessed a mile (2km) further west along the R757, close to the east end of the upper lake where there is a little pebbly beach. Misogynist storytellers say that St Kevin, who died in about AD620, chose this remote valley to get away from women. One in particular was so importunate that the saint had to beat her off with a bundle of stinging nettles. There are about ten churches, a tapering 100ft (30m) round tower and many crosses and other remains to examine. The original hermitage was on the shore of the upper lake and the remains — a rectangular church, and a man made platform where, it is thought, small mud-and-wattle houses once stood — can be reached only by hired boat. The road through the Wicklow Gap from Laragh (R756) follows the line of St Kevin's Road, a tenth-century pilgrim route to the Glendalough monastery.

Russborough House, near **Blessington**, designed by Richard Cassels (1741) for Joseph Leeson, first earl of Milltown, is open daily in high summer. It has magnificent plasterwork by the Francini brothers, Paul and Philip. The staircase walls and the ceilings of all the main rooms are gorgeously plastered and there is a collection of sculptures, paintings, porcelain, silver, carpets and furniture. From 1951 the mansion was the home of Sir Alfred Beit (died 1994) who inherited an immense fortune built on South African diamond and gold mines. Beit Bridge over the Limpopo river between South Africa and Zimbabwe was named after his entrepreneurial Uncle Alfred, a leading 'Randlord'. The Beit art collection at Russborough was famously raided in 1974 by a paramilitary gang led by Dr Rose Dugdale, a disaffected upper-crust Englishwoman, and again in 1986 when paintings worth £30 million were stolen. Some of the best pictures have yet to be recovered. Beit was president and benefactor of the Wexford opera festival for many years.

What is left of **Carlow's** Norman castle of 1207 stands on the east bank of the Barrow river flowing south to the sea at Waterford. It was an outpost of the Pale. Art MacMurrough Kavanagh (died 1417) burned it in 1405, Rory Og O'More (died 1578) did the same in Tudor times and in the 1640s it changed hands often. However, the cause of its present fragmentary state, two towers and a bit of wall, was an attempt in 1814 by a local doctor to turn it into a lunatic asylum. He was in a hurry to get his project under way and instead of dismantling unwanted walls, he used gunpowder. Old warehouses below the bridge are a reminder of Carlow's past importance as a link between the Barrow navigation and the Grand Canal. A sugar-beet refinery, still the town's largest employer, helped keep open the waterway up to Athy, beyond which it joined the Grand Canal, but below Carlow the system was allowed to deteriorate. In 1959 commercial traffic along the whole route came to an end and now it is used mostly by pleasure cruisers entering from the Grand Canal, and is navigable as far south as St Mullins, about 17 miles (27km) south of Bagenalstown.

A small museum at the rear of Carlow's town hall contains a

nineteenth-century press on which the *Nationalist and Leinster Times*, the weekly paper, was printed. Visitors will learn of an episode in 1789 when a ragged force of United Irishmen, 4,000 strong, was ambushed at Carlow. Over 600 insurgents were killed in the fighting or executed afterwards. A monument in the form of a modern high cross, in Church Street, is close to the place where they were buried. There are numerous folklife objects, such as a settle bed and Victorian cooking implements, and the trap-door used in public executions outside the prison up until 1820 is a prized exhibit. By the time of the 1829 Emancipation Act the large Gothic revival cathedral in Carlow was already half built. It is of aisleless cruciform design with a lantern tower 150ft (46m) high. In the nave a white marble memorial by John Hogan (1800-56) to Bishop James Warren Doyle (1786-1834), an energetic educationist and political journalist, depicts Mother Ireland rising from her knees. Beside the cathedral is an interesting, very early, Catholic seminary which opened in 1795.

Other buildings of note include an imposing courthouse by William Vetruvius Morrison at the Athy Road/Dublin Road junction and an eighteenth-century building, now the public library, donated to the town by George Bernard Shaw. The benefaction is acknowledged on a plaque. Shaw's aunt lived in Carlow. The main street has some small nineteenth-century shop fronts with good lettering, not much altered since they were built. A couple of miles west of Carlow (R430) stop at **Killeshin** church to inspect the fine Romanesque round-headed west doorway. It has four 'orders' — receding doorways-within-doorways.

The portal tomb known as **Browne's Hill Dolmen** is in the grounds of a handsome stone house (1763) a mile (2km) along the R726 east of Carlow. It has a huge capstone, estimated to weigh over 100 tonnes, the heaviest in Ireland — though the fact that one end is deeply embedded in the ground detracts from the significance of this superlative. One would like it to be supported by a stone leg! At the other end there are three stumpy legs, and a fourth one nearby. Altamont Gardens are signposted on the N81 5 miles (8km) south of **Tullow** and there are fine views from here of the Wicklow mountains to the north-east and, to the south, Mount Leinster (2,610ft/796m), highest peak in the Blackstairs range — but not the highest in Leinster, despite its name. There are at least two higher mountains in the Wicklows. Features at Altamont include a broadwalk lined with Irish yews and box hedging, a bog garden, old shrub roses, naturalised cyclamen and crocus displays in autumn and a flight of 100 hand-cut granite steps down to the Slaney river.

The N9 south from Carlow runs along the east bank of the Barrow, a scenic route as far as **Leighlinbridge**, where the Black Castle (1547) guards an important bridge across the river. The bridge dates from the fourteenth century. Stay on the east bank to visit **Bagenalstown** which has an picturesque drawbridge over the canalised river and sturdy industrial buildings, including a fine Maltings of 1868 and an imposing railway station. The Doric-porticoed courthouse is rather too impressive for a town with fewer than 3,000 inhabitants. It was part of an ambitious development plan by its founder, William Bagenal, which failed when the main coach road was routed elsewhere. The name Bagenalstown was sufficiently disliked for it to be changed by popular vote in the 1950s — to the equally unpronounceable Muine Bheagh (try Moonabeg). Despite voting to change it, many locals seem to use the old name.

Upstream from Carlow, the canalised Borrow follows the Laois/Kildare boundary to **Athy**, where a handsome eighteenth-century bridge, inscribed 'Sir James Delehunty, Knight of the Trowel' by its builder, spans the river. What is to be the fate of bridges such as this? Often, as at Athy, the most impressive feature of otherwise unexceptional towns, they suffer a relentless pounding by modern vehicular traffic, carrying what once went by rail or water, over their elderly arches. An earlier bridge at Athy was built by Sir John Talbot, first (and bravest) earl of Shrewsbury, who, although he was Henry V's lieutenant of Ireland from 1414, spent most of his time in France, defending English conquests there. He captured Bordeaux at the age of 65 and was still battling when he was defeated and slain at Castillon in 1453. Somehow he found time to build the bridge at Athy, and a castle on the bank now occupied by White's Castle, a hefty rectangular building, with sash windows, said to be sixteenth century. Half a mile (1km) upstream on the west bank are the battered remains of Woodstock Castle, which has very thick walls. Dating from about 1290, it was pummelled into ruin by confederate Catholic besiegers in 1649.

Two high crosses and the base of a third, all carved from local granite, so much harder to work than the more usual sandstone, stand in the old churchyard north of **Castledermot's** Franciscan friary. Carvings on the North Cross include David with his harp and the miracle of the loaves and fishes. It is an ancient site, with an accumulation of ruins from different periods, including a round tower 65ft (20m) high. All three crosses may predate the time when Cormac Mac Cuilleannáin, a celebrated tenth-century scholar-bishop of Cashel, was buried here after his head was struck off in a battle.

The upper portion of the rugged granite round tower was added in medieval times. A restored Romanesque doorway belonged to a long-vanished church and early and medieval grave slabs are littered around.

Driving north along the N9 through the Barrow valley, look out for the following places between Castledermot and the great hill fort at **Knockaulin**, which has been identified as Dún Ailinne, a seat of the kings of Leinster: best known is **Moone** high cross, which stands in the grounds of an eighteenth-century house, Moone Abbey. Over 17ft (5m) high, with 51 panels decorated with stylised flat carvings, this ninth-century cross has a strikingly modern look about it. Inside the ruined fourteenth-century friary church nearby is a fragmentary cross decorated with centaurs. Just beyond **Timolin**, with its busy pewterware workshop and a twelfth-century effigy of a knight in the churchyard, is the orderly village of **Ballitore** founded by Quakers in the 1700s. The Quaker school where the political thinker Edmund Burke (1729-97) learnt his Latin conjugations, has been restored as a library and museum. Burke's father was Protestant and his mother was Catholic. Two miles (3km) before the bridge over the Liffey at Kilcullen village, look out for a signpost to **Old Kilcullen**: there is a very good view of the surrounding countryside from the grassy cemetery with its ancient grave slabs, but the main reason for stopping here is to see the beautiful carved shaft of one of three fragmentary high crosses. The four apostles appear in three panels on the east face, and there are animals and Old Testament heroes on the west and north faces.

St Brigid of Kildare

St Brigid is the saint responsible for all those rush-plaited crosses. The first abbess of Kildare (AD490), one of rather few religious houses for women in the Celtic period, was called St Brigid. A Celtic goddess of the same name seems to have undergone a process of cultural metamorphosis, ending up as St Brigid, midwife to the Virgin Mary, sometimes called 'Mary of the Gael'. This lady saint's feast day, 1 February, coincides precisely with Imbolc, the second of the four great feasts in the Celtic ritual calendar — the others being Samhain (1 November), Beltaine (1 May) and Lughnasa (1 August). The Celts celebrated Imbolc with a fertility cult practice associated with lactating ewes. Brigid died at Kildare in AD523.

The **Kildare** monastery had separate sections for men and women. In common with almost every ecclesiastical centre in Ireland it was periodically burned, looted and its community slaughtered. In the twelfth century an Abbess of Kildare was abducted by a Wexford tribe and forced into bed with a common soldier, a calculated act of sacrilege. At about the same time, the Norman ruler of Ulster, John de Courcy, claimed that he had disinterred Brigid's bones and transported them to Downpatrick to be reburied alongside St Patrick and St Columba. A three-light west window in Kildare's Anglican cathedral depicts scenes from the lives of these first-division saints of Ireland. Nearby is a round tower which, apart from the top, dates to the tenth century and stands on the site of the ancient unisex monastery.

The north-west region of County Kildare is raised peat bog, part of the dreary Bog of Allen. Lying between the Liffey and Barrow river basins, west of Newbridge is the wide plain of the **Curragh**, the centre of Irish horse breeding and training. Everywhere you look there's a stud farm. At most times of the day but especially in the early morning, strings of thoroughbred horses, noble-looking creatures, are exercising on the short springy grass. You do not actually need to go anywhere to see them since the N7 runs right across the Curragh. This same open terrain has long been used for military manoeuvres and there is a large army training camp midway between Newbridge, a former British garrison town, and the little cathedral town of Kildare.

A curious, rather touching, exhibit in the horse museum at the Irish National Stud at **Tully**, outside Kildare, is the skeleton of Arkle, the great-hearted steeplechaser who won the Cheltenham Gold Cup three times in the 1960s. The stud was founded by an uncannily successful English breeder, Lord Wavertree, who always studied a horse's horoscope before deciding whether to train it or sell it. He won a great many classic races. A Japanese garden at the stud was created for Lord Wavertree by Tasa Eida, a Japanese gardener, between 1906 and 1910. The racecourse at the Curragh is the venue for the Irish Derby, and the most important bloodstock sales in Ireland are held at Goff's Kildare Paddocks, **Kill**, on the Dublin side of horsy Naas. **Punchestown** racecourse, where there is an extraordinary granite pillar stone 23ft (7m) high, is notable for a 3-day steeplechase event in spring. **Naas** also has a racecourse and a tiny bookshop with a huge stock of interesting titles, run by the Binchy cousins, Maeve and Dan. The N7 is a rather superior road at this point. In fact it is the best bit of motorway in Ireland (M7). Traffic goes romping eastwards into Dublin.

A steam museum in the grounds of Straffan Lodge, north of Kill, has a fascinating collection of model engines charting the development of the locomotive from the eighteenth century. One of the engines at **Straffan**, Richard Trevithick's 'Third Model', built in 1797, is claimed to be 'the world's oldest existing four-wheeled self-propelled object'. Such erudite facts have their connoisseurs in this part of Ireland. There is also a collection of full-size stationary engines working under steam.

At **Celbridge** on the Liffey an avenue of ancient lime trees leading from the eighteenth-century village to palatial **Castletown House** was more impressive before a housing estate was built in rather too close proximity. The house itself, rescued from decay in 1967 by Desmond Guinness, is the biggest of all the great Irish Palladian houses. It is also the earliest. The exterior was designed in 1722 for William Conolly, speaker of the Irish House of Commons, by the Florentine architect Alessandro Galilei. The interior and the two wings, one housing the stables and the other the kitchens, are by Edward Lovett Pearce. Dynamic Lady Louisa Lennox, who married Conolly's weedy nephew when she was only 15 and lived in the house for 63 years, was chiefly responsible for the decoration. Some of its 100 rooms have been recently restored and refurnished, including the drawing room which is decorated in green silk, an adjoining 'print' room with engravings stuck on to the walls, and an impressive long gallery with Venetian chandeliers and eighteenth-century portraits. Sumptuous 1760s' plasterwork in the staircase hall is by the Francini brothers who worked the likenesses of Conolly family members into their compositions. The hall has a black-and-white chequered floor and the staircase itself is a work of art. Interior decorator *par excellence*, Lady Louisa may have preferred the exterior since she arranged to die sitting in a tent erected on the lawn in front of the mansion, gazing at it as she faded away.

Only 14 miles (23km) from Dublin, Castletown is a venue for corporate entertainment and musical events. The American poet Robert Lowell (1917-77) stayed in the house for a while in the 1960s and the Irish Georgian Society had its offices here at one time. Conolly's Folly, a distant obelisk to the north seen from the rear of the house, was designed by Richard Cassels in 1739 for Catherine Conolly, the speaker's widow, to create employment after the severe winter of that year. It is 2 miles (3km) away. To examine its ingenious series of arches take the Maynooth road from Celbridge and turn right after a mile (2km). In Celbridge itself you may be able to get inside the disused Anglican church to inspect a fine monument by Thomas Carter the Elder to William Conolly.

Maynooth town is well within the Dublin ambit, with a suburban train service from Connolly station. The ruined castle beside the entrance to St Patrick's College, Maynooth, was the seat from 1176 of the most powerful family in fifteenth-century Ireland, the Norman Fitzgeralds. The castle was taken in 1535 when the tenth earl of Kildare, Silken Thomas Fitzgerald, rebelled against the king. Eventually, together with his five Fitzgerald uncles, he was persuaded to surrender by Lord Grey, marshal of Ireland, who guaranteed their personal safety. However, all six received what became known ironically as a 'Maynooth pardon', that is, they were executed. The castle remains include a massive keep and a gatehouse. For access, ask for the key at the caretaker's house across the road.

St Patrick's College, Maynooth, developed from a Catholic seminary founded in 1795 to provide an alternative to the practice of Irish priests going to train in post-revolutionary France. It is now a constituent member of the National University of Ireland, and particularly strong in the arts and humanities. Edmund Burke, who had lost his seat as MP for Bristol in 1780 because he supported Catholic emancipation and free trade with Ireland, was instrumental in establishing the seminary. He attacked the atheistical and violent Jacobinism of the French revolution in his famous *Reflections on the Revolution in France* published in 1790. Part of Burke's personal library is incorporated into the college library. Also at St Patrick's is a museum of ecclesiology which includes items belonging to Geoffrey Keating (1570-1650), the poet and historian who wrote a *History of Ireland* in Gaelic in about 1630 which he intended as an antidote to the unflattering portrayal of Ireland by Giraldus Cambrensis, Edmund Spenser, Richard Stanihurst and other 'foreign beetles' as he called them.

James Gandon, builder of Dublin's Custom House and the Four Courts, rarely ventured into the countryside. Rural settings for his buildings are limited to the stables at Carriglas, County Longford, and the two buildings he designed for the first earl of Portarlington, Emo Court and the nearby parish church of **Coolbanagher**, in County Laois. Pronounced 'leesh', the name is sometimes spelt 'Leix'. Laois was formerly called Queen's County after Mary Tudor. The mausoleum of the earls of Portarlington, also by Gandon, and a fifteenth-century font, can be seen inside Coolbanagher church which, although the interior has undergone alteration, retains its handsome exterior of 1786. It would be difficult to envisage a less rural-looking building than **Emo Court**, with its great copper dome and a monumental aspect, characteristic of Gandon's neo-classical style. It was begun in 1790 for John Dawson, earl of Portarlington, who had persuaded Gandon to come to Ireland, but it was not

Kilkenny Castle, the seat of the Butlers, stands above the river Nore

finished until 1836. At one time it was thought grand enough to be considered as a possible Irish residence for the Prince of Wales (Edward VII), a plan that came to nothing. Best features of the gardens are the Four Seasons and other classical statuary, a splendid avenue of Irish yews, many specimen trees and, aligned on the front of the house, a mile-long (2km) avenue of huge Wellingtonias. Five miles (8km) north of Emo Court, **Portarlington** was settled by Huguenots in the seventeenth century and has some fine if somewhat neglected townhouses from that time and, outside the town, a huge peat-gobbling power station that took 40 years to exhaust the nearby bog, at which point all the well paid jobs with Bord na Móna, the Peat Development Board, and the Electricity Supply Board disappeared. Many people now commute to Dublin for work. It is only 40 minutes on the train to Heuston station.

Stradbally steam and vintage machinery museum is a venue for traction engine rallies and railway events. Former Bord na Móna locomotives come puffing down the narrow gauge track, and massive steam rollers and road engines are maintained in good order. The railway operates at weekends March to October. At **Timahoe**, 3 miles (5km) south-west of Stradbally, a twelfth-century round tower is one of the best preserved in Ireland, 96ft (29m) tall, very sturdy, with an elaborately carved Romanesque doorway high up on the side. Its size and detailing gives some indication of the importance of the monastery founded here by St Cronan (also called St Mochua) in the seventh century. Going to see Timahoe may enable you to avoid Portlaoise, county town of Laois, and its traffic-clogged bit of a bypass; continue south-west towards Abbeyleix to join the N8 Cashel/Cork road. The main route from Dublin to Cork or Limerick is via **Portlaoise**, formerly called Maryborough (after Mary Tudor) and best known for its maximum security prison. It is 6 miles (10km) east along the N80 from Stradbally, past the castle-crowned Rock of Dunamase which was a stronghold of Dermot MacMurrough, king of Leinster, and later of the O'Mores, senior sept of the seven septs of Laois. It is an interesting ruin, easily reached and with good views of the countryside. You can reflect on the view later, as you fight your way past Portlaoise.

The road to Kilkenny (N8/N77) goes via pretty **Abbeyleix**, designed by the de Vesci family as an adjunct to their grand eight-eenth-century house and demesne (private), and the neat little village of **Durrow**. Durrow was planned round a green, with a castellated entrance gate into the grounds of Castle Durrow, now occupied by a convent school, an early eighteenth-century pink stone house with tall chimney stacks and a steeply pitched roof. This Durrow is not to be confused with Durrow Abbey, founded by St Columba, near Tullamore, County Offaly, where the precious *Book of Durrow* was written in the seventh century.

Walkabout in Kilkenny

Kilkenny, on the banks of the Nore, was the seat of the Butlers, dukes of Ormonde, whom Henry VIII thought he would cultivate to try to counter the influence of the Fitzgeralds, earls of Kildare (and Desmond). The Butlers did not need much encouragement. These two powerful Norman families were forever feuding, the Montagues and Capulets of the Pale. The tiny city, scene of numer-ous parliaments in medieval times, has managed to retain much of its medieval character. High above the streets, an enormous turretted iron-grey castle with drum towers contains more than enough history and art to sate the cultural curiosity of the thousands of tourists who are guided through the public rooms year round. Highlight of Kilkenny's 'arts week' at the end of August is an exhibition in the castle's art gallery when works by overseas artists are on display. The castle is one of Kilkenny's less medieval-looking buildings, and that is because it was virtually rebuilt in the nine-teenth century.

The most rewarding single visit in the town is St Canice's Anglican cathedral which contains numerous fine sixteenth and seventeenth-century tombs. The south transept in particular is full of Ormonde Butler monuments, including effigies of Piers Butler (died 1539) and Margaret Fitzgerald, his wife. The black marble font was made in the twelfth century and there is a grave slab of 1285 between the pillars opposite, easily overlooked. The cathedral was founded by the Cistercian abbot of Jerpoint and bishop of Ossory, Felix O'Dulany (1178-1202). An adjacent library contains rare books, some of which, like the Red Book of Ossory, date from the fifteenth century. There is access to the 100ft (30m) round tower outside the cathedral, and a bird's eye view from the top.

If your time in Kilkenny is short, spend it walking about. Notable features to look out for in the narrow winding streets include: a Tudor merchant's house, Rothe House, which is actually three houses cunningly built one behind the other to accommodate Mr Rothe's many children and their nursemaids; a sixteenth-century almshouse now occupied by the tourist office; a Georgian courthouse which was built over a thirteenth-century site; a Tholsel or parliament building of 1761, later the town hall. Medieval churches include the Black Abbey, now incorporated into the Dominican church, with a beautiful south window, and a ruined Franciscan friary. Parts of the old town walls survive across the river at St John's Augustinian priory church, and in the grounds of nearby Kilkenny College. The college succeeded the seventeenth-century St John's College, where Dean Swift, Bishop Berkeley, and Restoration dramatists George Farquhar and William Congreve were educated.

Guided town walks start from the castle entrance, a natural meeting place, where arty objects are on sale at design workshops occupying the former stable block. A passageway under the road links the castle's kitchens to the workshops.

Jerpoint Abbey on the Nore river, off the N9 12 miles (19km) south of Kilkenny, is said to have been a Benedictine foundation before being colonised by Cistercians from Baltinglass, Wicklow, in 1180. Be that as it may, the ruins are among the finest Cistercian remains anywhere in Ireland. The monasteries at Kilkenny and Kilcooly, County Tipperary, were founded from here and in 1227 it was affiliated to Fountains Abbey in Yorkshire. The extensive ruined monastery, its square tower with Irish battlements prominent seen from the road — and from the Dublin-Waterford train — is in a soft, pretty coloured stone and preserves a tremendous array of animated medieval figure sculptures in the fifteenth-century cloister, finely carved capitals in the nave, and some superb tomb sculptures including those on Bishop O'Dulany's tomb. The chapterhouse has a display of objects found on the site.

To see the old high altar from Jerpoint put your head into the Catholic church at nearby Thomastown, an early thirteenth-century settlement established by Thomas FitzAnthony Walsh, steward of Leinster. Defensive towers at either end of **Thomastown's** bridge and other massive stone structures in the town are a crumbled testament to its former importance when the town was encircled by a wall and fourteen towers. A mile (1km) south-east is Dysert Castle, where the philosopher George Berkeley was born in 1685. Despite not taking his clerical career very seriously, Berkeley was appointed dean of Derry in 1724 and bishop of Cloyne in 1734, sinecures which allowed him to devote more time to philosophising. Berkeley University, California, takes its name from his.

From Kilkenny the N76 runs to **Callan** where you might proceed to Green Street to peek at the strange interior of the Catholic church. The original architect (1834) spared a thought for the priest, incorporating a priestly bedsit into the design. Ruined St Mary's church

Jerpoint Abbey ruins are amongst the finest Cistercian remains in Ireland. There is a small museum in the chapter house

(1460) and, slightly to the north-east, the remains of an Augustinian friary built in 1467 by Sir James Butler, are reminders of the town's antiquity. The patronage of the Ormonde Butlers sustained the famous Callan workshops of sculptural masons throughout the fifteenth and sixteenth centuries. It is their work that you see at Jerpoint and Kilcooly. The R698/697 from Callan goes south via **Ahenny**, where two splendidly ornamented eighth or ninth-century high crosses, each surmounted by a curious conical hat like an Assyrian cap, stand in Kilclispeen graveyard, and on to **Kilkeeran** — more high crosses with caps — to end in **Carrick-on-Suir**, a market town on a lovely stretch of the river. Anne Boleyn is said to have been born in Carrick's thirteenth-century Ormonde Castle in 1507. Her grandfather was the seventh earl of Ormonde. An Elizabethan mansion, added to the castle by the tenth earl, Thomas Butler, has survived more than 400 years of Irish history, intact. Shorn of its demesne, which has been given over to a housing estate, the house is somewhat diminished but it is now being restored as a national monument and is open in summer. Carrick's main square has been renamed 'Sean Kelly' after the 1980s' champion racing cyclist who was born here. Kelly was rated number one in the world for five consecutive years.

The northern approach road (R429) to **Roscrea** is unpromising, distorted by traffic, with more time than enough to observe a hotchpotch of filling stations, mini supermarkets and terraced houses with wooden porches stained by exhaust fumes, but press on into town to see the thirteenth-century castle, with an imposing gatehouse tower, D-shaped corner turrets and, in the courtyard behind the curtain wall, one of the most appealing eighteenth-century townhouses imaginable. Joseph Damer, grandfather of John Dawson of Emo Court, bought the old Butler castle in 1715 and built this wonderful nine-bay house, three storeys plus basement, inside it. The Irish Georgian Society rescued it from dereliction and it is now a heritage centre, with a small Georgian-style formal garden. A notable feature of the interior is a charming pine staircase with a foliage-carved balustrade. On the single surviving façade of twelfth-century **St Cronan's church**, the west front, a sandstone-carved likeness of the bishop stands neatly between two rosettes over the round-headed doorway. A high cross of similar date nearby also carries the likeness of a bishop, probably St Cronan, on its east face, and there is round tower stump across the road. The Gothic-style Anglican church has a pleasingly elegant interior.

On down the N62 to Thurles via the pleasant small town of

Templemore, where ponies and traps clatter across the wide mall-like centre, with the Devil's Bit mountain a dramatic backdrop. In the middle of **Thurles'** long sloping central street, Liberty Square, a monument commemorates the men of 1798, Emmet, Wolfe Tone and Lord Edward. Nearby is the rambling comfortable Hayes Hotel — its bars and restaurants well patronised all day — where the Gaelic Athletic Association (GAA) was formed in 1884 to promote native Irish sports. The GAA's first patron was Thomas William Croke (1824-1902), the influential archbishop of Cashel, and his statue stands in Liberty Square among the parked and half-parked cars. Croke was an outspoken and compelling advocate of the Land League. Leo XIII suggested he should stick to religion and keep out of politics but he did not take the papal advice.

The last weekend in July sees the onset of *féile* (festival) fever, a three-day pop concert that brings thousands of young fans into town. From around Thursday midday the hoards are disgorged from Thurles' handsome railway station, or arrive by minibus, or thumb. Laden with bedrolls and backpacks, they make for Liberty Square.

The Cistercian house of **Holy Cross Abbey**, on the Suir river, is 5 miles (8km) south of Thurles (R660), well signposted from every direction, its compact outline and squat central tower visible from a distance across the flat country. Approaching, one is immediately struck by the beautiful stone tracery in the windows. Inside, the back half of the nave slopes down to the altar, giving people in the rear pews a good view of the low altar and low window. In the transept an early fifteenth-century wall painting endured Tipperary wind and rain for 200 years, when the church had no roof. The colours have long since gone but the black outline of a medieval hunter and his dog have survived. Avoid a hideous garden of meditation by stepping into the Old Abbey Inn for lunch or into an adjoining shop for film or an icecream. These convenient services are accommodated in part of the abbey fabric. The bridge over the Suir has eight arches. It carries a Latin inscription and the arms of James Butler, Baron of Dunboyne, and of Lady Margaret O'Brien, his wife. These two rebuilt the bridge, it says, in 1628. The abbey was founded by her ancestor, Donal Mór O'Brien in 1180. A great flock of wagtails inhabits the area downstream of the bridge, feeding on the river weed.

A few miles to the south, the **Rock of Cashel** appears on the horizon, a lump of limestone 200ft (61m) high rearing up from the undulating plain. The top of the rock is crowded with an astonishing collection of tall, imposing monuments inside a low retaining wall. The general impression is of a defensive fortress, with a battlemented central tower. Certainly this was a seat of the kings of Munster and a stronghold of Brian Boru, who became high king in 1002. Then you see the ruined gable wall and lancet windows of a large church. It is a thirteenth-century cathedral, with an eleventh-century round tower, perfect in outline and over 90ft (27m) high, attached to the north transept. The wall is a graveyard wall. Richard O'Hedigan, archbishop from 1406 to 1440, built a battlemented rectangular tower as his residence, at the west end of the cathedral and, for good measure, added battlements to all the parapets. There could hardly be a

The Rock of Cashel contains one of Ireland's most important and impressive historical sites

greater contrast with the quiet piety of Holy Cross. In the choir is the tomb of the remarkable archbishop Myler Magrath, a native of Clogher, County Tyrone, who started out as a Franciscan friar but then his career accelerated. He is recorded as holding four bishoprics and seventy other livings in 1604 and he was simultaneously Protestant archbishop of Cashel and Catholic bishop of Down. He was twice married and enjoyed life so much that he lived until 1622, when he was 100.

Huddled beside the big cathedral is a smaller, exquisite twelfth-century cathedral, Cormac's Chapel, with two towers and a heavy stone roof, steeply pitched, a grander version of the typical Irish stone roof found on St Mochta's House at Louth, St Columba's House at Kells and also on St Kevin's 'Kitchen', a similar tiny medieval chapel at Glendalough. Still on the rock but further down is the Brú Ború Heritage Centre, a kind of folk village which was built on the rock in the face of much public opposition. **Cashel** itself has an attractive main street, with harmonious slated roofs and brightly painted shop fronts, their proprietors' names hand-lettered. In the centre is an early Georgian mansion, once the bishop's palace and now a hotel. Across the road, in the grounds of the Anglican cathedral, is a small building housing the GPA Bolton Library, an outstanding collection of 12,000 printed books from 1473 to 1800, and also a few manuscript volumes, the earliest being an encyclopedia dating from 1168. The library was founded by the learned Theophilus Bolton, archbishop of Cashel 1730-44. The building (1836) is the work of a Clonmel builder-architect William Tinsley, who also designed the square at Cahir. He emigrated to the US in 1851 and was reponsible for handsome University Hall, Maison, Wisconsin, and the Ohio Institute for the Education of the Blind, in Columbus, Ohio.

West of Cashel, the N74 road to Tipperary undulates across rich pasture land, passing close to ruined **Athassel Priory**, the largest medieval priory in Ireland, founded in 1192 by William FitzAdelm de Burgo (William de Burgh) who succeeded Strongbow as governor of Ireland. The ruins of an enormous church 210ft (64m) long, a cloister and other thirteenth-century buildings are spread over 4 acres approached by two field stiles. William and his son and his grandson and many of their Burke descendants were buried here, though the grand thirteenth-century Burke tomb carved with figures of Norman knights has been removed to the Rock of Cashel. The statue of a Capuchin monk at Thomastown crossroads is Father Theobald Mathew (1790-1856), toiler among the poor of Cork and advocate of temperance, whose crusade against the demon drink reduced the exchequer's income from spirits to £0.8 million from £1.4 million. The picturesque ivy-draped ruin of Thomastown castle was his birthplace.

Tipperary's main fame comes from the old marching song, and the Tipperarians make the most of this fact: 'You have come a long way!' says a welcome sign at the edge of the town. Take the scenic twisty Cahir road (N24) from Tipperary and turn west at Bansha into the leafy green Glen of Aherlow, lying between Slievenamuck ridge and the foothills of the Galtees, red sandstone mountains rising from a limestone plain, with Galtymore mountain at 3,018ft (920m) the highest peak. The lower slopes are covered in dark firs and pine trees, a contrast with the heathery moorland further up. The head of the glen is in County Limerick and the Fitzpatricks of north Cork and the Tipperary O'Briens disputed the control of this important pass for many years. Galbally abbey, called Moor Abbey, a well tended little ruin at the Cork end of the glen, has a gloomy signboard about plunderings, suppressions and murders. The weary self-repetition of Irish history continues in **Galbally** village square, carved on a monument to Irish Volunteers who died on the scaffold, in the field and/or from hardships in the struggle for independence, plus a killing in 1920, an execution in Mountjoy jail in 1921, plus eight others. However, Galbally is a cheerful and hospitable little village with a tea shop, harmonious terraces of small houses and old-style fuel pumps that swing out over the pavement to reach your fuel tank.

More or less in parallel with the Glen of Aherlow, a pleasant stretch of the N8 runs from Cahir to Mitchelstown, north-east to south-west, between the shapely Galtees and the somewhat less interesting high moors of the Knockmealdown range. The fifteenth-century castle at **Cahir**, set on an island in the Suir river at the end of a long low bridge, has been restored and has an informative exhibition on the region's history. Limestone caves, called **Mitchelstown Caves** (though far from the town of the same name), are indicated off the N6 as you drive west. The curator lives in a house right in front of the entrance to the caves. **Ballyporeen**, ancestral home of US president Ronald Reagan, is a well signposted village, also off the N8.

To reach the 'Vee' road through the wide open uplands of the Knockmealdowns, take the R665 east from Ballyporeen and turn south on to the R666 at Clogheen, zigzagging up through pine trees to a very pronounced hairpin bend at the Vee Gap at 1,100ft (335m), descending thereafter to a fork. Whichever prong you take, you end on the R666 in green, well groomed County Waterford, which looks remarkably like Hampshire in southern England. One road brings you down past a Trappist monastery to Cappoquin where the Blackwater river makes an extraordinary ninety degree turn. After having flowed due east from Mallow for 40 miles (64km) with only the occasional wiggle, it suddenly turns due south at Cappoquin and makes a dash for the sea at Youghal. The other road runs directly down to a splendid eighteenth-century bridge across the river, with a pretty view of Lismore straight ahead. This bridge, the big trees and the open meadows indicate that one is approaching a particularly grand estate.

Irish Lismore and Viking Waterford

Lismore Castle stands at the edge of a high precipice overlooking the Blackwater, on the site of a monastery/convent founded by St Carthage in the seventh century. A castle of the medieval bishops of Lismore stood on the same spot and the towers of Lismore derive in part from that episcopal castle. Sir Walter Raleigh owned the estate for a time, and Edmund Spenser is said to have paced along the yew walk, composing parts of his interminable poem *The Faerie Queene*. In 1602 it was bought by Richard Boyle, the energetic Elizabethan adventurer who became first earl of Cork. Boyle rebuilt it and added a strongly fortified garden wall, so thick that you can walk along the top. He had the satisfaction of testing its usefulness in 1642 when the castle withstood a siege by confederate Catholics. They tried again in 1645 and this time succeeded and burnt the place but the earl was dead by then. Since 1748 Lismore has been the Irish home of the dukes of Devonshire (Cavendish). Lady Caroline Lamb, whose mother brought her to Ireland in 1812 in the hope that she would forget Byron, was one of many famous people to have stayed here. The present duke is in residence for part of the year. The rest of the time it is possible to rent the living quarters for around US $7,000 a week.

Outside the castle gate, the 1680 fabric of St Carthage's Anglican cathedral incorporates the chancel arch of a medieval cathedral and shelters numerous relics of earlier times. Six ancient cross-carved stones with Gaelic inscriptions are built into the west wall. They commemorate various Lismore abbots and hermits from the ninth century. The cathedral has a memorably light and airy interior, a fine oak pulpit of 1733, a stained glass window by the pre-Raphaelite painter Edward Burne-Jones (1833-98), many grave slabs with Norman-French inscriptions, the sixteenth-century carved altar-tomb of the Magrath family, and a splendid memorial to the Irish chemist Robert Boyle (1627-91) seventh son of the first earl. At the age of 16 Boyle went to Italy with his tutor to study with Galileo. Later he formulated Boyle's Law, namely, that the volume of a gas kept at constant pressure is inversely proportional to its pressure. There is a small heritage centre in Lismore's old courthouse and you may notice an unusual neo-Tudor Carnegie library in West Street. In the heyday of the see of Lismore, the village had twenty churches but little trace remains of any of them. There was intense rivalry between the sees of Irish Lismore and Viking Waterford which was not resolved until the middle of the fourteenth century.

The Blackwater river is particularly striking at **Fermoy**, across the county line in Cork, 15 miles (24km) upstream from Lismore. Once an important British garrison town on the Dublin-to-Cork road, it has a very substantial seven-arch bridge over the river, with herons, swans and ducks disporting themselves around the shallow weir. Many of the buildings in the town are on a generous scale, and so is the riverside promenade, and the designated parking areas beside the cavernous but comfortable Grand Hotel. In November 1930 a strange 'bird battle' took place over the river. A flock of 10,000 starlings, who normally roosted in a wood 1½ miles (2km) away, tried to oust Fermoy's colony of 300 rooks who lived in tall trees beside the river. Every evening for 2 weeks the homing starlings dive-bombed the rooks. The rook colony seems to have called in reinforcements because their number swelled to about 3,000 until the starlings returned to their normal roost and the danger was past.

Waterford is the chief town of the south-east, with a variety of industries. One look at its expansive waterfront tells you why it was strategically so important, first a Norse stronghold and then a Norman town second only to Dublin. It has a fine position on the Suir river, which is very broad and deep at this point, and is about 17 miles

The four-storey Georgian clock tower straddles the main street in Youghal

(27km) from the open sea. The modern bridge across the river, which you have to cross to get to the railway station, has a span of 700ft (213m). Throughout the Middle Ages Waterford was a flourishing port, trading with mainland Europe, and loyal to the English crown. Strongbow's marriage to Eva, daughter of Dermot MacMurrough, was celebrated in 1171 in the cathedral which stood where Christ Church cathedral (1779) is now. Henry II arrived in 1172 with a navy of 400 ships and King John landed in 1210 with a large army. Today Waterford is best known for its glassware, an eighteenth-century industry that was revived in 1947. To explore the old city turn up any of the narrow streets off the mile-long quay. The main feature is an extensive city wall. Reginald's Tower is the most notable of several fortified towers and formed a corner of the wall. A sturdy circular battlemented tower with a conical roof, it was founded by Reginald the Dane in 1003 but looks more like a twelfth or thirteenth-century Norman construction. Now a museum, it contains Waterford's civic collection, including royal charters up to the age of Queen Anne and ceremonial swords presented by King John and Henry VIII. A collection of Viking and medieval items is displayed in a heritage centre in Greyfriars Street.

The N25 west from Waterford passes through some of the most popular and populous holiday areas of the south coast. The 3-mile

Youghal harbour where the film Moby Dick *was filmed*

(5km) sandy beach at Tramore (Tra mór — Great Beach) is crowded in summer and there are the usual leisure facilities, including golf and sea angling, though a recent hi-tech installation called 'Celtworld' brings nothing to the area's amenities. Around **Dungarvan** there are more fine beaches, though not in the town itself. A pretty one is at **Ring** where there is a tiny Irish-speaking community. How it has survived in English-speaking County Waterford is a puzzle. **Youghal** (pronounced yawl) is a popular beach resort and fills up in summer with Dubliners on holiday. Part of the film *Moby Dick* was made here on location in 1954 and a pub of the same name down at the harbour displays fading photographs of the occasion. On the promenade, between the resort area and the old town, a large 1798 monument has a sternly worded inscription. But Youghal also has some tremendous medieval town walls, characterful architecture, including a four-storey Georgian clock tower straddling the main street, a striking red-and-white Dutch townhouse, gabled Jacobean almshouses — the oldest surviving in Ireland — a thirteenth-century parish church and a history that includes sieges, sackings and the comings and goings of flamboyant Elizabethans. Built by the Normans and refortified in the seventeenth century, the walls retain three of the original thirteen towers, and are in a good state of preservation. Sir Walter Raleigh (1554-1618), who owned 42,000 acres (168,000 hectares) of confiscated Desmond land around Youghal, was mayor of the town 1585-97. He is said to have lived in Myrtle Grove, an Elizabethan mansion just inside the walls. The house has been much altered but though the interior is mostly Georgian, a large chamber on the first floor has retained its original dark oak panelling and ornate chimneypiece and overmantel carved with the figures of Faith, Hope and Charity. Beside the house are four ancient yew trees, a reminder of the derivation of the town's name from *eochaill*, Gaelic for 'yew wood'.

The real Raleigh is a shadowy presence in Youghal compared with Sir Richard Boyle, later baron Youghal and earl of Cork, who purchased all Raleigh's Irish property, including Lismore, in 1602. A pleasant scenic road runs for about 17 miles (27km) up the west bank of the Blackwater river north from Youghal to **Lismore**, the seat of the first earl of Cork. Effigies of the 'Great Earl', his mother, his wives and many of his children are carved on a magnificent marble tomb in the south transept of St Mary's church. Boyle designed it himself more than 20 years before his death. The church dates from the thirteenth century and has a fine early English west door, a three-light lancet window, Norman-French grave slabs, a fourteenth-century eight-sided font, numerous memorials, including one to Robert Boyle (the chemist), and the Fleming grave, a beautiful fifteenth-century tomb in the north wall. Outside is a square tower contemporary with the church. From the churchyard, which has a cheerful if curiously horticultural appearance, with banks of dahlias and red-hot pokers, you are able to get up on to the top of a restored section of the town walls.

In 1649, along with Cork and Kinsale, the Protestant royalist garrison at Youghal declared for Parliament and gave allegiance to Oliver Cromwell during his vengeful Irish expedition. Having broken the back of the rebellion, which had been going on since 1641, Cromwell sailed from the harbour here in late May 1650. However, as the central character for the summer festival, the town council have settled for Raleigh, a somewhat less contentious figure. Raleigh, who introduced the potato into England, reputedly planted Ireland's first potatoes here in Youghal. The Walter Raleigh Potato Festival at the end of June is the highlight of the year.

Cork City

Cork city is the third largest city in Ireland, has a mild climate and a light-hearted approach to life. Strangers are positively encouraged to climb up the tower of the city's oldest (1722) church, St Ann of Shandon, and ring the eighteenth-century bells to the tunes of 'Amazing grace', 'Three blind mice' and 'On the banks of my own lovely Lee'. The high windows gives a fine view over the city, of the spires of many large nineteenth-century churches and houses and all sorts of other buildings climbing up the steep-sided valley in all directions. Immediately below the tower is Murphy's Brewery yard, stacked with beer kegs in long straight rows. Murphy's is now a subsidiary of the Dutch company Heineken, who are said to have invested up to £60 million renovating the huge brewery at Lady's Well, building offices on the site of the Foundling Hospital (keeping the old façade) and other commendable projects. Brewing is one of a diminishing number of indigenous industries in the city, and new jobs are mostly in electronics, engineering, pharmaceuticals and chemicals. Emerging on to the street, having rung the bells of Shandon, one notices three tiny pubs opposite the church entrance — The Chimes, The Steeple and The Shandon Arms.

The founder of Cork was St Finbar, who built a monastery near the source of the Lee, 40 miles (64km) away, and came downstream in about the year AD600 to build another one on the south bank of the river. The 'lovely Lee' flows through Cork in two unequal streams.

Kilkenny town centre, County Kilkenny (Chapter 8)

Shrines like this can often be found at the roadside. Beara Peninsula, County Kerry (Chapter 9)

Muckross Abbey just south of Killarney, founded for the Franciscans in the 1440s (Chapter 9)

Visually impressive Great Skellig off the Kerry coast rises more than 700 feet out of the sea. It provided a very rugged and isolated home for early Christian monks (Chapter 9)

Cork city, the third largest city in Ireland

The wider north channel is spanned by broad flattish bridges and the narrower south channel by small humpy bridges. The once-marshy area between the two channels is a dull modern business and shopping quarter, reconstructed after the district was burnt in 1920 by 'Black and Tans', rogue government auxiliaries. It has rather too many chainstore shopfronts but there are a few old passageways that shelter small restaurants, bars and the occasional quirky shop. The flea market off St Patrick's Street was Cork's eighteenth-century English market, and another covered market selling vegetables, fruit and meat at Princes Street was the old Root Market, first opened in 1788. It has pretty polychrome brickwork.

St Patrick's Street curves round to the river where a fine bronze statue of Father Mathew, 'apostle' of temperance (previously encountered at Thomastown crossroads on the N74) occupies a prominent position. Grand Parade, though not in the least grand, has some interesting eighteenth-century bow-fronted merchants' houses, hung with grey slates. These two thoroughfares, like all the city centre main roads, were waterways up into the nineteenth century. The old cannon in Grand Parade was used by boatmen as a bollard to tie up at. Near the houses is an appealing war memorial with a Gothic canopy. Called 'The Wars of Ireland', the inscription says it was erected in 1906 by Cork Young Ireland Society, to Irish patriots of the upheavals of 1798, 1803, 1848 and 1867. At the angles are statues of

'The Wars of Ireland,' erected in 1906 by the Cork Young Ireland Society

Wolfe Tone, Michael Dwyer, Thomas Davis and O'Neill Crowley, one for each war perhaps.

The car ferries from Swansea and Roscoff arrive at **Ringaskiddy**, a traffic-congested tongue of land with a martello tower at the tip, on the west side of Cork Harbour. They used to come into the main port, **Cobh** (pronounced cove), on Great Island in the middle of the harbour. Getting to Cobh by road from Cork is at least a dozen heavily trafficked miles and so the little ferry across the harbour is a boon for Cobh people. In the nineteenth century hundreds of thousands of emigrants embarked at Cobh — called Queenstown from 1849 until 1922 — for the often dreadful journey to America. Around 20 per cent of passengers on the 'coffin' ships from Cork to Quebec are recorded as having died on the journey or soon after landing. A mile south of Cobh is **Spike Island**, a large convict prison in Victorian times. It is still in use as a place of correction, for young offenders. John Mitchel, the celebrated republican convicted of treason-felony and transported to Botany Bay in 1847, was detained in a hulk moored off Spike. He describes the experience in his book *Jail Journal*. These stories are told in Cobh's visitor centre. On the promenade is a *Lusitania* memorial to the 1,200 people killed when a German submarine torpedoed the British liner in May 1915. Over 100 of them were American, a factor that helped bring the US into the war.

Further Information
— The South: Wexford to Cork City —

Places to Visit

Ballitore
Co Kildare
Quaker Schoolhouse
Open: daily 10am-6pm.

Blessington
Co Wicklow
Russborough House
Open: daily June to August 10.30am-
5.30pm plus Sundays in spring and
autumn.
☎ (045) 65239

Cahir
Co Tipperary
Cahir Castle
Open: May to September 10am-6pm,
longer hours in high summer, shorter
hours in winter.
☎ (052) 41011

Carlow
Co Carlow
Carlow County Museum
Town Hall
Open: every afternoon 2-5.30pm except
Monday.
☎ (0503) 31759

Carrick-on-Suir
Co Tipperary
Ormonde Castle
Open: June to September 9.30am-6.30pm.
☎ (051) 40787

Cashel
Co Tipperary
Rock of Cashel
Open: daily 9.30am-4.30pm, until 5.30pm
in spring and 7.30pm in summer.
☎ (062) 61437

Brú Ború Heritage Centre
Open: daily March to October 10am-
7.30pm but not Sunday morning.
☎ (062) 61122

GPA Bolton Library
Open: all year Monday to Saturday
9.30am-5.30pm and on Sunday afternoon.
☎ (062) 61944/61232

Celbridge
Co Kildare
Castletown House
Open: Monday to Friday 10am-5pm
(until 6pm April to September), plus Saturday (11am-6pm) April to September.
☎ (01) 6288252

Cobh
Co Cork
Queenstown Centre
Open: daily all year except January
10am-6pm.
☎ (021) 813591

Cork
Co Cork
Shandon Bells
Open: Monday to Saturday 9.30am-5pm.

St Finbarre's Cathedral
Open: Mon to Sat 10am-1pm, 2-5pm.
☎ (021) 963387

Crawford Art Gallery
Emmet Place
Open: Monday to Saturday 10am-5pm.
☎ (021) 273377

Cork City Museum
Fitzgerald Park
Open: Monday to Friday 11am-5pm
and 3-5pm on Sunday.
☎ (021) 270679

Cork City Gaol
Sunday's Well
Open: 9.30am-8pm in summer.
In winter weekends only.
☎ (021) 305022

Dungarvan
Co Waterford
Dungarvan Museum
Open: June to September Monday to
Saturday 10am-6pm.
☎ (058) 41231

Emo
Co Laois
Emo Court
Gardens are open: daily 10.30am-5.30pm all year.
House is open: Monday afternoons (2-6pm) March to October.
☎ (0502) 26110

Enniscorthy
Co Wexford
Wexford County Museum
Enniscorthy Castle
Open: every afternoon all year. From June to October 10am-6pm.

Enniskerry
Co Wicklow
Powerscourt Demense, Powerscourt Gardens & Waterfall
Gardens open: 9.30am-5.30pm March to October, waterfall open: 9.30am-7pm (10.30am-dusk in winter).

Ferrycarrig
Co Wexford
Irish National Heritage Park
Open: March to October 10am-7pm.
☎ (053) 41733

Glendalough
Co Wicklow
The monuments are always accessible. Visitor centre open: June to September 10am-6pm, until 7pm in summer. Shorter hours in winter.
☎ (0404) 45325

Jerpoint Abbey
Co Kilkenny
Open: Tuesday to Saturday 10am-1pm, 2-5pm, and Sunday afternoon, and 9.30am-6.30pm daily in summer.
☎ (056) 24623

Kilkenny
Kilkenny Castle
Open: daily April to September 10am-5pm (until 7pm in high summer). In winter closed Monday, and shorter hours.
☎ (056) 21450

Rothe House
Open: April to October Monday to Saturday 10.30am-5pm and Sunday afternoon. Rest of year open: Saturday/Sunday afternoons only.
☎ (056) 22893

Kilmore Quay
Co Wexford
Maritime Museum
Open: 2-8pm June to September.
☎ (053) 29655

Lismore
Co Waterford
Lismore Castle Gardens
Open: May to September 1.45-4.45pm daily except Saturday.
☎ (058) 54424

Lismore Heritage Centre
Open: 10am-6pm Monday to Saturday and Sunday afternoon.
☎ (058) 54975

St Carthage's Cathedral
Open: daily 9am-6pm (until 4pm in winter).

Maynooth
Co Kildare
St Patrick's College, Museum of Ecclesiology
To arrange a visit ☎ (01) 6285222

Mitchelstown Caves
Co Tipperary
Open: all year 10am-6pm.
☎ (052) 67246

Mount Usher Gardens
Co Wicklow
Open: March to October 10.30am-6pm (from 11am on Sunday).
☎ (0404) 40116/40205

New Ross
Co Wexford
John F Kennedy Arboretum
Open: all year 10am to 5pm (until 8pm in summer).
☎ (051) 88171

Roscrea
Co Tipperary
Damer House Heritage Centre
☎ (0505) 21850

Stradbally
Co Laois
Steam and Vintage Machinery Museum
The Green
Open: Easter to October Tuesday to
Saturday 10-12noon, 2-4pm.
☎ (0502) 25444

Straffan
Co Kildare
Steam Museum
Open: June to August afternoons
except Monday, plus Sunday afternoons in spring and autumn.
☎ (01) 6273155/6288412

Tullow
Co Carlow
Altamont Gardens
Open: Easter to October 2-6pm
Sundays and bank holidays only.
☎ (0503) 59128

Tully
Co Kildare
Irish National Stud and Horse Museum
Open: Easter to October Monday to
Saturday 10am-5pm and Sunday
afternoon.
☎ (045) 21617

Japanese Gardens
Open: same hours as stud.
☎ (045) 21252

Waterford
Co Waterford
Reginald's Tower Museum
Open: Easter to September Monday to
Friday 11am-7pm (closed for lunch
1-2pm) and Saturday morning.
☎ (051) 73501

Waterford Heritage Centre
Greyfriars Street
Open: Easter to September approx
same hours as Reginald's Tower.
☎ (051) 71227

Waterford Crystal
Kilbarry
Guided factory tours daily April to
October; Monday to Friday November
to March. Bookings ☎ (051) 73311

Wexford
Co Wexford
Westgate Heritage Centre
☎ (053) 42611

Youghal
Co Cork
Myrtle Grove
Limited opening hours.
☎ (024) 92274

Travel
Ferry to Saltee islands from Kilmore
Quay, Co Wexford, in summer.
☎ (053) 29714
Cruising restaurants on the river from
New Ross, Co Wexford. Booking/
information: ☎ (051) 21723/73752

Tourist Information Offices
Open: all year.

Cork
Co Cork
Grand Parade
☎ (021) 273251

Kilkenny
Co Kilkenny
Shee Alms House, Rose Inn Street
☎ (056) 21755

Rosslare Terminal
Co Wexford
Rosslare
☎ (053) 33232

Waterford
Co Waterford
41 The Quay
☎ (051) 75788

Wexford
Co Wexford
Crescent Quay
☎ (053) 23111

Wicklow
Co Wicklow
Rialto Centre
Fitzwilliam Square
☎ (0404) 69117

9 • The South West

North and West Cork, Kerry, Limerick, Clare

If north Cork is the least visited region of south-west Ireland, **Kanturk** rates as the least visited town. Grass grows in the streets, and yet the place has considerable charm, standing at the confluence of the Dalua and Allow rivers which are spanned by three fine bridges. The most imposing of these, an eighteenth-century six-arch humpback bridge over the Dalua, has a long inscription beginning:

'See Dalua roll its flood along
And Allow fam'd in Spenser's song'

— divided into couplets inscribed on panels set into the bridge. You can walk and read at the same time. Mature copper beeches shade the Dalua along O'Brien Street. A large Georgian house (now a private house, previously a hotel), prominently positioned at the end of Egmont Place, was built by Lord Egmont for his land agent. Strand Street, very wide at one end and very narrow at the other, is lined by an odd collection of buildings, including a canary yellow Clock House of 1838. A mile (2km) to the south is a huge semi-fortified three-storey structure known as **Kanturk Castle**, a cross between an Irish tower house and a Jacobean castle. MacDonagh MacCarthy, Lord of Duhallow, built it in about 1600 but his English neighbours were unnerved by its size and appearance. They thought he might be building a fortress. An order came from the Privy Council in London to stop the construction and it was never finished. It probably only was a house but even today its four massive corner towers have an undomesticated look.

In contrast with faded Kanturk, **Mallow** is a smart little spa town on the Blackwater, with a racecourse, a railway station, a sugar beet factory and an atmospheric old hotel. The mantelpieces in the hotel bar are graced by portraits of Mallow-men Thomas Davis (1814-45) and William O'Brien (1852-1928) — both Irish nationalists, one Protestant, the other Catholic. Davis was a poet and a founder of the *Nation* newspaper. O'Brien edited the Land League journal *United Ireland* and wrote novels. Plaques mark the houses where they were

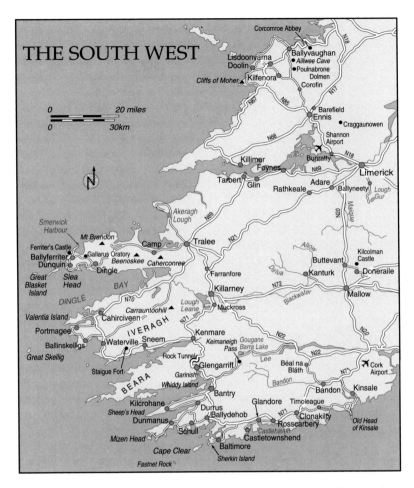

THE SOUTH WEST

0   20 miles

0   30km

Corcomroe Abbey

Lisdoonvarna
Doolin
Cliffs of Moher
Kilfenora

Ballyvaughan
• Aillwee Cave
• Poulnabrone
  Dolmen
Corofin

Barefield
Ennis
Craggaunowen

Shannon
Airport

Killimer
Foynes
Tarbert
Glin
Rathkeale

Bunratty

Limerick

Adare
Ballyneety   Lough
              Gur

Smerwick
Harbour

Mt Brandon
Ferriter's Castle
Ballyferriter
Dunquin
Gallarus Oratory
Beenoskee Caherconree
Dingle

Camp
Tralee

Farranfore

Killarney

Akeragh
Lough

Allow

Buttevant
Kanturk

Kilcolman
Castle

Doneraile

Mallow

Delua

Blackwater

Great
Blasket
Island

Slea
Head

BAY

DINGLE

Valentia Island
Portmagee
Ballinskelligs
Great Skellig

Carrauntoohill
Cahirciveen

Lough
Leane

Muckross

IVERAGH

Waterville Sneem

Kenmare

Keimaneigh Gougane
Pass   Barra Lake

Lee

Béal na
Bláth

Cork
Airport

Staigue Fort

BEARA

Rock Tunnel
Garinish
Whiddy Island

Glengarriff

Bantry

Bandon

Bandon Kinsale

Kilcrohane
Sheep's Head
Dunmanus

Durrus
Ballydehob

Schull

Glandore Timoleague

Clonakilty
Rosscarbery

Old Head
of Kinsale

Mizen Head

Cape Clear
Fastnet Rock

Castlehaven
Castletownshend
Baltimore
Sherkin Island

born, and a plaque on 139 Main Street identifies novelist Anthony Trollope's lodgings when his Post Office duties brought him to Mallow in the mid-nineteenth century. A novel-writing priest, Patrick Sheehan (1852-1913) who produced several bestsellers, was born at 29 O'Brien Street. A town with so many bookish connections needs a good bookshop, and indeed Mallow has one: Philip's Bookshop, opposite the Catholic church.

Like Kanturk, Mallow has a 'castle', a hulking great semi-fortified machicolated ruin of a house. This one is right in the town, just beyond a peculiar Victorian Hansel-and-Gretel building called the Clock House (not as nice as the one in Kanturk). Built in about 1590 by Sir Thomas Norreys, the castle was burnt in 1689 by order of James

*The clockhouse at Mallow,
a smart little spa town on
the Blackwater where
Anthony Trollope lodged in
the nineteenth century*

II. Facing the ruin is a delightful manor house (private), long and low, with ivy-covered gables and at one end, the estate's original stables. When the castle was burnt, the Norreyses moved into the stable block until, their fortunes restored, they were able to enlarge it by adding on the present house. It is nineteenth century but it looks the very model of Elizabethan authenticity. Sir Thomas was a well connected, rather ineffectual, administrator at the time of the Munster plantation, and his family had good reason to admire the Elizabethan style. His father was a life-long friend of Queen Elizabeth, and the deer in the park at Mallow are descendants of two white harts which she gave to Sir Thomas's daughter, her god-child. Such were the intrigues and vested interests of the period, however, that in due course his son-in-law, William Jephson, representative for Cork county in the second protectorate parliament, found himself proposing that Cromwell should be made king of England.

North-east of Mallow, 2 miles (3km) from Doneraile village, and close to the ruined thirteenth-century Buttevant Abbey, is the ivy-covered ruin of **Kilcolman Castle**, home of Edmund Spenser (1552-99), 'prince of poets in his tyme' as recorded on his memorial in Westminster Abbey, London. *Astrophel*, the beautiful pastoral elegy on the death of Sir Philip Sidney, was written at Kilcolman, and also much of *The Faerie Queene* — for which Raleigh, Spenser's neighbour at Youghal, wrote the opening sonnet 'Methought I saw the grave where Laura lay'. Spenser first came to Ireland in 1580 as secretary to Lord Grey, Lord Deputy of Ireland, and stayed on in various administrative posts. As an 'undertaker' for the settlement of Munster in 1588 he received a grant of 3,000 acres (1,200 hectares), and this castle on the main route from Limerick to Cork (N20). His wife, Elizabeth Boyle, who inspired his *Amoretti* sonnets, was a cousin of the Earl of Cork. Despite his rather unenlightened though well informed views of the laws and religion of sixteenth-century Ireland, Spenser created wonderful word pictures of the landscapes and the people. His life ended sadly. His health was not good and in 1598 Kilcolman was attacked by O'Neill insurgents under the earl of Desmond. The Spenser family had to flee the burning castle and the poet died in London soon after.

Perennially fashionable west Cork is stuffed with Dubliners (from Dublin 4) in summer, here for the fishing, yachting, and eating in gourmet establishments run by energetic German, Dutch, American, French, English, Welsh and, occasionally, Irish restaurateurs. Crowded in the high season but always pretty, **Kinsale** has a delightful position on the Bandon estuary, with narrow lanes, small slate-faced houses, some Georgian, a fishmarket of 1784 and a medieval parish church.

An interesting museum occupies the courthouse, now restored, which dates from the seventeenth century, an era when Kinsale seems to have been a favourite landing place for England's continental adversaries. Three thousand Spanish soldiers, allies of Hugh O'Neill, came ashore in September 1601 and occupied the port. They waited for 3 months, while O'Neill marched his army hundreds of miles south from Ulster, to confront the English in Munster. The victor at Kinsale was Mountjoy, Queen Elizabeth's deputy — with dire consequences for Gaelic Ulster soon to follow. A tourist trail of the battlefield is signposted around the town. Seven thousand French troops landed here in 1690, sent by Louis XIV to reinforce James II's faltering campaign. Spanish and French landings nowadays are mostly from deep sea fishing boats and yachts and the invaders head straight for Kinsale's fish restaurants and musical pubs.

Kinsale Old Head is reached across an expanse of undulating grassland, wide enough to swallow up several large holiday caravan settlements, to fine craggy scenery at the point and a sweeping white sandy beach at **Garrettstown**. This is one of a number of rewarding short visits in the coastal area south of the N71, which runs along the tops of the creeks, coves, harbours, bays, inlets and peninsulas of west Cork and on round to Killarney, but it is congested in summer, with frequent traffic gridlock in Clonakilty and Skibbereen. However, because of the absence of eateries and pubs, it is a fair bet that the beautifully situated Franciscan friary at Timoleague, approached by a splendid 10-arch bridge across estuarine flats, will not be afflicted in this way.

Timoleague was the burying place of the MacCarthy Reaghs, a distinguished branch of the MacCarthy clan of south Munster. The friary was noted for its hospitality, and for the fine Spanish wine which was easily landed here from small boats. Brother Michael O'Clery during his researches for the *Annals of the Four Masters*, came to Timoleague in 1629 on a visit from Donegal to consult a manuscript collection of saints' lives and secular histories, and the MacCarthys received extensive coverage in the *Annals* as a result. The collection was compiled for the scholarly Fineen MacCarthy Reagh and his wife Catherine Fitzgerald, the earl of Desmond's daughter. It must have been spirited away when the friary was burnt in 1642 because it was discovered 200 years later in Lismore Castle, hidden inside a wall. The destruction in 1642 signalled the end of the community. An eighteenth-century Gaelic poem recorded the scene 100 years later:

'Ivy sprouting in your eaves
Nettles on your cold flagged floor'

Clonakilty's most famous son is Michael Collins (1890-1922), the guerrilla leader who, with Arthur Griffith, negotiated the Anglo-Irish treaty of December 1921 which gave independence to southern Ireland. A brilliant organiser, very handsome, irresistible to women and exceedingly violent, he was assassinated in 1922 in the first months of the civil war. There is a memorial at Béal na Bláth, off the Bandon-Macroom road, scene of the ambush. Around Clonakilty you may come upon local road bowls teams in enthusiastic competition on rural side roads. Since 90 per cent of all the players of this ancient Irish game are to be found in the lanes of County Cork, Corkmen are the best authority on the pronunciation. It is 'bowling' as in 'howling', never 'bowling' as in 'rolling'.

Rosscarbery village, on a shallow coastal inlet, has a small seventeenth-century Anglican cathedral which, unusually for an Anglican church, is quite likely to be open when you pass by. Beside it is a fragment of the church of St Fachtna, who founded a monastery here in AD590. In its heyday the monastery's school was the most influential in Cork. A stone head on the wall below the bell tower window is said to be a likeness of St Fachtna who was so holy that when by mistake he left his book exposed on a hillside in the rain, it did not get wet. Local woodcarvers, James and Michael O'Regan, made the fine set of individual oak stalls for the Dean and Chapter, and there are three beautiful stained glass windows, one based on the pre-Raphaelite painting 'The Light of the World' by Holman Hunt.

The stone circle at **Drombeg** is the best of about sixty stone circles which have been found in west Cork. Though not as big as some, certainly not as impressive as say, the seven-circle complex at Beaghmore in Tyrone, Drombeg is very accessible, a turn-off on the R597 from Rosscarbery to Glandore. A cremated body in a pot was found at Drombeg but, as is usually the case with these mysterious monuments, nobody quite knows what it was doing there.

Castletownshend is a one-street village. The street is very steep and long, lined with some attractive well built houses and dividing briefly halfway down to bypass two large sycamore trees. At the top is Drishane House (private), home of the Somerville family where second cousins Edith Oenone Somerville (1858-1949) and Violet Martin ('Martin Ross') (1862-1915) wrote their popular *Irish RM* (Resident Magistrate) stories. At the bottom is the castellated house of the Townshend family, now a guesthouse, overlooking Castlehaven harbour. In 1601, this was a stronghold of the O'Driscolls who handed control of it, temporarily, to their Spanish allies who were here to fight the English. Three weeks before the main engagement at Kinsale there was a battle in this quiet harbour, which both sides claim to have won. After Kinsale, however, the O'Driscolls were supplanted.

The village was the creation of the Townshends (or Townsends — the 'h' crept in in 1870), the Somervilles, Bechers, Coghills and Chavasses, the Ascendancy, or Anglo-Irish, families who built the big houses up and down the street, intermarrying and enjoying a seigneurial lifestyle, mostly uneventful. The murder in 1936 by IRA terrorists of Edith Somerville's brother, a retired admiral in his seventies, is said to have shaken Castletownshend but even today, this must surely be the most concentratedly genteel place in Ireland.

On a hillock beside the castle, Somerville and Ross fans clamber around the graveyard of **St Barrahane's** parish church, looking for the final resting place of the famous pair. The clamberers include visitors from America where Edith Somerville had many friends. The interior of the church, where indefatigable Edith played the organ for 70 years, is very unspiritual, with genealogies, conquests and other achievements of the Townshends, Somervilles, Bechers, Coghills and Chavasses, fulsomely described on the walls. A stone tablet memorial records the admiration of Edith's American readers. The mosaic on the floor, the holy table and the reredos in the chancel, these were all Edith's doing. She also selected her own gravestone which, together with Violet Martin's, is out in the fresh air, immediately behind the church.

The Somerville and Ross literary partnership began in 1886 and they published about fourteen books before Violet Martin died. Afterwards Somerville continued to write under their joint names, producing thirteen more books. The exuberant, witty stories of Irish life as seen from the Big House are in line with the genre pioneered by Maria Edgeworth 100 years earlier. The televised *Irish RM* stories draw huge popular audiences when they are shown in Ireland, though even now some people feel personally targeted by their patronizing accuracy and will not watch on principle!

Peninsulas and Islands

The south-west corner of Ireland is a series of five long peninsulas — Mizen Head, Sheep's Head, Beara, Iveragh and Dingle — projecting out into the Atlantic, running roughly east to west, with some interesting islands offshore. This is good birdwatching territory, the first European landfall for transatlantic wanderers, all the way round from Cape Clear to the mouth of the Shannon, via the Blaskets at the end of the Dingle peninsula, up as far as the haven of little Akeragh Lough where exhausted vagrant wildfowl and waders flop down on the warm mudflats. From the bird observatory on the west side of **Cape Clear** island hundreds of bird species are tracked in their seasonal migrations. The observatory at North Harbour was set up by volunteers in 1959, a time when ornithologists were preoccupied with penetrating the mysteries of bird migration, and there are complete records from that time, kept at the observatory.

'The famished seabird past me sailed
Into the dim infinity'

wrote the Limerick-born poet Aubrey de Vere (1814-1902). Nowadays it is known where the birds come from and where they are going. The busiest, best bird season at Cape Clear is September and October, the time of the impressive autumn flypasts.

In high summer there are three daily ferries to Cape Clear from the harbour at **Baltimore**, with frequency dropping to one per day from October to May. The people-count varies similarly. It is a 45-minute journey, passing the nearer island of Sherkin — favourite venue for O'Driscoll clan gatherings, with pubs, good beaches, and crowded at holiday times — before the boat heads out into an exhilarating sea. Even on a day trip, you will see birds, and perhaps seals. At certain times of the year, there are pelagic birdwatching expeditions and the chance to see whales, dolphins, sharks and leatherback turtles.

Near the observatory is a ruined medieval church dedicated to Kieran the Elder (not to be confused with the more famous Kieran of Clonmacnois), a cross-carved pillar stone, a holy well, and three rather unreverential pubs. Newcomers are buying up derelict farms and cottages on Cape Clear, and breeze-block haciendas have sprung up in the usual haphazard way. Even so there remain some Gaelic speakers on the island — schoolchildren are sent here in summer to practise the language — and storytelling traditions have recently enjoyed a revival, with events and seminars in Gaelic and English for budding seanachies, or storytellers.

Fastnet Rock, 3 miles (5km) to the south, got its present lighthouse in 1906. Made of Cornish granite, it was first assembled in Cornwall, checked for fit, disassembled and put back together on the rock, its distinctive outline soon becoming a familiar sight to passengers on transatlantic liners. Nowadays Fastnet is the western turning point in the long-distance yacht race from Cowes, Isle of Wight, held every other year.

The N71 to Bantry makes a 90-degree turn at **Ballydehob** and runs due north past the top of Mizen Head peninsula, most southerly of the five peninsulas. After the tidy villages of the south coast, the countryside becomes all at once less protected, more desolate. If you have time, follow the north shore of Roaring Water Bay, past Ballydehob, Schull harbour and sandy Barleycove beach, to **Mizen Head** where there are fine views from the top of the head. Down below, an offshore lighthouse is linked to the land by a suspension bridge. Be careful not to go near the cliff edge. Three miles back the way you came, turn inland to ruined **Dunmanus castle**, a fifteenth-century O'Mahony tower house, one of many strongholds of this ancient west Munster clan, kinsmen of Brian Boru, who lost many of their fighting men at Clontarf in 1014. Another interesting cross-peninsula drive is from Schull to Drishane via bleak Mount Gabriel (1,336ft/407m). It is hard to believe that this was once a heavily populated area, but the archaeologists insist that it was. At Durrus, turn west for a scenic drive round the very thin, very deserted Sheep's Head peninsula, turning north at Kilcrohane past little Seefin mountain for some fine coastal panoramas and unexpected vistas.

The main square in **Bantry** is a long rectangle with a modern statue of St Brendan ('the navigator', founder of Clonfert) looking across the bay, his arms outstretched. Gulf Oil gave the statue to the town when they set up their oil terminal on Whiddy Island in the bay in 1968. The deep water was ideal for the petrol tankers, one of which, *Betelgeuse*, exploded in 1979. Brendan was a Kerryman, born near Tralee. He had a vision of paradise, an island out in the Atlantic, from a mountain top in Kerry and he does not look at home in Bantry.

The square is named after Wolfe Tone, the United Irishman who arrived in Bantry Bay in December 1796 with 16 French ships and 7,000 soldiers — less than half the huge Armada that had sailed from France. The rest had turned back in atrocious weather. Faced with the prospect of an imminent overwhelming attack from the ships anchored in front of his house, Bantry's English landlord, Richard White, is said to have mobilised local defences, capturing a scouting party that landed, and preventing a possible popular revolt in support of the invaders. Fortunately for him, the attack never came. The French commanders — including Tone, who had recently been made an adjutant general in the French army — could not agree what to do, and the weather was bad. After a few days they cut their cables and sailed away.

White was made a lord as a reward for his efforts. His son, second earl of Bantry, enlarged Bantry House and filled it with art, furniture and tapestries, some of which are on view to visitors to the house. There are some good paintings though the portraits of George III and Queen Charlotte are copies, as are the pair in the archbishop's palace in Armagh. Allan Ramsay painted them in 1762 and the king must have been pleased because he had copies made, to give away as appropriate. The Bantry House pair were presented to the first earl to mark his ennoblement. An exhibition on the French Armada, not to be confused with the Spanish variety, has been installed in the yard. There are Italian gardens around the house, with balustrades and statues, and fine terraces at the rear. The raised site is well above the level of the road, invisible from here. It gives a wide, low-level view over the bay to the Caha mountains on the far shore. Four black cannons still point their noses across the water.

The *Bantry Mariner* goes from the harbour every hour to **Whiddy Island**, 15 minutes away across the bay. The service is well used by the people living on Whiddy, some of whom seem to be in constant motion between the island and the mainland, en route to or from mass in Bantry. In summer there are cruises around this island which retains three large nineteenth-century military fortifications.

To visit **Gougane Barra**, where St Finbar built a hermitage on an island at the source of the Lee, take the R584 north-east of Bantry up the Owvane valley for about 12 miles (19km). The road rises to the scenic rocky Pass of Keimaneigh after which Gougane Barra forest park and lake are signposted.

It is a wild, dramatic place. The lake, with its small island where the saint's vanished oratory stood, is hemmed in by steep rocks and waterfalls. The courtyard and cells on the island are of eighteenth-century origin. The water is very deep, so deep that Finbar was able to drown a dragon in it — a cautionary tale for pilgrims coming here on the Sunday after St Finbar's feast day (25 September), a warning too for parties celebrating weddings in the modern Romanesque church.

The highest mountains in Ireland, Macgillycuddy's Reeks, are on the Iveragh peninsula but Beara and Dingle have some big mountains too. The wild hills of Caha west of Glengarriff are especially beautiful. The region's pleasant climate and lush greenness, mild and moist, with woods of old oak and berried holly, have been discovered by a large number of people from elsewhere who have come here to live.

Garinish Island, a rocky islet with a martello tower on the top 10 minutes by ferry from Glengarriff, was turned into an exotic 37-acre (15-hectare) garden just before World War I. Alan Bryce, a rich Scottish MP, bought it from the War Office and employed 100 men to move soil, blast rocks and build a series of walled gardens and follies, a pavilion, a clock tower, an Italian casita, a Greek temple, a Roman sarcophagus, a lilypond, a goldfish pond, almost everything except a big house. One was planned but was never built. Though not to everyone's taste, Garinish (or Ilnacullin) garden has many ornamental trees, shrubs, tender plants and colourful flowers growing in this sheltered inlet, a fine contrast with the bare tops of the Caha mountains beyond.

Take the Rock Tunnel route north, passing the Hedgehog Health Institute — a sign, if one were needed, that the West Sussex ethos obtains here — to classy **Kenmare**, a well planned village with a picturesque sheep market, where a left turn on to the N70 brings you on to the Iveragh peninsula.

With 30 hotels and 200 guesthouses and B&Bs going full blast in summer, **Killarney** can still be a hard place in which to find a bed — a measure of the unsentimental development of commercialised tourism in the area. Most of the estimated 1.6 million tourists who visit Kerry each year come to the south of the county. Holiday

Macgillycuddy's Reeks, west of Killarney, are Ireland's highest mountains

weekends are particularly busy and there are motor rallies, regattas, arts weeks, folk weeks, civic festivals, 'themed' festivals and many other well marketed year-round diversions to keep the visitors occupied, and also a succession of horse racing meetings, in Killarney itself in May and July, in Tralee in June and August, and Listowel in September.

An especially striking feature of Killarney national park is the glossy-leaved *arbutus*, or strawberry tree, which has waxy white flowers like lily-of-the-valley and prickly round scarlet fruit. A luxuriant vegetation, ferns, saxifrages and butterworts, flourishes in the mild damp climate. The park has three lovely lakes: Lower Lake (Lough Leane), Middle Lake (Muckross Lake) and Upper Lake. Around Lough Leane, largest of the three, the gardens of Muckross House, with Muckross Abbey nearby, and Ross Castle are rewarding visits. From Killarney town, go south on the N71 for a mile where **Ross Castle**, the last Royalist stronghold in Munster to hold out against Cromwell, is signposted. The castle stands at the end of a small peninsula in Lough Leane. It surrendered in 1652 when the attacking commander, Edmund Ludlow, got to hear of a prophecy that said the castle would be captured only when 'a ship should swim upon the lake'. In an act of rare imagination, Ludlow ordered a gun boat to be brought up the river from Castlemaine harbour.

The Blaskets and the Atlantic Ocean from Dunmore Head on the Dingle Peninsula, County Kerry (Chapter 9)

The only landing place on Great Blasket Island, uninhabited since 1953 (Chapter 9)

The majestic Cliffs of Moher, County Clare (Chapter 9)

Demoralised by this Birnham-Wood-come-to-Dunsinane scenario the garrison abandoned the castle.

At the same time, the friars down the road were being driven out of their friary which, now a well preserved ruin, adjoins the gardens of Muckross House. The friary took 40 years to build. Donal MacCarthy, prince of Desmond, founded it in 1448 — a period when the Fitzgeralds, earls of Kildare and Desmond, were constantly feuding with the Butlers, earls of Ormond — but he had to spend most of his money on fighting battles for years after. The changes in architectural fashions are detectable in the non-matching windows in the church and the different arcades in the cloister. The best feature of Muckross House, an 1840s Elizabethan-style mansion now used as a heritage centre, is its lakeshore gardens.

Visitors to Killarney converge from the three regional airports — Shannon, Cork, and Farranfore, a few miles north of the town, and oversized coaches bearing happy tour groups inch their way round the **Ring of Kerry**. The 110-mile (177km), very scenic route runs along the north bank of the Kenmare river estuary to Waterville, up to Cahirciveen and back along the south shore of Dingle bay to Killarney town. Inside the Ring is the great mountain range of **Macgillycuddy's Reeks**, with **Carrauntoohil**, at 3,414ft (1,041m) the highest peak in Ireland and, as such, irresistible to peak-baggers. At the north-east end of the range are the vistas of purple mountains and picturesque lakes which so affected the eighteenth-century Romantics and high priests of Victorian culture. Then, as now, the main activity in this beautiful place was looking at the scenery, with plenty of rowing about on the lakes, trips in jaunting cars and trails on horseback through the Gap of Dunloe. Somewhere along this narrow gorge Charlotte Brontë, on honeymoon, fell off her horse.

Big Bertha of Sneem

Sneem village derives its name from *snaidhm*, the Gaelic for 'knot'. It stands on the banks of the tumbling river Sneem that twists and wiggles its contorted way down the mountain side. Walkers on the Kerry Way, a rambler's version of the Ring of Kerry, find Sneem makes a congenial base, and anglers come here for the salmon fishing. A pretty village ranged round two squares, with two interesting churches and numerous hostelries, it has a generally elderly population. Many young people left in search of work and have not come back. Big Bertha, the world's oldest cow, who lived to be nearly 50, is Sneem's greatest celebrity. Born on St Patrick's Day 1944, she was of the rare Dremon breed, mother of 39 calves, fund-raiser for

A scene near Waterville on the Ring of Kerry road

local charities and a moderate Guinness drinker. She died at Christmas 1993 but can still be seen in the town, stuffed and mounted. The taxidermist returned her in time to lead the Sneem parade on St Patrick's Day 1994.

Staigue Fort is signposted north off the N70 just before Caherdaniel, up nearly 3 miles (2km) of bracken and fuchsia-flanked single-track lane. It is one of the largest, best preserved prehistoric stone forts in Ireland, with an 18ft (5m) high circular wall, 13ft (4m) thick in places, with two small rooms inside the wall, and surrounded by a large bank and ditch. Set near the top of a green valley, with a commanding seaward view, Staigue has escaped the heavy restoration work inflicted on that other magnificent stone fort, the Grianan of Aileach in Donegal.

Once a favourite holiday haunt of Charlie Chaplin, **Waterville** has the attributes of a traditional resort town — palm trees, a good beach, pleasant hotels, and golf. In 1991 it acquired its own full-blown Club Med village, the Club's ninety-ninth village, which overlooks Lough Currane. In summer there are boats from Waterville, and from tiny Ballinskelligs harbour across the bay, to the island of Great Skellig, or Skellig Michael, an important early Christian site 7 miles (11km) offshore. Only small boats, with a maximum of twelve passengers, are able to land on the island.

A massy rock, with two unequal pinnacles, 720ft (219m) and 650ft (198m) high, **Great Skellig** rises out of the sea like a bizarre medieval cathedral. It is one of a number of dramatic sea-girt rocks associated with the European cult of the archangel Michael. The Mont St Michel off Brittany is a famous example — and its daughter-house, St Michael's Mount in Cornwall, is another. In the eighth century, possibly earlier, a group of monks came to Great Skellig, climbed up to a high ledge and built six dry-stone beautifully corbelled beehive houses (*clocháns*), five oval ones and a square one, with a surrounding wall or cashel. To reach the enclosure requires some careful climbing, up a series of rough stairways hewn out of the rock, about 650 steps altogether. The square house has little wall cupboards like lockers and stone pegs for hanging up book-satchels, suggesting that this house was the monks' library and reading room. Nearby is a rectangular oratory or chapel shaped like an upturned boat. Below this group is a very ruined twelfth-century church, with only its east window intact. Among numerous other remains are more stone oratories, two fresh water wells and some primitive crosses. It is strange that the older structures should be in such good repair while more recent ones are so ruined, perhaps robbed of their stones in the 1820s when the lighthouse road was built, itself a considerable engineering feat. The monks lived on Great Skellig until the thirteenth century, though the meditative life was not without interruption. The Vikings made four attacks in the ninth century. On one occasion they carried off the abbot and, according to the *Annals of the Four Masters*, starved him to death in captivity.

There are also trips to Great Skellig from Portmagee and from Knightstown (Valentia Island). The boat journey takes about 2 hours, past the puffins of Puffin Island and the huge gannet colony on Little Skellig. There are no visitor facilities but people can spend 3 or 4 hours exploring the island before the boat leaves to return to the mainland. A large boat from Valentia carrying up to 175 people provides short (90 minutes) cruises around the islands but does not stop off anywhere — there is no need. The passengers have already seen it all, inside 'The Skellig Experience' visitor centre.

Visiting Irish islands is usually a leisurely, often prolonged affair and you must take pot luck with the weather. **Great Blasket Island**, 2 miles (3km) off Slea Head, Dingle, and uninhabited since the last people there were evacuated more than 40 years ago, is easier to get to. Boats depart every day in summer from the pier at Dunquin. An alien-looking heritage centre has been built at **Dunquin** on a 50-acre (20 hectare) piece of wild treeless valley close to the sea. Like Edward

Lear's poor Dong with a Luminous Nose, the Dingle peninsula now has an Experience at its tip, in this case the Blasket Centre. No peninsula should be without one!

Passengers transfer to dinghies for landing on Great Blasket since the island has no harbour, only a boatslip at the foot of the cliffs. In the 1960s Blasket Sound was the scene of a successful search for the wreck of the *Santa Maria de la Rosa*, an almiranta or vice-flagship of the Spanish Armada. The battered ship had staggered into the sound on 21 September 1588 and promptly sank to the bottom the same day. Great Blasket is especially prized for its vanished Gaelic cultural tradition, chronicled in timely autobiographical works by Tomas O'Crohan (Criomhthain) (1856-1935), Maurice O'Sullivan (1904-50) and Peig Sayers (1873-1958), a great storyteller and very old when she told her own story. All three wrote in Gaelic. Some of the buildings abandoned in the 1950s are to be conserved. The islanders' hardships seem to have been so extreme that surely only a sadist would want them to have stayed.

At the point where the Ring of Kerry turns east again, **Cahirciveen** was the birthplace of the Irish patriot Daniel O'Connell (1775-1847), most revered of all Irish leaders. The O'Connell Memorial Church in Cahirciveen was erected in his honour and, a special papal dispensation having been given, named after him. It is said to be the only Roman Catholic church in the world not named after a member of the Trinity, Holy Family or a canonised saint. It is an enormous edifice, big enough to excite the envy even of a saint.

The Dingle's bony backbone differs a little from those of the other four peninsulas of the south west. It too runs from east to west, but then turns abruptly north, rising up, to end dramatically with a great massy ridge, riven by a chain of pretty lakes in a long deep corrie, with **Mount Brandon** (3,127ft/953m), the highest point. There is a wonderful view of the mountain from the large carpark at the top of the Connor Pass, a 5-mile (8km) drive from Dingle town. One of Ireland's holy mountains, Brandon is associated with St Brendan and there is a pilgrim's path, with stations of the cross, from Cloghane village up to the top where someone has put up an aluminium cross made from bits of a German fighter plane that crashed on this misty mountain during World War II. Brendan Behan (1923-64) in his *Irish Sketchbook* writes affectionately of Brendan's Mountain, and 'the four good pubs resting snugly under its shadow', meaning the pubs of Ballyferriter, a little Gaeltacht village. Ballyferriter is well known too for its residential Irish-language courses.

Two miles (3km) north-west of the village and prominent on the far side of Ferriter's Cove, is the scant ruin of **Ferriter's Castle**, built in 1460, birthplace of the Old English Kerryman, Pierce Ferriter (1600-53), who served as a captain in the Catholic confederate army in the 1641 uprising. Ferriter wrote courtly love poems in Gaelic and, like that other poetical soldier, Sir Walter Raleigh, he seems to have been executed rather unnecessarily. He held out against the Cromwellians until the fall of Ross Castle in 1652. After he surrendered, his safe-conduct is said to have been dishonoured. Every beach on the Dingle peninsula is finer than the last one you saw, and just across the isthmus from Ferriter's Cove is the magnificent strand of **Smerwick** harbour. The name comes from two Norse words meaning 'butter harbour' and was conferred in the tenth century when butter was exported from here to the Norse settlement at Limerick. A modern stone sculpture by Cliodna Cussen, erected in 1980, commemorates a massacre at Smerwick when 600 soldiers, mostly Spanish, were put to the sword — not recently, thank goodness, but 400 years ago. In 1580 an English force under Lord Grey, newly arrived from England, came to Smerwick to dislodge a Spanish garrison from the Fort del Oro, built the previous year with assistance from the pope. It was to be a base of operations against the English. The fort was bombarded for 3 days, then surrendered and everyone in the castle except the officers were slaughtered. Sparing the officers and killing the ordinary soldiers was common practice at the time — not a policy calculated to appeal to prospective army recruits in a more democratic age. Sometimes, of course, no one at all was spared.

Historic Monuments of Dingle

The whole of the Dingle is extremely well endowed with prehistoric remains and early Irish Christian monuments, with a particular concentration at the west end, including numerous large crosses, scores of standing stones, churches and holy wells and hundreds of beehive houses. On the slopes of **Mount Eagle**, between Slea Head and Ventry harbour, there are more than 400 of these beehives although they are not all of great antiquity. Some were in use up to the nineteenth century and a few were even built in the twentieth century. 'Modern' stone-roofed beehive huts or *clocháns* make sturdy farm outbuildings. The corbelling method of construction is an ancient technique, known to the prehistoric builders of passage tombs and souterrains. Courses of flat stones are positioned so that as the building rises, each course projects further in than the one before, with the sides eventually meeting at the top to form the roof, or a single stone is placed on the top to form a flat roof. For the building to be stable, the walls have to be thick in relation to their height, so the space inside is invariably much smaller than you might expect from the outside. There is no more technically accomplished example of the corbelling method in Ireland than the **Gallarus Oratory**, a mile (2km) south-east of Smerwick harbour. Built on a rectangular ground plan, 21ft by 18ft (6m x 5m), about 16ft (5m) high and with a square-headed doorway, this small sandstone chapel measures 15ft x 10ft (5m x 3m) inside. It is similar to the boat-shaped oratory on Great Skellig except that its dry-rubble masonry is in near perfect condition, 1,200 years old and still no roof leak!

Like Iveragh, Dingle has its own designated long-distance footpath, the Dingle Way, and the mountains east of Mount Brandon, including big Beenoskee (2,713ft/827m), and the Slieve Mish peaks of Baurtregaum (2,796ft/852m) and Caherconree (2,713ft/827m), are equally interesting to climb, and rather less frequented.

On the southern slope of **Caherconree** is an impressive and unusual prehistoric fort at the 2,000ft (610m) level. Access from Camp village is along the R559, stopping at a small layby just before the highest point of the road. A waymarked path up the mountain is signposted from here. A great wall, very ruined, 350ft (107m) long and 14ft (4m) thick with a ditch on the outside, isolates the triangle

Beautifully corbelled Gallarus Oratory on Dingle is at least 1,200 years old

of land beyond. The rock falls sheer on two sides, the wall forming the third side. Promontory forts are not uncommon on sea cliffs in Ireland — there are fine examples on the Aran islands — but very rare inland. A legend relates how this fort was stormed by Cuchulain, the Hound of Ulster, after the local chieftain, Cú Roi, ravished Blathnad, his mistress (one of many), and carried her off to Kerry. Faithful though fallen Blathnad poured milk into a stream as a signal to Cuchulain. As soon as he saw the stream turn white he attacked, killed Cú Roi and got Blathnad back. Kerrymen from the county's mountainous areas used to be thought hardier, more rugged people than those from the lush green parts lower down. In the period following the 1916 rising, for example, IRA recruiting officers complained that while the 'glen' people had a fighting tradition, the 'flat' people of Kerry on the contrary were not suitable guerrilla material. They were too interested in peace, prosperity and so on, and were hopeless as revolutionaries.

The grand scenery of the Dingle left behind, the N69 from Tralee, chief town of County Kerry, runs north via Listowel across rather dull country for some 28 miles (45km) to Tarbert and the car ferry across the Shannon to Killimer, County Clare. There is a power station at **Tarbert** and the ferry is well patronised. It is the only river crossing west of Limerick city and runs every hour all year, more frequently in summer, and, should you wish to do so, enables you to avoid the Limerick conurbation.

From Tarbert the N69 passes through pretty countryside into County Limerick and the village of **Glin**, ancestral seat of the Knights of Glin, a branch of the Munster Fitzgerald tribe (headed by the earls of Desmond). The ruined keep of the old castle, battered in 1600, stands in the grounds near the present romantic white castle, built around 1800, which is the home of the twenty-ninth Knight of Glin, the architectural historian Desmond Fitzgerald. In the Republic country house owners' heavy repair costs attract tax relief provided the owner lets the public in on 30 days in the year, and Glin Castle is open all the month of May. The tax concession, though modest, allows tourists with an appetite for these things to inspect the interiors of big houses from which they would otherwise be firmly excluded. Some owners have greatly extended the limited opening, generating income from entrance charges and, increasingly, from bed-and-breakfast business. At Glin, for example, there is a shop and café inside one of the estate's gate lodges, open half the year, and summer visitors may find Glin open in June too.

From Glin there is a pleasant 8-mile (13km) stretch of road along the river to **Foynes**, where a flying boat museum recalls the small port's past importance as a transatlantic seaplane base, superseded in 1945 by Shannon airport on the far bank.

There is still an obligatory stopover at **Shannon** Airport for most transatlantic travellers, though the government was obliged to allow a limited direct New York-Dublin service in 1994. Most of the people you see drifting through the vast duty-free emporium are waiting to get back on their plane. The Shannon stopover — unpopular with airlines that are forced to make it — has long been part of official efforts to protect the fragile local economy and stem, even reverse, the drift of population eastwards. A large industrial estate associated with the airport provides employment, with suitable luxury housing to tempt head-hunted senior executives. The airport's usefulness as Europe's last refuelling stop on the north Atlantic route vanished 30 years ago with the development of long-range jet aircraft. However, it may be that neither Shannon's champions nor its detractors could have foreseen the phenomenal expansion of air travel: more and more people are choosing to fly from user-friendly airports like Shannon rather than endure congested journeys to the rebarbative environment of Heathrow and, to a lesser degree, of Gatwick and Dublin airports.

Nineteenth-century **Limerick** was renowned for lace and fine leather gloves. In the 1850s 900 girls plied their needles in Charles Walker's lacemaking factory. While the bottom has dropped out of the market for fancy gloves, a little lace-making still goes on, in the convent of the Good Shepherd in Clare Street, though the ladies are elderly and there are only three of them. There is nothing genteel about modern Limerick, the fourth largest city in Ireland, lying at the head of the Shannon estuary, where the preoccupations are computers and electronic engineering, rugby football and fishing, greyhound breeding and horse racing, disco dancing and hotel cabaret shows. The town was strongly fortified from early times and there was a city wall until about 1760. It then came to seem irrelevant, a hindrance to the development of the town, and most of it was dismantled. An impressive section survives at the back of Lelia Street, and the original massive town gate can be seen at the end of St John's Hospital grounds.

King John's Castle, built by the Normans in 1200 beside the river, came in for many severe batterings. Its walls are 10ft (3m) thick and the drum towers have a diameter of 45ft (14m), and it was intended to control what had been the territory of the O'Briens, kings of Thomond. The town and the castle were besieged four times in the seventeenth century, first in 1641 when the Irish captured it, then in

Limerick castle, on the banks of the river Shannon

1651 when the Cromwellians won it back, thirdly and most famously in 1690 when Patrick Sarsfield repulsed the Williamites, and lastly in 1691 when, after defending Limerick for the second time, Sarsfield negotiated a remarkable settlement.

After the Jacobite defeat at the Boyne, the Irish forces fell back on Limerick. William of Orange attacked the town with 26,000 men. The French commander, Lauzun, thought the case was hopeless. He abandoned the town to what seemed certain defeat and the Irish defenders braced themselves for the arrival of William's siege train, sent for from Dublin to finish the job. But Patrick Sarsfield, earl of Lucan, went out to meet the siege train at Ballyneety near Limerick and blew it up, eventually forcing William to retreat. The following year the Williamite commander Ginkel arrived, fresh from victory at Aughrim, and the fourth and final siege began. In the end the defenders had to treat for peace. Under the terms of the Treaty of Limerick, Catholics were to have the privileges they had enjoyed under Charles II restored to them and Sarsfield and 12,000 soldiers and their families were allowed to emigrate to France. The treaty was largely repudiated but not before Sarsfield and his Irish army were transported to France, all expenses paid.

There are neat brick patches in the castle walls where gashes made by Ginkel's guns have been repaired. You can see them clearly from

The Poulnabrone dolmen

Thomond Bridge, a solid nineteenth-century bridge with six arches, which has a large rough-hewn stone at the other end called the Treaty Stone, purported to be the stone on which the famous treaty was signed. The castle now houses a heritage centre. One of Limerick's bridges is named after Sarsfield and there is a bronze statue of him in the grounds of the Catholic cathedral, St John's. At the top of O'Connell Street is a bronze by John Hogan of Daniel O'Connell, 'the Liberator', who won limited Catholic emancipation 140 years after the treaty.

A campaign to erect a statue to the talkshow host Terry Wogan, a favourite son of modern Limerick, suggests the city's cultural values may have changed since those days. However, the establishment of the University of Limerick in the early 1990s may yet redress the balance. It was one of two new universities — Dublin City University was the other — created in the early 1990s to cope with the demand for higher education by the Republic's youthful population. The university is the home of the Hunt Museum, housed in a purpose-built gallery on the campus 3 miles (5km) north of the city centre. A gift of 1,000 items from the Celtic historian, John Hunt, forms the nucleus of the collection. (Hunt was the creator of the **Craggaunowen** centre, a recreation of various prehistoric structures, including a crannog and a ringfort, a few miles south-east of Ennis). However, if your time in the city is limited, **Limerick Museum** may be a more rewarding visit. It contains a quantity of items recovered from the important neolithic site at **Lough Gur**, a little horseshoe-shaped lake 12 miles (19km) south of the city, where there is a concentration of prehistoric monuments. The City Art Gallery in Pery Square, over-looking the little People's Park, has a growing permanent collection and also mounts a lively programme of temporary exhibitions. St Mary's Anglican cathedral, a twelfth-century foundation, much altered and restored, contains several fifteenth-century tombs. In the choir is the twelfth-century tomb of Donal O'Brien, the founder, and twenty-three misericords carved in black oak and dating from about 1490.

The prettiest village in Limerick is without doubt **Adare**, on the west bank of the Maigue river, with thatched cottages in the main street, beside the broad meadows and decaying big trees of a once influential great estate, and yet the place has a curiously tame and un-Irish look about it, more like an English West Country village. In the middle of the golf course — ask at Adare Golf Club house for access — is a fifteenth-century Franciscan friary, the finest of several interesting monastic ruins in the area. An Augustinian abbey of the fourteenth century stands beside the bridge and a Trinitarian abbey, thirteenth-century, now part of the Catholic church, further down the main street. At **Rathkeale**, south-west of Adare, **Castle Matrix** is a tall fifteenth-century keep built by the Desmond Fitzgeralds on the bank of the Deel river. Its older name is, curiously, Castle Mattress. Sir Walter Raleigh repaired it first, then it was modernised in 1837 and restored in the 1960s after being unoccupied for 30 years. It has a fine library in the great hall and is open to the public.

The N18 north from Limerick passes the Bunratty Castle turn and Shannon Airport before running through unexceptional country up to **Ennis**, county town of Clare, the parliamentary constituency of Eamon de Valera from 1917 to 1959, and where there is a ruined Franciscan friary with very fine tomb carvings of the fifteenth century. Four miles (6km) beyond Ennis, on the N18 is **Barefield** village where people come from miles around to celebrate mass in Gaelic on St Patrick's Day. The hymns are sung in Irish.

The strange topography of the Burren extends well beyond the old barony of Burren in the north-west corner of Clare. The Gaelic name for this landscape of mostly bare limestone rock is *boireann*, 'great rock', and it stretches from Ennis and the majestic Cliffs of Moher up to the Aran islands and inland to Gort, County Galway. There are many turloughs, seasonal lakes or pools, with no streams flowing

Ennis, the county town of Clare and parliamentary constituency of Eamon de Valera from 1917 to 1959

into them or out. The water is there one day and gone the next, vanished through the porous stone. The caves, swallow-holes and fissures are interesting to potholders and speleologists. There is one cave, at **Pollnagollum** in the high country north of Lisdoonvarna, which is 5 miles (8km) long. These underground caverns are dangerous to explore without an expert guide but **Aillwee Cave** at Ballyvaughan, a tunnel three quarters of a mile long, is open to the public. Beside the Ballyvaughan-Corofin road is a celebrated, much photographed portal tomb, the **Poulnabrone dolmen**.

Several dozen varieties of orchid and dazzling blue gentians flourish here. Montane species, in some places barely above sea level, grow happily alongside coastal plants, springing up between the fissures in the gun-metal-grey stone which, in certain lights looks a deep lilac. Tiny blackthorn trees and junipers, bonsai-like, grow just a few inches and stop.

The haunt of botanists and gardening clubs in spring and early summer, the region has much of interest all year round. Not far from **Burren** village, Corcomroe Abbey is a thirteenth-century Cistercian foundation with some exceptionally fine stonework. Carvings of human heads and flowers decorate the capitals in the choir, and the church is dedicated to Sancta Maria de Petra Fertili — St Mary of the Fertile Rock — which is what the Burren is: rocky but not barren. At **Kilfenora**, the community-run **Burren Display Centre**, explains all these things.

There is a strong musical tradition in Kilfenora village, which has a famous céilí band. Five miles (8km) north-west at rowdy Lisdoonvarna, a formerly elegant spa town, now rather less elegant, set dancing competitions attract squads of dancers. However, the real music enthusiasts make for **Doolin** on the coast, very crowded in summer, not so much because it is a jump-off point for the Aran islands, clearly visible across South Sound, but because of its traditional music, with sessions in all of the village's three pubs almost every night in summer. The whole place vibrates with the insistent rhythms of reels and jigs, combining innovation and repetition, of tin whistles, fiddles, *uilleann* (elbow) pipes, *bodhrans* (small single-skin drums) and accordions.

The **Cliffs of Moher,** rising vertically from the sea in huge layered slabs of limestone rock, are too steep to support the beautiful plants that make the Burren sparkle. Seabirds rest and even nest on the few ledges offered by these inhospitable and awesome cliffs in their dramatic stand-off with the Atlantic. This is one place where the most inveterate traveller will rejoice to find a little visitor centre!

The Cliffs of Moher in County Clare

Further Information
— The South West —

Places to Visit

Bantry House
Co Cork
Open: daily except 25 December 9am-
6pm (until 8pm in summer).
☎ (027) 50047

Blasket Centre
Co Kerry
Open: April to September every day
10am-6pm (until 7pm in high summer).
☎ (0667) 5113

Bunratty Castle/Folk Park
Co Clare
Open: daily 9.30am-4.15pm. Folk park
stays open until 6.30pm June to
August.
☎ (061) 361511

Burren village
Co Clare
Corcomroe Abbey
Always accessible.

Cliffs of Moher
Co Clare
Visitor Centre
Open: all year all day.
☎ (065) 81565/81171

Craggaunowen Project
Co Clare
Open: daily 10am-6pm April to
October.
☎ (061) 367178

Ennis Friary
Co Clare
Open: daily, May to September.
☎ (065) 29100

Foynes
Co Limerick
Flying Boat Museum
Open: 10am-6pm daily April to
October.
☎ (069) 65416

Garinish Island
Co Cork
Ilnacullin Garden
Glengarriff
Open: daily all year. Closed Sunday
mornings October to April.
☎ (027) 63040

Glin Castle
Co Limerick
Open: in May and June only, 10am-
12noon and 2-4 pm.
Enquiries: ☎ (068) 34173/34112

Kilfenora
Co Clare
Burren Display Centre
Open: 10am-6pm March to October.
Open until 7pm in high summer.
☎ (065) 88030

Killarney National Park
Co Kerry
Muckross House and Gardens
Open: all year daily 9am-6pm (until
7pm July and August).
☎ (064) 31440

Kinsale
Co Cork
Kinsale Museum
Courthouse
Open: Monday to Saturday 11am-
1pm in summer, and every afternoon
including Sunday in winter.
☎ (021) 772044

Limerick
King John's Castle
Open: 9.30am-5pm daily April to
October, and 11am-4pm Sunday
in winter.
☎ (061) 411201/361511

Limerick Museum
John's Square
Open: Tuesday to Saturday 10am-
1pm and 2.15-5pm.
☎ (061) 417826

City Art Gallery
People's Park
Open: Monday to Friday 10am-1pm
and 2-6pm (until 7pm on Thursday),
and Saturday mornings. Closed
holidays.
☎ (061) 310633

Hunt Museum
Limerick University
a mile (2km) east of city via N7,
signposted at Plassey Park Rd
Open: Monday to Friday 10am-5pm
May to September.
☎ (061) 361511

Lough Gur Centre
Co Limerick
Open: daily May to September 10am-
5.30pm.
☎ (061) 385186

Rathkeale
Co Limerick
Castle Matrix
Open: daily 11am-5pm May to
September.
☎ (069) 64284

Timoleague
Co Cork
Timoleague Friary
Always accessible.

Timoleague Castle Gardens
Co Cork
Open: Tuesday to Saturday 11am-5.30pm.
☎ (023) 46116

Valentia Island
Co Kerry
Skellig Experience (interpretive centre)
Iveragh peninsula
Open: daily May to September 10am-
6pm.
☎ (066) 72141

Youghal
Myrtle Grove
Co Cork
Open: in August, Monday/Wednes-
day/Friday 2.30pm and 4.30pm.
☎ (024) 92274

Travel
Ferries to Cape Clear Island, Co Cork
Daily ferry from Baltimore all year, 2-4
sailings in summer ☎ (028) 20114/
39135/39159. From Schull the ferry
operates June to August only: ☎ (028)
28138. Storytelling information: ☎/fax
(028) 39157. General enquiries: ☎ (028)
39119.

Boat trips to Great Skellig, Co Kerry
Daily sailings in good weather from
Portmagee, Iveragh peninsula.
☎ (066) 76115 or (066) 76124.

Boat trips to Great Blasket, Co Kerry
Boats in calm weather from Dunquin,
Dingle peninsula.
Enquire at Dunquin harbour or the
Blasket Centre, Dunquin.
☎ (066) 56371.

Tourist Information Offices
Open: all year.

Ennis
Co Clare
Clare Road
☎ (065) 28366

Killarney
Co Kerry
Town Hall
☎ (064) 31633

Limerick
Arthur's Quay
☎ (061) 317522

Shannon Airport
Co Clare
☎ (061) 61664

Tralee
Co Kerry
Ashe Memorial Hall
☎ (066) 21288

ACCOMMODATION AND EATING OUT

Accommodation is generally plentiful throughout Ireland and it is only during major festivals and public holiday weekends that you really do have to book ahead. In popular tourist areas at these times you can find yourself having to travel a long way out of town to locate a B&B if you leave it to the eleventh hour to start looking! Always check rates with the hotel or guesthouse and enquire about the proximity of potential sources of noise, such as discos, wedding parties and other late-night functions. If you are not satisfied with the answer, go elsewhere.

Outside main towns and popular tourist areas Ireland has rather few restaurants that operate independently of accommodation. Also be aware that many small family-run restaurants in country areas close on one or more days a week. Monday is the quietest day but Sunday evening can be patchy too. Avoid disappointment by calling ahead. If, after booking, you find you cannot go, remember to telephone the restaurant to cancel. For evening meals in country areas the best (sometimes, the only) food is very often to be had at the place where you are staying. All the hotels and guesthouses in rural areas listed here have good or excellent eating facilities.

Dinner with house wine will cost from about £40 although some hotels and restaurants offer special early evening menus which are good value. Midday meals invariably cost less than evening meals. At lunchtime most pubs provide soup, sandwiches, salads and, often, a complete meal for about £5. The tourist boards produce lists of restaurants and other places to eat, giving an indication of the kind of food available and also a price guide, useful for the independent traveller. Bord Fáilte – Irish Tourist Board publishes *Dining in Ireland* and a 'Tourist Menu Guide' listing restaurants that offer a set price menu. In Northern Ireland restaurants guaranteeing to use mostly local produce are listed in the annual *Taste of Ulster* booklet. The Northern Ireland Tourist Board also publishes a comprehensive *Where to Eat* guide. These guides are available from the tourist boards' offices listed on page 338.

Currency and Credit Cards

Mastercard (Interbank) and Visa etc are widely used in shops, restaurants, hotels and for car rental. Diner's Club and American Express are less widely accepted. Please note, however, that most guesthouses and even some small country hotels do not accept credit cards — so you will need cash. You can also use a US bank card (eg MAC) to get cash at some automatic teller machines. Currency in the Republic is the Irish punt (IR£). In Northern Ireland it is the British pound (sterling). In both the South and the North, currency notes are issued to the value of £5, £10, £20, £50 and £100. Coins are issued to the value of 100 pence (£1), 50p, 20p, 10p, 5p, 2p and 1p. Irish currency should only be used in the Republic and sterling in Northern Ireland.

International Telephone Codes and Telephone Services

The international code for the Republic of Ireland is 353. The international code for Northern Ireland, as for the rest of the UK, is 44.

When calling the Republic from Britain or Northern Ireland dial 010 353 plus the area code minus the initial zero, then the number. For example: (01) 6791977 = 010 353 1 6791977.

When calling Northern Ireland from the Republic dial 08 plus the local dialling code, then the number. For example: (01232) 246609 = 08 01232 246609.

It helps to know if the telephone is making the right sound when you make your first call in Ireland:

The dial tone is a continuous high-pitched tone.

The ringing tone is a repeated double-beat tone — burr - burr.

The engaged tone is a high-pitched beep-beep-beep.

Post offices, pubs, hotels, restaurants and large stores have public pay phones from which you can make local, long-distance and international calls. In the Republic you may still occasionally come across old-style coinboxes that operated on button A and button B: you put in the coins, then dial, and push button A when your party answers.

It is more convenient when calling long distance to use a telephone operated by callcard rather than by coins. Callcards can be purchased at post offices, newsagents and many retail outlets. Operating instructions are displayed in telephone boxes or on the telephone handset itself. For information on cardphones in the Republic call 1800-250250. If you have difficulty in making an international call, dial freefone 1800-680000 in the Republic, or 155 in Northern Ireland where British Telecom's international operator will help you. In Northern Ireland, the new Mercury telephones are good value for international calls.

Tourist Information

General tourist information on accommodation, restaurants, activity and special interest holidays and related subjects is available from the head office of Bord Fáilte – Irish Tourist Board and the Northern Ireland Tourist Board:

Board Fáilte – Irish Tourist Board (ITB)
Head Office
Baggot Street Bridge
Dublin 2
☎ 010-353 1 6765871/6616500

Northern Ireland Tourist Board (NITB)
Head Office
59 North Street
Belfast BT1 1NB
☎ 010-44 (1232) 246609

Bord Fáilte's other offices include:
GREAT BRITAIN
ITB
150 New Bond Street
London W1Y 0AQ
☎ 0171-493 3201

NORTHERN IRELAND
ITB
53 Castle Street
Belfast BT1 1GH
☎ (01232) 327888

ITB
8 Bishop Street
Derry City
Co Londonderry
☎ (01504) 369501

USA
ITB
757 Third Avenue
New York NY10017
☎ (212) 418 0800

CANADA
ITB
160 Bloor Street East
Suite 934
Toronto
Ontario
☎ (416) 929 27777

AUSTRALIA
ITB
5th Level, 36 Carrington Street
Sydney
NSW 2000
☎ (02) 299 6177

Other Northern Ireland Tourist Board offices are:
GREAT BRITAIN
NITB
11 Berkeley Street
London W1X 5AD
☎ 0171-355 5050

NITB
135 Buchanan Street
Glasgow G1 2JA
☎ 0141-204 4454

DUBLIN
NITB
16 Nassau Street
Dublin 2
☎ (01) 6791977

USA
NITB
551 Fifth Avenue, Suite 701
New York NY 10176
☎ (212) 922 0101

CANADA
NITB
111 Avenue Road
Suite 450
Toronto M5R 3J8
☎ (416) 925 6368

Accommodation and Eating Out

✳✳✳ Expensive
✳✳ Moderate
✳ Inexpensive

Chapter 1 •
Connaught

Accommodation

Achill Island
Gray's Guesthouse (McDowells) ✳
Dugort
Achill Island, Co Mayo
☎ (098) 43244/43148

Aran Islands
Ard Einne Guesthouse ✳
Killeany
Inishmore
Aran Islands, Co Galway
☎ (099) 61126

Faherty's ✳
Inishmaan
Aran Islands
Co Galway
☎ (099) 73012

Crowe's ✳
Inisheer
Aran Islands, Co Galway
☎ (099) 75033

Ballina
Imperial Hotel ✳✳
Ballina, Co Mayo
☎ (096) 22200

Belmullet
Western Strands Hotel ✳
Belmullet, Co Mayo
☎ (097) 81096

Boyle
Royal Hotel ✳✳
Boyle, Co Roscommon
☎ (079) 62016

Clare Island
Bay View Hotel ✳✳
Clare Island, Co Mayo
☎ (098) 26307

Clifden
Abbeyglen Castle Hotel ✳✳✳
Sky Road
Clifden
Connemara, Co Galway
☎ (095) 21201

Foyles Hotel ✳✳
Clifden
Connemara, Co Galway
☎ (095) 21801

Inishbofin
Day's Hotel ✳
Inishbofin, Co Galway
☎ (095) 45803

Louisburgh
Old Head Hotel ✳✳
Louisburgh, Co Mayo
☎ (098) 66455

Galway City
Brennans Yard Hotel ✳✳
Lower Merchant's Road
Galway
☎ (091) 68166

Skeffington Arms Hotel ✳✳
Eyre Square
Galway
☎ (091) 63173

Newport
Newport House ✳✳✳
Co Mayo
☎ (098) 41222

Black Oak Inn ✳
Medlicott Street
Newport, Co Mayo
☎ (098) 41249

Renvyle
Renvyle House Hotel ✳✳
Connemara, Co Galway
☎ (095) 43511

Roscommon
Abbey Hotel ✳✳
Co Roscommon
☎ (0903) 26240

Westport
Olde Railway Hotel ✳✳
The Mall
Westport, Co Mayo
☎ (098) 25605

Eating Out

Clifden
O'Grady's Seafood
Restaurant ✳✳
Market Street
Clifden
Connemara, Co Galway
☎ (095) 21450

Cong
Echoes Restaurant ✳✳
Main Street
Cong, Co Mayo
☎ (092) 46059

Galway City
Oyster Room ✳✳✳
Great Southern Hotel
Eyre Square, Galway
☎ (091) 64041

Malt House Restaurant ✳✳
Old Malt Mall
High Street, Galway
☎ (091) 67866

Inishmore, Aran Islands
Cliff House ✳
The Scrigeen
Kilronan
Aran Islands, Co Galway
☎ (099) 61286

Letterfrack
Rosleague Manor Hotel ✳✳✳
Letterfrack
Connemara, Co Galway
☎ (095) 41101

Louisburgh
Durkan's Hotel ✳✳
Chapel Street
Louisburgh, Co Mayo
☎ (098) 66140

Spiddal
Boluisce Seafood Bar ✳✳
Spiddal
Connemara, Co Galway
☎ (091) 83286

Westport
Quay Cottage Restaurant ✳✳
The Harbour
Westport, Co Galway
☎ (098) 26412

Chapter 2 •
The Midlands

Accommodation

Athlone
Shamrock Lodge Country
House Hotel ✳✳
Clonown Road
Athlone, Co Westmeath
☎ (0902) 92601

Ballinamore
Commercial & Tourist
House ✳✳
Ballinamore, Co Leitrim
☎ (078) 44675

Birr
Dooly's Hotel ✳✳
Emmet Square
Birr, Co Offaly
☎ (0509) 20032

Carrick-on-Shannon
County Hotel ✳✳
Carrick-on-Shannon
Co Leitrim
☎ (078) 20042

Carriglas
Carriglas Manor ✳✳✳
3 miles (5km) north-east
of Longford on Granard
road (R194), Co Longford
☎ (043) 45165

Cavan
Farnham Arms Hotel ✳✳
Main Street, Co Cavan
☎ (049) 32577

Edgeworthstown
Park House ✳
Edgeworthstown
Co Longford
☎ (043) 71325/6

Mountrath
Roundwood House ✳✳
Mountrath, Co Laois
☎ (0502) 32120
Convenient for Slieve
Blooms.

Mullingar
Greville Arms Hotel ✳✳
Pearse Street
Mullingar, Co Westmeath
☎ (044) 48563

Tullamore
Oakfield Guesthouse ✳
Rohan Road
Tullamore, Co Offaly
☎ (0506) 21385

*Moorhill Country Inn
Guesthouse* ✳✳
Clara Road
Tullamore, Co Offaly
☎ (0506) 21395

Virginia
Deer Park Lodge ✳✳
Virginia, Co Cavan
☎ (049) 47235

Eating Out

Athlone
Jolly Mariner Restaurant ✳
Abbey Road
Athlone, Co Westmeath
☎ (0902) 72892

Birr
The Stables Restaurant ✳✳
Oxmantown Mall
Birr, Co Offaly
☎ (0509) 20263

Cavan
Olde Priory Restaurant ✳✳
Main Street, Cavan
☎ (049) 61068

Glasson
*Glasson Village
Restaurant* ✳✳
Glasson, Co Westmeath
☎ (0902) 85001

Mullingar
Crookedwood House ✳✳
8 miles (13km) south of
Mullingar on Castlepollard
road.
Crookedwood,
Co Westmeath
☎ (044) 72165

Tullamore
Bridge House ✳✳
Tullamore, Co Offaly
☎ (0506) 21704

*Chapter 3 •
The North West:
Lakes and Mountains*

Accommodation

Ardara
Nesbitt Arms ✳
Ardara, Co Donegal
☎ (075) 41103

Ballybofey
Jackson's Hotel ✳✳✳
Ballybofey
Co Donegal
☎ (074) 31021

Donegal
Hyland Central ✳✳
The Diamond
☎ (073) 21027

Dunfanaghy
Carrig Rua Hotel ✳✳
Dunfanaghy, Co Donegal
☎ (074) 36133

Enniskillen
*Manor House Country
Hotel* ✳✳✳
Killadeas
Co Fermanagh BT94 1NY
☎ (013656) 21561

Tullyhona Guesthouse ✳
59 Marble Arch Road
Florencecourt
Co Fermanagh BT92 1DE
☎ (01365) 348452

Lisnarick
Drumshane Hotel ✳✳
Lisnarick
Co Fermanagh BT94 1PS
☎ (013656) 21146

Malin
Malin Hotel ✳
Inishowen, Co Donegal
☎ (077) 70606

Ramelton
McCrea's ✳
The Mall
Ramelton, Co Donegal
☎ (074) 51010

Rathmullan
Pier Hotel ✳
Rathmullan, Co Donegal
☎ (074) 58178

Port-na-Blagh
Port-na-Blagh Hotel ✳✳
Co Donegal
☎ (074) 36129

Sligo
Hotel Silver Swan ✳✳
Hyde Bridge
Sligo, Co Sligo
☎ (071) 43231/2

Stranorlar
Key's Hotel ✳✳✳
Stranorlar, Ballybofey
Co Donegal
☎ (074) 31018

Eating Out

Ballinamallard
Encore Steak House ✳✳
Main Street
Ballinamallard
Co Fermanagh
☎ (0136581) 606

Ballyshannon
Danby Restaurant ✳✳✳
Rossnowlagh Road
Ballyshannon
Co Donegal
☎ (072) 51138

Burtonport
Lobster Pot ✳
Burtonport, Co Donegal
☎ (075) 42012

Bellanaleck
Sheelin ❋❋❋
Bellanaleck
Co Fermanagh
☎ (0136582) 232

Collooney
Markree Castle ❋❋❋
Knockmuldowney
Restaurant
Collooney, Co Sligo
☎ (071) 67800

Enniskillen
Crow's Nest ❋
12 High Street
Enniskillen
Co Fermanagh
☎ (01365) 32522

Franco's ❋❋
Queen Elizabeth Road
Enniskillen
Co Fermanagh
☎ (01365) 324424

Fahan
Restaurant St John ❋❋❋
Fahan, Co Donegal
☎ (077) 60289

Irvinestown
Hollander ❋❋
5 Main Street
Irvinestown
Co Fermanagh
☎ (013656) 21231

Letterkenny
Carolina House ❋❋❋
Loughnagin
Letterkenny, Co Donegal
☎ (074) 22480

Mullaghmore
Eithna's ❋❋
The Harbour
Mullaghmore, Co Sligo
☎ (071) 66407

Ramelton
The Mariner ❋❋
Ramelton, Co Donegal
☎ (074) 51174

Rathmullan
Rathmullan House ❋❋❋
Lough Swilly
Rathmullan, Co Donegal
☎ (074) 58188

Chapter 4 •
Northern Ulster

Accommodation

Ballycastle
Marine Hotel ❋❋
1 North Street
Ballycastle, Co Antrim
BT54 6BN
☎ (012657) 62222

Glenhaven ❋
10 Beechwood Avenue
Ballycastle, Co Antrim
BT54 6BL
☎ (012657) 63612

Ballymena
Adair Arms Hotel ❋❋❋
Ballymoney Road
Ballymena, Co Antrim
BT43 5BS
☎ (01266) 653674

Ballygalley
Ballygally Castle Hotel ❋❋
274 Coast Road
Ballygalley, Co Antrim
BT40 2RA
☎ (01574) 583212

Bushmills
Bushmills Inn ❋❋
25 Main Street
Bushmills, Co Antrim
BT57 8QN
☎ (012657) 32339

Carnlough
Londonderry Arms Hotel ❋❋
20 Harbour Road
Carnlough, Co Antrim
BT44 0EU
☎ (01574) 885255

Castlerock
Golf Hotel ❋❋
17 Main Street
Castlerock
Co Londonderry BT51 4RA
☎ (01265) 848204

Coleraine
Camus House ❋
27 Curragh Road
Coleraine
Co Londonderry
BT51 3RY
☎ (01265) 42982

Cookstown
Greenvale Hotel ❋❋
57 Drum Road
Cookstown
Co Tyrone BT80 8QS
☎ (016487) 62243/65196

Cushendall
Thornlea Hotel ❋❋
6 Coast Road
Cushendall, Co Antrim
BT44 0RU
☎ (012667) 71223/71403

Dungannon
Inn on the Park ❋❋
Moy Road
Dungannon
Co Tyrone BT71 6BS
☎ (01868) 725151

Giant's Causeway
Causeway Hotel ❋❋
40 Causeway Road
Giant's Causeway
Co Antrim BT57 8SU
☎ (012657) 31226

Limavady
Gorteen House Hotel ❋❋
187 Roe Mill Road
Limavady, Co Londonderry BT49 9EX
☎ (015047) 22333

Londonderry
Waterfoot Hotel ❋❋❋
Caw Roundabout
14 Clooney Road
Derry City, Co Londonderry BT47 1TB
☎ (01504) 45500

Robin Hill ❋
103 Chapel Road
Derry City •
Co Londonderry
☎ (01504) 42776

Portballintrae
Beach House Hotel ❋❋
61 Beach Road
Portballintrae, Co Antrim
BT57 8RT
☎ (012657) 31214/31380

Portrush
*Ballymagarry Country
    House* ✳✳
46 Leeke Road
Portrush, Co Antrim
BT56 8NH
☎ (01265) 823737

Mount Royal Guesthouse ✳
2 Eglinton Street
Portrush, Co Antrim
BT56 8DX
☎ (01265) 823342

Rathlin
Rathlin Guesthouse ✳
The Quay
Rathlin Island
Co Antrim BT54 6RT
☎ (012657) 63917

Eating Out

Ballymena
Water Margin ✳✳✳
8 Cullybackey Road
Ballymena, Co Antrim
☎ (01266) 48868

Bushmills
Auberge de Seneirl ✳✳✳
28 Ballyclough Road
Bushmills, Co Antrim
☎ (012657) 41536

Coleraine
MacDuff's ✳✳✳
112 Killeague Road
Blackhill
6 miles (10km) south of
Coleraine on A29
Co Londonderry
☎ (01265) 868433

Londonderry
Schooner's ✳✳
59 Victoria Road
Derry City
Co Londonderry
☎ (01504) 311500

Portrush
Ramore ✳✳
The Harbour
Portrush, Co Antrim
☎ (01265) 824313

Chapter 5 •
Belfast & Environs

Accommodation

Antrim
Deerpark Hotel ✳✳
71 Dublin Road, Antrim
Co Antrim BT41 4PN
☎ (01849) 462480

Belfast
Europa Hotel ✳✳✳
Great Victoria Street
Belfast BT2 7AP
☎ (01232) 327000

Dukes Hotel ✳✳✳
65 University Street
Belfast BT7 1HL
☎ (01232) 236666

Stranmillis Lodge ✳✳
14 Chlorine Gardens
Belfast BT9 5DJ
☎ (01232) 682009

Camera House ✳✳
44 Wellington Park
Belfast BT9 6DP
☎ (01232) 660026

The George ✳
8 Eglantine Avenue
Belfast BT9 6DW
☎ (01232) 683212

Pearl Court House ✳
11 Malone Road
Belfast BT9 6RT
☎ (01232) 666145

Carrickfergus
Dobbins Inn Hotel ✳✳
6 High Street
Carrickfergus
Co Antrim BT38 9HE
☎ (01960) 351905

Downpatrick
Abbey Lodge Hotel ✳✳
Belfast Road
Downpatrick
Co Down BT30 9AU
☎ (01396) 614511

Hillsborough
White Gables Hotel ✳✳✳
14 Dromore Road
Hillsborough
Co Down BT26 6HU
☎ (01846) 682755

Holywood
Culloden Hotel ✳✳✳
142 Bangor Road
Cultra, Holywood
Co Down BT18 0EX
☎ (01232) 425223

Larne
Magheramorne House ✳✳✳
59 Shore Road
Larne, Co Antrim
BT40 3HW
☎ (01574) 279444

Portaferry
Portaferry Hotel ✳✳
10 The Strand
Portaferry, Co Down
BT22 1PE
☎ (012477) 28231

Templepatrick
Templeton Hotel ✳✳✳
882 Antrim Road
Templepatrick
Co Antrim BT39 0AH
☎ (01849) 432984

Eating Out

Bangor
Bryansburn ✳✳
151 Bryansburn Road
Bangor, Co Down
☎ (01247) 270173

Belfast
Roscoff ✳✳✳
Shaftesbury Square
Belfast 2
☎ (01232) 331532

La Belle Epoque ✳✳✳
61 Dublin Road, Belfast 2
☎ (01232) 323244

Clarence ✳✳
18 Donegall Square East
Belfast 1
☎ (01232) 238862

Nick's Warehouse ✴✴
35 Hill Street
Belfast 1
☎ (01232) 439690

Strand ✴✴
12 Stranmillis Road
Belfast 9
☎ (01232) 682266

Bittles Bar ✴
70 Upper Church Lane
Belfast 1
☎ (01232) 311088. Lunch
only.

White's Tavern ✴
Winecellar Entry
Belfast 1
☎ (01232) 243080. Lunch
only.

Crawfordsburn
Old Inn ✴✴✴
15 Main Street
Crawfordsburn
Co Down
☎ (01247) 853255

Hillsborough
Hillside ✴✴
21 Main Street
Hillsborough, Co Down
☎ (01846) 682765

Lisburn
The Wallace ✴✴
12 Bachelor's Walk
Lisburn, Co Antrim
☎ (01846) 665000

Newtownards
Gaslamp ✴✴✴
47 Court Street
Newtownards, Co Down
☎ (01247) 811225

Strangford
Lobster Pot ✴✴
The Square
Strangford, Co Down
☎ (01396) 881288

Chapter 6 •
From the Mournes
to the Boyne

Accommodation

Armagh
Charlemont Arms Hotel ✴✴
Lower English Street
Armagh BT61 7LB
☎ (01861) 522028/522719

Ashbourne
Ashbourne House ✴✴
Co Meath
☎ (01) 350167

Clones
Hilton Park ✴✴✴
Scotshouse
Clones, Co Monaghan
☎ (047) 56007

Drogheda
Boyne Valley Hotel
Stameen
Drogheda, Co Louth
☎ (041) 37737

Dundalk
Imperial Hotel ✴✴
Park Street
Dundalk, Co Louth
☎ (042) 32241/2

Kells
Headfort Arms ✴✴
Kells, Co Meath
☎ (046) 40063

Kilkeel
Kilmorey Arms Hotel ✴✴
Greencastle Street
Kilkeel, Co Down
BT34 4BH
☎ (016937) 62220/62801

Wyncrest Guesthouse ✴
30 Main Road
On A2 3 miles (5km)
north-east of Kilkeel
Co Down BT34 4NU
☎ (016937) 63012

Monaghan
Westenra Arms ✴✴
The Diamond
Monaghan
☎ (047) 81517

Navan
Ardboyne Hotel ✴✴✴
Dublin Road
Navan, Co Meath
☎ (046) 23119

Newcastle
Slieve Donard Hotel ✴✴✴
Downs Road
Newcastle
Co Down BT33 0AH
☎ (013967) 23681

Brook Cottage Hotel ✴✴
58 Bryansford Road
Newcastle
Co Down BT33 0LD
☎ (013967) 22204/23508

Slane
Conyngham Arms ✴✴
Slane, Co Meath
☎ (041) 24155

Eating Out

Ardee
The Gables ✴✴
Dundalk Road
Ardee, Co Louth
☎ (041) 53789

Carlingford
Jordan's ✴✴
Newry Street
Carlingford, Co Louth
☎ (042) 73223

Drogheda
Sennhoff Restaurant ✴✴✴
Boyne Valley Hotel
Stameen
Drogheda, Co Louth
☎ (041) 37737

Dundalk
Cellars ✴
Backhouse Centre
Clanbrassil Street
Dundalk, Co Louth
☎ (0142) 33745. Lunch
only.

Kilkeel
Fisherman ✴
68 Greencastle Street
Kilkeel, Co Down
☎ (016937) 62130

Newcastle
Mario's ❋❋
65 South Promenade
Newcastle, Co Down
☎ (013967) 23912

Percy French ❋❋
Downs Road
Newcastle, Co Down
☎ (013967) 23175

Newry
Brass Monkey ❋
Trevor Hill
Newry, Co Down
☎ (01693) 63176

Saintfield
The Barn ❋❋❋
120 Monlough Road
Saintfield, Co Down
☎ (01238) 510396

Waringstown
The Grange ❋❋❋
Main Street
Waringstown, Co Down
☎ (01762) 881989

Warrenpoint
Aylesforte House ❋❋
44 Newry Road
Warrenpoint, Co Down
☎ (0169 37) 72255

Chapter 7 •
Dublin & Environs

Accommodation

Dublin City
Buswells ❋❋❋
Molesworth Street
Dublin 2
☎ (01) 6764013

Gresham Hotel ❋❋❋
Upper O'Connell Street
Dublin 1
☎ (01) 8746881

Power's Hotel ❋❋
Kildare Street
Dublin 2
☎ (01) 6794388

Clarence Hotel ❋❋
Wellington Quay
Dublin 2
☎ (01) 6776178

Castle Hotel ❋
3 Gardiners Row
Dublin 1
☎ (01) 8746949

Kilronan House ❋
70 Adelaide Road
Dublin 2
☎ (01) 4755266

Howth
Saint Lawrence Hotel ❋❋
Harbour Road
Howth, Co Dublin
☎ (01) 8322643

Killiney
Killiney Court Hotel ❋❋
Killiney Bay
Co Dublin
☎ (01) 2851622

Malahide
Stuart Hotel ❋❋
Coast Road
Malahide, Co Dublin
☎ (01) 8450099

Eating Out

Dublin City
Commons Restaurant ❋❋❋
Newman House
85 St Stephen's Green
Dublin 2
☎ (01) 4752597

Patrick Guilbaud ❋❋❋
46 James Place
Off Lower Baggot Street
Dublin 2
☎ (01) 6764192

Grey Door ❋❋❋
22 Upper Pembroke Street
Dublin 2
☎ (01) 6763286

Kapriol ❋❋❋
45 Camden Street Lower
Dublin 2
☎ (01) 4751235

Lock's ❋❋❋
1 Windsor Terrace
Portobello
Dublin 8
☎ (01) 4543391

Restaurant Mahler ❋❋
Powerscout Centre
South William Street
Dublin 2
☎ (01) 6797117

Nico's ❋❋
53 Dame Street
Dublin 2
☎ (01) 6773062

Oisin's ❋❋
31 Upper Camden Street
Dublin 2
☎ (01) 4753433

Pasta Fresca ❋❋
3 Chatham Street
Dublin 2
☎ (01) 6792565

Gallagher's Boxty House ❋
20 Temple Bar
Dublin 2
☎ (01) 6772762

Hallin's ❋
Moore Mall
Ilac Centre
Moore Street
Dublin 1
☎ (01) 8729111

Kitty O'Shea's ❋
23 Upper Grand Canal
Street
Dublin 4
☎ (01) 6609965

Ryan's ❋
28 Parkgate Street
Dublin 8
☎ (01) 6719352

Stag's Head ❋
1 Dame Court
Dublin 2
☎ (01) 6793701

South of Dublin

Ballsbridge
Le Coq Hardi ❋❋❋
35 Pembroke Road

Ballsbridge
Dublin 4
☎ (01) 6689070

Blackrock
Park Restaurant ✳✳✳
40 The Mews
Main Street
Blackrock
Co Dublin
☎ (01) 2886177

Dun Laoghaire
Restaurant Na Mara ✳✳✳
1 Harbour Road
Dun Laoghaire
Co Dublin
☎ (01) 2806767/2800509

Goatstown
The Goat ✳
Dublin 14
☎ (01) 2984145

Sandycove
South Bank Restaurant ✳✳
Martello Terrace
Sandycove, Co Dublin
☎ (01) 2808788

Stillorgan
Stillorgan Orchard ✳
Co Dublin
☎ (01) 2888470

Dalkey
Guinea Pig ✳
17 Railway Road
Dalkey, Co Dublin
☎ (01) 2857202

North of Dublin

Howth
King Sitric ✳✳✳
East Pier
Howth, Co Dublin
☎ (01) 325235

Adrian's ✳✳
3 Abbey Street
Howth, Co Dublin
☎ (01) 391696

Skerries
Red Bank ✳✳
7 Church Street
Skerries, Co Dublin
☎ (01) 8491005

Chapter 8 •
The South

Accommodation

Carlow
Royal Hotel ✳✳
8 Dublin Street
Carlow
☎ (0503) 31621

Carrick-on-Suir
Cedarfield Country House ✳✳
Waterford Road
Carrick-on-Suir
Co Tipperary
☎ (051) 40164

Cashel
Cashel Palace ✳✳✳
Cashel, Co Tipperary
☎ (062) 61411

Kearney's Castle ✳
Main Street
Cashel, Co Tipperary
☎ (062) 61044

Cork
Imperial Hotel ✳✳✳
South Mall
Cork
☎ (021) 274040

Glenvera House ✳
Wellington Road
Cork
☎ (021) 502030

Dungarvan
Lawlor's Hotel ✳✳
Meagher Street
Dungarvan
Co Waterford
☎ (058) 41056/41122

Enniscorthy
Ballinkeele House ✳✳
Ballymurn
6 miles (10km) south-east
of Enniscorthy
Co Wexford
☎ (053) 38105

Fermoy
Grand Hotel ✳✳
Fermoy, Co Cork
☎ (025) 31444/31848

Glendalough
Glendalough Hotel ✳✳
Glendalough
Co Wicklow
☎ (0404) 45135

Kildare
Curragh Lodge Hotel ✳
Dublin Street
Kildare
☎ (045) 22144

Kilkenny
Newpark Hotel ✳✳
Castlecomer Road
Kilkenny
☎ (056) 22122

Lismore
Ballyrafter House ✳✳
Lismore, Co Waterford
☎ (058) 54002

Thurles
Hayes Hotel ✳✳
Liberty Square
Thurles, Co Tipperary
☎ (0504) 22122

Tipperary
Royal Hotel ✳
Bridge Street
Tipperary
☎ (062) 51204

Waterford
Granville Hotel ✳✳✳
Meagher's Quay
Waterford
☎ (051) 55111

Dooley's Hotel ✳✳
30 The Quay
Waterford
☎ (051) 73531

Wexford
White's Hotel ✳✳
Georges Street
Wexford
☎ (053) 22311

Youghal
Hilltop Hotel ✳✳
Youghal, Co Cork
☎ (024) 92911

Avonmore House ✳
South Abbey
Youghal, Co Cork
☎ (024) 92617

Eating Out

Cork
Oyster Tavern ✳✳✳
Market Lane
Cork
☎ (021) 272716

Glassialleys ✳
5 Emmet Place
Cork
☎ (021) 272305

Kildare
Silken Thomas ✳
The Square
Kildare
☎ (045) 21695

Maynooth
Leinster Arms ✳✳
Main Street
Maynooth, Co Kildare
☎ (01) 6286323

Midleton
Ballymaloe House ✳✳✳
Shanagarry
Midleton, Co Cork
☎ (021) 652531

Wexford
The Granary ✳✳
West Gate
Wexford
☎ (053) 23935

Youghal
*Aherne's Seafood
Restaurant* ✳✳✳
Youghal, Co Cork
☎ (024) 93633

Chapter 9 •
The South West

Accommodation

Adare
Dunraven Arms Hotel ✳✳✳
Adare, Co Limerick
☎ (061) 396633

Bandon
Glebe House ✳✳
Ballinadee
Bandon, Co Cork
☎ (021) 778294

Castletownshend
Bow Hall ✳
Castletownshend, Co Cork
☎ (028) 36114

Ennis
Queen's Hotel ✳✳
Abbey Street
Ennis, Co Clare
☎ (065) 28963

Kanturk
Assolas Country House ✳✳✳
3 miles (5km) from Kanturk
Co Cork
☎ (029) 50015

Kilkee
Halpin's Hotel ✳
Kilkee, Co Clare
☎ (065) 56032

Killarney
Conaberry House ✳
Church Street, Kilgarvan
Killarney, Co Kerry
☎ (064) 85323

Kinsale
Blue Haven Hotel ✳✳
3 Pearse Street
Kinsale, Co Cork
☎ (021) 772209

Old Presbytery ✳✳
Cork Street
Kinsale, Co Cork
☎ (021) 772027

Leap
Leap Inn Hotel ✳✳
Leap, Co Cork
☎ (028) 33307

Limerick
Greenhills Hotel ✳✳✳
Ennis Road, Limerick
☎ (061) 453033

Mallow
Hibernian Hotel ✳✳
Mallow, Co Cork
☎ (022) 21588

Rosscarbery
Carbery Arms Hotel ✳✳
Rosscarbery, Co Cork
☎ (023) 48101

Waterville
Butler Arms ✳✳
Waterville
Co Kerry
☎ (066) 74144

Eating Out

Bantry
Bantry Bay Hotel ✳✳
Bantry, Co Cork
☎ (027) 50289

Ennis
The Cloister ✳✳
Abbey Street
Ennis, Co Clare
☎ (065) 29521

Kenmare
Coachman's Hotel ✳✳
Henry Street
Kenmare, Co Kerry
☎ (064) 41311

Kinsale
Max's Wine Bar ✳✳
Main Street
Kinsale, Co Cork
☎ (021) 772443

Limerick
*Restaurant De La
Fontaine* ✳✳
Gerald Griffin Street
Limerick
☎ (061) 414461

Mallow
Longueville House ✳✳✳
3 miles (5km) west of town
on Killarney road (N72)
Mallow, Co Cork
☎ (022) 47156

Index